PLACE *and* **POLITICS**
in **MODERN ITALY**

University of Chicago Geography Research Paper no. 243

Series Editors
Michael P. Conzen
Chauncy D. Harris
Neil Harris
Marvin W. Mikesell
Gerald D. Suttles

Titles published in the Geography Research Papers series prior to 1992 and still in print are now distributed by the University of Chicago Press. For a list of available titles, see the end of the book. The University of Chicago Press commenced publication of the Geography Research Papers series in 1992 with no. 233.

PLACE *and* POLITICS
in MODERN ITALY

John A. Agnew

THE UNIVERSITY OF CHICAGO PRESS
CHICAGO AND LONDON

JOHN A. AGNEW is professor of geography at the University of California, Los Angeles. He is the author or coauthor of a number of books, most recently *Geopolitics: Re-visioning World Politics* and *The Geography of the World Economy,* third edition.

The University of Chicago Press, Chicago 60637
The University of Chicago Press, Ltd., London
© 2002 by The University of Chicago
All rights reserved. Published 2002
Printed in the United States of America

11 10 09 08 07 06 05 04 03 02   1 2 3 4 5

ISBN: 0-226-01053-8 (cloth)
ISNB: 0-226-01051-1 (paper)

Library of Congress Cataloging-in-Publication Data

Agnew, John A.
    Place and politics in modern Italy / John A. Agnew.
        p. cm. — (University of Chicago geography research paper ; no. 243)
    Includes bibliographical references and index.
        ISBN 0-226-01053-8 (cloth : alk. paper) — ISBN 0-226-01051-1 (paper : alk. paper)
        1. Italy—Politics and government—20th century. 2. Political geography.
    I. Title. II. Series.

    JN5451 .A63 2002
    320.945—dc21

                                                            2002017355

⊗ The paper used in this publication meets the minimum requirements of the American National Standard for Information Sciences—Permanence of Paper for Printed Library Materials, ANSI Z39.48-1992.

CONTENTS

FIGURES

TABLES

ACKNOWLEDGMENTS

In the 1980s I lived for several long periods in Florence and elsewhere in Italy. This experience introduced me to the politics of Italy from the perspective of different places in the country. At the same time, I was working on developing a geographical approach to understanding political identities and interests that challenged more dominant conceptions based on political science and sociology. After I attended a 1985 conference on the electoral geography of Italy organized in Parma by Carlo Brusa, my new friendship with him led me to his hometown of Varese. My interest in the Northern League blossomed out of that encounter and out of my travels in northern Italy in the late 1980s and early 1990s. The major parties of the Italian government at that time—the Christian Democrats and Socialists—collapsed while I was visiting Milan and Varese in 1992. That was an intriguing time, dashing with Carlo from one party headquarters to another to see which local politicians had been indicted for corruption and to find out what response the local activists were contemplating. The confluence of these experiences over several years brought about the work this book is based on.

The book itself has taken a long time to reach fruition. In 1992, when I was teaching at the University of Chicago, I spoke to Michael Conzen of the University of Chicago and Penelope Kaiserlian of the University of Chicago Press about writing on this topic, but I was diverted by other projects and by a move from from Syracuse University to UCLA in 1996. During the delay, however, my commitment to the idea of a place-based interpretation of politics was reinforced. Long advertised as a placeless realm par excellence, Los Angeles has proved to be anything but. Instead, it is incredibly differentiated and diverse with respect to persistent daily paths, residential segregation by class and ethnicity, and associated political outlooks and interests. Not only Italy, therefore, can benefit from thinking about its politics in place-based terms.

That the book has finally reached the light of day is due in no small part

to the interest, support, and encouragement of a large number of people: in
Italy, Carlo Brusa, Roberto Cartocci, Renato Mannheimer, Mario Caciagli,
Marco Antonsich, Luca Muscarà, Calogero Muscarà, Berardo Cori, Mauro
Palumbo, Giuseppe Bettoni, and Giovanna Zincone; and in the United
States, Michael Shin, Ferruccio Trabalzi, Beverly Allen, Naeem Inayatullah,
Mabel Berezin, Michael Barkun, the late John Nagle, Kristi Andersen, Fred
Frohock, Stephen Webb, David Bennett, Deborah Pellow, Louis Kriesberg,
and Manfred Stanley. Carlo Brusa and I worked together on the research for
what is now chapter 8. Michael Shin helped out with the data analysis in
chapter 7. The friendship of Carlo and Carla Brusa, Danilo and Vittoria
Croce, Benito Giordano, Pierguido Baj, Celia Gould, Stuart Corbridge, Jim
Duncan, and Zoran Roca has made the research and writing more pleasur-
able. Michael Conzen and Penelope Kaiserlian were instrumental in arrang-
ing publication by the University of Chicago Press. Christie Henry took over
as editor at a crucial stage in production. My copyeditor, Alice Bennett, improved the English. Chase Langford prepared the maps. Without the emotional support, spirited intellectual optimism, and editorial help of Felicity
Nussbaum, I fear the book would never have been completed. Of course, I
am solely responsible for what I have made of the advice offered by them all.

Several libraries provided sources I could not otherwise have found. The
Biblioteca Marucelliana and the Biblioteca Nazionale Centrale in Florence,
the Biblioteca Comunale Forteguerriana in Pistoia, and the Biblioteca dello
Stato in Lucca have been particularly important. I also thank the Interli-
brary Loan Department of Bird Library at Syracuse University. The mar-
velous collection of Italy-related books and serials in the Young Research
Library at UCLA has been nothing short of inspirational. Numerous people
in Lucca, Pistoia, Florence, Sicily, Milan, and Varese consented to interviews at various times between 1989 and 1997. I am particularly grateful to
Pierluigi Bartolini in Pistoia and the On. Sergio Dardini in Lucca for help
during my fieldwork in their provinces in 1989, 1992, and 1994.

The book's chapters have been composed in one form or another
largely since 1995, although I wrote a draft of what is now chapter 5 in the
late 1980s, and all of them are substantially different from their earlier
manifestations. Earlier versions of chapter 3 appeared in Brian Graham,
ed., *Modern Europe* (London: Arnold, 1998); chapter 4 in Beverly Allen and
Mary Russo, eds., *Revisioning Italy* (Minneapolis: University of Minnesota
Press, 1997); chapter 8 in *National Identities* (1999); and chapter 9 in *Political Geography* (1997).

The research for this book was funded by a grant from the Appleby
Mosher Fund of the Maxwell School at Syracuse University, a Faculty
Travel Grant from the Division of International Studies and Overseas Programs at UCLA, and funding from the Committee on Research of the Academic Senate of the University of California (Los Angeles Division).

ABBREVIATIONS FOR NAMES

AN   Alleanza Nazionale (National Alliance)

CGIL   Confederazione Generale Italiana del Lavoro (Italian General Confederation of Labor)

CISL   Confederazione Italiana Sindacati Lavoratori (Italian Confederation of Labor Syndicates)

DC   Democrazia Cristiana (Christian Democratic Party)

DP   Democrazia Proletaria (Proletarian Democracy)

DS   Democratici Sinistra (Left Democrats)

FDP   Fronte Democratico Popolare (Popular Democratic Front)

FI   Forza Italia (Go Italy!)

LN   Lega Nord (Northern League)

        Liga Veneta (Venetian League)

        Liste Verde (Green Lists/Ecology Party/Greens)

        Lega Lombarda (Lombard League)

M   La Margherita (The Daisy)

MSI   Movimento Sociale Italiano (Italian Social Movement [neo-Fascists])

PCI   Partito Comunista Italiano (Italian Communist Party)

PDS   Partito Democratico della Sinistra (Democratic Party of the Left)

PdUP   Partito di Unità Proletaria per il Comunismo (Proletarian Unity Party for Communism)

PLI   Partito Liberale Italiano (Italian Liberal Party)

PNM   Partito Nazionale Monarchico (Monarchist Party)

PPI/PP   Partito Popolare Italiano (Italian People's Party [pre-Fascist Catholic party, reestablished after the collapse of the DC in 1992])

PR   Partito Radicale (Radical Party)

PRI   Partito Repubblicano Italiano (Italian Republican Party)

PSA   Partito Sardo d'Azione (Sardinian Action Party)

PSDI   Partito Socialista Democratico Italiano (Italian Social Democratic Party)
PSI   Partito Socialista Italiano (Italian Socialist Party)
PSUIP   Partito Socialista Italiano di Unità Proletaria (Italian Socialist Party of Proletarian Unity)
        La Rete (Network)
RC   Rifondazione Comunista (Refounded Communism)
SVP   Südtiroler Volkspartei (South Tyrol People's Party [Bolzano])
UV   Union Valdôtaine (Valdotaine Union [Valle d'Aosta])

CHAPTER I

Introduction

Space is not the vague and undetermined medium which Kant imagined. Spatial coordination consists essentially in a primary coordination of the data of sensuous experience. To dispose things spatially there must be the possibility of placing them differently. This is to say space could not be what it was if it were not divided and differentiated. But whence come these divisions? . . . evidently from the fact that different sympathetic values have been attributed to different regions
—Emile Durkheim, *The Elementary Forms of Religious Life*

MAPPING POLITICS

Mapping politics involves showing how political identities and interests are structured geographically as the result of human agency in the places where people live. Human agency and the changing conditions under which that agency takes place, however, mean that mapping is never complete. Just as a map comes into focus, it is transformed into another one. In recent years the pace of geographical change in Europe and North America seems to have increased after a long period following World War II when the geographies of political identity and political interests looked fairly stable. This book provides a theoretical framework for addressing the conception of "mapping politics" and a set of historical-geographical case studies of modern Italy—since 1870, but with a more specific focus on the years since World War II—to illustrate the efficacy of the approach and to offer a distinctive perspective on the course of modern Italian politics. In so doing it also engages some of the major debates in contemporary political studies.

Perhaps the most important debate in contemporary political studies is over interpretations of the trend toward a world organized increasingly in terms of the flow of goods, messages, capital, and people across widely dispersed networks and, on the other hand, the continuing division of the world into national states that provide the main regulatory framework for these networks and the primary source of political identity for much of the world's population. There is something of an intellectual standoff between two sides in a debate over this tension: between those perhaps overstating the novelty and overall impact of networks and those who may remain too committed to the enduring significance of national territories. Part of the problem is the way the debate is posed, as if networks invariably stand in opposition to territories. This is the case only if networks are seen as a completely new phenomenon without geographical anchors in particular places and if all territories are seen as national ones.[1]

Yet there is another way of looking at politics without ending up in the current impasse of "networks versus territories." This approach is to see politics as organized in terms of the places where most people live their lives; settings that are linked together and across geographical scales by networks of political and economic influence that have been, and still are, bounded by but decreasingly limited to the territories of national states.[2] The novelty of globalization can be exaggerated, however. From one point of view, the social world has been global in various ways since the sixteenth century, when European imperialism began its global march. But social science in the twentieth century has resolutely privileged the national as a singular scale of analysis when actual domestic and international politics presuppose the coeval importance of other geographical scales (such as the local and the global).

Beyond the debate over networks versus territories and the national versus the global, current Anglo-American debates over the nature of politics are dominated by three schools of thought. These are called the rational actor, political culture, and multiculturalist schools, although there are different emphases within each grouping. To rational actor theorists, politics simply reflects and amplifies individual preferences. People are seen as perpetually engaged in maximizing their welfare whatever the context of life. The only "real" actors are individuals, who act politically by matching their preferences to this or that political ideology or to the promises made by this or that politician. Politics always reduces to the pursuit of individual self-interest. For political culture theorists, politics is more about the clash of values than the clash of interests. The "best" politics involves pursuing values that emerge from reasoned deliberation within social groups dependent on habits of mutual trust. Community and dialogue more than preferences and interests are the catchwords of this persuasion. But all politics is ultimately about the way groups associate to establish and articulate different values and then attempt to realize them through political action. Finally, multiculturalists see the groups we are cast into by virtue of race, ethnicity, language, or culture as fundamental to political mobilization and action. Such groups are ascriptive rather than voluntary. The identities groups provide precede both preferences and association. Politics is about gaining recognition for one's identity and then using it as a resource in struggles over material and symbolic interests.

A central claim of this book is not that these accounts are wrong but that they are radically incomplete in their understanding of how preferences, interests, values, identities, and thus politics come about. They abstract preferences, values, and so on from the spatial settings or places where they are realized. Politics is always part, but only part, of the complex lives of people who interact in a variety of groups that they cooperate with daily (families, associations, political organizations, fellow workers, businesses, churches) and that help socialize them into certain political dispositions rather than others.

The ties sustained by groups can be relatively strong if everyday life is dominated by a single group or by groups that have cross-memberships. But a feature of modernity is that most group memberships are extraordinarily fluid and crosscutting, with relatively weak ties between any one group and its members. Typically, therefore, values and preferences emerge from fractionated and differentiated group experiences in which identities are forged and remade through shifting voluntary self-affiliations. From day to day, the seemingly abstract processes of political disposition and mobilization are concretely grounded in the practical routines and institutional channels of the workaday world. For most people these are typically concentrated around definite geographical sites, though these are invariably linked into wider webs or networks through which groups and individuals are organized over larger areas such as regions, states, and the world. The identities, values, and preferences that inspire particular kinds of political action therefore are embedded in the places or geographical contexts where people live their lives.

The book develops this theory of "mapping politics" in relation to the empirical exploration of the politics of modern Italy. Italian politics is often seen as expressing either the timeless features of political culture (national or regional) whose origins lie in the primordial mists of the distant past or else the slow and agonized achievement of a national politics of individual preferences in the face of entrenched institutions and political practices committed to sustaining social and regional identities that work against national unity and common political purpose. Such perspectives are readily comparable to the political culture and rational actor theories mentioned previously. In their stead, and throughout this book, I propose a perspective that sees Italy's national space as being in historical flux, without presuming either fixed regional cultures or an emerging national politics of individual preferences.

Previous accounts have tended to see local geographical differences as representing the past either as inscribed in the contemporary political landscape or as residual to a present that is increasingly homogenized and nationalized. Alternatively, however, group membership is realized, identities are formed, and preferences are defined in shifting geographical settings, or places, that have different local and long-distance linkages over time. From this point of view geography is dynamic rather than static. It refers to the ways life processes impinge on politics as their local and long-distance components change over time rather than operating within fixed, permanent geographical parameters such as those set down by current national-state boundaries or historical regional designations.[3] Much contemporary social science depends implicitly on the prior and unexamined valorization of geographical units of account (the state, the city, administrative regions) and thereby occludes the possibility of seeing politics (or other phenomena) as geographically dynamic.[4]

WHY ITALY?

The focus on Italian politics might be seen as biasing the case in favor of the perspective of geographical dynamics. After all, Italy is usually seen as very unlike the rest of Europe or the industrial-capitalist world in general. It is notoriously divided geographically, socially, and politically. Consequently:

1. Only Italy has had an incomplete political integration with a weak sense of national identity and an overbearing national government that has failed to acquire a matching popular legitimacy. Other national states, of course, somehow have avoided these problems! Perhaps what sets the country apart is rather the lack of confidence in a national mission on the part of Italy's intellectual elites and Italy's subordinate position within international politics since the disaster of Fascism (1922–43).

2. Only in Italy did a blockage for over fifty years between 1947 and 1992 prevent alternation between the main progressive (the Communist) and center-right (Christian Democrat) political parties. Elsewhere, naturally, alternation has always been a matter of course! The Cold War geopolitical division of Europe ran through Italy in the sense that the main party of the left was Communist and thus potentially threatened the position of Italy within the west-east division of the continent if it ever acquired national office. This made Italy distinctive, but hardly unique. Other countries had powerful communist parties (if only for a time), such as the Parti Communiste Français in France, and other leftist parties in Italy and elsewhere in Western Europe were often skeptical of the benefits derived from continuous geopolitical alignment with the United States.

3. Only in Italy was there systematic corruption of society by political parties dividing up the spoils of government. The degree of corruption in

Italy has been truly remarkable, but it has reflected the country's dominance for so long by a set of "parties of government" rather than something simply inherent in the country itself. Italy is at most, then, an extreme case among industrial democracies rather than the total anomaly it is often made out to be.

Notwithstanding the limited appropriateness of a charge of bias, Italy does have a number of advantages as a focus for the general argument of the book. One is that Italian scholars have been intrigued by the differences between regions and localities within the country, from the *meridionalisti* (students of the South) of the late nineteenth and early twentieth centuries and the great Marxist thinker Antonio Gramsci (1892–1936) (on city/countryside and north/south development gaps) to contemporary political scientists, geographers, and sociologists addressing rural/urban, regional, and local differences. There is thus a vast storehouse of information available about Italy's internal geography and how scholars have tried to explain it. Another advantage is that Italy does contrast with other European countries (and the United States) in popular and intellectual self-consciousness about its political-geographical difficulties. In this respect, the only other example that immediately comes to mind is Canada, a country so perpetually on the verge of coming apart that the mystery of its continuing unity is the central question for Canadian social scientists. The question of political identity is more openly available for public discussion in Italy than elsewhere because of both the relative recency of Italian national identity (Italy unified only in the 1860s) and its problematic character. Finally, Italy has adapted to recent changes in the world economy, associated with the coming of the European Union and the explosion of economic transactions between businesses across national boundaries, in ways that seem to have increased geographical differentiation within the country. Local external economies of scale (associated with skilled labor pools, training schemes, artisan traditions, and supplier contacts) and local social interdependence have been important in producing specialized economies in many parts of the country. But other areas have lagged behind or have been left out of this trend, thus stimulating even more local and regional economic differences with potential political impact.

THEMES OF PLACE AND POLITICS

Four themes can be identified that cut across all chapters to provide the links between the empirical material on Italian politics and understandings of it (in chapters 3–9) and the theory of mapping politics (in chapter 2).

Place and Scale

The first theme concerns the way geographical differences are understood and interpreted. Rather than a "metric" space, divided into compact areas, place involves a conception of topological space in which diverse geographical scales are brought together through networks of internal (locale) and external (location) ties in defining geographical variation in social characteristics. People also invest meaning in the places they inhabit. The scales by which they identify themselves and their group memberships (national, local, international) vary both from country to country and over time. Since the nineteenth century in Europe the national scale has often been presumed as the scale for establishing primary political identity. But sense of place at the national scale can coexist with or be replaced by alternative ones. Existing geographical variation in a given phenomenon—party vote, geographical sense of political identity, and so forth—responds to changes in the interaction of networks that interweave the internal and the external to produce new geographical variation in the same phenomenon over time.

In other words, geographical variation cannot simply be read off one geographical scale, and it changes over time as the balance of influences across scales changes. Place differences therefore are a *necessary* concomitant to the interrelation of social, economic, and political processes across scales that come together or are mediated through the cultural practices of existing settings. In this way geography is inherent in or constitutive of social processes rather than merely a backdrop on which they are inscribed.[5]

Why has this sort of perspective rarely achieved much emphasis among social scientists or historians? For one thing, the concept of place became fatefully identified with that of community at the turn of the twentieth century when the current intellectual division of labor among social science disciplines was largely established. When community was viewed as in decline under the impact of industrialization and urbanization (and more recently the effects of new communication technologies such as cell phones and the Internet), place was eclipsed too. At the same time "society," rather than remaining solely an abstraction or ideal type, was defined in practical terms as coterminous with the national state. A single geographical scale—that of the national state—thus became the geographical base on which much social science was founded.[6]

In addition, dominant representations of terrestrial space have followed the identity that grew up in the nineteenth century between abstraction and scientific validity. Geographical variation, multicausal explanations, local specificity, and vernacular understandings are all antithetical to the concept of space either as national chunks or as the result of structural relations (for example, in the core/periphery relations of subordination and incorporation of world systems and dependency theories). "Science" is about finding causal relations that either are independent of time and space or vary predictably across area types or between time periods. In fact what often happens is that uniformity is imposed by selecting taken-for-granted geographic units and holding numerous potential causal variables ceteris paribus (as if their effects were not present) so that universality can then be discovered.

The distinction between different geographical scales or levels has also been a problem because they have served to distinguish various areas of study (such as international relations versus domestic politics or micro- versus macroeconomics) and levels of generalization and causality (ecological versus individual inference) rather than complexly related dimensions of the contexts in which actual social and political processes occur. Integrating scales is difficult or even heretical when different fields determine their specialty by basing their uniqueness on different scales and when analysis (reducing explanation to the simplest level) has tended to win out over synthesis (putting together elements of explanation that emerge across a range of scales).

Finally, representations of space and how we think they figure in understanding politics or other social phenomena are not merely epistemic—functions of how we just happen to think. They are closely related to the dominant political and material conditions of the eras when they are articulated. But they often live on after those eras have closed because of intellectual inertia and the closed character of the intellectual tribes that dominate different fields. Much contemporary social science is still steeped in the theories and representations of space of such nineteenth-century founding fathers as Marx, Durkheim, and Weber. Notwithstanding the legitimating quotation from Durkheim I offer at the beginning of the chapter, none of these luminaries had much to say to the enterprise of integrating scales of analysis into the concept of place. Yet the complexities of social life in a globalizing world require nothing less.

Historical Contingency

Since the late nineteenth century, Anglo-American political science has been trying to escape from the twin constraints of time and space by searching for empirical regularities that are independent of both. The goal has been to imitate an image of physics or mathematics as fields that made abstractions beyond the confines of the everyday and that were widely admired among academics for the causal simplicity, mathematical elegance, and aesthetic brilliance of their discoveries. Associated with this has been the drive to construct a state-centered applied social science that would better manage the various problems encountered during state formation.[7] These goals have largely failed, however, because of the need to engage with a social world that has resisted ready incorporation into schemes that insist on radical reduction of historical and geographical complexity to highly synoptic statements. In practice, history has been reduced to worldwide linear evolution toward a model represented by an idealized version of a particular geographical entity, typically England, France, or, latterly, the United States. This geopolitics of knowledge, reflecting whatever national group of social scientists or national experience was in the ascendancy, thus conditioned the understanding of time. As I discussed in the previous section, space was likewise reduced to the effect of the containers provided by the world's territorial states but taken for granted as the obvious units of social accounting.

This elimination of time and space as active components of social science analysis has recently undergone considerable criticism.[8] One important response has tried to return to historical narratives about states or localities in place of the "scientific" model. Such an idiographic response is limited, however, because it fails to address how space should figure in analysis. It is how time and space covary that matters in the constitution of social life, not privileging one over the other. What this book proposes is a social science that tries to use time-space variation as its basic point of departure rather than pretending to remove either from consideration or proposing that one is superior. This approach involves a dynamic mapping of shifts in political identities and actions, presuming as much change as stability in their substance over time and space.[9] A focus on place requires taking both space and time equally seriously.

Contexts of Political Action

The dominant conception of political action is that of individual actors belonging to groups (in practice, usually national census categories) that influence how they do or do not act. In this understanding, the purpose of political research is to find out what drives individual choices across enough individuals that we no longer need to rely on aggregate or geographically based evidence. Generalizing about individuals will then explain them. But explanation and generalization are not the same. Explanation is about the possible mixes of causes and reasons operating differentially across time and space rather than about generalizing across individuals independent of time and space, because individuals never exist independent of the historical-geographical contexts of their lives. The causes of political beliefs and actions are organized differentially across such contexts and are not deducible from frequency counts of the attributes of individuals abstracted from the contexts of political action.

Even recognition as an individual presupposes a social-geographical context in which that is possible. The affirmation of ordinary life as the source of the intersubjective understandings modern selfhood is based on is the centerpiece of the social philosophy of Charles Taylor.[10] From this perspective the individual self is irremediably social in origin:

[The] crucial feature of human life is its fundamental dialogical character. We become full human agents, capable of understanding ourselves, and hence of defining our identity, through our acquisition of rich human languages of expression. For my purposes here, I want to take language in a broad sense, covering not only the words we speak, but also other modes of expression whereby we define ourselves, including the "languages" of art, of gesture, of love, and the like. But we learn these modes of expression through exchanges with others. People do not acquire languages needed for self-definition on their own. Rather, we are introduced to them through interaction with others who matter to us—what G. H. Mead called "significant others." The genesis of the human mind is in this sense not monological, not something each person accomplishes on their own, but dialogical.[11]

Even without geographic variation in voting patterns or other political activity, therefore, this understanding presumes geographic variation in the causes and reasons of political activity as they come together in different places. If everyday life differs from place to place, then so too does the language of politics. One of the themes of this book is the need to replace the individualist account of political action with an adequate contextual one. The typical form that contextual approaches to political studies take, however—focusing on local deviations from a national average (as in the so-called neighborhood effect) that are then put down to local particularities—is not pursued here. Rather, I offer an approach that breaks completely with the individualist ontology and methodology, proposing that the national and the local are themselves always elements of a wider multiscalar context framing social causation and political agency.[12]

The Search for Normative Political Space

The world has not always been divided into territorial states. Indeed, all kinds of polities with distinctive geographies have existed at one time or another. It is only over the past few hundred years, and more especially since the American and French Revolutions, that the territorial state (after the English, French, or American model) has come to monopolize political debate and discussion of political action. This intellectual hegemony is now in doubt. There is an increasing disjuncture between the political spaces that are relevant to contemporary practical needs, often now at subnational or supranational scales, and the state-based ones on offer. In Europe in particular, the coemergence of regionalist movements and Europewide supranationalism suggest the limitation of totally statecentric accounts.

As Plato and Aristotle long ago recognized, politics is not just about who holds office and how it was acquired but also about the nature of office and the spatial arrangements under which government *should* operate. Scholars of politics have been slow to acknowledge the development of new conceptions of political spatiality (as in regionalist, trading bloc, and global-oriented movements) and also have remained largely tied to the national state as the locus par excellence of political life. This is because of a conception of political space as a fixed hierarchical grid, divided among states (suitably colored on a map) in a pecking order from least to most (the superpowers). Not only is this challenged by formal organizations operating at other geographical scales, it is also apparent in the failures of states around the world, from Colombia and Haiti to Sierra Leone, Rwanda, and Somalia.

To raise an alternative conception of political space is not to suggest that states are in imminent danger of disappearance, at least in the democratic capitalist parts of the world. On the contrary, it is to claim that the either/or of state centrism is extremely misleading. States have never actually monopolized politics in the way they have monopolized political theory. Now they do so even less. But if we allow political understanding to be dominated by a particular territorial form, then we remain oblivious to the emergence and the possibilities of other geographical entities such as politically reinvigorated cities, stronger municipalities, and supranational modes of political organization.[13]

OUTLINE OF CHAPTERS

Chapter 2 lays out the theoretical perspective of the book, linking it to contemporary debates over the nature of politics and identifying the sources of the perspective in recent literature in political theory. The main elements of the position are drawn out in relation to major strands of contemporary Anglo-American thinking about the nature of politics as reflected in discussion about agency, difference, association, and active socialization.

The weakness of Italian national identity as compared with other European national states is examined in chapter 3 in relation to the difficulty of acquiring and imposing a common "landscape ideal" or physical image for the country. A singular landscape ideal is viewed as a crucial component in erecting and communicating a sense of common nationhood. The rural Tuscan and ancient Roman idealized landscapes that came to the fore in the aftermath of Italian unification in the nineteenth century have not been able to provide the sense of national communality found in certain "exemplary" European states. Why has this been so, and to what effect?

By providing a critique of the common understanding of Italy and its north/south division in terms of the language of modern and backward, chapter 4 adopts a skeptical attitude toward the modernization approach that has dominated much thinking about Italian politics yet that has serious deficiencies. Why this approach has been so pervasive in the Italian case is the subject of close attention.

The focus changes in chapter 5 from the popular images and intellectual history of the previous two chapters to the dynamics of Italian electoral politics during the long postwar period in which the Christian Democratic Party and the Italian Communist Party had central roles in national politics. I identify three "geographical regimes" in which politics tended to be regionalizing (1948–63), nationalizing (1963–76), and localizing (1976–92). The key claim is that the different geographies resulted from changing group affiliations, shifting political and economic conditions, and the evolving external relations of Italy and its localities.

The important distinction between two territorial subcultures—the "red" or Communist of much of central Italy and the "white" or Catholic of the Northeast and pockets elsewhere—is examined in chapter 6 first in general terms and then in relation to two provinces of central Italy, Pistoia and Lucca, that represent the two traditions. A rather more complex picture of historical-geographical contingency emerges from the local studies rather than the somewhat simple one that has usually prevailed in Italian political studies. This chapter reinforces the idea of a dynamic place-based politics as opposed to fixed regional political subcultures.

Beginning in 1992 the Italian system of parties and elections underwent a dramatic change. Chapters 7, 8, and 9 examine aspects of the transformations still under way. Chapter 7 looks at the geography of how the Northern League, a regionalist party, emerged to replace the Christian Democrats in many parts of northern Italy. This chapter illustrates the more general question of how parties are replaced geographically during periods of intense political change. Chapter 8 returns more specifically to the Northern League to investigate the specific impact it has had on the political identities of northern Italians. The success of this regionalist party is examined with respect to what it says about the contemporary geography of political identity in northern Italy. Chapter 9 is concerned with the ways the new parties operating since 1992 have come to "imagine" Italy in terms of the geographical scales at which they operate and how they think it should be governed. In other words, my concern is to explore the reimagining of political space going on in Italy since the mid-1990s on the part of the main new political parties. Finally, chapter 10 draws together points from the other chapters in terms of the themes identified earlier in the introduction: place and scale, historical contingency, contexts of political action, and the search for a normative political space.

CONCLUSION

The overall purpose of the book is to use modern Italy, from its unification in the mid-nineteenth century to the present, as a laboratory for showing a geographical way of looking at politics that goes beyond the individualist and state-centered accounts that currently dominate. The idea is both to offer detailed critiques of conventional wisdom and to provide an alternative theoretical perspective that incorporates some of the main features of contemporary political theory. The book moves from the geographically more general to the more specific, from Italy as a whole to some of its parts, particularly in the Center and the North, and it is organized chronologically from a more macrohistorical frame of reference to more detailed studies of the recent past.

Versions of some of the chapters have been published previously, but they appear here in considerably revised form as parts of a sustained argument. Certain themes run across the chapters: a focus on places as constituted out of the workings of agents across multiple geographical scales, historical-geographical contingency, contexts of political action, and the search for normative political space. If the case of modern Italy is any guide, the division and differentiation of space are indeed as important as Durkheim suggested they are. It is a pity that he and his successors did so little to show how.

CHAPTER 2

Mapping Politics Theoretically

The first step in providing a coherent geographical perspective on Italian politics is to lay out a theoretical framework to which more specific empirical studies can be related. Recent history offers an opportunity to reevaluate the importance of geography—or the role of place-to-place differences within countries—in politics in Europe and North America. In many countries, established ideas about politics, based on assumptions about the high intensity and historical fixity of political party identification, the ideological range (left/right) and organizational characteristics of parties (mass/clientelistic), social class divisions and voting patterns, and common commitment to a national state and its territorial organization, are in question to a degree not seen since the 1920s and 1930s. In particular, the idea that any place within the boundaries of a specific country may well be more or less substitutable for any other place in terms of the main attributes of its politics (which parties are active, who votes for whom, and how local institutions mediate for national parties and their political messages), widely held at one time by many Anglo-American students of politics, is now much more questionable than it was ten or twenty years ago.[1]

Views have always differed, however, as to the extent of locational substitutability and how it came about. In respect to the first, my view is that the geographical homogeneity of any given nation or country was always exaggerated—more a normative commitment than an empirical fact.[2] The mass of people everywhere have always been locked into daily practices and routines that produce more limited perceptual horizons, locally focused interests, and limited political opportunities than those of the scholars who study them. In relation to the second, the much noted globalization of economic and, to a more limited extent, cultural life has not undermined the importance of the local and regional so much as it has *begun* reorienting them away from a primary focus on the local and the national to perceptions of and reactions to the supranational (e.g., the Euro-

13

pean Union) and the global (the situation of a region or locality in global trading and investment networks). So, though certainly not the creation of the recent intensification of globalization, regional and local *mediation* of politics in the presence of globalization has increasingly given rise to a greater variety of political forms (such as regional political parties), the erosion of national social cleavages and associated political affiliations, the breakdown of long-established regional voting patterns, and popular questioning of the limitations of current national political institutions in a globalizing world.[3]

These recent trends suggest a need to rethink the currently dominant model of national politics premised on a median national voter pursuing individual preferences or interests within a purely national space (the rational actor model), if only because the national space no longer entirely defines the limits of interest formation and hence a singular context for defining individual preferences. But more especially, this is necessary because the question of the political identity (national, class, ethnic, regional) around which preferences are decided can no longer be associated purely with the national or national–social class identities hitherto presumed to be crucial.

Of course, alternatives to this model are available that apparently do take the geographical basis of politics more seriously. These would include the idea of a set of socially constructed or primordial ethnic or social identities associated with different places determining political outlooks and action (multiculturalism) and that of geographically sedimented political cultures ranged along a continuum from the civic (or participatory) at one end to the passive or authoritarian at the other (political culture model). These two models have been widely accepted in Italy to account, respectively, for the distinction between regions long dominated by Catholic and socialist political affiliations (the northeast-white and central-red zones) and the North/South difference in the prevalence of political clientelism and active political participation.[4] Because both the alternative models see geographical variation in politics as derivative of either largely unchanging social identities or fixed political cultures, however, they offer no improvement over the rational voter model in accounting for contemporary changes in political outlooks and behavior.

What all three models (rational actor, multicultural, political culture) are missing is sustained focus on the mediating role performed for national politics, historically and today, by place-based processes of identity and preference formation. In other words, they all fail to consider the ways the spatial siting of people in relation to the uneven distribution of social, economic, and political opportunities and influences affects their political outlooks and activities.[5] To provide such a theoretical focus is my purpose in this chapter. I do so in two ways: by proposing a theoretical perspective on how places figure in national politics and by relating an important aspect of this perspective—active place-based socialization—to the major conceptual innovations of the three others identified previously (agency, difference, and association) to show how the place perspective can bring them together.

I use this theorizing about place and politics as the basis for examining the course of modern Italian politics. I understand theorizing as a form of praxis rather than logos. It is not a reified set of general propositions that fit all empirical cases but a set of general orientations and expectations drawn from past and contemporary thinking on which empirical analysis can be based and without which it would be impossible.[6] Though the arguments are general and can be applied elsewhere, in this book the empirical case in question is that of "Italy." Finally unified as a state only in 1870, Italy has been both an intellectual and a practical laboratory for numerous ideas about the best ways to organize politics in the absence of a strong existing national identity, from the interregional vote exchanges of early legislatures through Fascism to the competing visions of the postwar Communists, Christian Democrats, and other political movements. The lack of an existing nation on which to map the state has meant that projects for an Italian politics have always had to come to terms with a large number of social differences, political traditions, and distinctive economic interests that are not readily represented in simple national terms.

THE PLACE PERSPECTIVE

Place and Space

Terrestrial *space,* the earth's surface or some portion thereof, is often understood in the social sciences as the plane on which events take place at particular locations. It offers a concept of the general as opposed to the particularity of places. Space is also understood as commanded or controlled by powerful agents and institutions (such as states), whereas *place* is lived or experienced space. Space is the abstraction of places onto a grid or coordinate system as if an observer is outside it or looking down at the world from above. Sometimes space and place are not distinguished at all but are viewed as synonymous. Place can also be dismissed as an obfuscating term without analytic merit. In this usage one can write of particular spaces and general ones, thus reintroducing place but refusing to name it.

As a pair of terms, place and space reflect a tension that signifies their distinctiveness. Space represents a field of practice or an area in which an organization or set of organizations (such as states) operates, held together in popular consciousness by a map image or narrative story that makes the space whole and meaningful. Place represents the encounter of people with space. It refers to how everyday life is inscribed in space and takes on meaning for specified groups of people and organizations. Space can be considered as "top down," defined by powerful actors imposing their control and stories on others. Place can be considered as "bottom up," representing the outlooks and actions of ordinary people. Typically places are more localized, given that they are associated with the familiar, with being at home. But they can also be larger areas, depending on geographical patterns of activities, social network connections, and the projection of feelings of attachment, comfort, and belonging.

A place can be seen as having three necessary geographical elements. These combine both the particular qualities of a place and its situatedness in terrestrial space. The first is a *locale* or setting in which everyday life is most concentrated for a group of people. The second is a *location* or node that links the place to both wider networks and the territorial ambit it is embedded in. The third is a *sense of place* or symbolic identification with a place as distinctive and constitutive of a personal identity and a set of personal interests.

These three elements show up repeatedly, if unevenly, both in popular understandings of the word and in academic rumination about its content. Locale privileges the local, but location draws a place into a wider spatial field of reference. Sense of place brings in the symbolic significance of a place for those who live in and identify with it. This is not the same as community in the sense of a way of life based on personal intimacy and positive involvement with a localized moral order. If that is present it will reinforce the sense of place, but it is not necessary for a sense of place to exist and flourish.

The language of geographical scale is crucial in making the distinction between place and space. Geographical scale refers to the level of geographical resolution at which a given phenomenon is thought of, acted on, or studied. Conventionally, terms such as local, regional, national, and global are used to convey the various levels. Geographical scale is not the amount of information on a map, as with cartographic scale, but the focal setting at which spatial boundaries are defined for a specific social claim, activity, or behavior. Yet there is nothing very determinate about the terms typically used. The term local, for example, can in different cases refer to areas of vastly different size. For this reason, one scale makes sense only in relation to others. The terms are also inherently areal; they refer to territorial units of varying size and cannot adequately describe the character of networks and the spatial relationships they involve. As yet, however, even as the world globalizes, local and national scales of resolution remain dominant with respect both to institutional opportunities and to the sources of political action. Places are wedged between the local, the regional, the national, and the global, but with a continuing tendency to privilege the relations between the local and the national.[7]

Political power is the sum of all resources and strategies involved in conflicts over collective goods in which parties act with and on one another to achieve legitimate outcomes. It is never exercised equally everywhere. This is the basic law of political geography, for two reasons. First, power pools up in centers as a result of the concentration of coercive resources (instrumental power) and the ascription and seconding of power to higher levels in power hierarchies by groups at lower levels (associational power). Second, the transmission of political power across space involves practices by intervening others who transform it as it moves from place to place. Not only is the flow of power potentially disrupted in its actual spatial deployment, it is also subject to negotiation and redirection.

Geographical scale is constructed politically in three ways. One way is that political power is exercised from centers that vary in their geographical reach, defining global, national, regional, and local sites of power of differing geographical scope and political intensity. Often power flows hierarchically from one scale to another, but it can short-circuit one scale or more. Today, for example, regions and localities are thought of as interacting directly with globally effective seats of power with reduced national scale mediation. Another way is through the deployment of the language of scale itself. Geographical scales are intellectual constructs that are used to order the world in a meaningful way. In different political ideologies, different scales are given preference, reflecting their premises about the best or most appropriate level at which to think and organize politically. Thus nationalists privilege the national, regionalists the regional, non-Stalinist socialists the international, and so on. Finally, it is not so much the separate scales as the material and discursive balance between them that determines the constitution and effects of political power in a particular case or in relation to a particular issue. The balance between material and discursive processes operating from sites over different geographical ranges determines the way political power works. Historical shifts in the balance produce different political maps or place-based patterns of politics.[8]

The most typical modern European-American perspective on space, however, has been to ignore the question of scale. The preference is to divide space up into blocks of national spaces or territories. This approach expresses the central material and ideological significance for our time of nation-states, at least ideally, as the primary units of political, economic, and cultural organization. It is what the sociologist Herminio Martins has called "the rule of methodological nationalism."[9] Of course there is nothing necessary or inevitable about this. Today, in fact, the territorial division of the world into states is under increasing challenge from networks of power (associated with transnational business) emanating from and linking major world cities. In the past, centralized empires, territorial states, nomadic groups, and other distinctive types of political-geographical organization prevailed over large parts of the world or coexisted in close proximity. There is no good reason such geographical pluralism might not flower once again, if in distinctive ways, and collective action might be organized across geographical scales rather than confined within rigid territorial boundaries.[10]

The actual spatial organization of the world is of course already more complex than the simple assimilation of all social and political cleavages into a superordinate state-territorial spatial form assumed by most social science thinking. In particular, the spatial practices of everyday life have always maintained a local place specificity that defies sweeping up into national territorial containers. But today these are as much nodes in wider space-spanning networks as areal niches within national territorial spaces. Places, then, are at the same time territorial niches *and* network locations.

Some types of sociological theory have taken the spatial basis of social life very seriously, but usually without invoking the concept of place. From Simmel to Sorokin to Giddens, with a definite hiatus during the heyday of functionalist sociology in the 1950s and 1960s, spatial concepts and metaphors have been important.[11] Particularly during the past decade, spatial language and concepts have had increasing currency among sociologists. Pierre Bourdieu, Harrison White, and Anthony Giddens have been advocates of "spatially strong" theoretical discourses. All are involved, if in very different ways, in using the relational mapping of social onto biophysical space to transcend the major dichotomies (subject/object, material/ideal, etc.) that have long bedeviled sociology.[12]

Two other sociologists, Luciano Gallino and Arnaldo Bagnasco, have come closest to the concept of place proposed here with their idea of "territorial social formations."[13] By this they mean geographical areas with overlapping economic, social, and institutional assets integrated by means of local political hegemonies. In this understanding, the local-territorial provides the means of structuring the complex interactions between various influences that produce distinctive local economies and political modes of managing them. What is absent from this and other sociological literature, however, is an analysis of the precise elements of "place" and of how place can serve as a sociological as much as a geographical concept.

Places and National Politics

An empirical puzzle provides a simple way of starting to describe the importance of geographical context for national politics. National (or other aggregate) averages are more or less representative of specific observations depending on the degree of dispersion of all observations. National averages disguise a variety of local or regional differences that better represent the action of specific persons. In figure 2.1, for example, the relationships between different social classes and the vote for an imaginary political party are shown for an imaginary country's four regions. In each region the correlation between class and vote is perfect, but for the country as a whole there is no direct relation whatever. This extreme example illustrates the simple point the role of geographical context rests on: a national norm is constituted out of local situations.

Robert Putnam's much lauded 1993 study of the implementation of regional government in Italy rests largely on a series of quantitative comparisons at the national scale that are used to make interpretations about the political-cultural differences between northern and southern Italy but that do not hold up within the two parts of the country.[14] What appear to be relationships at the national scale (e.g., an inverse relation between "clericalism" and "civicness") turn out not to be so or are related differentially in the two parts of the country because the distribution of scores on the related variables within each region differs so much. In other words, within-group variation is so great that one cannot say much about between-group differences. The actual relations between the variables therefore differ between the two parts of Italy and cannot be bundled into a single relation for the whole without violating this fact.[15]

This is neither simply a statistical problem nor solely an Italian one but one that is theoretically and globally substantive. As social beings, people

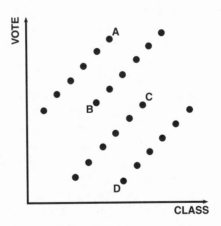

Figure 2.1 The correlation between class and vote for an imaginary political party in a country of four regions. Source: D. Derivry and M. Dogan, "Religion, classe et politique en France: Six types des relations causales," *Revue Française de Science Politique* 36 (1986): 158.

respond to the stimuli of their surroundings and thereby acquire the practical reasons that lead them to act in some ways rather than others. These social contexts are formed geographically. Social relations are made in physical settings or *locales* (everything from homes, schools, and shops to churches, workplaces, and places of recreation) that people constantly cross into and out of in the course of their everyday lives. Such locales are embedded in a wider territorial society according to *locational* constraints imposed by states and other institutions organized territorially and in node and network arrangements imposed by spatially extensive divisions of labor. Common experiences and identities create emotional attachments and self-definitions that are projected onto space to produce distinctive geographical identities or *sense of place*. This involves making distinctions between insiders and outsiders and often leads to exclusionary practices. Place thus cannot be valorized as inherently either "democratic" or "progressive" in its structuring of political practices.[16]

In a contextual view, therefore, human action is seen as threading out from the here and now of face-to-face social interaction into more extensive fields of mediated interaction managed by institutions and organizations with extended spatial reach. Social relations can be thought of as stretching out over space but linked tightly to the concrete interactions and intersubjective ties of persons rooted in the rounds of everyday life. So rather than adding together the categorical traits of individuals derived from national censuses or positing a set of group traits associated with a place from time immemorial to explain an action (such as voting), my purpose is to identify the mix or juxtaposition of a set of stimuli to action within a relevant space-time matrix or place.

People do not passively follow local rules and roles mandated by a set of social causes. They actively manipulate them, thus making them unique to the particular context. This inherently limits the possibility of explaining action by a set of determinate causes, a "social capital" or a "culture" unproblematically inherited from the past. At the same time, however, actors are never autonomous in the sense of being totally self-determining. Their very personhood (and what it means to them) depends on rules and roles established socially. What they make of them is a function of their agency—their ability to imagine action based on evaluation of how they live and how they came to live that way.[17]

This is a type of *configurational* explanation combining a focus on the action of human agents with accounts of the geographical settings in which the stimuli and reasons for action are grounded.[18] From this point of view, geographical context or place refers to funneling stimuli across space to produce specific types of action that are similar or different depending on the spatial covariation of the various stimuli. In other words, places are the cultural settings where localized and geographically wide-ranging socioeconomic processes that condition actions of one sort or another are jointly mediated. Although there must be places, therefore, there need not be this particular place.

By way of example, recent years have seen a dramatic reduction in electoral participation in Italy. Close analysis reveals, however, that the highest rates of abstention are among older voters (particularly women) in southern Italian cities and young voters in the metropolitan areas of the North. Different sets of reasons are at work in creating this geographical pattern, associated in the urban South with alienation from politics in general for the people in question and in the urban North with a protest against the existing political parties for the least-affiliated younger voters.[19] Not only are demographic differences in play, so are divergent experiences and understandings of politics for specific sets of actors in different places. Among the factors involved in the urban South are the decline of the "personal" character of politics with the removal of preference voting in elections and the overall decrease in clientelistic politics since the late 1980s and in the urban North the vilification and subsequent disappearance of such major political parties as the Christian Democrats and Socialists in the aftermath of the political corruption scandals of the early 1990s.

We might consider three important distinctions between the conception of context illustrated by this example and those predominant in the social sciences. For one thing, contextual effects are often seen as external effects on individual behavior arising from social interaction in a local environment. Typically, it is local neighborhood or group effects that are the object of analysis. Individuals are radically separated from the contexts around them, only to be related as if they have an existence independent of one another. For another, political movements and parties are usually exogenous to the enterprise. Emphasis falls on individual voters and their behavior while other actors are ignored or taken for granted. There is a bias against seeing institutions as involved in structuring contexts. Finally, there is a tendency to accept the claim that many social traits are really individual characteristics that we simply cannot yet methodologically deal with except as aggregate measures. Contextual effects are marks of our ignorance about real individuals and how they make decisions. This reductive psychologism can have no time for geographical context.[20]

Causes and Contexts

As the foregoing account should suggest, no single cause can be invoked to explain the interrelation between places and their politics. Grand theories based on single-factor explanations (technology, capital, class struggle, ethnic identity) not only are largely discredited as partial and overdetermined but also have no constitutive role for place. A potential causal matrix can be drawn from the existing literature on spatial variation in politics to explain the contextual scaffolding out of which places are made. As a result, I argue that places in contemporary European and North American politics can be configured in terms of six sets of causes.[21] Together these causes can be viewed as potentially producing the cultural contexts for the range of possible actions directed toward national politics by human agents in particular places. But they engage with the three dimensions of place (locale, location, and sense of place) in distinctive ways, as shown below.

The relative weight and mix of each type of cause varies, of course, from country to country and from place to place within countries. The ordering reflects a working outward from the pathways and barriers of everyday life into the wider spatial worlds they are embedded in. But their relative importance shifts as geopolitical, cultural, economic, and technological conditions change over time. They thus draw together the conventional wisdom from a wide range of the contemporary geographical literature on the multiple ways human actors make places. To reiterate, my listing of significant causes reflects my preference for multicausal analysis within a common ontological framework that privileges the concrete settings of everyday life. In these particular quotidian instances, however, causes do not determine but condition the choices made and the actions undertaken by active human agents.

First of all, the microgeography of everyday life (work, residence, school, leisure) defines the more-or-less localized settings where patterns of social interaction and personal socialization are realized. Even individuals without strong social associations must navigate the constricted and directed pathways of daily life. A sense of local distinctiveness or of wider territorial affiliation (including adhering to somewhere as large as a nation-state) can be a feature of an emotional attachment to a particular place. This is especially true when a place is seen as a "community of fate" in which a person's material life chances and emotional well-being are caught up with the condition and prospects of a local area.[22] Social groups also form through local ties and by extralocal linkages to similar groups elsewhere. Not everyone in a given place is socialized in exactly the same way with the same outcome. Class, gender, and ethnic differences are created and also have specific political effects through the particular local and extralocal ties they reflect.[23] Sociologist Georg Simmel argued that socialization into group membership through instilling norms of conduct usually took place spatially because social boundaries had to be spatialized to be effective: "The proximity or distance, the uniqueness or the plurality that characterize the relations of social groups to territory are therefore often the root and symbol of their structure."[24] Socialization does not happen once and for all, as in accounts that emphasize childhood to the exclusion of all other phases of life; it occurs repeatedly over the course of a lifetime with the possibility of new memberships and intersubjective relations as people move around or groups (in particular, the differences the groups define and the associations they give rise to) are reformulated in and across places.[25]

Second is the influence of the wider social division of labor in establishing the character of different places and identification with them. The social division of labor takes a spatially differentiated form and evolves in rhythm with changes in the world economy. There is unevenness in the spatial distribution of investment, labor skills, input sources, and markets. Places develop relatively specialized economic bases because of their accessibility, labor force, and production assets. Some localities and regions are branch plant economies, dependent on flows of capital and decisions from elsewhere. Others are the headquarters of transnational businesses or engaged in the specialized production for a range of national and international markets but largely dependent on their endogenous capacities. All places also have economic sectors that depend largely on local markets, a point emphasized in so-called community power research. A large part of local politics is concerned either with conflicts over the interests of parochial capital or with the need to make the local area attractive to footloose business investment. These spatial-economic characteristics have important effects on the social structures of specific areas and the nature of local politics. In particular, class and community affiliations take on meaning in relation to the geographical contexts defined by the social-spatial division of labor. National economies came into existence in Europe and North America in the nineteenth and early twentieth centuries, setting geographical limits to investment and business organization. Since then, nationwide wage agreements, increased labor force participation by women, common rates of taxation, and the provision of similar levels of public services have helped diminish local and regional differences in conditions of employment and human welfare. Economic globalization, however, in emphasizing competition for mobile capital between states and localities, has introduced a wider geographical framing into the workings of spatial divisions of labor.[26]

Third, and of increased importance in recent years, is the nature of communications technologies and access to them. Transportation and information technologies create geographies of isolation and accessibility that draw places differentially into wider networks of communication. Such networks are frequently hierarchical across settlement systems and sharply limited by linguistic boundaries and customs barriers. The relative presence or absence of communication network ties, then, provides another contextual dimension to national politics by limiting or enhancing interaction across space. Today, social groups and political affiliations rely more on flows of information and images over space than on immediate spatial propinquity.[27] Powerful media of communication, especially television, exert a particularly important political influence. The messages of the media in many countries are strongly defined by the territorial boundaries of the national state because of language constraints and either state ownership or concentrated corporate control (Italy's Silvio Berlusconi, media baron and leader of his own political party, Forza Italia, is an obvious example). The arrival of global media enterprises, such as MTV and CNN, has the capacity to disrupt this established relationship between mass media and national territory, but except for those who understand English, this has so far had a limited direct effect on the conduct of politics.

Fourth, all places today are embedded in territorial states. States are congeries of localities and regions held together in central-local tension. Though most obvious in federations, this tension is implicit in all states. When popular legitimacy counts, as it does in all but the most repressive states, governments must pursue policies and redistribute resources in ways that maintain or enhance the legitimacy of the state or current regime. In the presence of economic and political inequality between places, this will involve conflict over which places get what. To challenge or change the institutions of government requires becoming involved in their operation. De facto, this legitimizes governments by producing repertoires of collective action that are directed toward them, such as organizing and supporting political parties that run in national elections rather than simply engaging in local protests and rebellions. In this way local and regional politics are drawn toward the center. At the same time, however, the center remains dependent on the periphery, to causally reverse the terminology typically adopted by those who see the central government successfully homogenizing localities around a national standard or norm for culture and politics.[28] Local politicians must be recruited for national office and must satisfy local constituencies with what they achieve. In other words, local populations negotiate their own terms of engagement with the center. National politicians must speak their language, both literally and in terms of issues and policies that concern different local constituencies. Peasants (and others), therefore, have never been entirely turned into Frenchmen in the sense of a typical or average French (Parisian) person with the exact same interests and preferences distributed by class, gender, age, and so forth. Local governments can also strike out in various directions, even while constrained by national-level policies.[29] For example, they can enter into coalition with international or local business interests to foster place-specific economic growth and provide different packages of public goods and services than those characteristic of the country as a whole.

Fifth, ethnic, class, and gender divisions and antagonisms have national (and international) histories as promulgated by political movements and influential commentators and leaders. Such divisions become reified in political discourses that then serve to anchor political ideologies (nationalist, socialist, liberal, etc.). The relative weight and various meanings attached to the social divisions, however, and hence the appeal of different ideologies, are not the same everywhere. They vary from place to place in patterns of external economic dependence, work authority structures, local cultural forms, and the history of local experience with respect to the use of social divisions by political movements.[30] Popular collective memories are common, in which regional and local identities combine with national ones. The national story is seen through local eyes. Various geographical scales of political identity, and connections to social ones, therefore are not necessarily mutually exclusive. The imagination of the nation does not contradict the local image of "homeland." Indeed, the latter can flow into the former, as has long been the case with the German *Heimat* or integral national political community made up of local communities.[31] In recent times, however, identity politics has become both more complex and more important to national politics across a range of countries. This is a result of the breakdown of totalistic and unreflexive identity schemes, such as the purely national or the familial, in which people always know their place. New movements for racial civil rights, ecology, feminism, and gay rights are not simply about material interests but are "struggles over signification; they are attempts simultaneously to make a nonstandard identity acceptable and to make that identity livable."[32] These identity struggles are often pursued by associating them with places where potential supporters are concentrated and where historic battles took place or with images of places (such as a distant homeland or a utopia) that can serve as a common point of reference. But older movements too, such as trade unions, also rely on places as a focus of collective identity. This is illustrated clearly by the geographical pattern of support for the coal miners' strike in Britain in 1984–85, which depended critically on the extent to which mining settlements were geographically isolated, on local histories of work organization, and on the character of local labor relations.[33]

Sixth, political movements make claims about nation, region, and locality as well as ethnicity, class, and gender in their manifestos and rhetorical pronouncements. These claims generate different responses in different places and can tie movements, and political parties as formal types of movement, to particular representations of the national space and how it is internally differentiated.[34] Even putative nationwide parties, for example, declare themselves for states' rights or municipal interests in addition to the identity or interests of particular regions and localities. Just as the Republican Party in the United States has become the party of the South and devolution to the states, the British Labour Party, run by politicians from its electoral fortresses in Scotland and the north of England, has become the party of devolution and local solutions to global problems. Of course, historically the Republicans were the party of the Union and the United States business establishment, with its main electoral base in the Northeast, and Labour was a working-class party supportive of state-centered solutions to a wide range of social problems. Shifts in the identities of parties reflect shifts in the ideological divisions around which they compete for popular support and the match of new political divisions with the places where parties can hope to achieve success and capture national office.

By way of summary, the geographical context of place channels the flow of interests, influence, and identities out of which emanate political activities such as organizing movements, joining parties, and voting. This understanding assumes that political action is structured by the geographical configuration at any moment of a complex set of social-geographical causes. Rather than a static or fixed geography constraining action, geography is the dynamic constellation of causal stimuli and reasoned action. Even when causal stimuli are similar in mix across places, the impact, mediated by the historical experience of particular places, can be quite different.[35] So whether outcomes are the same or different, the way they are produced varies from place to place. One of the tasks of contemporary political geography is to show empirically how this works.

This theoretical perspective requires operating simultaneously with several modes of analysis with an eye to overall synthesis. There is simply no adequate justification for a "one size fits all" methodology. The typical opposition drawn between qualitative and quantitative approaches is particularly problematic. The idea that any one methodology can answer all types of question is one of the most bizarre features of modern Anglo-American social science. To meld the production and pattern of political outcomes necessary for mapping politics requires a number of different empirical approaches. In the first place, large-scale quantitative analysis is most appropriate for detecting trends over time at various geographical scales in relation, for example, to electoral stability and change. Second, available accounts of popular and elite political interests and identities must be subjected to critical historical scrutiny. Third, local studies involving interviews and local written sources anchor understanding of the intersubjective worlds of daily life out of which politics is finally mapped.

BRINGING TOGETHER KEY CONCEPTS

Each of the theoretical perspectives noted at the beginning of this chapter (rational actor, political culture, and multiculturalist) offers an area of strength as an analytical approach to politics. But each tends to privilege a specific facet of national politics at the expense of others, and all neglect something that the place perspective takes particularly seriously. They tend to argue past one another, therefore, yet each can be seen as offering something important to a more complete account. Through reconstituting what the others offer, the place perspective is capable of incorporating the others' main areas of strength. In this section I take each of the main conceptual contributions in turn, beginning with the rationalist *agency* of the rational actor model, moving on to the focus on *difference* of multiculturalism and on the *association* of the political culture model, and ending with a conception of *socialization* as the specific contribution of the place perspective in bringing the others together. Along with a discussion of each one's conceptual contribution, I attempt to show how each can also be brought under the rubric of the place perspective.

Agency

The rational actor model of politics rests on two major premises: that individuals engage in a reasoned calculation of the costs and benefits of adopting positions on different political issues, and that they match their positions to those of organizations and parties so as to decide which to support. This approach has a number of advantages over those that presume identification with either a party (the Michigan model, named after the university where national surveys linking party identification to voting behavior were pioneered) or a class position (as measured by national census variables such as occupation or income). The most celebrated advantages are that it claims universal applicability, focuses on persons as knowing agents rather than automatons, lends itself to modeling behavior based on a few assumptions about how preferences are formed, privileges recent experiences more than long-term normative commitments, and is not tied to a particular substantive theory of political action (such as class or ethnicity), although the census characteristics of individuals may be used as surrogates for patterns of preferences and interests. Two versions of the model are identifiable: the wide and narrow versions differ in terms of whether individuals are restricted to egoistic preferences, have limits on their cognitive capacities to process information, and face only obvious objective constraints or also are limited by perceived ones.[36]

Even if one adopts the wide version, however, aspects of the rational actor model are still questionable. Two critical deficiencies concern the treatment of preferences and the notion of rationality. Preferences are deduced from what is defined as material self-interest. Reasoning therefore is restricted to optimizing individually ranked preferences. That such preference rankings might arise socially and as the result of moral reasoning raises little or no concern. This can lead to interpretive trouble when identity commitments and social influences interfere with a simple translation of presumed preferences into political interests.[37] The cautionary tale of Japanese consumers, supportive of restrictive government trade policies seemingly opposed to their interests, suggests that ideological commitments and moral reflection can interfere with the simple formula of preferences equal interests.[38] Rationality is seen in narrow utilitarian terms such as the maximization of utility or profit rather than as a process of efficiently applying means to any number of ends.[39] For example, strivings for status, power, and the approval of others may be important motivations of political action, but they do not make that action irrational. That term should be reserved for the inefficient matching of means to ends, not for the character of the ends themselves.[40]

What, then, is the main conceptual contribution of the rational actor model, broadly construed? It is the focus on active agency responding to lived experiences and situational characteristics, including institutional opportunities, political capacities, and responses to recent events, that sets the approach apart from more deterministic ones such as social class or political culture or multicultural models. There is an expectation of change and volatility in political outlooks and action rather than stasis and tranquillity. This certainly fits recent political experience in Europe and North America. It also opens the approach to the role of different contexts in providing different menus of choice for political agents by means of the specific mix of institutional opportunities, current socioeconomic circumstances, and recent political histories found in different places.[41]

Difference

Multiculturalists and some feminists privilege the invention and perpetuation of differences or distinctions between groups and their effect on orientations to and participation in political activities such as organizing movements, pressuring institutions, and supporting political parties. Since the 1960s, and in response to civil rights struggles by minorities and women's groups and the growth of "unmeltable" immigrant groups resistant to conventional cultural assimilation, a range of perspectives has arisen that calls into question both the stability of established political identities (particularly national ones) and their relative significance. Group identity is seen as depending on drawing radical social distinctions between your group and an external other by means of stereotyped images and sweeping generalizations about the profound differences that exist between you and all the others. Common to the various viewpoints on group definition by "othering" is the position that, since the Enlightenment, Western political thought has associated political order with cultural homogeneity and political chaos with cultural diversity.[42] Though understandable in the aftermath of Europe's vicious religious wars in the sixteenth century, such an orientation does not vindicate what James Tully calls "an empire of uniformity" within states.[43] Rather, Tully argues that the modern ideal of a uniform national constitutionalism impedes the recognition and accommodation of cultural diversity. Addressing difference has been deferred by associating political community with states and viewing political community as underpinned by cultural uniformity. Only between states is cultural difference theoretically possible.

Notwithstanding the virtues of this historical account of the rise of state-centered politics, within this framing other group identities simply push national identity out of its dominant place. Individuals become mere carriers of their cultural heritage, not true actors in their own right. Though the degree of essentialism as opposed to social construction ascribed to group membership is controversial, the hostility to the idea of personal agency is pervasive. This has at least three consequences: a tendency to totalize identities (ethnic, racial, gender, sexual orientation, etc.) other than national ones in a way remarkably similar to the way national identities have been conventionally treated, a dismissiveness toward national identities, as if they are at least incipiently authoritarian whereas the ones championed are not, and a tendency in practice to purify preferred identities by downplaying or disallowing their hybridity and complexity.[44]

What is most useful about this way of thinking is its clear focus on what has been called the labor of division, or the importance of the parallels between social distinctions made by intellectuals, political practices, and divisions of political space.[45] The effects of difference can be understood as invariably *taking place*, always involving a drawing of social boundaries and either a territorialization or a networking of cultural differences. The dominance of the national as the geographical level or unit par excellence for making and bounding distinctions is thus historical rather than natural. The surveillance power of states (through census taking and taxation as much as through violent coercion) has subordinated cultural-geographical differences within states. But incorporated places have never been entirely removed from political agendas, and they have recently experienced something of a revival in response to new pressures from the world economy and increased immigration. Today, therefore, the making of difference is taking place in ways that transgress the equation of political community with established nation-states and groups with singular identities, linking groups across national boundaries and partitioning the internal space of states into a mosaic of places associated with different groups and their (mixed) identities.[46]

Association

Advocates of political culture models typically explain political action not by reference to individual actors or social groups (primordial or socially constructed) but with respect to normative orientations learned largely, but not entirely, in childhood from families and other primary groups and as members of secondary organizations. These approaches emphasize shared values, beliefs, and preferences shaped by common historical experience that are reproduced through membership in primary groups. The so-called subjectivist approach tends to focus on the long-term continuity of political dispositions and the values that underpin them. Civic republicans tend to privilege the role of group memberships or association for encouraging active political involvement. They differ, however, in how far they prefer organized groups or more informal types of association and how much they identify historical path dependency as vital to the emergence of civic and noncivic cultures.

I argue here that the general approach has serious problems, not least its sociological vacuity and its tendency to reproduce old ideas about national character in more neutral-sounding language. A commitment to national-level analysis is not inevitable. Indeed, any geographical unit with a high degree of presumed cultural uniformity fits the bill. Irrespective of the geographical scale of analysis, however, reasonably rigorous empirical research shows how problematic political culture studies tend to be, demonstrating that indicators of short-term experiences have more power in explaining political attitudes than does evidence of long-term dispositions[47] and that path dependency introduces a "geographical lock-in" that obscures the role of recent as opposed to historically distant institutional and cultural factors in accounting for contemporary political activity.[48] When linked to the idea of social capital, association in groups often takes on an even more questionable role in explaining political involvement.[49] For one thing, group associations are frequently identified as individual traits when they are in fact contextual in nature. For another, social capital cannot be reduced solely to associationism, given its provenance as a concept designed to incorporate a range of noneconomic factors into models of political and economic behavior.[50]

Among American political theorists, the civic republican (or communitarian) version of the political culture model has undergone a significant expansion in recent years, related particularly to a revival of interest in Alexis de Tocqueville's *Democracy in America*.[51] As is well known,

Tocqueville was sensitive to differences in spaces of association. The contrast between Europe and America was judged to result from the more open horizon in America, the opportunity to make places from scratch, whereas in Europe established systems of land tenure, settlement, and inheritance restricted the circulation of the population. Tocqueville invoked this American pattern to explain the greater social egalitarianism of Euro-Americans and their greater propensity to involve themselves in social groupings and civic life than found among contemporary Europeans.

Those currently invoking Tocqueville either decry the loss of the world of civic engagement and political efficacy Americans once enjoyed or, failing to learn from Tocqueville's own sensitivity to the political consequences of different spatialities of communication and movement, try to expropriate the Great Traveler for projects of rehomogenizing the nation's map of social solidarities and civic-mindedness.[52] They also miss the extent to which early American civic culture depended on "the representative institutions and centrally directed activity of a very distinctive national state."[53] In particular, the high levels of extralocal information that Tocqueville thought characterized the inhabitants of rural Michigan came from letters and newspapers delivered by the United States Post Office. Local association did not occur in a national geographical vacuum.

What is compelling about this revival is the renewed attention to social mediation in political life. The focus on association, however, needs closer integration with the spatial structures of the present day. Not only are places now more closely integrated economically and bureaucratically, they are also more segmented culturally and ethnically than was the case historically.[54] Partly this is a function of differential surveillance and subordination, indicated, for example, by the military-style policing and high levels of incarceration in inner-city black neighborhoods in the United States, but it is also a result of the growth of more fleeting and partial forms of association such as support groups and other forms of social sustenance. What is clear, however, is that politics in the United States and elsewhere involves individual self-transformation (increased sense of efficacy, etc.) as well as organizing for collective action, and that this is invariably promoted by association with others, not necessarily just in evidently political groups.[55]

Socialization

What brings agency, difference, and association together? As defined above, each seems pretty much exclusive of the others. Agency implies individual action, difference emphasizes group identity as the overriding determinant of behavior, and association suggests group membership as the crucial parameter of political activity. What glues them together is the possibility of active socialization of persons through identification with various social groups and chosen membership in various associations and the places connected with them. Agency therefore does not necessitate the total autonomy or rigid separation of individuals.[56] Rather, through social contexts individuals learn agency and acquire the resources to practice it: the ways and means of associating with and dissociating from others in pursuit of diverse and shared ends, which is what politics is all about.[57]

This understanding of socialization differs profoundly from the sense of "cultural zapping" that the term often signifies, implying an external effect from the cultural environment internalized by individuals. The meaning here is closer to Georg Simmel's idea of *sociability,* suggestive of the concrete social networks in which people are born, raised, and live their lives and from which they acquire primary orientations to both their own "life world" (selfhood) and the larger world.[58] The densest informal and spontaneous network ties are intensely localized even today. They are traced by the most geographically concentrated circuits of everyday life. Older and younger people are particularly dependent on such localized ties. Families and friendships are especially important sources of sociability at the beginning of life and toward the end. But as sociologist Eviatar Zerubavel argues in his analysis of how social distinctions are learned and practiced in everyday life, the spatial content of sociability remains high throughout the life course:

> We . . . associate selfhood with a psychological "distance" from others, and experience privacy (including its non-spatial aspects, such as secrecy) as having some "space" for ourselves or as a "territory" of inaccessibility surrounding us. We experience others as being "close" to or "distant" from us and portray our willingness or unwillingness to make contact with them using topological images such as "opening up" (or "reaching out") and being "closed" (or "removed"). We also use the image of "penetration" to depict the essence of the process of becoming intimate.[59]

This spatial language is deeply revealing not only of practices of exclusion, separation, and bounding personal and group space but also of how we continue to talk about and experience selfhood, always in relation to both alien others and the groups we belong to. Overall, "we basically experience reality as a 'space' made up of discrete mental fields delineated by 'fences' that define and separate them one from another."[60]

Even in the age of the Internet, most electronic communication still falls away rapidly with distance, implying that such potentially anonymous network linkages depend on prior face-to-face relations. Most children who have access to a computer, for example, e-mail their school and neighborhood friends more often than they tap into bulletin boards with unknown persons. Likewise, most workplace electronic message distribution is local.[61] Formal organizational and group memberships are also heavily oriented to the physical nodes and routes followed day to day, even if they are less localized and more diffuse than more informal and spontaneous ties.[62] More generally, "entry to hyper-space necessitates access to the technology and nomads require passports if they are not to be sent back whence they came."[63]

When the globalization associated with a shrinking world of communication is neither uncritically embraced without adequate empirical support nor uncritically excoriated without attending to its positive consequences (not least the prospect of a more open world with less socioeconomic exclusion), it can be understood as potentially transforming the sense of place.[64] If the local is still the primary site for human co-presence, phenomenologically based in bodily activities, the spatial extension of communication actively works to undermine a clear sense of social isolation and self-sufficiency as it also enhances the importance of interactions across space. Such spatial stretching is by no means new; it can be thought of as an essential feature of modernity.[65] But its intensity and pervasiveness across a wide range of places are new and can be seen as depleting the sense of place as localized and subverting the apparent distinctiveness of different places to a greater extent than in the past.[66]

However intense and disintegrative the disembedding of places may be, it is invariably held in check by what the anthropologist Ulf Hannerz calls "the glass of milk syndrome."[67] Bodily needs and everyday physical routines anchor the otherwise unbounded imagination to place. Indeed, the rush of new stimuli from distant points may encourage an enhanced identification with local place amid what can be perceived as a corrosive flow of media and money. Such identification is both physical and discursive, framing social action on both practical and ideological grounds. The word grounds signifies precisely the place-based character of active socialization into political and other dispositions.

"Embodiment" is the key to how engaged agency remains embedded in places. The world is shaped by how people engage with it from *where* they sit or stand. The locatedness of human bodies provides the immediate locus for any action that is undertaken. Consequently, people are *never* disengaged thinkers (as a narrow rational actor model would have it) but are agents whose experiences can be understood (by them and others) only in relation to the contexts or backgrounds in which their lives are embedded. This is not just a question of general dispositions or "languages" (in Charles Taylor's sense of "modes of expression") that are learned once, presumably early in life, and can be ignored later. The contribution of significant others throughout the life course, from parents and family to teachers, friends, and influential acquaintances, is crucial simply because humans are social animals. Identities and interests are worked out through dialogical relations with others, not alone as calculating agents.[68]

People actively choose where to concentrate their social energies and in turn receive different stimuli from the settings they invest in. They are not simply passive recipients or carriers of social messages but are active participants in their own social lives. Individuals do not come before or stand outside society. As actors, individuals are creative beings, capable of engaging in moral agency based on compelling reasons acquired from their surroundings. But their creativity occurs only in social contexts that influence the possible courses it can take. These are the product of reactions to and influences on material flows, ideas, and practices emanating from sources with a variety of geographical ranges, from the local to the global, that vary in their relative intermixing over time and from place to place.

The word culture can be used to represent the structure or system of signification (set of symbols, understandings, and commitments) that defines the *common sense* of a particular place. It is in this context of intersubjective understandings and meanings that political action is realized. Of course, the danger of the word culture lies in its frequent use to represent a set of eternally fixed traits in which groups and individuals alike are trapped. Its advantage lies in the way it draws attention to the complex flow of social, economic, and political influences and how these are always engaged concurrently by strategies of action drawn from stories, symbols, rituals, and worldviews that people both learn from and contribute to.[69]

A focus on active socialization in place allows a potential escape from the "murky world . . . of social determination in which practices are embedded and which sustain them" to one in which "practices is a word not for some sort of mysterious hidden collective object, but for the individual formations of habit that are the condition for the performances and emulations that make up life."[70] It does so by allowing a clear focus on the ways distinctive sets of causal influences bring about different outcomes in terms of individual behavior in different place contexts.

Two very different ideal types of socialization can be identified. The first, the *collective,* is constructed between a strong singular group identity tied to a focused image of place, a powerful attachment to certain voluntary associations, and an intense pattern of sociability. The second, the *conjunctural,* is characterized by relatively "light," multiple group identities without a strong sense of place, weak or no attachments to voluntary associations, and limited day-to-day engagement with others. There is therefore no need to posit a single one size fits all conception of socialization. The first usually implies a strongly territorial pattern of socialization, in which agency, difference, and association reinforce one another through dense and interconnected ties of sociability that bind people to places. Contemporary Italy still seems to have a high degree of this type of socialization, in spite of the pressures to fit in with a world of increasingly ephemeral affiliations. The second implies a much weaker pattern of socialization with looser connections to place. This is the model of American socialization that many scholars seem to have, notwithstanding evidence for the persisting importance of local and regional social and political ties and differences in the United States. In any actual case, of course, the character of socialization and the connection to place may well be somewhere in between the two ideal types.

CONCLUSION

I propose, then, two tracks to establish a place perspective as an approach to understanding politics in a wide range of countries, though Italy is given prime consideration in this book. The first is a straightforward statement of the theoretical position and its varied assumptions about space and place, the nature of geographical context, and the causes that condition place-to-place differences in political activities. The second is a drawing together of concepts from various currents of contemporary Anglo-American political thought to show how they can be made compatible with the place perspective, both enriching it and suggesting that it is possible to overcome seemingly insuperable theoretical differences if a suitable vehicle is available. The point is to show that while there is much of value in contemporary political thought, the conceptual contributions can sometimes be placed in a fresh light if they are reformulated and related to one another. In this case the geography of socialization is seen as providing an overarching framework in which to place conceptions of agency, difference, and association that are at the center of contemporary disputes about the roots and course of political action.

CHAPTER 3

Landscape Ideals and
National Identity in Italy

A world divided up into national territories that people identify with is not a natural given. National identities are based on the creation of "imagined communities" among people who do not know most of their conationals or much of the national territory beyond what they encounter in the course of their lives. Although some national identities have old roots in places within present-day national territories, national identities as they are known in Europe today are usually traced to the period in the late eighteenth and early nineteenth centuries when political elites invented traditions of group occupancy of a given national territory and began to associate this with popular rather than purely monarchical sovereignty.[1]

Based on the creation of national communication networks and vernacular literatures in national idioms, the circulation of common stories about national origins and tribulations, the casting of national definitions of taste and opinion, and commemoration of the heroic and tragic sides of a common past, by the close of the nineteenth century national identities became basic components of self-identities for the burgeoning middle classes and segments of the working classes across the whole of Europe. Everything from the orientation of railway networks around capital cities to military conscription and mass elementary education conspired to produce political identities in which the national was increasingly dominant in relation both to other geographical scales and to social identities such as class or religion.

None of this happened, however, without intensive political struggle and rhetorical dispute. In his classic book *The Country and the City,* Raymond Williams showed that literary and cultural production, in the form of anthems, political pamphlets, and novels, derived much of its aesthetic appeal from conflicts arising from the changing geography of the times.[2] New classes, interests, and ideas about national identity contended with existing ones in a struggle for control over territory. There was nothing inevitable about the outcome of this process. It took quite different paths in different countries. We err when we insist on making all cases conform to the history of a particular ideal type, whether that is England, France, or even the United States.

Identifying the means of producing national identities is one thing; the content of those identities is another thing entirely. Much of the recent understanding of national identities rests on the spread, by mass education, of nationalist versions of history and the commemoration of nationhood associated with periodic rituals and "sites of memory," places where the past of the nation is represented in the present, thus preserving in concrete form the *collective* achievements and sufferings of people unknown to one another who have served and sacrificed for the nation.[3] These sites range from monuments to national heroes and uprisings against foreign rule to war cemeteries and the built form of capital cities (Whitehall and Trafalgar Square in London, the Arc de Triomphe and the Champs Élysées in Paris). Emotional investment in the visual map image of the national territory and an idealized three-dimensional physical landscape of the national state have attracted much less interest.[4] In particular, limited attention has been given to the images of the national territory (the national landscape) that people might carry around with them—what can be called national landscape ideals. These are not necessarily designed for popular consumption, although competing groups may well endorse particular landscape ideals as part of the struggle over the expropriation of the national territory. It is more that they emerge into popular consciousness by means of both propaganda and that "common sense" that the famous Italian Marxist theorist-activist Antonio Gramsci saw as the social glue of an emerging nationalist hegemony. In the Italian case, as we shall see, Gramsci's overall indictment of the failure of the country's nationalizing intellectuals (and political leaders) is also true of its failure to construct a hegemonic consensus about a national landscape ideal.[5]

STORIES OF LANDSCAPE AND IDENTITY, SIMPLE AND COMPLEX

Since the nineteenth century dominant images of landscapes in Europe for outsiders and nationalizing intellectuals alike seem to have been national ones. Often these are quite specific vistas turned into typifications of a national landscape as a whole. Quaint thatched cottages in pastoral settings (England), cypress trees topping a hill that has been grazed and plowed for an eternity (Italy), dense village settlements surrounded by equally dense forests (Germany), and high-hedged fields with occasional stone villages (France) constitute some of the stock images of European rural landscapes conveyed in landscape painting, tourist brochures,

school textbooks, and music. Ideas of distinctive national pasts are con-
jured up for both natives and foreigners by these landscape images. They
are representative landscapes, visual encapsulations of a group's occupation of a particular territory and the memory of a shared past it conveys.[6]
They can also be thought of as one way the social history and distinctiveness of a group are objectified through reference (however idealized) to
the physical settings of the everyday lives of people to whom we "belong,"
but most of whom we never meet. Yet these landscape images are both
partial and recent. Not only do they come from particular localities within
the boundaries of their nation-states (respectively, southern England, Tuscany, Brandenburg, and Normandy) their visualization as somehow representative of a national heritage is a modern invention, dating at most to
the nineteenth century. The history of these landscape images therefore
parallels the history of the imprinting of certain national identities onto
the states of modern Europe.

The agents of every modern national state aspire to have their state represented *materially* in the everyday lives of their subjects and citizens. The
persisting power of the state depends on it.[7] Everywhere anyone might
look would then reinforce the identity between state and citizen by associating the iconic inheritance of a national past with the present state and
its objectives. Yet this association is harder to achieve than it might first
appear. Where the past can be readily portrayed as monolithic and uniform, as with the English case, consensus about a national past with un-
broken continuity to "time immemorial" suggesting a comfortable, even
casual, association is easily accomplished. But nowhere else in Europe is
landscape "so freighted as legacy. Nowhere else does the very term suggest
not simply scenery and *genres de vie,* but quintessential national virtues."[8]
Even in England, however, not all is as it seems. The visual cliché of sheep
grazing in a meadow, with hedgerows separating the fields and neat villages nestling in tidy valleys, dates from the time in the nineteenth century when the landscape paintings of Constable and others gained popularity among the taste-making elite.[9] Nevertheless, though invented, the
ideal of a created and ordered landscape with deep roots in a past when
people all knew their places within the landscape (and the ordered society
it represents) has become an important element in English national identity, irrespective of its fabulous roots in the 1800s.[10]

Elsewhere in Europe, capturing popular landscape images to associate
with national identities or inventing new ones has been much more difficult. The apparently straightforward English case therefore is potentially
misleading, one good reason for turning to other examples.[11] It suggests a
simple historical correlation between the rise of a national state and a singular landscape imagery, however insecure this may now be in the face of

economic decline, North/South political differences, the revival of Celtic nationalisms challenging the English hubris to represent something they alone now call "British," the immigration of culturally distinctive groups unwilling to abandon their own separate identities, and the devastation wrought on the rural landscape by agribusiness.[12] Nation-state formation elsewhere in Europe took a very different direction than in England—not to say that everywhere else it was the same. Two aspects of the difference are vital.

One aspect was the complex history of local and urban loyalties in many parts of Europe, particularly those later unified as Italy and Germany.[13] In these contexts there was often a long history of city independence and local patriotism with little or none of the early commercialization of agriculture and industrialization that swept English rural dwellers into national labor markets and national–social class identities at the very same time a state-building elite was strengthening and extending national institutions. The image of a bucolic past tapped the nostalgia of those experiencing the disruptions of industrialization, reminding them that not everything had changed. Such landscapes could still be found, even if no longer experienced daily. Later industrialization often also involved less disruption of ties to place. In particular, as electricity replaced steam power, industries moved to areas of existing population concentration rather than, as in the case of the English coalfields, requiring that people move to where the industry was.

Another aspect was the external orientation of the English state and economy. Not only were English merchants, industrialists, and travelers increasingly dominant within the evolving world economy of the nineteenth century, they were often nostalgic for what they had left behind when they traveled abroad and needed to compare what they saw with a datum or steady point of view. This led many of them to idealize in their mind's eye an England that was largely the product of a merging of their own experience and the renderings of England in paintings and other visual representations. This produced a unified vision that was much harder to achieve in those contexts where influential people had less empire, traveled less, and thus had less need of a single, stable vision.[14]

Not only the idea of a national landscape but also that of national identity is also more complex than the simple English story might make it appear. A national identity involves a widely shared memory of a common past for people who have never seen or talked to one another in the flesh. This sense of belonging depends as much on forgetting as on remembering, reconstructing the past as a path to the national present in order to guarantee a common future.[15] National histories, monuments (war memorials, heroic statues), commemorations (anniversaries and parades), sites of institutionalized memories (museums, libraries, and other archives), and representative landscapes are among the important instruments for ordering the national past. They give national identity a materiality it would otherwise lack. But such milieus of memory must coexist with other memories and their identities. National identity does not sweep away all others. Some local identities, such as the German attachment to *Heimat* (homeplace), while remaining distinct, also feed into a wider national identity.[16] Some diasporic groups, however, such as Scottish Hebrideans in North America or recent immigrants to Europe, retain local or religious identities rather than adopting the national ones they are usually associated with by outsiders.[17]

The "sacralization" of the nation-state has never been total: even within totalitarian states, sites of religious and local celebration have had their place, even as states try to exploit them.[18] The totalization of national identities has faced a number of barriers. One difficulty is what to select from the past to identify and emphasize as distinctive and peculiar. National pasts are fraught with conflicts over dynastic claims, boundary disputes, religious pogroms, and the meaning of historical events and personalities. What to emphasize, therefore, is also fraught with potential conflict. Whose national past is it, anyway? As a result, national identities can have multiple definitions and are constantly in flux. Allied to what to select from the past must be the self-conscious conviction that a bounded national space with considerable internal cultural homogeneity actually exists. Attaining this conviction requires a readily available other against whom to define one's national identity.[19] Without this widely shared belief there is little that is "national" for the identity to express. Another barrier to the totalization of national identities is the existence of alternative identities (such as class, region, ethnicity, and religion) that do not always flow into or easily coexist with clear and coherent national ones. As the world economy has become more integrated and political boundaries have lost some of their force in regulating economic and cultural flows, these alternative identities have become increasingly potent.[20] A third obstacle has been the reemergence of powerful transnational identities, usually associated with religious beliefs and transculturated migrants, but also related to groups adhering to dominant ideologies such as neoliberalism and its agents, namely international banks, multinational firms, and large-scale regulatory organizations (the European Commission and the International Monetary Fund, to name just two). Finally, the idea of identity is itself an intellectual imposition, implying that there are singular, stable, and essential divisions that people identify with.[21] Yet there are societies in which conceptions of the self or person do not require the spatially bounded reference groups and physically bounded individuals that much academic discussion of identity presupposes. Identifying *with* a particular group is not a necessity of life. Nor, therefore, is national identity. At the same time, identity can also be analytically problematic, obscuring the varied social processes of categorization, group identification, and self-understanding that the term is meant to capture.[22]

ITALIAN UNIFICATION AND THE PROBLEM OF A NATIONAL LANDSCAPE IDEAL

Italy provides a good case for examining the connection between landscape and identity. Italy was at the center of the visual revolution of the Renaissance, in which visual representation became a vital part of the modern means of communicating the meanings and significance of religious and political messages. And it has also been a country where state formation was long delayed by the existence of alternative foci of material life (in particular, city-based economies), the home base of the papacy and the Roman Catholic Church, and local cultural identities alternative to "Italian." It may be at the opposite pole from England, in that creating a match between a representative landscape and an Italian national identity was a difficult and obviously artificial process from the start. It thus draws attention to the *process* of linkage between identity and landscape in more complex ways. Also, much has already been written about the English case,[23] so looking at the other extreme of European experience as a whole (a late-unifying state with much internal cultural heterogeneity) has much to recommend it.

An Italian state formed only in the second half of the nineteenth century. Although this tardiness in establishing a single state for the peninsula and islands had numerous causes, the strong municipal, city-state, and regional-state governments (particularly in the North) held off the forces pushing the country toward unification. Most important, in the late Middle Ages and during the Renaissance, at the same time that the great Western monarchies were consolidating territorial states in England, Spain, and France, the politics of northern and central Italy was characterized by a fragmented mosaic of city-states and localized jurisdictions of a variety of types, from principalities to republics. It was the "extraordinary energy and growing capacity of urban centers [that] led paradoxically to the early elimination from central and northern Italy's political firmament of any *superior*—king, emperor, or prince. The cities transformed themselves precociously into city-states with corresponding territorial dimensions and political functions."[24] This is not to say that they did not try to turn themselves into territorial states—but they failed to do so. As their economic strength faded in the eighteenth century, with Europe's center of political-economic gravity moving northwestward, the

Italian ministates proved easy prey to the expansionist ambitions of Austria and Spain. Even with foreign domination, however (and this was a major stimulus to the development of Italian nationalism before unification), the capacity of Italian cities to penetrate adjacent territories but with no one city winning control over the others was relatively undiminished. When European politics in the nineteenth century opened up the possibility of a national state for Italy, the initiative came from a regional state, Savoy-Piedmont, "whose social and political structure was different, and of less glorious tradition, from that of the city-based states. Inversely, the rapid fall of the city-based states signals the absence of effective power to sustain them, even though their long survival testified for centuries to the vitality of medieval urban civilization."[25]

It was from northern Italy and, initially at least, by northern Italians that Italy was made. The traditions of the city-states and the Europeanness of the Savoyard regime gave unified Italy the monarchy that provided the "new" Italy with its mythic resources. The South, and the zones the Austrians had controlled in the North, had been won from foreign domination, but foreign domination, particularly in the South, was seen as having created a society that was now doubly disadvantaged: geographically marginal to Europe and politically marginal to the "high" Italy of Renaissance city-states from which the new territorial state could be seen as having descended.

Foreign political-constitutional models, particularly those provided by England, France, and the new Germany, were also important to the nationalizing intellectuals who set up shop in Rome after the final annexation of that city to the new state in 1870.[26] Acceptance by other Europeans as a rising great power became a particularly important element in national policy that was to last until 1945. This meant taking very seriously what foreigners found exceptional in Italy. The new state could then build on foundations that would lead to respect from the others. It was to ancient Rome, both republican and imperial, and to certain Renaissance landscape ideals articulated by foreign visitors to Italy as well as by local savants, that the visionaries of the new state turned. Both of these represented powerful images that would serve double duty: to mobilize the disparate populations of the new state behind it and to impress outsiders with the revival of a glorious past, only now in an Italian rather than a Roman or a Renaissance form.

FLORENCE AND THE TUSCAN LANDSCAPE IDEAL

Turning first to the Renaissance inspiration, the Italian Risorgimento (revival through unification) of the mid-nineteenth century was largely concerned with reestablishing Italy as a center of European civilization, as "it"

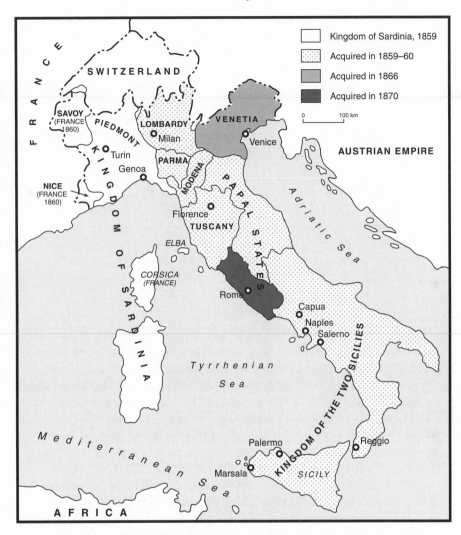

Figure 3.1 The political geography of Italian unification, 1859–70. Source: Author.

had been during the Renaissance. Florence was, of course, the preeminent center of the Renaissance, long since consigned to the role of *città d'arte* or storehouse for all that Italy had been. It was in Florence in the 1850s that a group of landscape painters set about putting their talents into the service of the new state. The Macchiaioli painters (from the various meanings of *macchia:* spot, sketch, dense underbrush) set about defining a representative landscape for Italy. Not surprisingly, they saw Tuscany as the prototypical Italian setting. This was what they were most familiar with. Of course, it had great Renaissance connotations. It also fit the foreign (particularly English) romantic attachment to Tuscany and other locales in northern and central Italy, as expressed by the early nineteenth-century generation of poets and writers.[27] The city of Dante, Michelangelo, and Machiavelli was the appropriate center for a national revival. The Macchiaioli used their Renaissance forebears and European contemporaries (particularly English painters) as their guides. They expressed their nationalism through a search for images that could be used to tie the noble past to the developing present. Art historian Albert Boime writes that

> they searched the riverflats along the Arno, the orchards and farms of the suburbs of Florence, the hill pastures around Pistoia, and the wild Maremma region (with its thick *macchie* of scrub pine and underbrush) for motifs appropriate to their fresh viewpoint. Their topographical specificity and personal response were totally integrated in what might be called a *macchia-scape*—the landscape that retained the sincerity of vision they admired in the Tuscan artists of the Quattrocento, but that also conveyed the modernity and nationalism of contemporary Italian life.[28]

Like the Risorgimento itself, the Macchiaioli idea had both Italian and European dimensions. For all their other differences, leaders of the movements for Italian unification such as Giuseppe Mazzini and Count Camillo Cavour of Piedmont wanted to bring Italy up to date and to a social and political equality with the rest of Europe. The Macchiaioli were also both nationally and internationally oriented. In Boime's words, "By asserting Italian individuality they hoped to contribute to a release of energies needed to make Italy a great nation, able to assume a role in the affairs of Europe."[29] Their "sketch tradition" drew directly on Renaissance prototypes but also was linked by the Macchiaioli to the French Barbizon school, just as the Risorgimento appealed for legitimacy to the French Revolution and the two Napoleons. But the self-attached label of the school also had subversive overtones, if Boime's analysis has merit. Some of the painters were notorious punsters and self-defined "outlaws." The word *macchia* can mean hiding out in the woods (*farsi alla macchia*), living as an outlaw (*vivere alla macchia*), or publishing illegally (*stampare alla macchia*). In Florentine dialect *macchia* has the additional meaning of a "child of the woods," signifying someone without parents, marginal and disinherited. The wild and wooded Maremma region of southern Tuscany fit this aspect of the Macchiaioli vision; associating the painters with the secret societies (such as the Carbonari) that had stimulated the first efforts at Risorgimento. The Carbonari took their name from the charcoal burners of the forest who labored in secret away from the gaze of the authorities.[30]

The bible of the Macchiaioli movement, Telemaco Signorini's *Carica-*

turisti e caricaturati al Caffè Michelangiolo (Caricaturists and the caricatured at the Michelangiolo Café), first published in 1893 but based on articles written in 1866–67, recreates the atmosphere of the popular café in Florence where the Macchiaioli congregated.[31] There were ten core members: Giuseppe Abbati, Cristiano Banti, Odoardo Borrani, Adriano Cecioni, Vincenzo Cabianca, Vito D'Ancona, Giovanni Fattori, Silvestro Lega, Raffaelo Sernesi, and Telemaco Signorini himself. Underlying the book's gossip about who said what to whom is a narrative linking the history of the Macchiaioli to that of the Risorgimento. One connecting influence was romanticism, even though the Macchiaioli were relentlessly realist in their artistic representations. As early as 1813 Laurence Sterne's preromantic masterpiece *A Sentimental Journey through France and Italy* was translated into Italian (Tuscan) by Ugo Foscolo, himself a famous poet and writer. Walter Scott's novels were also translated and widely read by literati in mid-nineteenth-century Italy. The great Italian patriot Giuseppe Garibaldi was later often compared to Scott's hero Rob Roy, from the 1817 novel of that name. In 1827 Alessandro Manzoni came to Florence to purge his allegorical novel of Italian unification (*I promessi sposi* [The betrothed]) of its Lombard expressions and rewrite it in the Tuscan (Italian) dialect.[32] All these works marked a break with the formal and pedantic writing that preceded them. They all accept nations as natural forms whose literary canons should reflect this status. They also appeal to a certain naturalism that finds in physical landscapes an important source of the "spirit" of particular nations. Manzoni, for example, was fond of saying that he came to Florence to bathe his masterpiece "in the waters of the river Arno," as if the rewriting required his own presence in the physical surroundings, sounds, and smells of Florence. Incidentally, this also gave a tremendous boost to the cause of the "Tuscanizers," those who wanted to establish the Tuscan dialect (because of its historical connection to such great *Italian* writers as Dante) as the national language of the new state.[33]

Another element in Signorini's story of the Macchiaioli is a critique of previous landscape painters, who are seen as preferring foreign (particularly French) scenes to Italian ones. In particular, Signorini praises the autobiography of Massimo D'Azeglio (*I miei ricordi* [Things I remember]), an older historical novelist and painter, which was published in 1867. Though a social conservative, D'Azeglio (famous for his aphorism after unification: "We have made Italy, now we must make the Italians") argued strongly for a patriotic landscape ideal. This is what attracted the Macchiaioli to him. He celebrated the indigenous (Tuscan) landscape and shared their cultural aims. He was heavily critical of his own generation of painters:

> We love independence and nationalism, we love Italy; further, the landscape painters all chant together "Rome or death," but when

Figure 3.2 Silvestro Lega, *Paese con contadini* (Landscape with peasants), c. 1871. Private collection, Montecatini.

they take up their brushes the only thing they don't paint is Italy. The magnificent Italian landscape, the glorious light, the rich hues of the sky over our heads and the earth we tread; no one considers these things worthy of being painted. Go to exhibitions and what do we see? A scene from the north of France, imitation of so and so; a seascape at Etretat or Honfleur, imitation of someone else; a heath in Flanders; a wood at Fontainebleau, copied from God knows who! . . . They prefer a nature without a soul, without character, weak and tempered like a muted violin. For this they renounce Italy, her sky and the beauty which once brought so many enemies into our land, but today, thank God, brings only friends who never tire of acclaiming it.[34]

Much of Signorini's story, however, is taken up with relating the history of the café and its patrons to the ups and downs of the campaign to unify Italy. Even the recollections of friends killed in the wars or the ideals of the Risorgimento conjure up landscape images when at certain moments he recalls them. Especially

during a beautiful autumn morning, or on a balmy spring day, or in a winter mist, or amid the sultry passions and strident song of the harvest-time crickets, when it happens that I climb alone the smiling hills of memories which crown our city [Florence]; or stroll along the fields and gardens populated with farmhouses and villas, along the banks of the Mugnone or the Arno, the Mensola or the Affrico,

Figure 3.3   Rafaello Sernesi, *Radura nel bosco* (Forest glade), c. 1862–63. Private collection, Montecatini.

and come upon a small grassy area, off to the side and in the shade; then, having put down my old paint box, the faithful custodian of my personal impressions, inseparable companion of my distant voyages and nearby excursions, I lie down on my back next to it, and gazing intently at the profound blue of the heavens, I return with my thoughts to the past, now having become more significant to me than the future! . . . And my entire past unfolds, not only its mad joys and its daring undertakings, but also its profound sadnesses and its infinite vexations.[35]

Figure 3.4 Telemaco Signorini, *Sul greto d'Arno* (On the bed of the Arno), c. 1863–65. Gallery of Modern Art, Florence.

What Signorini finally reveals, therefore, is the deep relationship that existed for the Macchiaioli between landscape and the development of the Risorgimento. But it is not just any landscape. The landscape impressions are those of Signorini's native Tuscany; of the river Arno, the hills surrounding Florence, the sharecropping peasants who are part of the landscapes where they appear. The outstanding memories of his life return to him when he recalls the sites depicted by the Macchiaioli. The passage ends on the sad note with which many Italian patriots greeted the way Italian unification evolved: dependent more on conquest and external (non)intervention than on popular uprising and revolt. Compensation is found in the private moments when art merged with life in the depiction of landscapes that expressed one's ideals and aspirations (figs. 3.2 to 3.4).[36]

This culture of the Risorgimento associated closely with Florence and Tuscany was not to outlast it. Even as Florence became (temporarily) the capital of the new Italy in 1865 and was beginning to assert its position as a national cultural center, the Macchiaioli started to lose their social cohesiveness and their common political commitments.[37] Tuscany was not a smaller version of the whole of Italy. Tuscan history was not national history. Florence was not to be the permanent capital of the country. Their images did not stick, much like the promise of the Risorgimento itself. Quickly the Macchiaioli were redefined as precursors of Impressionism or simply another school of provincial Italian painters. Only during Fascism were they once again raised as proponents of an idealized Italy, this time, of course, as precursors of the chauvinistic and ultranationalist vision of an older rural Italy beloved of the most reactionary Fascists.[38] With such unfortunate friends, rehabilitation has been a long time in coming.

ROME AND THE ROMAN LANDSCAPE IDEAL

A better-known attempt at creating a representative landscape for Italian national identity than that of the Macchiaioli came to fruition after unification was achieved. This involved looking to the ancient past of Rome as the seat of empire to find inspiration for a new Rome around which the new Italy could be built. The selection of Rome as the capital certainly suggests that the Roman past was in the minds of Italy's unifiers even before unification was finally achieved. "For me Rome is Italy," wrote Giuseppe Garibaldi, the great hero of unification, in his memoirs.[39] As early as 1861, although not yet part of the new state, Rome was declared the capital. The annexation of Rome and its surrounding region provided not only the last chunk of the national territory claimed by Italian patriots but also a "neutral" city not associated, as were Turin, Milan, and Florence, with the local elites who had taken hold of the process of Italian unification.[40] In other words, as Massimo Birindelli puts it, Rome "became the capital not for the qualities that it had but for the ones it was missing."[41] This political advantage plus the obvious associations with a glorious past gave Rome crucial points over its competitors. Rome's international visibility also counted. Italian unification was more the result of international diplomacy than of nationalist revolt. Consequently, attracting outside support was critical. By way of contrast, German unification during the same period (1850–70) was much more internally oriented. The choice of Berlin reflected both the Prussian dominance of the new state and the Prussian state's prior commitment to economic and military growth as manifested in the growth of Berlin itself. Rome was very different. Rather than a center of national prestige or strength, Rome was widely viewed in the new state as a parasitic city that consumed but did not produce.[42] It was an ecclesiastical city without either manufacturing industry or modern bureaucracy.

But the choice of Rome was vital to the architects of a new Italian identity. First, across all the movements for unification the city of Rome was itself a unifying force.[43] If there was a single tradition that the population of the peninsula and islands held in common, it was that of ancient Rome. The myth of a unified past, however different from the present, underwrote the unified future that the Savoyard monarchy and its aristocratic allies who had taken control of the Risorgimento saw for the new state. Rome at least presented a strong image for a group concerned that the new

Italy might turn out to be too decentralized for their political and economic interests. It also represented a vision at odds with the more parochial ones emanating from local elites in Turin, Milan, and Florence. Rome represented a central link in a country in which local and municipal attachments were strong. It was, in Bruno Tobia's words, "the meeting point through which it became possible for municipalism to be projected directly towards a *national* dimension."[44] Locating the capital in Rome also took on directly the pope's claim to be a temporal as well as a spiritual ruler. The pope remained the one local ruler of preunification Italy to reject the spirit and purpose of Italian independence and unification. As the capital, therefore, Rome symbolically embodied various aspects of the Jacobinism and centralism that were hallmarks of Italian unification: the myth of Rome as a strong center to counteract the centrifugal pressures emanating from the real political divisions of the country represented by other places such as Florence and powerful institutions such as the papacy.

From the outset, the new rulers tried to make Rome a symbolic center for their regime. Initially there was an attempt, under the patronage of the Piedmontese politician Quintano Sella, to establish a new center of gravity for the city to the northeast, beyond its 1870 core. This largely failed. It was easier and more profitable to local interests to concentrate government offices in the historical core. In this they largely succeeded, expropriating convents, monasteries, palaces, and other buildings from the previous papal regime. Another and more important symbolic method was "patriotic building." This involved locating monuments and public buildings to celebrate the new regime, recall its historical connections, and challenge the singular association of the Roman Catholic Church with the most sacred sites in the city. From one point of view, however, these efforts at securing a new monumental Rome in the years 1870 to 1922 largely came to nothing.[45] As Tobia has argued in some detail, impressive ideological-rhetorical debate produced little physical change in the city's landscape.[46] Within the historical center only the subversive placement of the Vittoriano (the monument to King Victor Emmanuel II, the first king of the new Italy) on the edge of the Capitoline Hill (the historical core of the city, next to the seat of the commune and the Roman Forum) and midway between the pope's two seats—at the Vatican and, as bishop of Rome, at San Giovanni in Laterano—provided a powerful symbol of the new national identity in the new Rome (fig. 3.5). Even then the monument was to a person rather than to some abstract ideal of the nation, though during Fascism attempts were made to turn the monument into something more representative. The identification with the person of the monarch was particularly questionable, since many of the proponents of unification had been republicans or opponents of the Savoyard monarchy.

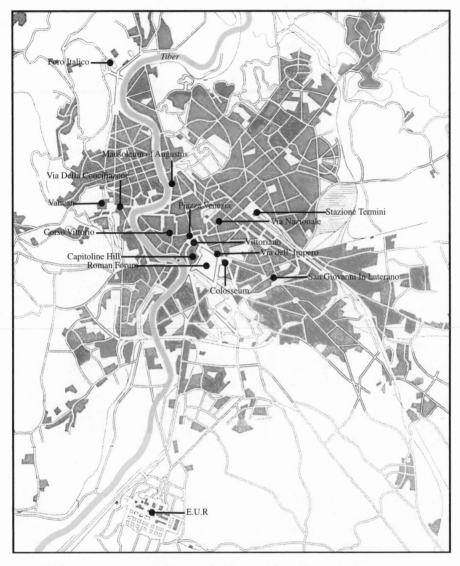

Figure 3.5 Rome in 1951 with major sites mentioned in the text. Source: Author.

Though the Vittoriano may well have been the "only true national monument" that "aroused a common national feeling,"[47] its symbolic power drew attention to the *lack* of commemoration of the real heroes of the Risorgimento: Giuseppe Garibaldi and Camillo Cavour.

From another point of view, however, less focused on individual monuments, the changes in the fabric of the city representing the arrival of a new nation can be seen as more considerable. The reorientation of the axis of the city and the placing of monuments did create a new secular image for the city at odds with the ecclesiastical one that had hitherto predominated. In particular, the placement of the Vittoriano and its construction in white Brescian marble, at odds with the brown tones of surrounding buildings, provided a new visual anchor for the city. Via Nazionale and its western extension, Corso Vittorio, plowed a new east-west axis through the historical center, making Piazza Venezia, in front of the Vittoriano, the central hub for traffic as well as the new symbolic center of the city. Other changes, such as the embankment of the river Tiber, the straightening of streets and "regularizing" of piazzas into Euclidean shapes, and the clearing of archaeological sites to set them off monumentally (e.g., fig. 3.6), also represented successful attempts at both remaking the city and associating the changes with the glories of the angular and rational city built by the ancient Romans before the "decadence" of later times.[48]

Fascism continued what had begun under the liberal regime (fig. 3.7). Two new anchors to the city as a whole emerged over time: the Foro Mussolini to the northwest of the historical core (where the Olympic Stadium now stands) and the EUR complex to the southeast (built beginning in 1937 for an exposition that was never held, finished in the 1950s). Possibly Benito Mussolini's most important manipulation of urban space for political purposes was transferring his office from the Palazzo Chigi to the Palazzo Venezia in Piazza Venezia in 1929. Thereafter, Piazza Venezia became the key space in Rome for performing the ceremonies and the ritual speechmaking that were the hallmark of Italian Fascism. Broadcast to central piazzas in towns and cities throughout Italy, Mussolini's speeches from the balcony of the Palazzo Venezia created a sense of national "togetherness" that Italy had never had previously and, apart from when the national football team takes the field, has not enjoyed since.[49]

Mussolini, more and more the personification of Fascism as the years wore on, increasingly turned to ancient Rome to provide a pedigree for his otherwise modernist movement. Reconstructing Rome according to an imperial image became a vital part of the agenda of Fascism. Plans were often compromises between different factions and architectural viewpoints. As a result, the outcome in terms of real changes was not always coherent. Segments of roads were built, but they never went all the way to where they were intended to go. For example, a road was punched through the Roman Forum between Piazza Venezia and the Colosseum (today called the Via dei Fori Imperiali), but the extension of this road, intended to lead inland and to the Adriatic, was never completed. Drawing the city toward the sea, to celebrate a renewal of an outward, imperial orientation and claim the Mediterranean for Italy as *mare nostrum*, was perhaps the most

Figure 3.6 Excavations of the Roman Forum at the turn of the twentieth century.
Source: M. Sanfilippo, *Le tre città di Roma: Lo sviluppo urbano dalle origini a oggi*
(Rome: Laterza, 1993), 181.

successfully realized goal, once it was defined. The *autostrada* linking the
outskirts of Rome to Ostia, opened in 1928, was the earliest manifestation
of this strategy. This was followed by the Via del Mare, linking Piazza
Venezia to the southern outskirts, and the EUR project to pull the growth
of the city seaward.

However successful they were as architectural projects, the impact of
both Liberal and Fascist attempts at making over Rome as a representative
landscape for the new Italy was severely limited.[50] For one thing, Rome
was naturally polycentric. The city in 1870 had a complex structure from
its variegated past of eras of expansion and contraction. One consequence
was that it lacked a single monumental center that could be captured for
the new national identity. The city was still the seat of the pope, who, until 1929, refused to recognize the new state. As the headquarters of the Roman Catholic Church, Rome was still symbolically connected to the world
"in between" ancient Rome and modern Italy that the architects of the

Figure 3.7   The Via dell'Impero (now the Via dei Fori Imperiali) shortly after its opening in 1933. Mussolini could now see the Colosseum from his balcony in the Palazzo Venezia, just to the right of the Vittoriano (right rear). This new road best symbolizes Mussolini's choice of associating his regime (and Italy) with the Roman past. Source: M. Sanfilippo, *Le tre città di Roma: Lo sviluppo urbano dalle origini a oggi* (Rome: Laterza, 1993), 389.

new Italy had wanted to erase from popular memory in order to celebrate the arrival of the new state. Another problem with Rome as the setting for a representative landscape for Italy as whole was that there was too much past present in the city to offer singular interpretations of what was there. Consisting of layers of ruins built up over the centuries, Rome lends itself to the image of Eternal City, but this image is at odds with that of a new national identity. The eclectic mixture of epochs and influences in the physical fabric of the city leads more toward universalistic than nationalistic interpretations. Rome is a city for the ages and for all (at least Christian) peoples.[51]

THE DIFFICULTY OF REALIZING A SINGULAR NATIONAL LANDSCAPE IDEAL IN MODERN ITALY

Italy's very Europeanness worked against achieving a long-lasting association between a particular landscape ideal and an Italian national identity. It remained forever associated with the glories of ancient Rome and the Renaissance, which the whole of Europe (or even more expansively, the whole of Western civilization) claimed as part of its heritage. Italianizing these also suffered from a number of features of Italian geography and society that point up the difficulties of realizing singular landscape ideals.

The first feature is the obvious one that Italy does not have an integrative physical geography. Its geographical identity as a singular unit is undermined by strong separations between the Po basin in the north and the mountainous spine–coastal plain pattern and islands to the south. As a result the physical landscapes available for expropriation are remarkably varied, reflecting the terrain, the climate, and the vegetation of a peninsula stretching from the heart of continental Europe almost to the shores of Africa. This range, working against the effective integration of a modern state, also produced a widely accepted continental/Mediterranean dichotomizing of Italian population and society that made a singular landscape image difficult to accept.[52] By way of example, Simon Schama points out the importance of the ancient metaphor of rivers as the "arterial bloodstream of a people" in bringing together facts of physical geography and national landscape images.[53] Unlike England with the Thames, France with the Seine and Rhône, the Austro-Hungarian Empire with the Danube, and so on, in Italy rivers divide the country rather than bring it together. The Po and the Tiber, the two principal rivers, never fit the bill. Sharing Italy with the Po, the Tiber had lost its imperial reputation. The mountainous spine of the country also works to disrupt west-east connections, making communication across the peninsula particularly difficult. A strong localism has been the result. As Enrico Castelnuovo and Carlo Ginzburg note for the history of Italian art, "Italian polycentrism [has shown] itself to be far stronger than all attempts at centralization."[54]

Certain features of Italy's historical geography also worked against the successful creation of a national landscape ideal. One of these is the absence of a dominant city, such as London or Paris, to subordinate the country to a singular vision. Rome was only the fifth largest city of the new state in 1871, exceeded in population by Naples, Milan, Genoa, and

Palermo. As the capital city it grew vigorously, but it still is politically and culturally predominant only in its immediate hinterland and in parts of the South. Indeed, it suffers from a very negative reputation in other parts of the country, particularly in the North, where it is associated with corrupt politics and inefficient bureaucracy. Related to this is the continuing importance of local and regional identities in Italian culture and society. Dialect differences, local economic interests, and attachment to local customs and traditions remain very strong in Italy. Unlike England, Scotland, France, and Germany, and more like Spain, in Italy class and status distinctions are expressed in local as much as in national terms of reference. "Folk" religious beliefs with strong localist connotations have remained strong—and resilient—in some regions even in the face of massive urbanization and social change.[55] A powerful *campanilismo* or localism has persisted, therefore, rather than fading away in the face of pressures for nationalization.[56] It has also proved impervious to ready co-optation, as in the German case, into reinforcing a larger national identity. At the moment in northern Italy a political movement (the Northern League) is attempting to use local identities as the basis for a program of either radical federalism or secession from Italy.[57]

Yet at the same time, an Italian mass culture has developed that ties together what would otherwise be a disparate set of places. Two types of influence have been particularly important. One was the system of political parties that Italy acquired at the end of World War II. With strong regional and local constituencies, the parties enabled the creation of strong local-national connections by means of both the allocation of government jobs and contracts and the division of national-level resources (such as the state television channels) between the various parties and their supporting groups. This system of *partitocrazia* is now waning with the collapse of the main parties after the corruption scandals of the early 1990s.[58] The other is an Italian culture industry that markets films, television, art, and music in the country as a whole. Certain ideas of Italianness, associated with taste, design, style, and beauty, emerged in the aftermath of World War II and have substituted for both the country's defeat and the continuing absence of other unifying symbols. National obsessions with television, football (soccer), and a cult of feminine beauty have been identified as particularly crucial components of this Italywide mass culture.[59]

The two words for "country" in standard Italian, *paese* and *patria*—the first used easily and frequently, the second self-consciously and infrequently—offer an interesting perspective on the balance between these polarized local and national identities. The first is typically used to refer to the local area you come from and identify with. *Paese* can be used to represent Italy as a whole (as in *Bel Paese*), and then it represents a fusion of the local with the national. The second use refers to Italy as a whole and is a formal term that would rarely come up in everyday conversation. In neither usage does it translate as "countryside"—which is the alternative meaning to that of country as *patria* in English—and strongly associated with the English national landscape ideal.

Part of the problem for an Italian national ideal of any kind has been that the national institutions created at the time of unification have been seen by significant minorities as foreign impositions. Not only were the Savoyard monarchy and its affiliated institutions carried to Rome, the state brought novel practices to regions where the writ of any sovereign was historically weak (Sicily, for example) and many groups (such as serious Catholics and anarchosyndicalists) regarded the state itself as illegitimate. The absence of a widely accepted civic nationalism or patriotism made inventing a singular vision of the state next to impossible. Fascism was, among other things, a way of trying to *force* unification, of bringing about the national uniformity and autarky that the dominant royalist strand of the Risorgimento had promised. Its failure, then, is revealed by the ready reversion to localism and particularistic identities that followed its wartime defeat.[60]

Perhaps most significant in accounting for the absence of a singular landscape ideal, however, is that Italy has lacked the dominant heroic event or experience on which many singular landscape ideals are based. In England the shock of industrialization produced a romantic attachment to a rural-pastoral ideal that has outlasted the original historical context. In the United States the myth of the frontier and the subjugation of wilderness has likewise focused national identity around themes of survival, cornucopia, and escape from the confines of city life.[61] In Italy only the recycling of the idea of the Risorgimento serves a similar purpose.[62] The problem is that the Risorgimento has multiple messages that have varied from the start, depending on which side of the unification process one chooses to emphasize. Its landscape legacy is likewise divided: Florence versus Rome. When allied to disputes over later mythic episodes such as the impact of Fascism, the Resistance to Fascism (1943–45), and the political unrest of the period 1968–85, the net effect is to produce multiple interpretations of Italianness and its essential landscape that persist but mutate over time following dramatic events rather than a stable, singular interpretation that knits all Italians together.[63]

Finally, Italian unification was never able to successfully capture the religious beliefs and practices of the Italian population. From 1870 until 1929 the state remained alienated from the Church, denied access to its spiritual authority. Fascism tried to sacralize the state by building an alternative civic religion, but this had to coexist with existing religious affiliations and the physical presence of the pope.[64] As a result the ritual power of the Italian state remained compromised, never able to obtain that symbolic investment in its attempts at designating certain sites as sacred to the nation and landscapes as representative of the spirit of the people that seem to arise so effortlessly in, say, the English or German case.

CONCLUSION

As a new, more politically integrated Europe seems set to arise, Italians are its most fervent supporters. They have long been ready to operate at the geographical scale of Europe. Their most important myths—ancient Rome and the Renaissance—are broadly European more than narrowly Italian. The difficulty in achieving what some other European nation-states have so easily acquired—a singular landscape ideal—suggests that such ideals are historically contingent and not without their own problems. When British "Eurosceptics" lament the loss of sovereignty in the "new" European Union, they point almost intuitively to a material or *physical* England that is also under threat. In this view, therefore, the strong visual image of an unchanging rural England has become a major political resource *and* liability, encouraging intransigence over further moves toward European unification yet undermining rational discussion about the pros and cons of centralized and decentralized governance at the level of Europe as a whole. Italy, whose small-firm manufacturing industry was also always seen (particularly by English commentators) as a symptom of backwardness before it became the engine of Italy's economic renaissance, has no such singular landscape (or other) ideal of "how it is" and "what it is like" to hold it back. This not only fits better the evolving world economy as it is reorganized around localities and city/hinterlands more than national economies,[65] it also undermines the simple story about national identities and representative landscapes that many geographers (and others) tell themselves. History does not end with a representative landscape for a secure national identity. This modernist story is one we have been telling ourselves for so long that we have forgotten it is only one story.[66] Italy tells another one, which may have much more to say to the Europe of today and tomorrow.

CHAPTER 4

Modernization and
Italian Political Development

Italy now has by most accounts the third or fourth largest economy in Europe and is one of the world's most developed societies in terms of levels of consumption, life expectancy, and possibilities for individual expression. But it is not unusual to read in the Italian press with respect to some feature or another of Italian life that Italy is "lontani dal continente" (distant from the Continent) or "fuori dall'Europa" (outside Europe).[1] With the bribery and corruption scandals in 1991–92 enveloping many of the politicians and the political parties that ruled Italy after World War II, the sense of geographical alienation from political conditions elsewhere has deepened further. Nor is it rare to find in scholarly writing on Italy recourse to the metaphor of backwardness as an appropriate description of the social and political character of the peninsula (and islands) and its population. Indeed, the struggle against backwardness, both national and specific to certain regions (particularly in the South), has become a leitmotif of Italian politics, a rallying cry of all efforts to forge a singular national territory and associated identity out of the disparate places inherited from the past.

In much contemporary social science either time and space are opposed to one another as alternative templates or, more typically, time is translated into space. That is, blocks of space (countries or regions) are labeled with the essential attributes of different periods relative to the idealized historical experience of one of the blocks. Hence territories are named as primitive or advanced and backward or modern. Progress occurs when the backward start to become like the modern. The terms are always applied at a single geographical scale (usually world regions, national states, or regions within states) while "bracketing" (assuming away) the others. An implicit comparison with an ideal type unit (at the same scale) is then used to make generalizations about the condition of the backward one.

Of course the critique of modernization theory has made note of the labeling before, but usually at a global scale with reference to East/West and North/South differences in culture and economic development.[2] My point is to extend the critique in three ways. First, I argue that the conversion of time into space usually produces a timeless space in which geographical differences are traced to time immemorial. Denying a dynamism to geography also renders history inert. Second, I mean to show how this understanding is applied both to the question of national political development and to the question of regional and local political differences within a European state as well. Third, I claim that the conversion of time into space derives from a European geopolitical imagination that denies place—as an intermingling of the effects of multiple geographical scales in the practices of everyday life—an active role in explaining politics. Places are only spaces on a map drawn by those with the power to do so, slotted into a worldwide schema of places that are either backward or modern.[3]

The Italian case also touches on a more general question in historiography: how to deal with the particular experiences of different national territories in relation to a standard account of national development. This is often referred to as the issue of geographical exceptionalism and takes its meaning in relation to the dominance of English, French, American, German, and (until recently) Soviet experience as norms against which the historical evolution of other national spaces should be compared. This chapter can be seen as an exploration in the genealogy of the metaphor of backwardness and its metamorphosis into a myth about Italy and its internal geography. The metaphor fuses a set of understandings about people and their places that are at the same moment both analytic and normative. Historically, however, the normative component or moral judgment has faded from view and the analytic claim of the metaphor, to *explain* difference, has become paramount.

Projecting qualities drawn from a rendering of a specific historical experience of one place (England, the West, or the United States for Italy; northern Italy for the Italian South) onto terrestrial space in general promotes three dominant tendencies in social science. One is the tendency to *essentialize,* or identify one trait as characterizing a particular spatial unit (e.g., caste in India; Mafia in Sicily; political instability in Italy as a whole). A second is a temptation to *exoticize,* or focus on differences as the single criterion for comparison between areas. Similarities or universal conundrums (e.g., barriers to political participation, difficulties of social mobility) are thereby ignored. The third is the tendency to *totalize* comparisons, or turn relative differences into absolute ones. The whole of a society is thereby made recognizable by any one of its parts. The whole block of space occupied by the society is suffused with a character that is defined by the social totality (usually a culture understood as a spatially indivisible unity at a national or civilizational scale that has been around more or less forever).[4]

METAPHORS OF BACKWARD ITALY

How widespread is the invocation of backwardness and the backward/ modern metaphor in relation to Italy? As Tim Mason has pointed out, discussion of modernity and modernization has been central to much contemporary Italian history and social science, but without self-consciousness as to terminological precision or explicit attention to the implication that Italy is somehow behind other countries and needs to modernize.[5] Adopting the vocabulary of backward and modern is not restricted to a particular school or political grouping. Across the political spectrum there is common recourse to the language of the modern and modernization even though there may be differences over the substantive components of modernity. For example, debate over Fascism from both left and right has been dominated by claims and counterclaims as to its modern and traditional qualities. In other countries this vocabulary has been much more contestable and contested than it appears to be in relation to Italy. In Italy it has become central to *conceptions of the country* and to Italy's place in the world of nation-states.

The vocabulary of backwardness and modernity can be found everywhere, though there is no consistency in the concrete particulars used to exemplify it. Some arbitrary examples can be drawn from both academic and political sources. Discussion of Italy's economy is dominated by the theme of the country's lagging behind and catching up relative to the economies of northern Europe. To economic historians Nicola Rossi and Gianni Tonioli, for example, "given Italy's relative backwardness around the turn of the century, a higher long-term growth rate might have been expected."[6] A one-volume history of postwar Italy, published to rave reviews in Italy and England, is portrayed by its author, historian Paul Ginsborg, as "charting the country's dramatic passage to modernity."[7] Although he writes from a standpoint sympathetic to the problems of the growing working class in postwar Italy, the author has frequent recourse to the language of modernization and backwardness in characterizing Italy (and particularly the Italian South) by its lack of "civic trust" and the "precariousness" of its modernization. A book by historian Domenico Settembrini traces Italy's political backwardness to a prevalent "antibourgeois" ideology that the author finds in both Fascism and anti-Fascism.[8] Italy is treated as an *anomaly* to Europe's destiny with liberal democracy when, as Roberto Vivarelli points out in a devastatingly stinging review, Italy precisely symptomatizes the universal dilemmas and difficulties involved in gaining and deepening democratic practices.[9]

A 1986 "cultural anthropology" of Italy by Carlo Tullio-Altan provides an extreme example of the use of the metaphor of backwardness. Indeed, from this point of view Italy represents a case study in the total failure of modernization.[10] Tullio-Altan presents Italian national history as a continuous unfolding of "sociocultural backwardness" as clientelism, anarchistic rebelliousness, organized crime, and lack of civic consciousness have conquered ever larger public spaces. Everything that is distinctively Italian about Italy is backward when compared with the successful countries to the north. What is more, the struggle for modernity is hopeless in the face of the strengthening forces of backwardness. Finally, in 1987 the sociologist Luciano Gallino sees in Italy the absence of a "fundamental ingredient of modernity . . . the interest of the individual in public action."[11] This is seen as a product of the peculiar mix of traditional and modern elements in Italian society rather than the singular victory of backwardness.

In many political circles in the 1970s and 1980s the language of modernization completely replaced older terminologies privileging social class and religion. This was especially obvious with the Socialists after Bettino Craxi became their leader in 1976. But elements in the Christian Democratic Party, particularly activists close to the former prime minister Ciriaco De Mita, also adopted this language as a substitute for older pastoral and Catholic themes. On the political left there was an appearance of not wanting to be left behind. Alberto Asor Rosa, an intellectual affiliated with the then Communist Party, was quoted as saying that "altogether the Left has never had as a value at the core of its project, control over innovation and modernization," implying that it now should have such a value.[12] Renato Curcio, one of the founders of the left-wing terrorist group the Red Brigades, reported in an interview from prison in 1987 that "if Italy has changed and modernized itself in so radical a way, this is due to the social conflict of the 1970s of which the Red Brigades were a component."[13]

Some political scientists had already hailed the victory of modernity based on some empirical evidence for a nationalization of Italian electoral politics beginning in the 1960s. A trend toward more homogeneous levels of support across the country for the two major political parties, the Christian Democrats and the Communists, and increased volatility between elections were interpreted as signaling the appearance of the modern "opinion" voter, rationally weighing the options between candidates and parties rather than voting because of identification with a political subculture (such as the white-Catholic or red-socialist) or in an exchange of favors (clientelism or patronage voting).[14] Borrowing from American electoral studies such methodological innovations as national opinion polling and the idea of the median national voter, Italy was seen as potentially on course from its anomalous past toward a future indistinguishable from that of other advanced democracies. Beginning in the 1980s, however, the emergence of new parties organized around local and regional issues, from the Leagues in the North to La Rete (Network) in Palermo and Milan, and the revelations of systemic political corruption in the early 1990s tended to undermine optimism about the permanence of electoral nationalization according to an English or an American model.

The idea of backwardness had not disappeared, only now it was increasingly applied to regional differences within the country. This was not new. The Italian South had long been the subject of Italian politicians and intellectuals who, from the earliest days of unification, had seen it as a drag on the modernization of the country as a whole. An intellectual tradition of *meridionalismo,* or studying the South, had grown up to account for the economic underdevelopment and cultural distinctiveness of "the South." An influential 1993 book by Robert Putnam, referred to previously, putatively about the relative administrative success of the regional tier of government introduced to Italy as a whole in 1970, revived attention to backwardness, only now the focus was on why the South remained mired in stasis, as indicated by the failure of regional governments in that region compared with the relative success of the regional reform in much of the North. Notwithstanding the tendency of Putnam's book to invoke the distant past, particularly the medieval political differences between North and South, rather than more recent history to account for present political differences, its largely positive reception suggests that the political-cultural logic of backwardness could still be applied within Italy even in the face of evidence for the nationalization of electoral politics.[15]

Based on such a wide range of sources, I therefore propose that the image of a backward Italy struggling (somehow) with modernity is a dominant representation of the country in the eyes of both Italian and foreign commentators. Before turning to the origins of this understanding of Italy, both generally and in relation to Italian intellectual history, I want to give closer attention to two of the sources mentioned previously, the books of Paul Ginsborg and Carlo Tullio-Altan. I do not claim that these books provide a true sample in a statistical sense of all writing about contemporary Italy. My argument is that they represent two leading genres of writing about Italy. One, largely English in origin in its reliance on an unfolding narrative of a precise historical period, implicitly (through the concepts it uses) compares Italy to a reading of English experience; the other, more typically Italian in origin, expresses an exasperation with the failure of Italian institutions to match the perceived success of similar institutions elsewhere.

Ginsborg's detailed narrative account of Italian history from 1943 to 1988 works around a series of oppositions through which he interprets movement from backwardness to modernity. In order of degree of abstraction, these are weak state/strong society; familism/collective action; class and regional dualism: workers/bourgeoisie, north/south; corrective/structural reform; and militance/*riflusso* (retreat into private life). Ginsborg operates from a standpoint sympathetic to the condition of workers and peasants in the early postwar period. He sees 1943–48 as a time when opportunities to redistribute wealth and power were lost, and he reads subsequent history in terms of the consequences of this fateful failure. A reader cannot but see an implicit comparison between this diagnosis and the typical British reading of what happened in Britain during the same period and its consequences for postwar Britain; the "corrective" reforms of the first postwar Labour government marked a clear watershed with the past and the beginnings of the modern welfare state. Yet in spite of the mistaken road taken in the 1940s, by the 1980s the nationalization of values taken for granted in the case of postwar Britain has finally captured even the most recalcitrant of Italians, though Ginsborg is doubtful about its permanence. This is because Italy's modernity is uniquely fragile, threatened by the persisting possibility of *reversal* of the current balance of oppositions. The path to modernity chosen in the immediate postwar years therefore is still subject to unpredictable shifts and pathological turns. Consequently, as Ginsborg concludes on "Italy in the 1980s," Italy remains a country with a "deformed relationship between citizen and state," where "neither from civil society nor from the state has there emerged a new and less destructive formulation of the relationship between family and collectivity" and more particularly, "the lack of *fede pubblica* (civic trust) continues to bedevil southern society."[16] True modernity, in this naturalized discourse of a country changing in spite of its essential self, is always around the corner or elsewhere, not in Italy.

"The cult of modernity," Mason suggests, "may grow out of a concern with its opposite."[17] Rather than the drive toward modernity, even if it is precarious, it is the persistence of backwardness that then takes center stage. Tullio-Altan sees Italy as condemned to perpetual repetition of a primordial condition of civic immaturity. He attributes this to the temporal persistence and geographical spread into the rest of Italy from the South of the syndrome of "amoral familism" first diagnosed by the American political scientist Edward Banfield in *The Moral Basis of a Backward Society*.[18] Banfield was later to gain notoriety for his claim that the riots in American cities in 1965–68 were mainly for "fun and profit."[19] Banfield's 1958 book is still widely used in introductory university courses on Italian politics and society in the United States and serves as a basic source for Putnam's more recent writing about regional differences in Italy.

To Tullio-Altan the roots of Italy's backwardness lie in the initial failure at the moment of unification in the nineteenth century to overcome the "national dualism" between a developing North and a backward South. He makes much of Giuseppe Mazzini's prophecy that "Italy will be that which the Mezzogiorno will be."[20] Even though Italy as a whole is backward, therefore, the origins of this condition lie in the South. Two influences in particular are identified as responsible for the diffusion of backwardness within Italy: clientelism (votes exchanged for favors) and *trasformismo* (collaboration among politicians by the exchange of favors). Because these practices were so pervasive, a bourgeoisie with a national orientation capable of overcoming local and regional outlooks failed to develop, perpetuating the cultural backwardness of Italy as a whole.[21] It is a strange inversion of Antonio Gramsci's argument about *la questione meridionale* that unification failed to produce a true revolution because northern workers and southern (and other) peasants did not make common cause against the unifying northern bourgeoisie. But it parallels arguments common to historians of Germany that compared (implicitly) with England or France, Germany failed to have a proper bourgeois revolution. The specificity and tragedy of German history are thereby explained by comparing what German history was *not* with idealized English and French national histories.[22]

Tullio-Altan thus reduces the fusion of what may be old and new in any particular epoch and nation-state to a straightforward manifestation of *absence* put in temporal terms as backwardness. The Italian political class, in particular, is seen as embodying both a culture that is particularistic and a parallel political practice that is clientelistic and transformist. But what if this is not to any extent a heritage of the past? What if these elements are part of a "modern and effective system of power designed to integrate into the national society masses of people who are dangerously inclined to claim democratic participation and their own emancipation"—in other words, "a modern political culture"?[23] Both Tim Mason and Rosario Lembo offer arguments for this reversal of Tullio-Altan's thesis.[24] As Mason suggests, the "civic maturity" of Tullio-Altan's (absent) modernity would not be popular with the dominant groups in most modern polities.[25] Encouraging withdrawal from active participation in politics and the widespread subversion of political institutions for personal gain are not unique to contemporary (and backward) Italy.

The attribution of backwardness makes sense, therefore, only if the backward features of Italian politics and society are implicitly compared with some ideal of modernity. For Tullio-Altan this appears to be defined largely by the *absence* of those features that identify Italy as backward (clientelism, *trasformismo*). But there are some more positive clues to the essence of modernity. The social conscience based on individual responsibility produced by the Calvinist branch of the Protestant Reformation—

and, of course, missing from Italian historical experience—is a concept introduced early in Tullio-Altan's analysis to frame later discussion of the specific features of Italian cultural stasis. In fundamental opposition, a concept drawn from Banfield's report of his fieldwork in one southern Italian village in the mid-1950s (Italian "amoral familism," the inability to act collectively for a common good beyond the bounds of a nuclear family) is identified as the conceptual key to understanding Italian difference from the Calvinist's modern conscience. Yet as numerous commentators have pointed out, Banfield misrepresents the social order of the village he studied, and one village does not a nation make, even when it appeals to prejudices widespread within that nation itself.[26] More pertinent, given that Italy is the seat of a powerful church with universal claims, might be the role of the Catholic Church in denying legitimacy to the new Italian state and its long-standing hostility to democratic politics. It is not so much an *absence*, again, such as having missed out on Calvinism, as a significant *presence*, the location of the Vatican in Italy, that has helped turn Italian political development along the path taken.[27]

FROM METAPHOR TO MYTH

This criticism is all very well, one might say, but surely the vocabulary of backward and modern is nothing more than a stock of evocative metaphors that helps to communicate the differences between Italy and two ideal types of society—the backward and the modern? I would argue that the vocabulary is now much more than this; that it organizes and directs thinking about the nature of Italy. From this perspective backward Italy has become a *myth*, the idealization involved forgotten as the metaphor has substituted for analysis. This is not to say that the metaphor is necessarily false in all its usages, only that it functions more as a fable than as a mere communicative device.

The literary scholar Frank Kermode makes a distinction between myth and fiction that may be helpful here. In his view, a fiction is "a symbolic construct ironically aware of its own fictionality, whereas myths have mistaken their symbolic worlds for literal ones and so come to naturalize their own status."[28] The line between the two is fuzzy rather than hard and fast, since all fictions can become myths once established and widely disseminated. This is what has happened to the metaphor of backward Italy.

It is conventional wisdom among European and American intellectuals that modernized societies (Europe, particularly England, and the United States are the paradigms at a global scale) are rational and secular to the exclusion of traditional-metaphysical myths about their founding and nature. As I argue later in the chapter, this position has become a central element in the backward/modern metaphor itself. Modernity is by definition life without myth. As sensitive a commentator on contemporary American society as political theorist Sheldon Wolin appears to endorse this position. Modernization is seen as destroying the mythology that is necessary for political community.[29] But perhaps it is more that our most cherished European myths, such as backward/modern, are simply ones without eschatological hope of a better world *in its entirety,* merely naturalized fictions that give meaning to historical and political speculation about the trajectory of particular societies contained by the boundaries of territorial states.

But how has mythmaking been possible in the case of backward/modern? What is it about this particular metaphor that has turned it into myth? My response falls into two parts: first sketching out the origins in European thought of the metaphor of backwardness (and its polar opposite, modernity), then offering an understanding of why the metaphor has acquired the status of myth specifically in relation to Italy.

SPACES OF BACKWARDNESS

One consequence of Columbus's famous voyage of 1492 was a heightened sense among European intellectuals of a hierarchy of human societies from primitive to modern. It is surely no coincidence that in conventional historiographies modern history begins with the era of Columbus. However, the simple juxtaposition of newly discovered and primitive worlds against a familiar and modern "old world" that the discoverers came from is an altogether too simplistic if currently popular view of what happened.[30] All societies define geographical boundaries between themselves and others.[31] Sometimes the world beyond the horizon is threatening, sometimes it is enticing. But not all portray the others as backward.

In fact, little has been written on exactly how early modern Europeans assimilated exotic peoples into their understanding of historical geography. In a major review of scholarship covering the sixteenth and seventeenth centuries, however, Michael Ryan suggests that the major means was assimilating the exotic into Europe's own pagan and savage past: "In the triangular relationship among Europe, its own pagan past, and the exotic, the principal linkage was between Europe and antiquity."[32] The categories of pagan and barbarian, discovered as an inheritance from the European ancients, were deployed to differentiate the new worlds from the old.[33] Thus a conception of the *temporal* transition through which the European social order had been transformed was imposed on the *spatial* relationship between the new worlds and Europe in its entirety. The religious dimension was especially important in reading the new pagan worlds as standing in a relation to the (European) Christian world the way that world stood in relation to its own pagan past.

This is not entirely surprising if we remember that discovery of the new geographical worlds coincided with the rediscovery of Europe's own ancient past.[34] Indeed, as Robert Mandrou recounts, "the new worlds that fascinated the intellectuals of the sixteenth century were not so much the Indies—West or even East—but those ancient worlds which the study and comparison of long-forgotten texts kept revealing as having been richer and more complex than had been supposed."[35] Of course Italy was the center for this new activity, associated as it was with monastic libraries, universities, and the recovery of ancient texts. Ironically, given the challenge to ecclesiastical authority that the rediscovery of the ancients could entail, it was from within the Church that the "new learning" arose: "Italian cities, richer in Churchmen than any others in Europe, and closer to the papal authority, constituted the setting that was most apt to stimulate the study of ancient texts and pre-Christian thought."[36]

The articulation of spatial differences in temporal terms was reinforced by the taxonomic lore that Renaissance-era Europeans learned from the ancients. As Edward Said has suggested, much ancient Greek drama involved demarcating an "imaginative geography" in which Europe and Asia are rigidly separated: "Europe is powerful and articulate; Asia is defeated and distant. . . . Rationality is undermined by Eastern excesses, those mysteriously attractive opposites to what seem to be normal values."[37] An image of essential difference with roots sunk deep in the primordial past was used to invent a geography that had no real empirical points of reference.[38] In terms of such categories as race, property, oligarchy, etiology, and economy, the Orient (and non-Europe in general) was claimed as "the negation of all that was being claimed for the West, by polemicists knowing, in fact, very little about it."[39] The "Ottoman peril" of the Renaissance gave particular credibility to vulnerable Europeans' sense of a profound chasm between the familiar world of Europe and the exotic world of the Oriental other. In Europe "the Turkish threat worked toward reviving a waning loyalty to the *Respublica Christiana* and gave new life to the old cry for peace and unity in a Christendom subject to the pope."[40]

As the European states emerged from the dynastic struggles and religious wars of the seventeenth century and embarked on their schemes of empire building outside Europe, comparing themselves with the ancient world, especially the model provided by Rome, proved irresistible. Baron Lugard, the British ruler of northern Nigeria, was to maintain that Britain stood in a kind of apostolic succession of empire: "As Roman imperialism . . . led the wild barbarians of these islands along the path of progress, so in Africa today we are re-paying the debt, and bringing to the dark places of the earth . . . the torch of culture and progress."[41] Perhaps the peak of this Romanist historiography is found in the writing of Hegel, especially in the *Philosophy of Right,* first published in 1821. Based on the relative extent of the absolute sovereignty of the state and its "ethical substance," the nation, Hegel divided the world into four historical realms arranged hierarchically, with the Oriental (India seems to have figured prominently in his thinking) as the lowest, the Germanic as the highest (surprise!), and the ancient Greek and Roman worlds, as the precursors of the Germanic, in between.[42] Effective state sovereignty was a necessary condition for achieving personal moral identity.[43]

Beginning in the late eighteenth century, the resort to classical precedent to understand spatial differences in social order was also put on a scientific foundation. Pragmatic common sense was backed up by explanation in terms of natural processes or by analogy to natural processes. It became increasingly popular to see social change as a transition from one stage or level of *development* to another.[44] As the nineteenth century wore on, and in imitation of discourse within biology, this view was elaborated on as an evolutionary movement from a lower to a higher level of organization. In terms of economic growth and social and political progress, some parts of the world were at levels of development that Europe had previously experienced.[45] The idiom of what Ranajit Guha terms "improvement" came to prevail over that of "order."[46] The distinction no longer lay primarily in essential difference that could not be transcended but in the possibility of overcoming backwardness through imitation. The future of the backward lay in repeating, if they could, what Europe had done.[47]

By the close of the century, modernity was increasingly conceived of as the form of society in which social interaction is rationally organized and self-regulating. Max Weber's theory of rationalization provided the most important account of this modernity within an evolutionary historiography. For Weber the rationalization of social life involved the increasing regulation of conduct by instrumental rationality rather than traditional norms and values. Weber himself was less than enthusiastic about this process of modernization, but many of his sociological disciples have had few doubts. The version of Weber's theory disseminated in the English-speaking world by Talcott Parsons, as Jürgen Habermas notes, "dissociates 'modernity' from its modern European origins and stylizes it into a spatio-temporally neutral model for processes of social development in general."[48] This modernity, subsequently often confused with the post–World War II United States, then became a social model to which other less developed societies, such as Italy, could aspire.[49]

A final boost to the designation of areas as backward or modern came from the ideological combat of the Cold War, in which the two modern worlds of capitalism and communism struggled for dominion in the backward or traditional Third World.[50] Although later adopted as a symbolic referent for the solidarity of formerly colonized peoples, the term Third World was never a particularly useful empirical designation. Its meaning was premised on the prior existence of two competing models of development that would allow for no alternatives. The backwardness of the Third World was necessary to define the modernity of the other two. *They* are what *we* used to be like. Only by having a backward could there be a modern.

WHY BACKWARD ITALY?

Italy is very much part of the Europe that figures in this outline history of the concept of backwardness. But the conceptual grid of which it is a component, figuring spatial differences in temporal terms, has become so universalized, considered applicable in diverse circumstances, that differences *within* Europe have also come to be thought of in terms of backwardness and modernity. So even while at a global scale Italy is considered modern, within Europe it can be seen as backward. Reality may be one thing; perception is something else again. A more poverty-stricken vocabulary for dealing with sameness and difference between places is hard to imagine! Yet its attractiveness for treating spatial differences in terms of temporal ideal types has been so great that it has spread from its original global context of use to other scales without much comment.

There are a number of reasons Italy has become prone to characterization in terms of backwardness. The first is its alleged failure to live up to its earlier promise. The signs of an incipient modernity associated with the Renaissance never produced the universal state that Hegel would later see as a prerequisite for true modernity. From this point of view Italy has been plagued by a persisting disunity based on geoeconomic and linguistic fragmentation. Unlike Germany in the nineteenth century, where identification with a *Heimat* (homeland) allowed for widening identification with territorial state and nation,[51] local identity in Italy has not led easily toward a wider sense of national identity.[52] The very city-states that are associated so intimately with the Renaissance failed to produce the integrated national state that would have taken Italy to the next level of modernity.[53] The variety and density of urban centers in Italy worked against the ready creation of a territorial state with a dominant capital city. Foreign potentates found in Italy almost unlimited possibilities for a strategy of divide and rule. The power of the Universal (but also Roman) Church has continually frustrated attempts at creating a national state in its homeland. The common identity of Italians as Catholics made the achievement of a more circumscribed national identity seem redundant for large segments of the population. Not even the pious Alessandro Manzoni could successfully challenge this paradox. Because of its difficulties with the papacy, the monarchy of unified Italy was not able to fuse religious symbolism with dynastic history in the ways common elsewhere in Europe. Recent Christian Democrats did not really try to fuse religious with national identity. They looked to locality or to "Europe" for their political identity.[54]

The stories told of Sicily in united Italy are instructive for what they say about the use of the backward/modern pairing within the country as an indicator of failure to live up to promise.[55] One story is usually about the Mafia, a word now charged with more than Sicilian application but that refers to the historical development of a specific type of criminality based on a code of silence and, at least classically, a secret organization and code of conduct reflecting both a long history of absentee landownership and popular resentment of state police power.[56] In a more nuanced version, the story is about the long-term difficulties of creating an integrated Italian polity from above, when Italian unification in the mid-nineteenth century was essentially imposed by the northern state of Piedmont on the rest of the peninsula, Sicily, and Sardinia rather than desired from below by a substantial part of the population. These accounts, both stereotypical and more historically subtle, lead to similar conclusions. One is that Sicilians have had little or no history of self-rule, either aristocratic or democratic. The second is that this lack of familiarity with self-governance has opened them up for exploitation by small, determined groups such as those associated with the Mafia, able to promise material favors in return for popular social and political support. From this point of view, therefore, Sicily is backward politically because it never acquired the cultural traits that were necessary for its successful assimilation into the Italian body politic. That Sicily was coerced militarily into Italy rather than welcomed as an established sociopolitical entity is left without mention, as is the fact that Fascism, hardly a manifestation of modern "civic democracy," was entirely northern in origin.[57]

In addition to the "special case" of Sicily and the South, the sense of Italy's general failure to mature as a political entity has deep roots among Italian intellectuals. The major theme of Niccolò Machiavelli in such works as *The Prince* and *The History of Florence* was the civic corruption of his epoch compared with the civic excellence of the ancient Romans. Papal power along with manipulation and penetration from outside were indicted as the main culprits.[58] Again, the heroes of the Risorgimento in the early nineteenth century blamed the reactionary Austrian and Bourbon regimes that governed large parts of the peninsula and islands for the pervasive political and economic stasis they were operating against. The image of subordination to neighboring states became a fixed element in the national consciousness as conveyed through Manzoni's influential 1827 novel of the Risorgimento, *I promessi sposi*.[59] Generations of Italians have been exposed to the making of Italy by reading this allegory of inner purity and tenacity struggling with external tyranny and exploitation.

The failure of unification to live up to expectations, because it came about through conquest and subterfuge rather than popular insurrection and replaced a set of reactionary governments with a single one, has added a further blow to the fragile Italian collective identity. A permanent feature of Italian historiography became argument over the "failure" of unification. Each new failure—the Liberal governments of the late nineteenth century for failing to match the colonial and economic achievements of the contemporary great powers, the failure of the Italian military in both world wars, the failure of Fascism as a developmental dictatorship to help Italy catch up with the rest of Europe—gave rise to new attempts at Risorgimento. As these themselves, particularly Fascism, then the anti-Fascist Resistance of 1943–45, and finally the student and worker struggles of 1968–72, failed to deliver an eschatological promised land, further disillusionment has been assured.[60]

Carlo Collodi's *Pinocchio*, first published in 1880, captures in allegorical form the fate of backward Italy, always awaiting its true liberation to modernity. Collodi was a disenchanted supporter of the original Risorgimento. The mischievous puppet aspires to true childhood, but his bad behavior seems to condemn him to perpetual puppethood. Only after demonstrating human virtue does he become a real boy. His path of metamorphosis follows the track of Italian history, from a puppet forced to move at the control of others to a donkey (a symbol for adherence to Church doctrine favored by nineteenth century anticlericals), to an autonomous personality (courtesy of a completed Risorgimento).[61]

Comparison with an external standard has been fundamental to the image of failure. No longer the seat of modernity after the sixteenth century, lost first to the English, then to the Germans and more recently to the Americans, Italy became synonymous for many intellectuals with the decadence of a Mediterranean world that had once again turned its back on its inheritance. The French defeat by Prussia in 1870, the Italian defeat by Ethiopia in 1896, and the Spanish defeats by the Americans at the turn of the century conspired to produce the idea of a link between military effectiveness, political development, and ethnicity. This was bolstered by the growth of a positivist sociology based on environmental and racial determinism. Southern Italians (as a Mediterranean rather than a continental European people) were characterized as particularly primitive—unpredictable, unreliable, rebellious, and criminal. They were a drag on the development of Italy as a whole. The image of a tragic fall from grace relative to success elsewhere became rooted in Italian as well as foreign accounts of Italy. The historian Silvio Lanaro, in a brilliant book on the self-images of Italians, notes cynically that "admiration for foreigners has been the principal ingredient of Italian nationalism."[62]

The late-nineteenth century politician Francesco Crispi has been perhaps the only Italian political leader except for Mussolini to create a rhetoric that saw modern Italy in apostolic succession to previous periods of national greatness and as a body overcoming its fragmentation.[63] But the danger of pointing to the past was that it reminded everyone of the gap that now existed between the noble past and the degenerate present. The massive emigration from the southern regions, the failure to emulate the apparently effortless colonial successes of the British and the French (symbolized above all by the military defeat at the hands of the barbarian Ethiopians at Adua on 1 March 1896), and persistent political and military mismanagement were especially galling. When the rhetoric of Roman-imperial reincarnation turned out to be hollow, as with both Crispi's colonial adventures and Fascism's claims as a developmental dictatorship, the conception of Italy as a spiritual idea in the process of becoming realized in a modern form was also discredited.[64]

There have been some important, more specific classical influences on thinking about Italy's place on the backward/modern continuum relative to other countries. The important influence of Hegel on Italian historiography has reinforced the idea of Italy's lagging behind the rest of Europe in the development of a modern political identity. This is not an influence in the straightforward sense of borrowing Hegel's philosophy of history.[65] Rather, it is the peculiar Italian rendering of the Hegelian *Weltgeist,* above all by the influential philosopher Benedetto Croce, as the need to abandon sectional material interests for a higher national interest. Increasingly opposed both to historical materialism as a theory of history and to socialism as a political ideology, Croce argued for the primacy of political will in creating a sense of national purpose.[66] Croce read German experience as the successful pursuit of interests embodied in the idea of a culture, of a common sense that would inspire people to a new way of life.[67] This vision inevitably pictured Italy as a pupil of the more advanced northern Europeans, to whom Italians should look for inspirational models.

The late industrialization of Italy and the persistence of traditional norms and values (above all, suspicion of the state and its works) have also provided prima facie evidence for a Weberian reading of Italian backwardness. Compared with most other European countries, Italy appears to have retained a greater element of those nonrational values, associated with ascription rather than achievement, specific loyalties rather than the general value commitments that Parsons associated with tradition, especially in the continuing importance of family ties for the economy and the role of clientelism in the national bureaucracy.[68] Gift and redistributive transactions do not easily fit into evolutionary schemes based on the presumed victory of market exchange and economic rationality,[69] yet these have remained of particular importance within the Italian political economy. What sociologist Marcel Mauss named "noble expenditures" that bind rich to poor in the displacement of class struggle have been an important mechanism for maintaining social order but have worked against the emergence of an impersonal state based on an abstract equal citizenship as its operating ideal.

The three major social groupings of postunification Italy with possible roles in creating a breakthrough to a stronger national identity—the capitalists, the workers, and the middle class—elaborated alternative institutions (e.g., the Case del Popolo for the workers) and regarded the state as a client rather than as an object of commitment or affection.[70] Fascism's identification of *la patria* had to work with a mosaic of identities and expectations rather than an integral texture based on the prior diffusion of a singular cultural vision.

The absence from the peninsula and islands of the heroic feats and sharp historical breaks that have lain behind so much sociological theorizing, such as that of Weber and Parsons—the Protestant Reformation, the French Revolution of 1789—have also encouraged a sense of an unheroic or even cowardly history that has not escaped from a past of traditional-local ties and sentiments. The major irony in this hand-wringing is that many of the social indicators associated with backwardness have deepened as the country has modernized. For example, the welfare state has increased the importance of political-family connections as disability pensions have *increasingly* been awarded on a particularistic basis.[71] The opposition of backward and modern thus dissolves as "we discover continuity in change, tradition in modernity, even custom in commerce. Still, not all that was solid now melts into air, as a certain post-modernist reflexive anthropology has prematurely supposed. There remain the distinctive differences, the cultural differences."[72]

Finally, the two political cultures that grew in Italy at the turn of the century and reappeared after Fascism, the socialist and the Catholic-popular, have been largely without sentiments of national identity and solidarity. To them Italy has been the site of struggles over grand ideas that transcend any one national space. In the postwar period this has often involved looking outside Italy for models of social development. On one side, at least until the 1960s, the Soviet Union was seen as a paragon of modernity. Some of the student revolutionaries of 1968 looked to China and Maoism for their model (the Milan newspaper *Corriere della Sera* referred to the student revolutionaries en masse as *i cinesi*). On the other side, if also with increasing uneasiness during the years of the Vietnam War but seemingly without much choice in the context of the Cold War, was the United States. All groups used the United States as their measure, whether as a challenge or as a threat. Rather as in the Third World, there was a struggle over the model of modernity in postwar Italy. The major political parties and their associated intellectuals defined their goals largely in terms of Italy's backwardness in relation to the two foreign models of modernity.

Within Italian society and among many intellectuals it is evident that the American model proved the more enticing. American standards became the ones that Italian performance was measured by and that defined the road to follow. As Silvio Lanaro emphasizes, "an arsenal of symbols and objects represented by the United States" came to substitute for the absence of an effective center within Italian society.[73] The American perspective on modernization (Americanization) spread widely as the American social sciences, especially a political science of a particularly American provenance, expanded within the Italian universities in the early 1970s.[74] The nationalization of political values relating to the achievement of high mass consumption became an indicator of Italy's emulation of American modernity. This fits well the imperatives of a political class that put its faith in material progress to neutralize concerns about the contemporary moral order of clientelism and insider dealing that they represent. The persisting failure of significant groups and regions to experience the fruits of material progress and (more significantly given the often explicit comparison with the United States) the lack of an American civic virtue, the popular celebration and adulation of existing political institutions without much active participation in them, only reinforced the idea that Italy, with its popular contempt for existing institutions yet deeply politicized Weltanschauung, not only was different but was still backward, even after all these years.

CONCLUSION

One of Italy's most renowned astrologers, Francesco Waldner, describes to the German writer Hans Magnus Enzensberger his view of Italy's perpetual political impasse: "The Italian peninsula as a whole may be under the dynamic sign of Aries, but the republic's horoscope is dominated by Gemini. Apart from that, every horoscope consists of four elements: earth, water, fire, and air. But the republic was declared on June 18 1946, and there were no planets in earth signs on that date. That's why this state lacks authority. It's unable to act effectively. Alternatives exist only for the individual. That makes survival possible."[75] For Enzensberger, in comparison with assorted social scientists, journalists, and pundits, the astrologer emerges as one of the more sober commentators on the Italian condition.

One might note that there is little difference between the empirical analysis of the astrologer and that provided by the discourse of backwardness and modernity. In neither case is Italy the actual object of analysis. For one it is the position of birth signs, for the other it is comparison with ideal types that become confused with empirical referents (such as England or the United States). Yet we scoff at the astrology as unscientific while seeing the backward/modern polarity as unquestionably sound, scientific, or commonsensical.

It is precisely the commonsensical quality of the polarity that gives it mythic power. Since Columbus first returned, we have become so used to characterizing geographical differences in idealized temporal terms that we cannot see any problems with this way of thinking. We assimilate empirical information to the polarities. We read the whole world through them. The ultimate irony, given Columbus's own origins in an Italian city-state, is that in a European context Italy has been more readily portrayed as backward than as modern. A temporal metaphor initially applied to make sense of the spatial gap between the new worlds and the old has become a preferred way of dealing with Italian differences relative to an idealized European modernity. In so doing, the intrinsically *normative* character of the terms backward and modern has been obscured.

This has served, however, to underpin the project of designating Italy as a self-evident territory with an easily communicated goal: to overcome its inherent backwardness relative to more advanced states elsewhere. At the same time, designating regions within the country as exhibiting different degrees of backwardness—particularly the South and its component parts—highlights internal others who can be portrayed both as a drag on the national project as a whole and also as to blame for the continuing instability and persisting failures of national political institutions.[76] Recognizing differences between places, however, does not necessitate turning them into instances of universal modern/backward categories whose invocation obscures far more than it illuminates understanding of those very differences.

CHAPTER 5

The Geographical Dynamics of Italian Electoral Politics, 1948–87

The term geographical usually conveys a misleading sense of permanence, of fixity, that is antithetical to concepts such as social change or dynamics. The usage reflects the widespread image of geography as an encyclopedic inventory of immutable physical features and social attributes. This "common sense" has passed into fields such as political science that see geography merely as either a stage on which social and political dynamics are played out or a map of political outcomes determined by nationally constituted social forces. In neither case is geography seen as inherently involved in producing such outcomes. More particularly, as national states develop politically they are viewed as increasingly characterized by national political processes organized by national political parties appealing to and drawing support from individual voters around the national territory based on rational weighing of options (opinion voting).

The focus of this chapter is on how trends in the electoral geography of Italy over 1948–87, the period when a specific set of political parties and a division of national power between them dominated Italian electoral politics, indicate an active or dynamic geographical constitution of electoral politics. By this I mean that even nationalization is mediated geographically by a meshing of influences on electoral behavior in different places within Italy that give rise to geographically differentiated patterns of election results, including nationalization. But nationalization is only one among a number of possible options, as this chapter makes clear: regionalized and localized patterns are also possible.

To be sure, aspects of the nationalization thesis are unimpeachable. The locus of political activity and the repertoires of collective action, for example, have expanded from the entirely local to the national, from the patronized (dependent on local power holders) to the autonomous and anonymous.[1] As a result, national political parties and national-scale institutions have assumed increased significance as mechanisms of political incorporation and expression at regional and local scales. But the nationalization thesis implies much more than this. It suggests that local political voice is the result of nationally defined social cleavages and communication channels that have totally replaced influences emanating from other geographical scales.

After first surveying the typical understanding of nationalization in the Italian case, I describe the political consequences of the main ways Italy is divided geographically and the political parties and electoral system that prevailed from 1948 to 1987. I finally turn to the evidence for three successive electoral-geographical regimes (regionalizing, nationalizing, and localizing) rather then a single linear trend toward nationalization over the entire period.

THE NATIONALIZATION THESIS AND ITALIAN POLITICS

A widely accepted premise of modern political science is that political outlooks and alignments are increasingly organized around individual voters choosing between parties based on their political preferences to produce national patterns of political mobilization.[2] Political differences are increasingly seen as nationalized as membership in crosscutting national census categories, representing sets of preferences, displaces geographical location or region as the primary predictor of political behavior. In Italy this point of view became popular among political scientists beginning in the late 1960s.[3] A major study of Italian political behavior conducted from 1963 to 1965 argued that a nationalization of Italian politics had occurred between 1946 and 1963.[4] The pattern of an electorate divided into two parts, left and right, and spread more or less homogeneously throughout the country—as in other representative democracies—had come to Italy. From this point of view, individual opinion voting had replaced identification with regional subculture, social group, or locality as the main source of political identity. Modern voting behavior is seen as an expression of individual opinion constrained only by access to information and by particular sociodemographic characteristics such as class, age, and education. Consequently, support for specific political parties is increasingly and equally volatile everywhere as voters shift from party to party to satisfy their political preferences.[5]

Certainly, national and province-level election results in 1963–76 can be used to support this perspective. There was a tendency toward homogenization of support for the main Italian political parties of the time: the Christian Democrats (DC), the Communists (PCI), and the Socialists (PSI). This could be explained partly in terms of the saturation of support for parties in some areas and partly in terms of common national processes of political mobilization leading to shifting party affiliations. In particular, there was a sense of greater electoral instability as voters became more volatile in their political affiliations.[6] In fact, homogenization does not seem to have been paralleled by much of an increase in electoral volatility. Evidence from Bologna, assumed to be a stronghold of PCI "identity voting," shows a degree of shifts in voting over the entire period 1946–83 that is not that far off the figures for a number of Italian cities in 1976–79 (table 5.1).

Neither homogenization nor electoral volatility in itself, however, can be taken as a signal of a permanent shift from a geographically fragmented process of political mobilization to a nationally homogeneous one.[7] The idea of the individual opinion voter was crucial to this logic, suggesting that opinion voting would give rise to a process of electoral choice in which the old social influences associated with regional subcultures would retreat. Voters, national media, and national campaigns were seen as the three moments around which electoral politics was now organized.

As the huge literature on local contextual effects in voting suggests, however, the opinion voting that is alleged to lie behind the other trends is not an isolated individual act but is itself the outcome of social influences. Opinions are formed as a result of active socialization from family, friends, workplaces, churches, schools, media outlets, and political communication.[8] Consequently, in the absence of evidence for the isolated

Table 5.1   Estimates of Electoral Mobility in Selected Italian Cities

Bologna	%		%
1946–48	22.8	1968–72	22.9
1948–53	n.a.	1972–76	23.8
1953–58	21.1	1976–79	18.8
1958–63	25.5	1979–83	25.8
1963–68	22.0		
Other cities (1976–79)			
Turin	28.9		
Milan	29.3		
Genoa	21.2		
Verona	22.7		
Padua	27.5		
Perugia	17.8		
Naples	32.1		
Salerno	29.8		
Taranto	29.1		

SOURCE: Percy A. Allum and Renato Mannheimer. "Italy," in *Electoral Change in Western Democracies: Patterns and Sources of Electoral Validity*, ed. Ivor Crewe and David Denver (New York: St. Martin's Press), 1985, 295. Data for Bologna, Turin, Genoa, Padua, Perugia, Salerno, and Taranto supplied by P. G. Corbetta and H. M. Schadee of Istituto Cattaneo, Bologna, those for Milan and Naples by ADPSS, Milan.

NOTE: The estimates for the cities in the second list are available only for 1976–79.

opinion voter (as opposed to the opinion voter operating within social networks), evidence for homogenization and volatility has been insufficient to justify total abandonment of models of political behavior involving recourse to geographical social influences. Even proponents of the trend toward nationalization based on opinion voting stress the important residual role of identity (belonging) and clientelistic (vote-favor exchange) voting as expressive of local histories and interests.[9]

In fact, considerable empirical evidence now suggests that nationalization of voting patterns was a feature of the years 1963–76 rather than a permanent trend over the entire period since the collapse of Fascism and the end of World War II.[10] This realization led to something of a revival of "geographical" models of political behavior that emphasize regional subculture and the persistence of regional types of voting: briefly, opinion voting in the Northwest, identity voting in the Center and Northeast, and exchange voting in the South.[11] Such models identify historical-cultural rather than socioeconomic factors as the primary determinants of political cleavages. The rootedness of parties in particular areas through their organization and institutional strength is given special weight as a factor producing socialization into different political traditions. Key periods in the past—medieval communal organization, the years after unification, the period of labor organizing early in the twentieth century, and the civil war in central and northern Italy during the collapse of Fascism, 1943–45—are viewed as critical in establishing regional political traditions. The Catholic subculture of northeastern Italy, the socialist subculture of the Center, and the clientelistic subculture of the South and Sicily are regarded as the major traditions that have resulted.

There are three specific models that rely on fixed subculture-regional conceptions of political action: regional taxonomies of cultural traditions; historical studies of local political cultures; and sociological studies of party-government and political-subculture links. The problem is that these subcultural models tend to see regionalization as a structural precondition of Italian electoral politics when the evidence for its permanence is as limited historically as is that for nationalization as an emerging trend across the entire period 1947–87. I examine these models in chapter 6 in relation to a classic case of apparent identity voting: the two provinces of Lucca and Pistoia in central Italy and their long-term affiliations, respectively, with Catholic and socialist voting traditions.

LOCALITIES AND REGIONS IN MODERN ITALY

Since the end of World War II Italy has been transformed from a relatively poor country into one of the world's major industrial powers. The changes in economic development there occurred more rapidly and were more geographically widespread than anywhere else in Western Europe during the same period. Two inheritances from the past, however, have had important effects on this transformation. One is the relatively short history of political unification, dating from 1861 and finally realized only in 1870; the other is persisting geographical disparities in wealth, industrialization, and social organization. The geographical dynamics of Italian electoral politics over the postwar period have been largely the result of the interplay between historical inheritance and the recent transformation of the Italian economy.

The short history of unification is important in a number of respects.[12] First, it was a unity imposed on the Italian peninsula and islands rather than one arising from a popular base (see fig. 3.1). Unification lacked widespread peasant support, and along with a lack of recognition given the new state by the Catholic Church, the legitimacy of the parliamentary monarchy established in 1861 was seriously compromised by opposition from republican opponents. The legitimacy crisis has persisted down the years, partly because major political movements, from the Fascists to the Christian Democrats and Communists, have had their own ideas about what the state should be and partly because many Italians have come to associate the state and its agencies with stultifying bureaucracy, ineptness, and corruption. After World War II the state very quickly succumbed to domination by a single political party, the Christian Democrats, that ruled in coalition with smaller parties, if in different combinations, from 1947 until 1992. A system of party-dominated government replaced the dictatorship of Fascism and the older tradition of *trasformismo* or vote exchange among representatives. Affiliation with the government parties was required for access both to government resources and to many jobs. Unsurprisingly, the "division of the spoils" (*lottizzazione*) favored groups and places giving persistently strong electoral support to the governing parties, particularly the Christian Democrats and, after 1976, the Socialists of Bettino Craxi. Bastions of the PCI or the neo-Fascist Movimento Sociale Italiano (MSI), parties shunned in the process of national coalition formation, could hardly expect equal treatment.

Second, however, regional and local sentiments (sense of place) helped forge political identities before unification that national political parties and institutions have had difficulty undermining. The differentiation of territorial identities has been underwritten by important linguistic and social differences between parts of Italy. In the social realm, for example, many northern Italians greatly value a wealth of associations aimed at political, commercial, recreational, and special interest (e.g., veterans, trade unions) activities. Elsewhere, but particularly in the South, kinship and clientelistic relationships hold relatively greater sway, both in politics and in daily life. These divergent patterns of social life, based on divergent histories of settlement patterns, agricultural systems, and degrees of social isolation, have adapted and endured rather than faded away under the onslaught of a single national pattern.[13]

Finally, until unification large parts of Italy were ruled either by foreign empires or from the Vatican. The Papal States of central Italy, in particular, had long been a major barrier to Italian political unification. As secular as well as religious rulers, in the nineteenth century the Catholic clergy became the subject of an intense anticlericalism that was absent elsewhere in Italy. It is therefore little surprise that it is in central Italy, where the power of the Church was most associated with the interests of the landholders, that a socialist (after World War II a communist) social and political consciousness took root. In the former Austrian lands of the Northeast, however, where the Catholic clergy was identified with the interests of the peasantry, the Church took on the role as a representative of the populace, similar to the one it adopted more recently in Poland. The prosperity and local chauvinism of the city-states of northern and central Italy further strengthened the centrifugal tendencies of political organization across the peninsula and islands as a whole.

As a result, the achievement of unification has been unable to mask an older political and social fragmentation. It amounted to the incorporation under one banner—Italy—of a variety of territorial forms of social organization and levels of economic development. In the general terms laid out by Antonio Gramsci in his writings on Italian political development, unification united a capitalist and industrializing North with a largely feudal South into a single political unit under the leadership of the northern elite.[14] This *blocco storico*—historical alliance between northern capital and southern land—created an economy in which the industry of the South was subjected to vigorous and deadly competition from the more efficient businesses of the North. Initial advantage, control over fiscal policy, and geographical proximity to other industrialized areas in Europe combined to give northern business a permanent edge. Unable to defend its assets, industry in the South collapsed, and the region became an agrarian periphery from which taxes and labor were extracted to support the continued industrialization of the North. The social consequences of unification reverberate still in Italy. While an industrial bourgeoisie and working class emerged in the Northwest, in the South there took root a system of patron-client relations amid a social structure dominated by landlords, peasants, and a petit bourgeoisie dependent on state employment and their role as intermediaries between localities and the state apparatus.[15]

If anything, this bifurcation was reinforced by the way Fascism collapsed and Italy was liberated from German occupation at the end of

World War II. The South was invaded by the Allies and wrested from the Fascist regime by military conquest. But the area north of Rome, particularly around and to the north of a line that represented the front between the two sides for much of 1944, was liberated in part by the activities of clandestine armed bands and by passive resistance to the German occupiers and their neo-Fascist allies in the so-called Republic of Salò. These experiences meant that after the war totally different memories of the years 1943–45, and thus of Fascism and its costs, prevailed in North and South. This was reflected in the results of the 1946 referendum on the monarchy, with the North largely against its continuation and the South largely in its favor. As a consequence, the idea of the Resistance against Fascism by Italians could take root only in the North, where it became a leitmotif of postwar politics, particularly on the part of the Communist Party, which had played an important role in opposing the occupying power and its local collaborators.[16]

Notwithstanding recent charges that the role of the Resistance in national liberation has been exaggerated and that the part armed bands affiliated with the Communist Party played in eliminating political opponents as well as war criminals and protecting selective turncoats has been largely unexamined, the new Republican constitution of 1948 was undoubtedly a major achievement for the mix of political forces associated with the Resistance. That it was also therefore a victory for the republican sympathies of the North is less frequently noted.[17]

The terms the North and the South, however, overgeneralize the geographical complexity of Italy. In the late nineteenth and early twentieth centuries, industrial development was concentrated in the northwestern regions of Lombardy, Liguria, and Piedmont and in scattered nodes elsewhere. There was tremendous geographical differentiation and specialization. Fascism reinforced the existing pattern of industrial concentration. In 1939, 30 percent of all industrial employees lived in Lombardy, 12.8 percent in Piedmont and 4.8 percent in Liguria. Only 12.1 percent resided in the South and a net total of 15.9 percent in the Veneto and Tuscany combined.[18] These patterns underline the fact that Fascism was in its origins a northern movement committed to restoring stability in northern industrial and commercial-agricultural areas that had experienced widespread labor unrest and revolutionary agitation in the aftermath of World War I.[19]

Italy in general and the Center and the South in particular suffered enormous economic losses during the last two years of World War II. Most of the worst fighting, and the greatest damage, was concentrated in the areas of Rome-Naples and Florence-Bologna. The industries of the Northwest emerged relatively unscathed and in a position to reestablish their dominance. Recovery was rapid. In 1948 the national index of industrial production stood at 102 (1938 = 100), and it climbed steadily in the ensuing years, reaching 164 by 1953. Much of the new and expanded industries were in the Northwest, in part as the result of a tight credit policy instituted in 1947 that extended credit only to firms that were "good risks."[20]

By 1951 Italy had largely recovered economically from the war and stood exactly in the middle of the list of fifty-five countries that supplied per capita income figures to the United Nations.[21] This figure, however, masked major regional and local variation. Though per capita incomes in the major industrial centers of the western Po Valley (such as Milan and Turin) resembled those of northern Europe, incomes and living conditions in the South and in most rural areas were more akin to those in Latin America or the Middle East (fig. 5.1). Southern provinces, such as Avellino, Potenza, and Agrigento, had average incomes less than 20 percent those of Milan. Regional industrial contrasts were especially clear. The South, with 42 percent of the land and 38 percent of the population, had only 19.5 percent of the manufacturing labor force and 20 percent of the national income.[22]

Over the postwar period, however, even as the Northwest retained its hold on the main industrial sectors, the highest rates of economic growth occurred in the Center and Northeast, where small firms clustered in specialized industrial districts gave rise to the "Third Italy" that has received so much comment in relation to the course of Italian economic development. Italian entry into the European Community, opening up export markets for small appliances, clothing, and other consumer goods, and the increased economies associated with flexible production by small firms were important stimulating factors. The existence of artisanal traditions of production, local governments oriented to economic growth policies, loosely enforced tax and environmental regulations, and the ability to exploit family labor were necessary preconditions.[23]

Although national economic development policies consistently favored industrial growth in the South, either through subsidies or through infrastructure investment, these largely failed because the industries were capital intensive and without much stimulating effect (e.g., petrochemicals in eastern Sicily) or because, for political reasons, the proceeds were channeled into housing and public works projects that had little long-term impact on economic development. At the same time, however, national government income transfers (pensions, unemployment benefits, etc.) have raised southern incomes and improved regional levels of consumption. By the 1980s parts of the South such as Abruzzi, Lazio, and sections of Puglia, Basilicata, and Campania increasingly began to experience something of the type of small-scale economic development associated with the Third Italy. Interestingly, this coincided with the ending of the

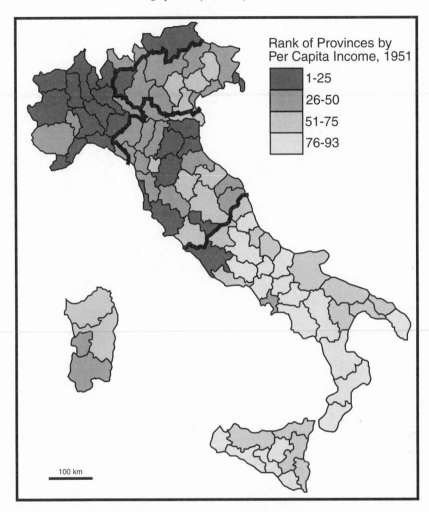

Figure 5.1 Groups of provinces ranked by per capita income, 1951. Source: based on Guglielmo Tagliacarne, *Il reddito nelle province italiane nel 1973 e confronti con gli anni 1951, 1971, e 1972* (Milan: Istituto Tagliacarne, 1975), 72.

special treatment of the South as a whole by Italian governments through the instrument of the Cassa del Mezzogiorno, suggesting that the politicizing of this agency may well have retarded rather than aided southern development.[24]

The geographical complexity of serious regional and local economic disparities has been reinforced by a remarkably diffuse settlement structure (fig. 5.2). Unlike many European countries, in Italy the distribution of population and urbanization are not and have not been centered on a

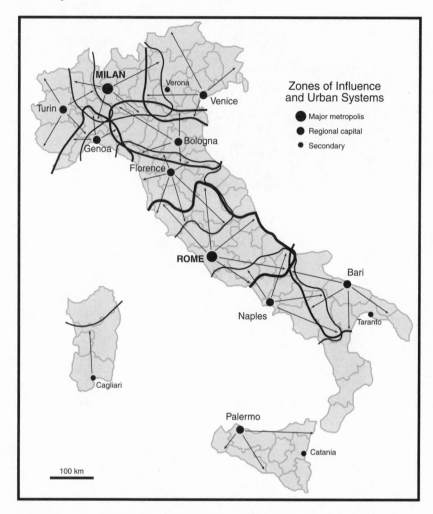

Figure 5.2   The Italian urban system and the spheres of influence of major cities.
Source: redrawn from Jacques Béthemont and Jean Pelletier, *Italy: A Geographical Introduction* (New York: Longman, 1983), 38.

single city or metropolis with regional capitals gravitating around an un-mistakably dominant political-economic center. Rather, the Italian urban hierarchy is diverse and complex, with two dominant metropolises (Rome and Milan), eight regional capitals (Turin, Genoa, Venice-Padua, Bologna, Florence, Naples, Bari, and Palermo), and six secondary regional centers (Brescia, Verona, Taranto, Messina, Catania, and Cagliari).[25] This hierarchy is geographically asymmetrical—complete in the North but with fewer intermediate-sized cities in the Center and South. Moreover, whereas the northern hinterlands or zones of influence are coherent, dense, multi-functional, and interlinked, the southern hinterland boundaries are weaker and zones are less interconnected.[26] The character of the Italian urban hierarchy thus pinpoints the contrast between the North and the South and the decentralized nature of urban development throughout the country.

Within the geographical framework of this diffuse urban system, Italy has experienced a massive redistribution of population since unification, most especially since World War II. There has been a large-scale movement of people off the land throughout the country, but especially from the mountainous interiors of the South. In the 1950s and 1960s many of these migrants moved to the industrial cities of the Northwest, to Switzerland and Germany (replacing the older destinations of North America and Argentina), and to southern cities. Migration from South to North, a hallmark of postwar Italian society, compensated for underdevelopment in the former by movement of population to the latter.[27]

Finally, the social and economic inequalities between localities and regions in Italy have been reinforced by a system of local government that divides the country territorially into communes, provinces, and in 1970, after many years of dispute, administrative regions.[28] Though notoriously centralized, Italian government does allow, particularly at the regional level, for some autonomy in initiating policies. This means that local governments can adopt policies in areas such as urban planning, agriculture, and industrial development independent of national government control and in response to perceived local economic and social problems. Thus geographical differences in economic and social conditions also owe something to differences in local political capacity and mobilization. For example, some regions, such as Emilia-Romagna, have invested much more successfully in various public services and economic development than have regions such as Puglia and Calabria.[29]

In Italy, therefore, a relatively short history of unification within a single state has combined with a variety of social and economic forces to produce, by European standards, a relatively decentralized and fragmented economy and society. It is within this framework that political parties, and associated agencies, have had to create national politics.

PARTIES AND ELECTIONS, 1948–87

In the immediate aftermath of World War II three large political parties (the Christian Democratic Party, DC; the Communist Party, PCI; and the Socialist Party, PSI) and a number of smaller ones emerged to replace the single-party system of Fascism. Most of the parties traced their organizational and ideological roots to the pre-Fascist period. Episodically new parties might appear, but none had the staying power of the big three and a number of long-standing ancillary parties that entered into alliance with one or other of the big ones, particularly the DC.

The DC was initially dominant in terms of share of the total vote, and it remained so until its demise in 1992 (table 5.2). From 1948, when the 1946 constitution largely went into effect, until 1981 it always provided the prime minister, and between 1947 and 1987 it was the largest partner in all governments. But it could never govern alone and frequently abandoned coalitions to favor the interest of internal factions in occupying different cabinet offices or to discipline relations with Parliament, among other factors influencing the longevity of governments.[30] More broadly based than the Popular Party, its forebear in the pre-Fascist period, it was a religious party but also much more than that. The DC drew support from a wide range of social strata, particularly in rural areas and small cities in the Northeast and in the South. In ideological terms, the DC was divided into a set of factions from left to right, whose influence at any particular instant determined the overall position of the party. Initially a party of local notables in the South and a mass party in the Northeast, it increasingly became a "syndicate of political machines" across the country as a whole.[31] Increasingly geared toward redistributing the resources of the state in return for electoral support, the DC attempted to be both a Catholic and a national party without becoming nationalistic.[32] With the DC a party-based *trasformismo* replaced the dictatorship of Fascism and the classic representative-based *trasformismo* of the pre-Fascist period.

The main electoral competition for the DC from the secular and nationalist right came from the Liberal Party (PLI), the Monarchists (PNM), and the neo-Fascists (MSI). The PLI represented a secular, conservative tradition that was important in late nineteenth-century politics but was in decline thereafter. Its appeal in the postwar period was largely to upperclass groups. The Monarchist Party, absent after the 1960s as a force in national politics, was largely confined to Naples and a few other southern cities (such as Lecce in Puglia) where antirepublican sentiments were exploited to advantage by local notables. The MSI represented another atavistic tradition, that of the Fascists. It appealed to a strange alliance of aging Fascist Party members and officials, southern notables, some government employees, military officers, and, in some places, such as Rome, adolescents drawn to the party by its antiforeigner and militaristic image.

The DC's major competition on the political left came from the PCI, the PSI, the Social Democrats (PSDI), and the Republicans (PRI). The Republicans, the most centrist of the group, assumed a radical position more than a socialist one. They espoused a modern Italy of limited but efficient, technocratic, and honest government rather than government as an agent of

Table 5.2 National Elections, 1946-2001, Constituent Assembly (1946) and Chamber of Deputies, Percentage of Total Votes by Parties (numbers of seats in parentheses)

Party[a]	1946	1948	1953	1958	1963	1968	1972	1976	1979	1983	1987
DC	35.1 (207)	48.5 (305)	40.1 (263)	42.4 (273)	38.3 (260)	39.1 (266)	38.8 (267)	38.7 (292)	38.3 (262)	32.9 (225)	34.3 (234)
PCI	18.9 (104)	31.0 (183)[b]	22.6 (143)	22.7 (140)	25.3 (166)	26.9 (177)	27.2 (177)	34.4 (228)	30.4 (201)	29.9 (198)	26.6 (198)
PSI	20.7 (115)	—	12.8 (75)	14.2 (84)	13.8 (87)	14.5 (91)[b]	9.6 (61)	9.6 (57)	9.8 (62)	11.4 (73)	14.3 (94)
PSDI	—	7.1 (33)	4.5 (19)	4.5 (22)	6.1 (33)	—	5.1 (29)	3.4 (15)	3.8 (20)	4.1 (23)	3.4 (17)
PRI	4.4 (23)	2.5 (9)	1.6 (5)	1.4 (6)	1.4 (6)	2.0 (9)	2.9 (14)	3.1 (14)	3.0 (16)	5.1 (29)	3.7 (21)
PLI	6.8 (41)	3.8 (19)	3.0 (13)	3.5 (17)	7.0 (39)	5.8 (31)	3.9 (21)	1.3 (5)	1.9 (9)	2.9 (16)	2.1 (11)
PR	—	—	—	—	—	—	—	1.1 (4)	3.5 (18)	2.2 (11)	2.6 (13)
DP	—	—	—	—	—	—	—	1.5 (6)	0.8 (—)	1.5 (7)	1.7 (8)
PdUP	—	—	—	—	—	—	—	—	1.4 (6)	—[c]	—
MSI	—	2.0 (6)	5.8 (29)	4.8 (24)	5.1 (21)	4.4 (24)	8.7 (56)	6.1 (35)	5.3 (30)	6.8 (42)	5.9 (35)
PNM	2.8 (16)	2.8 (14)	6.9 (40)	4.8 (25)	1.7 (8)	1.3 (6)	—	—	—	—	—
Others[d]	9.5 (50)	2.5 (5)	2.7 (3)	1.7 (5)	1.3 (4)	6.0 (26)	4.0 (4)	0.8 (4)	2.7 (6)	3.2 (6)	5.8 (10)

Party[a]	1992	Party	1994[e]	1996[e]	Party	2001[f]
DC	29.7 (206)	FI	21.0 (99)	20.6 (123)	FI	29.5
PDS	16.1 (107)	PDS	20.4 (109)	21.1 (171)	DS	16.6
RC	5.6 (35)	RC	6.0 (14)	8.6 (35)	M	14.5
PSI	13.6 (92)	Lega	8.4 (117)	10.1 (59)	RC	5.0
PDSI	2.7 (16)	AN	13.5 (109)	15.2 (93)	Lega	3.9
PRI	4.4 (27)	PPI	11.1 (33)	6.8 (71)	AN	12.0
PLI	2.9 (17)	Others	19.6 (139)	17.1 (78)	Others	18.5

(continued)

Table 5.2   (continued)

Party[a]	1992	Party	1994[e]	1996[e]	Party	2001[f]
MSI	5.4 (34)					
Lega	8.6 (55)					
Others[d]	10.8 (41)					

SOURCE: Ministero dell'Interno.

[a]DC = Democrazia Cristiana, PCI = Partito Comunista Italiano, PSI = Partito Socialista Italiano, PSDI = Partito Socialista Democratico Italiano, PRI = Partito Repubblicano Italiano, PLI = Partito Liberale Italiano, PR = Partito Radicale, DP = Democrazia Proletaria, PdUP = Partito di Unita Proletaria per il Comunismo, MSI = Movimento Sociale Italiano, PNM = Partito Nazionale Monarchico (Monarchists), PDS = Partito Democratico della Sinistra, RC = Rifondazione Comunista, FI = Forza Italia, AN = Alleanza Nazionale, Lega = Lega Nord, PPI = Partito Popolare Italiano, DS = Democratici Sinistra, M = La Margherita.

[b]Parties presented on joint election lists.

[c]Ran on PCI lists.

[d]Includes South Tyrol People's Party (SVP), Sardinian Action party (PSA), Valdotaine Union (UV), and Socialist Party of Proletarian Unity (PSUIP). The SVP generally accounts for 3 seats; the PSUIP won 23 seats in 1968. The Greens won 13 seats, with 2.5 percent in 1987. After 1992 various center-right factions and the anti-Mafia (Rete) vote are important

[e]New electoral system. Percentages are from proportional contests, seats are total seats from majoritarian and proportional contests

[f]Percentages are from proportional contests. FI and its allies, AN and Lega, won 368 seats (86 in proportional seats, of which 62 for FI and 24 for AN). DS and its ally, M, won 250 seats (58 in proportional seats, of which 31 for DS and 27 for M). RC won 11 seats and others 1.

social change or revolution. The latter, of course, are the espoused goals of the Italian socialist tradition going back to the late nineteenth century. Though committed to such goals, these parties have been chronically divided over political priorities and organizational strategies. All had roots in Marxism, but for most of the postwar period none was an orthodox Marxist-Leninist party. All were "revisionist," but rarely did they agree on foreign policy, party organization, and parliamentary democracy. It is probably accurate to say, however, that the PCI's positions edged toward the others' from the 1960s on.[33]

Of the four parties, the PCI had the strongest organizational base and increasingly the most electoral strength. Although always appealing to workers, it also enjoyed substantial peasant and lower-middle-class support in some localities and regions (particularly some of the regions of the former Papal States—Romagna, Marche, and Umbria—and in Emilia and Tuscany). Over time its base of voters diversified through appeals to employees in general and to some sectors of small business in particular (retailers and small-scale manufacturers). The PSI and PSDI came to have weaker working-class support. As they lost votes to the PCI they drifted to the center and came to rely increasingly on the patronage politics used so effectively by the DC.[34] This required access to government office. After the early 1960s they became, along with the PLI and PRI, the most important potential national coalition partners for the DC.

The late 1960s and the 1970s were a period of reaction against party politics in Italy, as elsewhere.[35] But even as extraparliamentary politics exploded onto the streets with revolts from the left and counterrevolution from the far right and its Mafia allies, new political parties attempting to straddle the gap between the cultures of revolt and electoral politics came into the political marketplace. Most of these were on the left and gained most of their support in northern cities, notably Proletarian Democracy (DP), critical of the compromises of the PCI with the "system"; the Liste Verde (or Green Lists/Ecology Party); and for the 1979 and 1987 elections, the Radical Party (PR), mobilized around the inequities of the Italian criminal justice system, social issues such as divorce and abortion law reform, and state involvement in the terrorism of the 1970s and early 1980s.[36]

One reason there were so many small parties is that, unlike the United States and other countries with simple majority voting in single-member constituencies, Italy presented few barriers to entry into electoral competition. Under a system of proportional representation with multimember districts, a vote for a small party need not be a wasted vote. At the same time, parties also served important mediating functions in such a highly differentiated society. This encouraged coalition formation to balance ideological representation against political effectiveness. It also eventually produced the systemic corruption of the so-called *partitocrazia*, or party-based political economy, around which many other features of Italian life increasingly revolved. Particularly from the mid-1970s, as the DC and PSI shared the key positions in national government and formed coalitions with one another and smaller parties at other levels of government, the parties colonized Italian society by exchanging government contracts and public sector employment for financial contributions and electoral support.[37] Local-national political links were increasingly oiled nationwide by an exchange of favors that was no longer as localized or regionalized, or based on conflict between factions in the DC, as corruption had tended to be before the 1970s.[38] Judicial exposure of this system finally brought it tumbling down in 1992, along with the two parties most implicated in it—the DC and the PSI.

What were the electoral rules whereby the parties competed with one another for popular support before the collapse of the First Republic in 1992 and the imposition of a new electoral system for the national election of 1994?[39] The electoral system was one of proportional representation. Without any threshold of votes needed to qualify for a seat and thereby open to the representation of minority interests, this system encouraged the proliferation of political parties and the need to negotiate cross-party coalitions after elections in order to form national governments. National political elections (*elezioni politiche*) involved selecting a number of members to the Chamber of Deputies and a single senator. Voting was by party list and until 1987, if desired, by expressing preferences for particular candidates. Election to the Chamber of Deputies was by party list in districts ranging from four to forty-seven members. These districts generally group all the provinces of a small region or segments of a large region. They closely follow the administrative divisions of the country, so it was fairly easy to see the support for specific party lists by commune, province, and region. Counting votes involved distributing preference votes among parties and candidates. In districts electing fewer than sixteen members, up to three names could be marked; in those with more members, up to four. Preference voting was always indulged in on a much larger scale in the South than in the North (a northern maximum 19.5 percent rate of preference voting in 1972 compared with a southern minimum of 44.3 percent in 1976) and by DC voters in Italy as whole and DC, PSI, PSDI, and right-wing voters in the South. Preference voting correlated highly with clientelistic politics.[40]

Turnout in national elections was exceptionally high, ranging as high as 93.8 percent in 1958. After 1979 turnouts dropped, but they remained above 80 percent until 1992.[41] Indeed, true rates of participation may have been higher because official figures were based on electoral rolls that included people who had moved or died. Registration was and still is automatic. Geographical differences in turnout were always small (5 to 10 percent) and probably reflect dated electoral rolls more than systematic differences in attitudes to electoral participation. Rates were lower in areas of heavy emigration and in the South. Turnouts in all elections (local, national, and European) have been much the same. Relatively high rates of participation thus were characteristic of all Italian elections and all parts of Italy across the period 1947–87. The main parties competed everywhere, though their claims and strategies often varied significantly across constituencies.[42]

THE GEOGRAPHICAL DYNAMICS OF ITALIAN ELECTORAL POLITICS, 1947–87

Italian electoral politics from 1947 to 1987 has been viewed either in terms of nationalization and the rise of the individual opinion voter or in terms of regional cultures with static political profiles. Alternatively, however, it can be interpreted in terms of three political-geographical "regimes" in which the places Italy is made from have had different degrees of political similarity and difference at different times. This periodization of the dominant geographical scale at which electoral politics is expressed draws on a number of studies that more or less explicitly adopt the same approach but that are largely silent about the idea of a dominant geographical dimension for a given period.[43]

It is important to note that throughout 1947–87 changes in the levels of support for Italian political parties from one national election to the next were small compared with those in such countries as France and Britain. But certain realigning elections can be identified when changes were greater than usual and involved flows of votes beyond the confines of parties grouped into the left, right, and center "families" within which votes were more typically exchanged.[44] The major shifts occurred in 1948 and 1953, when the PCI emerged as the main party of the left and the DC as the main party of the center; 1963, when the DC lost votes to the right and began its collaboration with the PSI and the PCI began its long march toward the center; and 1976, when the PCI increased its vote from new voters and voters from the center and the DC received votes from the right.

No previous study has tied these frequently noted national shifts to changes in the political geography of electoral choice. Yet these dates seem to be critical in the geographical composition of votes as well as to signal important realignments at the national scale. Indeed, the general stability in votes cast for the main parties at the national level seems to mask important shifts at other scales in the overall geographical makeup of voting blocs. This best explains what can be called "Mair's paradox" in the Italian case, the tendency for many commentators to note changes in the overall fortunes of parties without much demonstrable change in the national shares of votes cast.[45]

One way of seeing if realigning elections correlate with changes in electoral geography is to decompose the variance of votes for a major party (the DC) in all national elections to the Chamber of Deputies from 1953 to 1987.[46] Doing this shows that provincial standard deviations around national means go up from 1953 to 1968 but drop substantially from 1968 to 1976, with an ensuing increase from 1979 to 1987 (fig. 5.3). The drop is an indicator of nationalization. Before 1963 the regional standard deviations (regional means around the national means) of the DC vote are higher than those within regions (provinces around regional means), which, with the exception of 1972–79 when they show a parallel drop, become ever larger than the regional ones over time. This is an indicator of localization after 1979 rather than a reestablishment of the regionalization characteristic of the period before 1963.

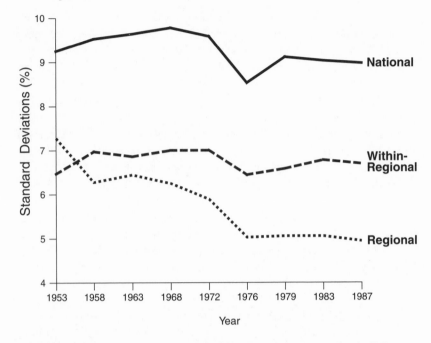

Figure 5.3   Decomposition of geographical variance in votes cast for the DC, 1953–87, at national, regional, and within-regional levels. Source: Author.

The trend for the PCI is similar except that the regional standard deviations are consistently larger than those for the DC, particularly after 1979. This more powerful regionalization effect is not surprising, given the well-known retreat of the PCI back into its central Italian heartland after the big national success of 1976.[47]

I interpret these findings as follows: a period of high national variance for both the DC and the PCI from 1953 to 1963, with regional clustering accounting for a significant but declining share of total national variance; a period of nationalization from 1968 to 1976 in which the standard deviations at all scales went down; a period of increased national variance after 1976 largely accounted for by increased within-region variance, particularly for the DC.

The approach is based on a behavioral notion of degrees of homogeneity in vote percentages at different geographical scales. A more abstract view, more in keeping with the discussion in chapter 2, would involve how places differ in the ways politics is structured cognitively and emotionally by the people who live in them. In this view, place directly structures the domain of discourse (and choice) and only indirectly structures the domain of behavior. Thus there can be a different structuring of choice with similarity in behavior. Detailed discussion focusing on what went on in different places during the different periods attempts to deal with this criticism.

The Three Geographical Regimes

Whatever its empirical limitations, the periodizing does help fit together elements of the conventional wisdom about the course of Italian electoral politics over the postwar period that have remained fragmented and inchoate rather than joined together within a larger narrative drama.[48] The geography of Italian politics since 1947 can be characterized in terms of three distinctive geographical regimes that have dominated in different periods. The first regime, dominant from 1947 until 1963, involved a regional pattern of support for the major political parties based on place similarities that clustered regionally. The second, in effect from 1963 until 1976, witnessed the expansion of the Communist Party out of its regional strongholds into a nationally competitive position with the Christian Democratic Party. This had different causes in different places, but the net effect was to suggest a nationalization of the two major parties. The third, characteristic of the period since 1976, has seen increased support for minor parties, including regional parties such as the Northern League (Lega Nord), the geographical "retreat" and political disintegration of the PCI and DC, and a more localized pattern of political expression in general, reflecting the increased patchiness of Italian economic growth and social change and the crisis of the system of parties after 1992.

The Regionalizing Regime

The period 1947–63 is that of the classical electoral geography of Italy established most definitively by Galli and his colleagues.[49] They divided the country into six zones based on levels of support for the three major parties, the PCI, the DC, and the Socialists (PSI), and on the regional-local strength of the major political subcultures, the socialist and the Catholic:

Zone 1, the "industrial triangle," covered northwestern Italy and included Piedmont, Liguria, and Lombardy. This was the region where industrial production was concentrated before World War II and where most new industrial investment was concentrated in the 1950s. Socialists, Christian Democrats, and Communists were all competitive in this region.

Zone 2, *la zona bianca* (the white zone) covered northeastern Italy and included the provinces of Bergamo and Brescia in Lombardy, the province of Trento, the province of Udine, and all of the Veneto except the province of Rovigo. The Christian Democrats were most strongly entrenched in this region, and opposition was divided among a number of parties.

Zone 3, *la zona rossa* (the red zone) covered central Italy and included the provinces of Mantova, Rovigo, and Viterbo; the whole of Emilia-Romagna except the province of Piacenza; Tuscany except for Lucca (an *isola bianca*); Umbria; and the Marche except the province of Ascoli Piceno. In this region the PCI was most strongly established, especially in the countryside but increasingly in the cities.

Zone 4, the South, included the province of Ascoli Piceno and the regions of Lazio (except Viterbo), Campania, Abruzzo e Molise, Puglia, Basilicata, and Calabria. This zone was historically the poorest and the most marked by clientelistic politics. In the 1950s the Christian Democrats and the right-wing parties dominated the zone, but they were faced with increasingly strong challenges from the PCI and the PSI.

The final two zones, zone 5, Sicily, and zone 6, Sardinia, had more complex political alignments than the peninsular South. Though the DC was dominant, other parties also had a presence. For example, the PCI was well established in the southern provinces of Sicily (especially the sulfur mining areas), while Sardinia had a strong regionalist party (fig. 5.4).

There were strongly rooted cultural "hegemonies" (party-based consensus building) in only two of these zones, *la zona bianca* and *la zona rossa* (fig. 5.5). However, in electoral terms, support for specific political parties was remarkably clustered regionally in 1953: the PCI in the Center, the PNM (Monarchists) and MSI (neo-Fascists) in the South and Sicily, the DC in the Northeast and the South. In the 1950s Italian politics followed a regional regime reflecting a similarity at the regional scale of place-based social, economic, and political relationships.[50]

But a true regionalism, in the sense of a majority dominance within a region by a single party, applied only to the Northeast (for the DC) and the Center (for the PCI). This was the result of a true cultural hegemony in these regions in which the respective parties stimulated support for themselves and colonized local society through the organization of affiliated farm cooperatives, banks, artisanal associations, and recreational facilities. This helped stimulate economic development in these regions (what was later to flower as the Third Italy), but it also made the basis of the parties' electoral support much more one of identity or belonging that extended beyond the act of voting into other spheres of life.[51]

Elsewhere, parties might experience local dominance, perhaps based on the charisma or favors of a local politician or notable, but this was not akin to the cultural links between party and place in the Northeast and the Center. Only in the Northwest were major parties competitors that could hope to unseat their opponents. A set of subcultures therefore could plausibly be seen as structuring and limiting political choices in different regions but were hegemonic only in the two regions identified as *la zona bianca* and *la zona rossa* (see chapter 6).

Figure 5.4 Map of Italian provinces and the voting regions used by Galli and Prandi. Source: redrawn from Giorgio Galli and Alfonso Prandi, *Patterns of Political Participation in Italy* (New Haven: Yale University Press, 1970), 114.

The Nationalizing Regime

The second period, 1963–76, marks a break with the regional pattern characteristic of the 1950s. Two electoral shifts were especially clear: the expansion of support for the PCI outside *la zona rossa* (along with its consolidation inside), particularly in the industrial Northwest and parts of the South, and the breakdown of *la zona bianca* as a number of small parties made inroads in the previously hegemonic support for the DC in parts of

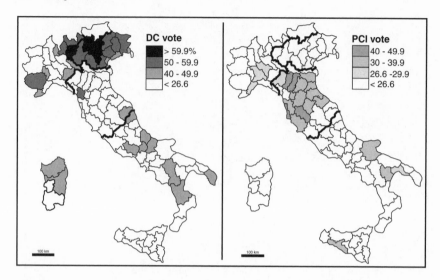

Figure 5.5   DC vote as a percentage of total vote by province, 1953 national election (Chamber of Deputies); PCI vote as a percentage of total vote by province, 1953 national election (Chamber of Deputies). Source: Author.

the Northeast. The net effect of these changes was a seeming nationalization of the major parties, even though they still maintained traditional areas of strength.

These political changes were the fruit of the major economic and social changes Italy underwent in the late 1950s and early 1960s. A major expansion occurred in manufacturing and industrial employment, especially in the Northwest, as an extraordinary boom or "economic miracle" drew the Italian economy away from its predominantly agrarian base. At the same time that the industrial centers of the Northwest were experiencing such dramatic economic and social change as a result of the economic boom and massive immigration, the rest of the country was experiencing shock waves emanating from the Northwest. The extreme south of the peninsula (Puglia, Basilicata, and Calabria), with the exception of Taranto, the site of a major steelworks built under government auspices, had little industry and was a major zone of emigration to the Northwest. Where industry was established it created pockets of new social and economic relationships in the midst of a rapidly depopulating rural society. In all these places and among immigrants from the South now living in the North, the PCI expanded its support in the late 1960s and early 1970s.[52]

The boom of 1959–63 was led by exports, which had accounted for the greatest share of growing production from 1955 on. The major products were cars, domestic appliances, and office equipment—mass-produced goods not requiring particularly sophisticated technology. Although exports surged, the domestic market remained depressed until 1965, when the growth of private consumption finally began to run ahead of GNP. By the late 1960s, the material quality of life of many Italians, particularly in the Northwest, had improved significantly. An Italian consumer society based on nationwide advertising and consumption norms was born.[53]

The economic boom of the early 1960s initially reinforced the historical concentration of industry in the Northwest. Some investment went into new technologically innovative sectors, but much new employment was in older factories that had expanded production without much technological change. These industries provided many unskilled jobs with low wages and poor working conditions. By the late 1960s workers in these factories, many of them recent immigrants from elsewhere in Italy, became important participants in the strikes and social unrest that enveloped the industrial centers of the Northwest. These protests marked the onset of a long period of social conflict that lasted until the early 1980s and involved terrorism and counterterrorism as well as strikes and street protests.[54]

The cities of the Northwest were completely unprepared for the immigrants who arrived at a dizzying rate in the 1960s. There were not enough jobs, schools, housing, or public services. Immigrant ghettos proliferated, sometimes in decaying quarters on the fringes of city centers, more frequently in shantytowns on the outskirts. Their inhabitants faced unpleasant living conditions, unfamiliar and exacting work discipline, and persistent hostility from local populations. Not only did they participate in strikes and other forms of protest, they also became recruits for the PCI and other parties that promised social change. The expansion of the PCI in the Northwest in 1963–76 can be traced in large part to these new immigrants.

The PCI probably also benefited, at least initially, from the explosion of new political issues, particularly those associated with the ecological and women's movements. These peaked in their national political impact in 1975–76.[55] Though relatively open to the questions of environmental degradation and women's social inequality raised by these movements, the PCI also had to square its newfound enthusiasm for these issues with old constituencies more concerned with economic growth and income distribution or with maintaining the environmental status quo, particularly in relation to pollution by small firms in PCI-dominated areas such as along the river Arno in Tuscany, and to hunting birds and other wildlife in its rural strongholds in central Italy. On many social issues, such as divorce and abortion, the PCI was also very conservative, compared in particular with the new Radical Party, for fear of alienating the Church and possible Catholic voters. Because the larger parties, particularly the PCI, had trouble overcoming these divisions, the demands of the more activist ecologists led to the growth of new specialized Green parties and motivated some women activists to create such groups as the Federcasalinghe (Housewives Association). An initial boost to the PCI in the early 1970s therefore was followed by disenchantment and political fragmentation by the end of the decade.

In addition to the geographical expansion of the PCI, the other major feature of 1963–76 was the so-called breakdown of the Catholic subculture or dominant position in *la zona bianca* or Northeast and the subsequent loss of DC voters. The argument is that the DC, being largely an electoral party rather than a mass party with a large membership, had relied heavily on affiliated organizations, many of a religious nature, to mobilize its support. In the late 1960s, however, as a result of heavy out-migration from rural areas in the Veneto, Trento, and Friuli, the constituent subregions of *la zona bianca,* and the growing industrialization of some areas such as Venice, Treviso, Trento, and Pordenone, the traditional social networks and communal institutions DC hegemony was based on began to collapse. Other parties could now make inroads into what had hitherto been a region totally dominated electorally by the DC.[56]

The nationalizing political-geographical regime peaked in 1976, when the DC and PCI together accounted for 73 percent of the national vote. Although this trend had distinctive causes relating to the geographically differentiated social and economic effects of the economic miracle and their interplay with political and organizational traditions, it was widely interpreted as a permanent nationalization of political life. To be sure, the DC and the PCI were now national political parties. The 1976 election seemed to seal once and for all the PCI's penetration of constituencies where it had previously been weak or where support had stagnated (but not much in the former DC strongholds in the Northeast). The party registered gains over 1972 of 10.6 percent in Naples-Caserta, 10.9 percent in Cagliari-Nuoro (Sardinia), 9.6 percent in Rome-Viterbo-Frosinone, and 9.2 percent in Turin-Novara-Vercelli. By the standard of Italian national elections since World War II, where swings of 1 to 2 percent were regarded as "victories" or "defeats," these were immense swings indeed.[57]

The Localizing Regime

The 1979 election indicated a much more complex geography of political strength and variation than had previously been characteristic. The PCI in particular lost ground nationally relative to the most recent elections. But since then all parties have been less nationalized than in 1963–76. The

1983 and 1987 elections suggested a trend toward a localization or increased differentiation of political expression that continued until the even greater political and electoral changes of the early 1990s. In 1983 the DC lost 5.4 percent nationally, but the PCI was not the beneficiary. Rather, it was smaller parties such as the Republicans (PRI) in the North and the PSI and MSI in the South that gained the most. The PSI in particular picked up votes and seats in the South from the DC (and in places the PCI), to the extent that the PSI's traditional base of support in the Northwest was increasingly eclipsed by its gains in the South. This "southernization" of the PSI had national ramifications in that it turned another party with potentially national support toward the patronage model of electoral support hitherto dominated by the DC as its "southern strategy" of gaining exchange voters affected its nationwide operation. In 1987 the DC recovered somewhat from 1983, but without a major geographical expansion. The major loser this time was the PCI, which lost ground in the Northeast, the Northwest, and some provinces of *la zona rossa* to the PSI and a variety of smaller parties including the Radicals (PR), the Greens, and Democrazia Proletaria (DP).[58]

Regional-scale change in this period was modest. Most change was localized, with DC and PCI votes, as well as those of smaller parties, experiencing opposing shifts in adjacent districts (for 1979 see fig. 5.6). In addition, regionalist parties, such as the Liga Veneta in the Veneto and the Partito Sardo d'Azione in Sardinia, and national parties with a reputation for honesty, such as the MSI and the PRI, achieved local success but without much net increase in their total national support.[59]

I examine the localizing regime in two ways. One way is to show how increased electoral differentiation followed a restructuring of economic and social life during the late 1970s and early 1980s. The second involves exploring the failure of the PCI to build on its success in 1976 and linking this to locally distinctive social and economic changes.

One factor in electoral localization was the increasingly differentiated pattern of economic change after a previous era of geographical concentration of industry. Although the economic boom of the early 1960s concentrated economic growth increasingly in the Northwest, by the late 1960s there was considerable decentralization of industrial activity out of the Northwest and into the Northeast and the Center. This new pattern of differentiated economic growth led some commentators to write of the emergence of "three Italys"—a Northwest with a concentration of older heavy industries and large factory-scale production facilities, a Northeast-Center of small, family-based, export-oriented and component-producing firms, and a still largely underdeveloped South, reliant on government employment but with some of the small-scale development (for

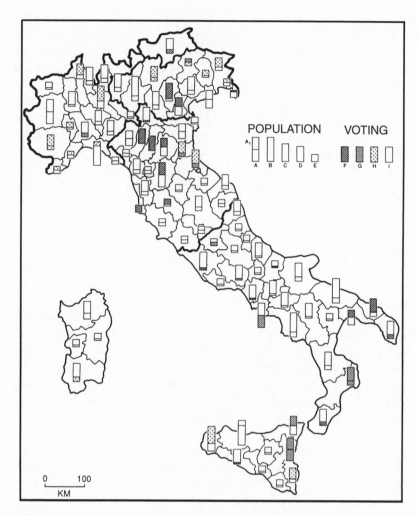

Figure 5.6 Localization of high levels of support for parties, 1979 national election (Chamber of Deputies). A, total inhabitants of province; A1 = percentage of residents in provincial capital; B, if number of inhabitants is more than 1 million; C, if number is between 600,000 and 1 million; D, if number is between 350,000 and 600,000; E, if less than 350,000; F, if a party surpasses a threshold of 50.3 percent of the vote; G, if a party surpasses 9.06 but gains less than 18.82 percent; H, if a party surpasses 3.85 but gains less than 8.51 percent; I, provincial capitals and dependent areas in which no thresholds are passed. Source: Carlo Brusa, *Geografia elettorale nell'Italia del dopoguerra: Edizione aggiornata ai risultati delle elezioni politiche 1983* (Milan: Unicopli, 1984), 72.

example, in the vicinity of Bari or Caserta) characteristic of the Third Italy (Northeast-Center).[60] This terminology, though useful as a general characterization of a new economic geography, masks both a much more uneven and differentiated pattern at a local scale and the linkages between localized development and the big firms of the Northwest. High concentrations of employment in major growth industries have, in fact, been widely scattered. Regional patterns are no longer clear-cut.[61] What is apparent is that the heavy concentration of industry in the Northwest has diminished at the expense of new growth industries in the towns and countryside of the Center and Northeast and in scattered locations in the South (fig. 5.7).

Organizationally, however, the net result has been a reinforcement of the national economy's dual structure: the division between relatively few giant firms, overwhelmingly headquartered in the Northwest, and myriad small workshop businesses in the Northwest and in the Third Italy. The big firms that propelled the boom of the early 1960s entered into crisis in the 1970s as a result of higher wages prompted by the labor militancy of 1969–70, the imposition of national cost-of-living increases, and the deep world recessions of 1973–74 and 1979–81. They responded by investing in automation and laying off main production employees and by decentralizing production away from large factories, where labor unions remained strong, to the emerging small-firm sector. The large firms still remain critical to important sectors of the Italian economy such as textiles, steel, chemicals, automobiles, and electronics, but they no longer have the antagonistic labor relations they once had. Their factories are no longer centers of radical politics or even of necessarily strong support for parties of the left.[62]

At the same time, the increasing need for consumer goods industries to respond to rapid shifts in product demand led to a massive direct stimulation of the artisanal and small businesses that were based in industrial districts scattered across northern and central Italy, producing clothing, shoes, metal goods, musical instruments, and household appliances for increasingly global markets. The emergence of long-distance ties, sensitivity to the failures of the Italian public economy to deliver adequate infrastructure, worries about competitive advantage in global competition, and the assertion of local identities against the idea of a southern dominance over national government and its agencies (such as the post office, the railways, and the schools) produced a very different orientation to national politics in those places now tied directly into the world economy.[63]

The geographical shifts in manufacturing industries were closely correlated with growing per capita incomes where they are situated. Those provinces that experienced the greatest income growth in the late 1970s and early 1980s tend to be in the Center and Northeast (e.g., Pordenone,

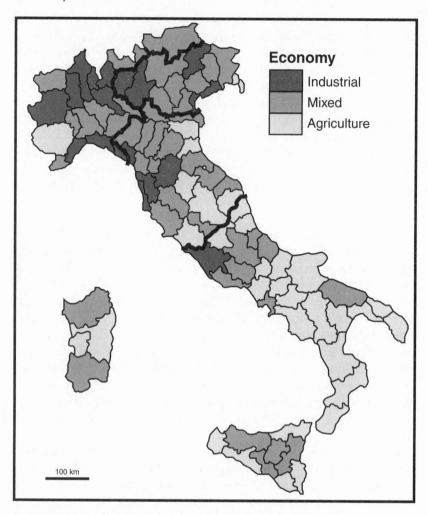

Figure 5.7   Economic localization in Italy in 1981: three types of provincial economy. Source: Brusa, *Geografia elettorale nell'Italia del dopoguerra,* 75.

Bologna, Modena, Arezzo) or in the vicinity of Rome (e.g., Latina, Frosinone), precisely the areas where new industrial development has been most concentrated (the prealpine belt from Bergamo to Pordenone, the Emilian corridor from Milan to Bologna, northern Tuscany from Pistoia to Arezzo, and certain provinces of the northern Mezzogiorno).[64] This trend has brought greater disposable incomes to hitherto deprived areas and changed the basis on which people orient themselves to politics. In some places this has involved greater secularization, elsewhere it has meant a retreat from forms of recreation dependent on organizations affiliated with the Communist Party, such as the *case del lavoro* (local centers for recreational and political activities), into more private pursuits. Either way, opinion voting has opened up for those previously locked into either exchange or identity voting. However, this has produced not nationalization but, on the contrary, a more fragmented and localized electoral politics.[65]

Other factors have also contributed to the localizing political-geographical trend from the late 1970s to the present. One was the failure of the parties to successfully adapt to social and economic change. In Trento and Udine (in the Northeast), for example, the DC had problems adapting to the new economy. In large parts of the South and the Northwest, the PCI was unable to capitalize on earlier successes mainly because in the South it neither had control over the state resources that lubricate the politics of many parts of that region nor was able to build a permanent following. In the Northwest its major vanguard of unionized workers was much reduced in economic importance at the same time that the other parties had become better organized and that the particular problems of the southern immigrants, whom the PCI had previously recruited as voters, had largely receded from the political agenda.[66]

The emergence of effective regional governments in Italy as whole since 1970 also reinforced the localization of interests and sense of place. Where parties have achieved some strength and legitimacy through control over regional governments, they have been able to build local coalitions for national politics based on the pursuit of local interests. The PCI, for example, benefited from its control of or participation in the regional governments of Emilia-Romagna, Tuscany, and Umbria, but it suffered elsewhere, and other parties such as the DC and the PSI benefited, because of its lack of control over patronage jobs and inability to write regional political agendas.[67]

The former successes of the DC in *la zona bianca* and the PCI in *la zona rossa* rested to a degree on the social institutions they were affiliated with (unions, cooperatives, clubs, etc.) as well as on social isolation. However, the shifting orientations of these institutions and the rise of the consumer society opened up possibilities for smaller parties. There is some evidence that, after the late 1960s, ties between the DC and the PCI and their supportive organizations, especially the unions for the PCI, had weakened.[68] The parties themselves were responsible for some of this. To expand nationally, they often had to abandon or at least limit the ideological appeal that served so well in areas of traditional strength. They also had to respond in some areas to new movements such as the Greens, which opened them up for both factionalism and essentially localized forms of organization and ideology.[69]

More generally, political parties do not always travel well. Thus, in comparing northeastern with central Italy, the question of compatibility between party style and local style arises. In the mid-1970s, in a comparison of the two regions where the DC and the PCI exerted their greatest influence in the 1950s and 1960s, *la zona bianca* in the Northeast and *la zona rossa* in the Center, Alan Stern noted

> the evolution of two very different forms of political hegemony, each with distinct characteristics that necessitate sharply contrasting forms of maintenance. The Christian Democratic variety that flourishes in northeastern Italy is fueled efficiently by stable social organization that deemphasizes the place of politics in community life. In comparison the communist variant thriving in central Italy accents the urgent attention that political matters should command among the local citizenry and thereby constantly reaffirms the relatively recent sense of legitimacy that underlies PCI control.[70]

Of course these hegemonies always had local roots, and in some localities their power has been quite visible and persistent, although, as Mario Tesini has suggested for Bologna, things could have turned out quite differently if key politicians had made different choices.[71]

Finally, between 1987 and 1992 the system of parties in place since the end of World War II unraveled (see chapters 7–9). As a result of the end of the Cold War and disputes over the meaning and appropriateness of the term communist, the PCI regrouped as two new parties, the larger Partito Democratico della Sinistra (PDS) and the smaller hard-line Rifondazione Comunista (RC). As a result of investigation of systematic corruption in their operations, the PSI collapsed and the DC disintegrated into three separate parties, the Partito Popolare to the center-left and two smaller factions to the right. The Fascist MSI was reborn as a new "post-Fascist" conservative party, Alleanza Nazionale, and in 1994 a new party organized by the media tycoon Silvio Berlusconi, Forza Italia, attempted to replace the DC on the center-right. The proliferation of smaller parties continued. But a new electoral system, in effect for the first time in 1994, forced parties to look for coalition partners *before* elections so as to run more effectively for the 75 percent of seats decided by majority votes in single-member districts. The other 25 percent of seats remain under the previously dominant system of proportional representation for candidates from party lists in multimember districts. By 1996, with the federalist-separatist Northern League a potent electoral force in many parts of northern Italy, all parties save Forza Italia and the PDS were now largely local or regional in strength.[72] Even these two parties must coalesce with some of the others to achieve national-government office. In 2001 Forza Italia allied with the

Alleanza Nazionale and the Northern League to achieve a winning coalition against the Democratici Sinistra (former PDS) and La Margherita, an electoral alliance made up of the Partito Popolare and others on the center-left. Even though in 2001 Forza Italia achieved success in large parts of Italy in its own right, the local strength of different parties means that support for all parties today is more obviously localized than it was in 1976 or in the 1950s.

A second type of exploration of the localizing regime focuses more specifically on a major aspect of the period between 1976 and 1987: the decline of the national PCI vote in the critical period immediately after its success in 1976. This is often put down to the disillusionment of new PCI voters with the PCI's historical compromise with the DC (quietly supporting the government but having no direct role in it) between 1976 and 1978. After that initial setback, however, the trend of retreat continued in the 1980s, with the Center and, somewhat ironically, the Northeast as the only regions in which earlier gains were largely retained. But the pattern of losses was not a simple reversal of previous geographical expansion. The loss pattern was variegated, with 1976–79 losses greater than 1972–76 gains in Puglia and Sicily and in Trieste, proportionate losses in Lazio and a number of southern provinces, and losses smaller than earlier gains in Liguria, in parts of the Northeast, and in the Center.[73]

As a guide to what might have been responsible for this variegated pattern of gains and losses, stepwise multiple regression analysis is of some use.[74] A number of variables indicating social and economic conditions by province can be used to predict PCI losses: the presence and intensity of various economic sectors, unemployment, level of schooling, urbanization, the availability of public assistance, and the number officially unemployed but "unavailable"—a measure of those working unofficially or off the books. Analysis can be conducted nationally and by region to see to what extent results are different at different geographical scales.

Of nine variables that survive elimination from the original ten, different combinations of five variables best predict the PCI losses at the national and regional scales (table 5.3). Nationally, two occupational variables are noteworthy: PCI vote loss varies inversely with working unofficially and directly with unemployment rate, indicating lighter losses where the underground economy is strongest and heavier losses in areas of high unemployment. These results mask a more complex geographical picture, however. The precise relationships of the variables to losses differ from one region to another, suggesting the limitations of national-level analysis in the absence of nationalization.

Different processes seem to have been at work in bringing about PCI losses in different regions. In the Northwest, vote loss was positively asso-

Table 5.3   Predicting the Loss of PCI Votes, 1976–79, at National and Regional Levels

	(1)	(2)	(3)	(4)	(5)	(6)	(7)	(8)	(9)	r^2
Northwest	−0.50	+0.36	−0.26			−0.54		+0.66		0.71
"Zona bianca"	+0.73	+0.18			−0.11	−0.34				0.96
"Zona rossa"	+0.42	−0.53		+0.22	−0.26		−0.61	−0.57		0.67
South	+0.22	+0.41	+0.12			−0.26	−0.24			0.46
Italy as a whole		+0.45			−0.10	−0.15	−0.44		−0.09	0.61

SOURCE: Renato Mannheimer, "Un'analisi territoriale del calo comunista," in *Mobilità senza movimento: Le elezioni del 3 giugno 1979*, ed. Arturo Parisi (Bologna: Il Mulino, 1980), 88.

NOTE: Results use nine independent variables by province.

(1) Rate of urban concentration (population resident in communes with more than 100,000/total resident population).

(2) Rate of unemployment (unemployed/resident population, 1977).

(3) Cost of living increase (percent increase 1976–77)

(4) Percentage of value added in agriculture.

(5) Percentage of value added in industry.

(6) Percent of value added in services.

(7) Percentage of those listed as "not available" on list of those unemployed (1977).

(8) Number occupied in industry/resident population (1975)

(9) Minimum pensions/total pensions, 1976 (a measure of indigence).

ciated with socioeconomic variables such as prevalence of industrial employment and higher unemployment rates, signifying greater losses in industrial provinces with higher unemployment. Lesser losses occurred in urban centers with higher levels of value added in services. In all other regions, however, urbanization and vote loss are strongly associated, signifying perhaps greater electoral mobility among those regions' urban voters.

In the South, the regression model has poorer fit to the pattern of PCI vote loss ($r^2 = 0.46$), though vote loss again correlates positively with unemployment and inversely with the underground economy and service employment. Other factors not measured in this analysis, such as a demobilization of 1976 voters as a result of general alienation and the increased trend toward voter volatility in the South as old exchange networks broke down, may also be important in the region.

In *la zona rossa* losses were greatest in provinces that were most urban and least where unemployment was higher and more people were employed in industry and in the underground economy. In *la zona bianca* losses were greatest in more urbanized areas and in those with high unemployment and high value added in agriculture. Interestingly, therefore, PCI losses between 1976 and 1979 varied inversely with unemployment in *la zona rossa* and positively in *la zona bianca*. Equally curious is the absence of much of a relation between the underground economy and loss of PCI votes in *la zona bianca* but a powerful inverse one in *la zona rossa* (indicating lower losses where the number of unofficially employed is higher).

This can be explained in terms of the continuing mediating effects of local social networks and community traditions in the two zones. Under conditions of dramatic economic restructuring and rapid social change such as affected Italy in general and the two zones in particular in the 1970s, the unemployed and those in irregular employment in *la zona rossa* continued to look to the PCI. In *la zona bianca,* however, the unemployed and those insecurely employed turned away from the PCI after previously being drawn to it in 1976.

The contrasts between provinces captured by the regional-level analysis indicate the plurality of processes associated with electoral choice leading to the loss of votes for the PCI in 1979. The analysis also reveals that the onset of the localizing regime involved the appearance of different balances of processes in different places that could not be captured by a single Italywide conception of what had happened. A "one size" national model could not fit the complex processes governing the emergence of the new geographical regime. Rather, the regional differences in paths to the loss of votes by the PCI suggest "the existence of distinct logics that, in different contexts, govern the process of the formation of the vote."[75]

CONCLUSION

The nationalization of electoral politics has been a major theme of recent political science. It is certainly clear that what happens locally and regionally cannot be divorced from consideration of forces emanating from national-scale institutions and processes. In particular, in Sidney Tarrow's words, "penetration, standardization, and incorporation" by national states have transformed the nature of what goes on anywhere, however imperfectly and unevenly.[76] But this does not mean that processes of political socialization and action now are essentially national. To the contrary, local socioeconomic settings and long-distance influences (including national-state ones) now create the contexts for continuity and change in popular political behavior. Agency and social influences come together in place.

The Italian case illustrates the importance of the geography of political behavior. The balance between places and the national state is uneasy and unstable. Places can throw up politics that are not functional for the state; for example, support for antisystemic, antiregime, separatist, and ethnic movements. Italy has often attracted the attention of foreign commentators precisely because of the dysfunctional attributes of its electoral politics. But the possibility of a geography to its dysfunctionalism has never attracted equivalent attention. It was the inability of the major parties to make themselves sufficiently attractive in enough places across the country that produced the coalition governments characteristic of Italian electoral politics. Conversely, smaller parties with specific local or scattered constituencies failed to appeal elsewhere. The lack of alternation between conservative and progressive governments in Italy over the period 1948–87 was symptomatic not simply of an institutional blockage that could be resolved by constitutional tinkering[77] or by admission of the PCI into coalition government,[78] but rather of enduring and emerging sociogeographical differences that have frequently resulted in regional and local rather than truly national political parties.[79]

This point has been missed by "nationalizing intellectuals." The national state is not a transcendental object that empowers "its" population to make political choices. It is dependent on the political patterns that places construct. It is as much at their mercy as they are at the national state's. Political nationalization therefore is not an immanent force overcoming yesterday's local communities in the interest of national modernity. Rather, it is a historically contingent result of electoral choices made under the pressure of distinctive socialization processes in different places.

CHAPTER 6

Red, White, and Beyond: Place and Politics in Pistoia and Lucca

Intense loyalty to local football (soccer) clubs has become an important feature of everyday life for people all over Europe, especially young men. Nowhere is this more the case than in Italy, where fanatical adherence to "the team" recalls older forms of identification with the local community generally referred to in Italian as *campanilismo*.[1] In the region of Tuscany (Toscana) in central Italy, the Florence team, Fiorentina, has the largest mass following of any major Italian football team, reflecting the prominent position that the city of Florence has occupied historically within the region. However, in the province of Lucca, to the west of Florence between the Apennines and the Ligurian Sea, Juventus of Turin, one of the archenemies of Fiorentina in contemporary Italian football, has thirteen supporters' clubs to Fiorentina's five, a figure roughly three times as great as for any other Tuscan province. This is because the population of Lucca, a separate republic independent of Tuscany until 1847, has a political history and identity distinct from the other Tuscan provinces. Even when there is no local team capable of challenging Florence's, many *lucchesi* throw in their lot with a successful team in distant Turin rather than convert to support for Fiorentina.

Lucca therefore appears to contrast with the rest of Tuscany. This is not news. Lucca is famous in Italy in other respects than its football affiliations. Above all, Lucca has long been seen as an *isola bianca,* a white island, in the sea of *la zona rossa.* It is the most important geographical outlier of a *zona bianca* largely confined to the Northeast. In the years from World War II until its collapse in 1992, the Christian Democratic Party was the majority party in both national and local politics in the province of Lucca. The province immediately to the east, Pistoia, was for many years seen as a stronghold of the Italian Communist Party. They can be considered adjacent examples of the two territorial subcultures that many commentators have seen as dominating Italian politics down the years. In fact, the hold of the two political traditions in the two provinces has long been less than total. In particular, the domination of the Christian Democrats in Lucca diminished beginning in the 1950s, while Pistoia's Communist Party increased in strength from the 1950s to the 1970s. This chapter explores the political history of the two provinces to establish an alternative to two largely fixed subcultures as a way of thinking about the origins and course of political affiliations.

In recent social science local political difference has been viewed either as residual, fading under the onslaught of modernization and its political twin national identity (as in the nationalization thesis explored in chapter 5) or as primordial, related to a cultural drive in which culture is viewed as a fixed bundle of traits and beliefs formed in the distant past and reproduced unwittingly by local populations (explored in this chapter). In studies of Italian politics these have been the dominant perspectives. The residualists, the majority group among students of Italian politics, have stressed the slow emergence of the modern individual engaged in opinion voting, with a decline in political action based on group identity or clientelism. The primordialists have emphasized the impact on political activities and voting behavior of relatively fixed regional cultures or subcultures, especially the Catholic subculture of northeastern Italy, the socialist subculture of central Italy, and the clientelistic subculture of the South and Sicily.

After a review of these positions, I shall briefly propose an alternative perspective drawn from the argument of chapter 2. This approach sees local political difference as an aspect of the working of place in which culture is dynamic—a set of practices, interests, and ideas subject to collective revision, changing or persisting as places and their populations change or persist in response to locally and externally generated challenges that are never trapped at a single scale of expression but are the result of a historical formation and restructuring of processes across a range of geographical scales. I then turn to interpreting Italian electoral politics since World War II, first in terms of the ideal types of red and white subcultures and then in relation to the local histories of the two Tuscan provinces. These two provinces are chosen to illustrate the two interrelated themes of this chapter: that what is possible politically is defined by the evolving cultures of specific places, and that these neighboring provinces, representing an example of each of the two territorial subcultures of postwar Italy, the red and the white, illustrate the ways distinctive local cultures were established and have evolved rather than remained fixed in place as local exemplars of white and red territorial-subcultural ideal types.

MODELS OF TERRITORIAL SUBCULTURES

There are perhaps three specific models that rely on fixed territorial-subcultural conceptions of political action: regional taxonomies of cultural traditions; historical studies of local political cultures; and sociological studies of party-government and political-subculture links. For reasons outlined later, none of these models is satisfactory.

The first involves identifying the most fundamental geographical divisions in voting behavior in terms of subcultural homogeneity. A number of taxonomies have been proposed, the earliest being that of Mattei Dogan in 1967, the most influential that of Vittorio Capecchi et al. in 1968, and the most recent those of Roberto Cartocci in 1987 and Fausto Anderlini in 1987.[2] Over time, the taxonomies have shifted from a tripartite regional division—Northeast, Center, and South, with the Northwest as a "residual" region not easily characterized in subcultural terms—to an emphasis on the importance of the North/South division (Cartocci) and local functional regions defined partly in cultural terms (Anderlini).[3]

A second primordial model focuses on local areas with a long history of political homogeneity, such as red areas with strong support for the Communists (PCI) in central Italy[4] or white areas with strong support for the Christian Democrats (DC) in the Northeast.[5] Emphasis is placed on the persistence of political alignments in the face of economic and social change, suggesting that political cultures defined in the past continue to control later political behavior.[6] Unlike the American literature, there is a positive tendency to see political culture as rooted in and emanating from local social institutions (especially clubs and associations) rather than as directly internalized psychologically by individuals.[7]

The third model focuses on local institutions, particularly the dominance in them of particular political parties and particular organizational cultures. For some commentators local political systems, elsewhere as well as in Italy, when dominated by a single political party and political entrepreneurs of a particular complexion, use jobs, personal favors, and a dominant local ideology to produce local populations with commitments to that party.[8] The tautological nature of this position (dominance produces dominance) has led others to introduce subcultures as a kind of social glue or mediating variable for particular parties and their appeal. In examining the recent economic success of northeastern and central Italy, for example, Carlo Trigilia and Arnaldo Bagnasco argue for the importance of local party dominance and social traditions in jointly creating the conditions of consensus and mediation of diverse interests necessary for the development of the dynamic small firms that have prospered in these Italian regions.[9] Subcultures, party dominance, and economic growth thus form a virtuous circle in these regions, whereas by implication they do not do so elsewhere, especially in the South.[10]

AN ALTERNATIVE PERSPECTIVE

All these models share a primordial definition of culture and an orientation toward continuity rather than change in political behavior. There are four specific drawbacks. First, they give little if any attention to the re-construction of historical-geographical sequences in the development of Italian politics. Geography is seen in static rather than dynamic terms. Once established at a critical juncture in the past, cultural differences simply reproduce themselves through their association with some places rather than with others. Second, there is little emphasis on the local area as a theater of activities from which emerge social and political commit-ments and political change influenced by events and processes emanating elsewhere. Rather, the local is seen in terms of isolated cultural emergence and persistence, resistance to change, and the overwhelming weight of tradition.

Third, only some regions or localities are viewed as integrated com-munities with territorial subcultures. Elsewhere, again especially in the South, communities are viewed as without the consensus or bonds of faith and trust that are taken as indicative of true subcultures.[11] The problem here is that those who cannot have a subculture pinned on them are left with no culture at all! David Kertzer has suggested that the term hege-mony be reserved for those settings where political parties have acquired a certain role in consensus and institution building and that the term sub-culture be dropped altogether so that all Italians can be thought of in cul-tural terms rather than just those in the Northeast and the Center.[12]

Fourth, culture, especially political culture, is seen in static and deter-ministic terms. Opinions, captured in surveys at particular points in time, are regarded as constitutive of political culture, which in turn becomes a black box of values and beliefs used to explain the selfsame opinions. To avoid this tautological dead end, culture is better thought of as a structure or system of signification (set of symbols and commitments) defining the range of possible actions (political and other) that a group or individual can undertake in a given society.[13] More particularly, a political culture can be thought of as defining the limits of the possible in political life, the intersubjective framework to which individual actors bring their own at-titudes, values, interests, and personalities.[14] Percy Allum brilliantly sum-marizes this perspective:

It can be affirmed, by reformulating a noted saying, that, "culture proposes, man disposes." Further, however, I would underline that political culture is not static, even if it is persistent: it changes over time even if slowly, as taught in the 18 Brumaire of Marx, and changes above all in the course of political struggles that totally re-structure practices and "systems of signification," so that the "sense" of yesterday is not always the "sense" of today, and alternative politics that were unthinkable yesterday become suddenly possible today.[15]

What is possible politically, therefore, is defined by the evolving cultures of specific places. Over time these can be more or less distinctive, but however similar or different, they are formed from the bottom up, out of everyday life. This does not mean that political dispositions are created in geographical isolation. That has been the fallacy of so many community studies.[16] Different places have different relationships to the national state, international economy, and secondary social organizations such as churches, labor unions, and political parties. These differences affect the nature of local political cultures as local life adjusts to external challenges. The outcome of this process of social structuring is the geographically differential appeal of different political parties and movements that changes over time as changing local cultures propose and local people dispose.

RED AND WHITE TERRITORIAL SUBCULTURES

The so-called red and white subcultures in Italy have been viewed predominantly as regional-territorial entities in which voting has been largely based on identity or sense of belonging as a result of the political and extrapolitical domination exercised in the red and white zones by a single political party—the DC in the case of *la zona bianca* and the PCI in the case of *la zona rossa.*

The studies of Carlo Trigilia are perhaps the most sophisticated among established approaches in formulating a clear definition of the concept of *territorial political subculture* as expressed in the two zones.[17] He identifies four fundamental elements to the concept: localism or local identity (a center-periphery fracture); a widespread and ideologically oriented network of associations; a sense of belonging to the territory and the network of associations that represents and rules it; and a local political system based on consensus around a specific political force capable of aggregating and mediating different local interests and representing them at the national level.

The major origins of both subcultures are traced to the agrarian crisis of the 1880s, the birth of mass politics in northern and central Italy at that time, and subsequent developments in the establishment of political movements and affiliated organizations in the years between 1880 and the onset of Fascism. Their consolidation as distinctive territorial subcultures is seen as reflected in the voting patterns that emerged after the collapse of Fascism (beginning with the 1946 election) and the significant differences between the two zones and between both and the rest of the country in referenda on political, economic, and social issues.[18]

The following three sets of indicators represent the empirical counterparts of these historical-geographical claims:

1. The organized presence of Catholic and socialist movements in the pre-Fascist period, with particular emphasis on mass participation in local associations (illustrated by the occurrence of and memberships in chambers of labor, producer and consumer cooperatives, rural banks, unions, religious associations) but also involvement in national and local elections (shown by the composition of local councils and by election results).

2. The results obtained by the DC and by the PCI plus the Socialists (PSI) in the Constituent Assembly election of 1946. Provinces are considered part of the respective territorial subcultures if for the two groupings they have votes above a 45 percent threshold. The 1946 election is chosen because it was the first free election after Fascism with universal adult suffrage (all men and women over twenty-one) and had a high turnout (89.1 percent).

3. The results of referenda by province indicating the substantive ideological difference between the territorial subcultures (e.g., on divorce, abortion, electoral rules, government wage policy) and their differences from elsewhere, particularly their high degree of internal consensus.[19]

Using these criteria, the following provinces can be classified as in *la zona bianca:* in the Veneto and Friuli regions of the Northeast, Padova, Vicenza, Verona, Treviso, Belluno, Trento, Udine, Pordenone, and Gorizia; in northern and eastern Lombardy, Como, Sondrio, Bergamo, and Brescia; in Tuscany, Lucca; in Piedmont, Cuneo and Asti; in Liguria, Imperia; and in Abruzzi, L'Aquila. Often, however, it is the geographically contiguous provinces of the Northeast (from Como in the west to Gorizia in the east) that tend to be associated primarily with *la zona bianca* as a territorial subculture. But the concept should be extended to cover all the areas the criteria apply to even if they are not contiguous with the core area in the Northeast.

La zona rossa is more difficult to define definitively because the relative weights of the PCI and PSI in the aftermath of World War II indicated somewhat divergent strains in the general socialist subculture. Giordano Sivini claims there are two subareas to *la zona rossa,* depending on the different historical roots of socialism.[20] The first, the Mantova model, covering the Po Valley provinces of Rovigo, Mantova, and Parma, is one where the PSI share of the vote held up after 1948. The area has a tradition of class politics based on agricultural laborers and their unions. The second, the Reggio model (covering the provinces in Emilia-Romagna of Reggio Emilia, Modena, Bologna, Ferrara, Ravenna, and Forlì; La Spezia in Liguria; Pistoia, Firenze, Pisa, Siena, Livorno, Grosseto, and Arezzo in Tuscany; Perugia and Terni in Umbria; and Pesaro e Urbino in Marche) is one where the PCI increasingly dominated from 1948 to 1976 and is characterized by a long history of sharecropping (*mezzadria*) and a strong connection between town and countryside.

Notwithstanding their obvious differences, the two territorial subcultures have also emerged from similar social and economic processes. There are perhaps four major historical-geographical similarities, as noted by Trigilia and others.[21] First there is the tendency to privilege the communal-territorial, particularly city/countryside differences rather than class in social mobilization, but also the defense of local society against the impact of the market and the state (the periphery against the center). Second, there is a powerful territorial institutionalization of social movements both by means of social control over members and by the extension of that control into power within local and regional political institutions. Third, this locally based cross-class solidarity has been rewarded by a polity that functions by mediating between social forces and the state administration. The organized representation of particularistic demands emanating from the institutions (and parties) of the two territorial subcultures permits a leverage over the central government that more disorganized interests and geographically diffuse social groups are unable to command. Finally, each of these territorial political subcultures has grown in counterpoint to the other. Their mutual ideological antagonism, based respectively in Catholic anticommunism and socialist anticlericalism, received a powerful fillip from the international situation after World War II, when the Cold War division between a capitalist-Christian West and a communist-atheist East actually ran through Italian national politics, with the DC claiming the former side and the PCI the latter.

Typically, however, the stories of the two zones diverge in the details, even as each is seen as the outcome of a set of path-dependent conjunctures and crises reaching back to time immemorial. The characteristic story of *la zona bianca* combines a history of small-scale peasant proprietorship with strong ties to local Catholic institutions (particularly the parish and its priests) and the Catholic political party (the Popular Party before Fascism, the DC afterward). The agricultural crisis of the 1880s was mitigated by the activities of parish priests in developing linked institutions to provide services to small-scale farmers in the countryside and to organize their production. During the years of Fascism the influence of the Church led to a decisive break with the oppositional politics of the pre-Fascist period. In its place Catholic Action, a direct instrument of the Church hierarchy, provided a continuing link between Church and local society in the areas previously organized from the bottom up. This activity was particularly important in extending the political role of the Church from the countryside into the towns. After the collapse of Fascism, the Church led a crusade to establish the DC as its primary agent in the new republic, using the party as a means for aggregating local interests and mediating them before representation in Rome. The towns remained rather less integrated into the white subculture than did the countryside, revealing the continuing importance down the years of the agrarian crisis of the 1880s.[22]

The typical story of *la zona rossa* emphasizes the first years of the twentieth century, when socialist organizing on a large scale became legally possible; the division between the socialists and the communists after the schism of Livorno (1921); the targeted destruction of socialist institutions by Fascism; the resistance, active and passive, to Fascism that reemerged in the countryside and consolidated in the last years of World War II; and the advantage the PCI gained as a result of its role as the primary organizer of the defense of localities against the remaining Fascists and their German allies during the hostilities in central Italy in 1944–45.[23] These events produced quite different political affiliations in different areas. In the Po Valley, where capitalist agriculture had created a strong class politics based in rural labor unions the PSI inherited this older class-based socialist tradition. The PCI was the beneficiary in those areas, particularly where sharecropping was widespread, in which the intransigence of rural wage laborers "was subordinated to the possibility of betterment of the working class though the development of a more rational use of productive assets."[24] In this latter case, more strictly analogous to the characteristics of *la zona bianca,* after World War II the PCI became the mediator between a variety of local interests and attracted support from across social classes. A municipal socialism based on efficient and honest local government became the ruling model in these areas and found expression in an increasing political hegemony for the PCI.

La zona rossa therefore has both more variety than *la zona bianca* and a very different institutional history. The differences between the two zones on the whole, however, can be identified fairly systematically (table 6.1). This has been done at some length by Patrizia Messina.[25] I provide an overview of the main points she makes. For *la zona bianca,* she isolates as fundamental the identification with the Church rather than the state, the defense of small-scale private property, and the role of the DC as instrumental in helping the local social world rather than as consummatory (an end in itself). Two specific aspects of the white political subculture are regarded by Messina, and the writers she draws from, as crucial to the white subcultural zone. First is the type of *political socialization* characteristic of the zone. This emphasizes private solutions based on predominantly Catholic values in which local government responds to specific demands and conflicts left over by private efforts at resolution. The second aspect is *antistate localism,* which refers to the tendency to limit politics to essentially negative activities such as the defense of property and of local tradition against the power of the national state. This creates local politics of an *aggregative* type, exchanging votes for favors across a range of local in-

Table 6.1 The Territorial Subculture Model: A Comparison of the Main Features of the White and Red Zones

Characteristics	Sources of cultural identity	Founding dimension of identity	Relations with party of reference	Local means of reproducing proxies	Antagonistic values and prevalent modes of protest	Means of subcultural integration/type of community participation
Subcultura politica bianca	Catholic Church (network of associations) Peasant world (small owners) Predominantly rural settlement (city/country fracture)	Fracture church/state Identity founded on social (private) Defense of local tradition Conservative orientation	Proxies instrumental to DC Indirect political affiliation	Nonintervention policies DC recognizes hegemony of Catholic world in return for electoral support Antistate localism Aggregative political institutions	Anticommunism Antistatist Abstentionism (exit)	Social integration around values of small farmers The social (private) predominates over the public Absence of civil religion High social participation and development of voluntary sector
Subcultura politica rossa	PCI and unions Peasant world (sharecroppers/wage laborers) Urban and rural settlement (welding of city and country)	Fracture of capital and labor Identity founded on political (public) Proposes social change Reformist orientation	Identification with PCI and the left Direct political affiliation	Interventionist policies PCI used public resources to guarantee reproduction of subculture Integrative political institutions	Anticlericalism Anti-Fascist Blank ballot (voice)	Political integration around values of civic cooperation and solidarity Political (public) predominates over private Strong civil religion Strong political participation

SOURCE: After Patrizia Messina, "Persistenza e mutamento nelle subculture politiche territoriali," in *Le elezioni della transizione: Il sistema politico italiano alla prova del voto, 1994–1996*, ed. Giuseppe Gangemi and Gianni Riccamboni (Turin: UTET, 1997).

terests. Apparently based on attachment to Catholic teaching, this system is reinforced by the absence of a civil religion or by attachment to a set of public values. Without the glue provided by the matrix of Catholic institutions, the conception of politics is suited solely to the defense of particularistic interests.

For *la zona rossa,* on the contrary, it was the centrality of the cleavage between capital and labor, united by a social base in a population drawn from sharecroppers and agricultural wage laborers and, above all, by the historical experience of anti-Fascism, that created the conditions for a local politics favorable to the left and its main agencies, the PSI, the PCI, and the unions. In other words, the red zone has a politics based in political experience rather than reflecting prior social affiliations. Two features of the red subculture stand out. First is the *politicization of society.* By this is meant the predominance of the public and the political over the private and the social. Identification with the PCI and the historical left is based on their commitment to the public sphere as the arena where inequalities will be addressed. The second aspect, *municipal socialism,* is based on the direct intervention of government in local life to favor the unemployed and poor but also to provide financial help to cooperatives and public services (such as elementary education). This local politics is of an *integrative* type in which political choices are made locally and intervention follows based on a set of priorities. Political participation is highly valued, to the extent that protest involves deliberately leaving ballots blank in elections rather than abstentionism, or failing to go to vote, as in *zona bianca.* An increase in abstentionism in *la zona rossa* could be read as an indicator of subcultural crisis, showing how far political participation has ceased to have the centrality it once had in a highly politicized setting.

This approach to the two types of political subculture is undoubtedly helpful in laying out the main dimensions of similarity and difference between two Italys whose political affiliations provided the geographical heartlands for the two political parties that dominated Italian national politics from 1948 to 1992. But as with all ideal types, this way of thinking encourages a greater sense of historical path dependence than recent history suggests is wise.

Long before the renaming and division of the PCI (1990) and the disappearance of the DC (late 1992), both parties had begun to lose their hold within their territorial subcultures.[26] In its increased ideological drive to the political center to succeed nationally, the PCI had to sacrifice both its ideological purity (such as its Soviet affiliation) and its utopian cast. At the same time, the changing economy of its strongholds (including the shift from agriculture to small-scale industry), consumerism, and the decreasing hold of affiliated organizations over leisure time undermined its cultural centrality and decreased the politicizing of society. By the 1980s the DC was in even greater trouble in maintaining its central role in a society where Catholic values, the traditional way of life, and the network of local associations to which it had committed itself were all disintegrating under pressure from secularization, consumerism, and a Europeanized export economy that the local type of politics was not created to respond to.

LUCCA AND PISTOIA

Lucca and Pistoia are interesting provinces from the perspective of this chapter because in conventional primordialist terms each represents a particular territorial subculture: Lucca, the Catholic subculture (*la zona bianca*) and Pistoia, the socialist subculture (*la zona rossa*). Although each, especially Lucca, can be reasonably portrayed as culturally distinctive, it is important to stress three points at the outset:

1. Their political complexion has not remained static over time with a simple onset followed by a set pattern, implying a simple historical path dependence based on a set of relatively fixed territorial traits

2. Different communes (*comuni*) within the provinces have changed over time politically in ways different from as well as similar to other communes, suggesting much more local variation than the model of territorial subcultures implies

3. The perspectives of local politicians and locally based writers offer interesting insights into the dynamic character of political affiliations and their basis in changing social, economic, and political realities

The major purpose of this section is to explore these three points and suggest from the "place perspective" how the cultural contexts of Lucca and Pistoia have changed to help produce the sequence of regimes at a national level described in chapter 5. This is a complement to the approach of the previous section and draws from it in offering a more dynamic account of red and white Italys in the evolution of Italian electoral politics in 1948–92.

The Provinces

The provinces of Lucca and Pistoia are in northern Tuscany, north of the river Arno to the west-northwest of Florence (fig. 6.1). One of the oldest *autostrade* (four-lane highways) in Italy, dating from the 1930s, the Firenze-Mare, runs through the two provinces and connects them to Florence. In 1981 Lucca had a population of 388,904 and Pistoia one of 267,151. The six communes chosen for study, all of which grew in population between 1960 and 1990 and experienced considerable economic development, especially small-scale industrial development, had the following populations in 1981: Lucca, 91,246; Capannori, 44,041; Porcari,

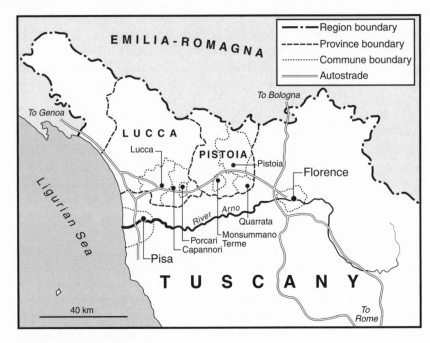

Figure 6.1   Map of northern Tuscany showing the provinces of Lucca and Pistoia, the six communes referred to in the text, and the communes of Florence and Pisa. Source: Author.

6,699; Pistoia, 92,274; Quarrata, 20,350; and Monsummano Terme, 16,511.

Politically, the two provinces and the six communes are diverse (table 6.2). In terms of electoral support for the two largest Italian political parties over the period 1946–92, Lucca and its communes have been more dominated by support for the Christian Democrats than have been Pistoia and its communes by support for the Communist Party. However, each province tended to go through three phases. In Lucca, 1946–58 was a period of consolidation of support for the DC. From 1963 to 1976 the PCI emerged as a major competitor as the DC vote initially fell but thereafter generally was maintained. After 1976 support for the DC fell, much more in communes other than the three selected here, but parties other than the PCI, especially the PSI and the Greens, gained in support. In Pistoia 1946–58 was a time of balance between the two major parties, except in Monsummano Terme, where there was an early dominance by the PCI. From 1963 to 1976 the PCI moved ahead of the DC, even though the DC remained the major opposition party. After 1976 the PCI vote stagnated and then declined and the DC vote decreased substantially, with other

Table 6.2 Results of National Elections, Constituent Assembly (1946) and Chamber of Deputies (1948–2001) in the Provinces of Lucca and Pistoia and in Three Communes in Each

	1946			1948			1953			1958		
	T	DC	PCI	T	DC	PCI	T	DC	PCI	T	DC	PCI
					(FDP)[a]							
Lucca	87.6	48.0	13.6	91.3	61.2	21.6	93.1	51.9	17.8	92.4	54.1	15.7
Lucca	85.4	49.5	12.2	92.5	63.8	16.2	94.8	54.9	15.8	94.8	56.5	12.5
Capannori	89.3	48.8	9.9	92.9	63.1	16.6	93.1	55.8	16.7	91.7	61.0	14.6
Porcari	92.6	46.5	11.8	93.7	60.9	21.4	95.3	55.8	22.8	94.0	56.6	21.4
Pistoia	94.5	29.8	34.5	95.2	40.1	47.2	96.4	35.0	37.1	96.1	34.5	37.8
Pistoia	93.4	28.7	34.4	97.1	39.7	47.2	96.9	34.4	37.3	97.0	34.4	37.5
Quarrata	94.0	24.3	42.3	95.7	50.3	39.3	97.4	46.6	28.3	97.5	46.8	29.2
Monsummano Terme	94.2	20.8	46.9	96.1	32.5	55.2	96.9	26.4	49.4	96.7	24.0	50.4

	1963			1968			1972			1976		
	T	DC	PCI	T	DC	PCI	T	DC	PCI	T	DC	PCI
Lucca	93.5	47.2	17.7	94.1	45.8	21.0	94.6	47.3	23.0	95.1	47.6	29.9
Lucca	95.2	49.7	13.3	95.5	49.2	15.6	95.9	51.6	16.8	96.5	54.2	22.8
Capannori	94.6	55.7	15.7	94.2	53.6	20.6	94.6	57.5	21.4	94.2	56.5	27.0
Porcari	94.1	49.7	23.4	94.6	48.4	28.8	96.0	49.6	30.2	96.6	47.9	38.3
Pistoia	96.6	30.2	42.7	96.3	30.3	44.6	96.5	30.2	45.3	96.5	30.7	50.5
Pistoia	98.5	30.1	41.5	96.9	30.1	43.4	96.9	30.2	44.1	97.2	30.4	49.8
Quarrata	97.1	43.6	36.5	97.5	42.0	40.9	97.2	41.8	42.0	96.3	40.1	47.3
Monsummano Terme	96.0	20.3	56.0	96.2	21.6	56.4	96.3	20.1	56.4	96.5	22.6	62.2

	1979			1983			1987			1992		
	T	DC	PCI	T	DC	PCI	T	DC	PCI	T	DC	PCI
Lucca	92.5	45.1	27.9	90.7	39.0	28.1	90.6	38.7	26.1	—	—	—
Lucca	94.8	50.3	21.4	91.5	42.9	21.6	90.9	42.1	19.8	83.7	36.6	11.6
Capannori	92.2	54.4	25.3	90.4	49.9	25.4	90.6	48.3	23.6	82.7	45.9	13.2
Porcari	95.4	45.2	35.1	93.4	42.6	34.3	94.0	41.5	30.8	86.0	41.4	17.9
Pistoia	94.5	29.8	48.7	92.5	25.4	48.9	93.3	35.7	45.4	—	—	—
Pistoia	94.7	29.3	47.2	91.7	25.2	47.6	94.0	25.5	44.2	85.6	21.9	27.9
Quarrata	95.2	39.3	45.6	93.2	34.6	45.8	93.5	34.9	41.7	84.3	30.3	25.0
Monsummano Terme	95.1	23.6	58.6	93.8	17.8	57.7	93.1	20.1	54.0	84.9	16.9	36.1

	1994			1996			2001			
	T	FI	PDS	T	FI	PDS	T	FI	DS	M
Lucca	—	—	—	—	—	—	—	—	—	
Lucca	—	19.8	15.8	79.3	16.5	16.7	81.2	27.3	15.7	17.7

(continued)

Table 6.2   (continued)

	1994			1996			2001			
	T	FI	PDS	T	FI	PDS	T	FI	DS	M
Capannori	—	21.1	17.6	75.7	17.9	18.3	79.8	27.0	17.7	16.5
Porcari	—	21.9	21.1	81.6	16.2	19.8	79.8	27.0	17.7	16.5
Pistoia	—	—	—	—	—	—	—	—	—	—
Pistoia	—	16.7	32.2	83.9	14.4	33.8	86.4	22.4	30.8	12.3
Quarrata	—	19.6	28.9	81.8	16.8	29.2	86.4	22.4	36.8	12.3
Monsummano Terme	—	19.5	38.2	82.5	18.3	37.6	85.6	24.5	29.2	10.0

SOURCES: 1946, 1948: M. Gabelli, "Toscana elettorale 1946 e 1948," *Quaderni dell'Osservatorio Elettorale* 20 (1988): 199–308; 1953–68: Giunta Regionale, *Dalla costituente alla regione: Il comportamento elettorale in Toscana dal 1946 al 1970* (Florence, 1972); Giunta Regionale, *Il comportamento elettorale in Toscana: Una prima interpretazione*, Regione Toscana, (Florence, 1975); 1976–83: Giunta Regionale 1976, 1979, 1983, 1987, *Elezioni Senato e Camera* 1976, 1979, 1983, 1987, Regione Toscana, Florence; 1992, 1994, 1996: Regione Toscana, *Elezioni 1992, 1994, 1996; 2001*: Ministero dell'Interno.

NOTE: Table shows turnout (percentage of eligibles voting) and percentages DC, PCI, FI, PDS/DS, and M (see table 5.2).

ªFDP = Fronte Democratico Popolare (including PCI), 1948

parties such as the PSI acquiring the "lost" votes. However, in one of the communes, Quarrata, the DC maintained its position much more than in the others. Since 1992 the DC has disappeared in both provinces, replaced electorally to a very limited extent by Forza Italia, which now must share the former DC vote with the three factions into which the DC disaggregated, and the PCI has given way to the Partito Democratico della Sinistra (PDS) and Rifondazione Comunista (RC). Though PDS (DS in 2001) is by far the dominant party on the left, RC has acquired some local strength in the province of Pistoia, particularly in more rural areas. The coalition of the DS and La Margherita (incorporating the left-of-center of the former DC) was a winning one throughout much of Pistoia and Lucca in 2001, suggesting that Forza Italia is not the natural successor to the DC in either province.

Overall, these trends are similar to those for Italy as a whole described in chapter 5. Save for the general lack of balance between the parties in sharing the total vote across the two provinces, there is no *total* electoral domination over the entire period by either party in either province. By British and American standards, dominant party majorities are relatively modest. In the 1950s, however, DC and PCI hegemonies (ascendancy in social and political life based on social consensus) were in formation, although the DC hegemony in Lucca was much the stronger of the two. In the 1960s the DC and the PCI became competitive on what had been each

other's turf, even though one-party dominance was maintained or enhanced. After 1976 a greater heterogeneity in patterns of support for all
political parties is apparent. Today neither the DC nor the PCI exists,
though each has descendants that vie for popular support. The old hegemonies are gone, but differences persist in local politics, if of a much lesser
subcultural importance.

What was it about the two provinces that drove them in such opposing
directions politically from the 1940s to the 1980s? Interviews with local
politicians in 1989 and again in the early 1990s, some active in the 1950s
and others in the 1980s, a survey of local party newspapers, and a number
of local scholarly studies suggest the importance of six themes, although
the last three are more subject to dispute among the sources than are the
first three. These themes are the role of the Fascist period and its aftermath
following from the political organizing efforts of both whites and reds at
the close of World War I; the local sense of place or identity with historical roots; the nature of associationism; the degree of party organization;
the character of industrial relations; and the history of connectivity to the
larger Italian and world economies. In approximate order of importance,
these are the themes that local sources suggest are crucial in understanding the post–World War II political courses of the two adjacent provinces
in northern Tuscany.[27]

The themes parallel, if in a different order and with some overlap between them, the six sets of causes of place-based variation in political dynamics laid out in chapter 2 (numbers in parentheses refer to ordering of
causes in the list in chapter 2, pp. 21–26): first (6, 4), the role of political
movements (socialist, Catholic, and Fascist) in stimulating local political
and social organization and appealing to local interests at the same time
that they integrate places into the country (Italy) as a whole; second (1),
the microgeography of everyday life, sense of place, and the creation of
communities of fate; third (1), social group formation through place-
based associational memberships; fourth (6), the post–World War II dynamics of party organization (particularly of the DC and the PCI); fifth (5),
local labor/capital antagonisms and their reflection in industrial relations;
and sixth (2, 3), the changing linkages of the places (Pistoia and Lucca)
within wider spatial divisions of labor and communication networks (particularly transportation). Obviously, in each case the three dimensions of
place as described in chapter 2—locale, location, and sense of place—are
implicated in different degrees and to different effect.

Both Lucca and Pistoia were the scene of major social and political organizing in the countryside in the years immediately before and after
World War I. In the areas where small peasant proprietorship prevailed,
the Plain of Lucca and between Pistoia and Prato (Quarrata), rural savings
banks affiliated with the Partito Popolare Italiano (PPI) put down roots un-

der the powerful influence of Don Orazio Ceccarelli, an activist Catholic priest in Quarrata.[28] But the PPI also addressed itself to the problems of the sharecroppers who predominated elsewhere by encouraging membership in the *leghe bianche* or white leagues. Indeed, the dominance within the PSI of maximalist socialists, with little interest in local institution building and much in the powers of revolution, meant that the PPI was more successful because it was more realistic and more concrete in its proposals. What is more important here, however, is that it was competitive in Pistoia in the way that socialist organizations were not in Lucca. At least in this part of *la zona rossa,* how red the area would finally be was up for debate and struggle.

In the town of Pistoia a strike at the San Giorgio railway works in 1919 signaled the local arrival of the workplace conflict over wages and working conditions then afflicting large parts of industrial Italy. This was followed by layoffs in most of the major industries in both Lucca and Pistoia that had been stimulated by wartime demand for their engineering and textile products. Invasions of shops by workers and others led shopkeepers into the arms of local Fascists looking for opportunities to intervene. But total industrial employment was still relatively small and situated in large factories such as the textile mill of La Cucirini Cantoni Coats, outside Lucca, and the railway carriage factory of San Giorgio (later La Breda) in Pistoia. The resistance of rural proprietors to reform of the sharecropping system was a much more important source of local Fascism than the odd local industrial strike. In 1920–21 Fascist *squadrismo,* involved in the intimidation and destruction of both socialist- and Catholic-affiliated organizations, came to Lucca and Pistoia. Fascist recruits came primarily from the urban middle class (war veterans, students, public employees, shopowners in the city centers), whereas the leaders were usually lawyers, pharmacists, and businessmen. August 1921 saw the invasion of Pistoia by Fascists from Prato and Florence. By 1922 Catholic as well as socialist and communist buildings were attacked and destroyed; for example, *il circolo comunista* in Serravale on 10 January and *il circolo cattolico* in Spazzavento on 13 August. The Valdinievole district of western Pistoia was a particular target of Fascist violence, because the local resort town of Montecatini was congenial to Fascists and many of the surrounding areas, such as Monsummano Terme, were strongholds of the PSI.[29]

Most of the enterprises founded in the preceding years by both Catholic and socialist-communist organizations disappeared under Fascism. Of the more than sixty rural savings banks in the province of Pistoia in 1920, only ten were left by 1945. As one Pistoia DC politician put it in the local party newspaper in 1975, "Fascism laid bare the work of the Catholic movement in Pistoia."[30] The devastation wrought on socialist-communist organizations was even more complete. These had to start from scratch during the resistance period of 1943–45. Catholic Action did provide a legitimate outlet for Catholic recruiting activities, which was to the advantage of the DC after World War II. But this hardly compensated for what had been lost. In particular, Fascism saw the deepening of hostility between sharecroppers and proprietors without the possibility of the self-help of the rural organizations for the sharecroppers that had briefly revealed their promise immediately after World War I.[31]

It was the memory of this resentment and the dreadful events of the "civil war" or anti-Fascist struggle in northern Tuscany in 1943–45 that figure so prominently in local accounts of the appearance of such different political trajectories in Pistoia and Lucca once peace arrived in late 1945.[32] Typically, the Resistance is pictured as a Communist myth, a vital part of the image that the Communists stood largely alone in their active and subversive opposition to the Fascist regime. It is also tied to the idea that out of the experience of the Resistance came an affiliation with the Soviet Union as the model communist society. Certainly this aspect of affiliation with the PCI seems to have had significance for the postwar generation of Communist militants. Places in Tuscany where membership rates for the PCI were highest in 1945–46 were also those where PCI votes were highest in the 1946 national election, indicating a high degree of popular mobilization. This appears to correlate in turn both with a high incidence of Resistance activity in 1943–45 and with previous support for socialist and PPI candidates before Fascism, the garnering of the newly enfranchised female vote, and the successful recruitment of support by the Communists from among extended sharecropping families.[33]

But in both Lucca and Pistoia, politicians across the political divide— not surprisingly most vociferously those who came of age in the 1940s— wished to establish their credentials as resisters of Fascism. So it is not just PCI militants who want to claim a heritage in 1943–45 when locals battled Fascists and German Nazis in the hills of Pistoia and Lucca. One writer in *La Provincia di Lucca* (a publication of the DC-oriented Lucca Chamber of Commerce), for example, argues that the Resistance was not a red phenomenon at all. Using letters from condemned resistance fighters, he shows their idealistic focus on patriotic themes—a sort of second Risorgimento rather than a precursor to either revolutionary government or local autonomy.[34] The myth of the Resistance, therefore, has been exploited to advantage by the two provinces' DC politicians, even if it has been less central to them than to the PCI politicians of Pistoia.

A second theme is that of local sense of place or identity. This is common to both written sources and interview subjects. Lucca's social distinctiveness is particularly addressed in this way. Lucca's long independence as a separate state, the containment of the historic city by splendid walls, the preservation of possibly the most numerous Romanesque churches of any single Italian city, the physical distinctiveness of the Plain of Lucca with its small farms scattered about the generally flat landscape, and the great mansions of Lucca's merchant elite distributed around the countryside define a landscape quite different from the small cities, mountains, and intensively cultivated valleys and slopes of much of the rest of Tuscany.[35]

This Luccan sense of difference is said to encourage a certain political complacency, even among the poor. The clerical presence, rather than being hierarchical and alien, is fused into the everyday life of city and countryside. According to one informant, a longtime Communist activist in Lucca, the city and its environs provide an "absorbent setting" for conflicts: differences are "never brutal," and although by the 1980s local business boosters had taken control of the DC, the spirit of the *popolari* (the pre-Fascist Partito Popolare) and a cautious attitude toward religious dogma characterized even the most partisan of the Catholic population.[36] This understanding helps explain why in the divorce referendum of 1974, an issue on which the Church took a hard stand, many DC activists and voters in Lucca drifted away from the party opposition to legalizing divorce and supported maintaining the divorce law in place since 1970.[37] The creation of a new tier of regional governments in 1970, after years of national DC opposition for fear it would further institutionalize PCI strength in regions such as Tuscany and Emilia-Romagna, further isolated Lucca as an *isola bianca*, at least initially. By the late 1970s, however, increased support for the Socialist Party in Lucca could be put down to an attempt at indirect *lucchese* rapprochement with the PCI-dominated regional government (the PCI and the PSI were allies in the regional government from 1970 on), proving that local identity need not always be allowed to work against local interests.

The more characteristically Tuscan landscape of the Valdinievole and the Apennine valleys to the north and west of Pistoia, with their associations with the *case coloniche* (characteristic farmhouses) of extended sharecropping families, seem to physically represent the collectivism implicit in that type of agriculture and the wide range of skills it stimulated and that later were harnessed in the growth of small-scale industries. The hard life of the sharecroppers (*mezzadre*) is a recurring theme of the PCI newspaper in Pistoia, *La Voce*, in the 1950s, as is Pistoia's lagging behind other Tuscan provinces in its average standard of living. In 1966 Pistoia had the lowest per capita income of all Tuscan provinces and was fiftieth out of ninety-two in the whole of Italy.[38] It is in this context of a relatively high level of poverty among a population with collective work habits that we can find at least part of the appeal of the PCI's collaborative approach to economic development. At the same time, however, little or nothing can be said about widespread anticlericalism across the province. Relatively low levels of church attendance in heavily communist areas do not translate into an equivalently high level of anticlericalism. Particularly since the 1950s, the antagonism between Church and state that supposedly was one inspiration for the socialist subculture of central Italy has been largely missing from the province of Pistoia.[39] In addition, unlike the province of Lucca, whose border has had a long history as a state boundary, Pistoia was created as a province only in 1927. As an administrative product of Fascism, therefore, Pistoia's administrative history has rather run against its increasingly PCI political complexion in the postwar years. Subdivisions within the province, such as Valdinievole, the area around Montecatini, and Quarrata, have a greater salience in popular place identities than do small areas in the province of Lucca, where even the residents of the mountainous northern Garfagnana seem to identify with the province as a whole and the city of Lucca in particular.[40]

The nature of associationism is a third theme that many local politicians and local studies identify as important to the difference between the two provinces. It is not that associationism (a high level of participation in locally oriented social groups and voluntary associations) is present in one and absent in the other. Both Lucca and Pistoia have relatively extensive participation in voluntary organizations and such entities as cooperatives. The main difference between the provinces seems to lie in the greater importance of cooperatives and work-related associations in Pistoia and of voluntary, often Church-related organizations in Lucca. But even this contrast is not absolute, and much recent associationism is without either formal Church or PCI sponsorship or linkage.

The more rural and, traditionally, largely sharecropping parts of the province of Pistoia, such as the communes of Monsummano Terme, Larciano, and Lamporecchio and the periphery of the commune of Pistoia have had the highest rates of membership in cooperatives since the 1950s, when they were first formed under PCI auspices. Since 1979 Unicoop, a "superco-op," has displaced older consumer cooperatives in response to the challenge of new commercial supermarkets. But on the whole Pistoia has a lower level of involvement in cooperatives of all kinds than other parts of Tuscany (except Lucca) and Emilia-Romagna.[41]

Coldiretti, the organization for Catholic owner-occupier farmers, served a role in Lucca similar to that of the cooperatives in Pistoia until the 1970s. Other Catholic-affiliated organizations oriented more to leisure and cultural activities also began to lose public support in the 1970s. But the *volontariato* (charitable organizations) have maintained more of a role than have the economic ones. Some of these are officially sanctioned by the Church; others, particularly ones of a cultural nature, such as theatrical and choral groups, have sprung up from dissenting groups and from outside Church influence altogether. At the same time, charitable entities, such as the Church-sanctioned ambulance service Misericordia, are active in Pistoia as well as in Lucca and, at least in the early 1990s in Pistoia, involved open Communists as well as DC supporters among their active members. Disillusionment with shifts in party policy has also produced open breaks between local associations and the parties. A good example of this was the defection of local hunting groups in the Valdinievole and elsewhere in Pistoia from the PCI in the late 1980s because of the party's national stance against hunting, a policy designed to attract largely urban Green voters to the party. The new associationism of the years since the 1970s is therefore intensive, but without the political-sectarian overtones of the older variety discussed in models of the territorial subcultures.[42]

Three other themes are more disputed by local interviewees with respect to their effect on the electoral geography of the two provinces. The first is party organization. This is where path dependence or, better, institutional inertia plays a role. A fairly common refrain is that those places where parties put down roots most successfully at auspicious moments are precisely the ones where those parties have maintained a hold. Where parties did not manage this, electoral politics has been a more competitive affair, without the built-in bias in favor of one party at the expense of others. The provinces of Lucca and Pistoia each offer good examples of both. In the first case, there are communes, such as Monsummano Terme for the PCI in Pistoia and Capannori for the DC in Lucca, in which at critical moments after World Wars I and II party capacity and local conditions formed a virtuous circle. In the second case, as with the seaward communes of Lucca (La Versilia) and with Quarrata in Pistoia, neither the DC nor the PCI achieved a stranglehold on outlooks and votes at critical moments. On balance, however, the DC in Lucca managed to establish a stronger hold in its province much earlier than did the PCI in Pistoia. There are limits, therefore, to seeing the red and white provinces as mirror images. If the two provinces are any guide, party organization and local electoral strength are much more contingent on very localized historical-geographical conditioning than suggested by the causal arrow from social-geographical characteristics to electoral outcomes in the models of the two territorial subcultures.[43]

It is also reasonably clear that the two parties also began to lose their capacity for popular mobilization around singular party images at about the time, between 1958 and the early 1970s, they achieved electoral domination within their respective provinces. This is indicated by declining numbers of party memberships for the PCI as a result of immigration and the slow dissolution of the PCI's link with the Italian General Confederation of Labor (CGIL) and increased factionalism within the DC caused by local businesses and ideological differences (over, for example, the Vietnam War), challenging Church affiliations as the centerpiece of the DC coalition. Even as they peaked electorally, therefore, the PCI and DC organizational-ideological foundations were beginning to crack.[44]

Not surprisingly, the character of industrial relations, or more broadly capital-labor relations, is emphasized by the PCI interviewees and sources. Since many of them had backgrounds as labor organizers for the Communist-affiliated CGIL unions, they provide considerable knowledge of labor relations in the two provinces. Some DC politicians in Pistoia, however, also highlight the importance of labor struggles between their affiliated Italian Confederation of Labor Syndicates (CISL) unions and the CGIL ones on the fortunes of the party in the province.[45] But they and their political opponents agree that it is the memory of labor struggles in the past, particularly in the late 1940s and early 1950s, as much as contemporary conditions that drives the impact of labor relations on political affiliations and voting behavior.

The two most important points made are that conflicts between landowners and sharecroppers took place in Pistoia rather than in Lucca and that there was a more successful organizing of industrial workers by PCI-affiliated CGIL unions in Pistoia. The first point is seen as obvious because except in a few areas (such as the communes of Altopascio, Montecarlo, and Porcari) the province of Lucca had a smaller share of its agricultural land devoted to sharecropping than did the province of Pistoia. Even though sharecropping has faded enormously as an economic fact of life in contemporary Pistoia, the memory of its depredations and the PCI role in challenging it lives on and helps fuel political attachments to this day. Bear in mind, however, that the province of Pistoia was never totally dominated by sharecropping as a type of landholding (compared, say, with the province of Florence) and that Lucca and Pistoia were similar in having much more fragmented patterns of landholdings than such Tuscan provinces as Siena and Florence.[46]

The second point requires more elaboration. Neither province has ever had much of an industrial working class in the classic sense. What existed before World War II was concentrated in a few large factories in the provincial seats: the textile mill of Cantoni Coats and the tobacco factory in Lucca and the San Giorgio (later La Breda) works in Pistoia. In Pistoia, however, the workers were organized earlier and affiliated with socialist unions before Fascism. Union organizers also endeavored to politicize sharecroppers and agricultural laborers. In Lucca, where many of the factory workers were women, what organizing there was tended to focus on local issues and working conditions rather then the more general working-class issues stressed by trade unionists in Pistoia. After World War II the San Giorgio works in Pistoia became particularly politicized and was the site of bitter struggle between DC- and PCI-affiliated metalworkers' unions. Until the 1980s the memory of strikes, union elections, and layoffs colored political positions in the province. The main division was over the nature of unions and their activities. Even politicians on the left of the DC who were generally supportive of unions and the interests of peasants and workers, such as Gerardo Bianchi in Pistoia, spoke out throughout their careers against "political strikes" and "sterile agitation" that struck them as going beyond local issues.[47]

Since the 1960s this scenario in the two provinces has been transformed by the massive growth of small-scale manufacturing industries spread around the countryside, using labor formerly employed in agriculture and, increasingly, immigrants from southern Italy and North Africa. Much of the new industry is indigenous, in contrast to the historical situation when the main employers were either foreign (the headquarters of La Cucirini Cantoni Coats in Lucca was in Glasgow) or from other parts of Italy (the headquarters of San Giorgio in Pistoia was in Genoa). In addition, the union federations, particularly the CGIL, retreated from a subsidiary position in their relations to the parties and by the 1980s had become largely independent of party influence. The net effect has been to reduce the amount of conflict around the workplace, particularly in Pistoia, though the memory of such conflict still lived on in the early 1990s.

Finally, one theme mentioned in chamber of commerce publications and in studies of Tuscany's economic geography, and also by several interviewees, is that the two provinces have had different economic histories in terms of their connection to Italy as a whole and beyond. In this construction, Lucca has long been more externally oriented than Pistoia, going back to the days of merchant capitalism. It is Pistoia that has experienced the greatest relative disruption of its economic base, particularly since World War II, switching from a largely localized agrarian economy with a few large industries to one fueled by the export of manufactured consumer goods and other items (such as nursery stock and cut flowers) from myriad small-scale producers. The province's economy has had to adjust rapidly to the introduction of industrial capitalism, first in the form of some limited factory industrialization and more recently in the form of small-scale manufacturing production. Lucca has followed a much more evolutionary economic course, with a more mixed economy (in the size of industrial firms and the range and size of its service sector) and with a long tradition of emigration and linkages to other parts of Italy and around the world. Not surprisingly, therefore, the *pistoiesi* have had to deal with greater social disruption and turned to that political movement promising an active response to it rather than those standing pat and waiting for providence to take its course. If this sounds suspiciously like "opinion voting" all along, then so be it.[48]

The Selected Communes

Turning from the provinces as a whole, a systematic focus on the communes selected perhaps help explain in more relevant detail what happened electorally in the two provinces over the postwar years. The communes were chosen to illustrate certain distinctive electoral tracks within the provinces. Porcari (province of Lucca) and Quarrata (province of Pistoia) changed the most politically. In 1953 the DC was the majority party in each, then it steadily weakened, most clearly in Quarrata, largely to the benefit of the PCI. In each case economic transformation and immigration played major roles. Before Fascism, Quarrata was a stronghold of the Partito Popolare Italiano (PPI), whose activists were founders of the local DC after World War II.[49] However, the economy of the area changed from agricultural to industrial. Today it contains an important industrial district specializing in household furniture and some textile production associated with the neighboring province of Prato. Moreover, the area has experienced considerable immigration over the past thirty years, especially from other parts of Tuscany and the Italian South. The PCI worked to extend its support in the area, partly through ancillary organizations such as social clubs. This strategy was successful for a time, but today these clubs attract mainly older men and are not major instruments of political mobilization.

Porcari is likewise an area whose economy was transformed and that has also had a large immigration from southern Italy. Historically, it was one of the areas of the province of Lucca with the highest percentage of agricultural land under sharecropping, a typical predictor of PCI orientation in the territorial subculture model. In the 1960s it had the highest rate of population and new job growth of all communes in Lucca, taking advantage of its location adjacent to the Firenze-Mare superhighway to attract papermaking and other businesses from outside the region.[50] In this case, however, the PCI was not particularly well organized to exploit the grievances and aspirations of new voters, perhaps because PCI organization in the province of Lucca was much inferior to that in the province of Pistoia. But none of the parties are well organized in Porcari, and there is a much lower level of politicization of local and national issues than is apparent in Quarrata. Perhaps this reflects the lack of either PPI or PSI organizing in the area at key times early in the twentieth century.

This degree of political change is less true of the communes that are seats of provincial government. They have relatively more diversified economies, although Lucca has a greater preponderance of larger firms and a weaker small-firm sector than Pistoia. This reflects Lucca's relatively greater dependence on outside capital and its long history of ties with northern Italy and overseas. Pistoia's recent economic development has been much more endogenous in origin, based on local artisans and share-cropping farmers transforming themselves into small entrepreneurs. Also, in the communes of Lucca and Pistoia, affiliation with the dominant local party has been an important prerequisite for appointment to a wide range of jobs in the public sector. Local industries and local organizations, such as chambers of commerce, were strongly tied to the two major parties. For example, banks and the chambers of commerce in both Lucca and Pistoia were strongly DC in orientation. There is also, perhaps, the most continuity in local social-spatial identity or sense of place. In both Lucca and Pistoia, but especially in Lucca, the historical center of the city provides an emotive reference point for identity that is missing from the amorphous communes surrounding it. The walls of the city stand as an everyday reminder of Lucca's glorious past and its political independence.[51] A merging of the civil and religious in a concentration of physical symbols such as the walls and churches of the city helps cement the self-image of *lucchesi* as citizens of a separate world with its own distinctive politics (fig. 6.2).[52] Given the Tuscan context of PCI dominance, the DC was the major beneficiary of this Luccan "separatism."

In Pistoia the physical damage to the city in the last years of World War II, still apparent in places, is a constant reminder of the importance of those who resisted Fascism. This has abundantly benefited the PCI, which not only played the leading role in local resistance efforts but managed to convince voters it had.[53] The PCI has also been successful in politicizing the working-class population of Pistoia to its advantage. This was partly due to its success among the CGIL-unionized workers of the major local employer, Breda Costruzioni Ferroviarie (formerly San Giorgio, a major producer of railway vehicles and buses), but it also reflects the ability of the local party organization to adapt to changing economic conditions—for instance, through its strong support for expansion of the small-firm sector among local artisans and former sharecropping families (fig. 6.3). But it was not until 1975 that the PCI gained an outright majority on the commune council (twenty-one seats out of forty), suggesting how slow and contested the rise of PCI hegemony actually was in this part of red Italy.

Interestingly, the DC in Lucca was all but invisible between elections, suggesting that the population there has lower aptitude for everyday political mobilization than that of Pistoia and thus reinforcing at least one element of the ideal typical contrast between white and red Italys. Ironi-

Figure 6.2   An aerial panorama of the city of Lucca looking east to west, the famous walls clearly demarcating the old city. Source: Author.

cally, there appears to be an overall lower level of activity in voluntary organizations (such as social clubs and the volunteer ambulance corps) and cooperatives in Lucca than in Pistoia, including DC and PCI activists and their replacements, even though Lucca has a long history of involvement with Catholic aid societies and is dominated by political language emphasizing mutual aid and an active social life based on parties and neighborhood.

In Capannori and Monsummano Terme the hegemony of one or the other of the two major parties was long maintained against the trends in their respective provinces. Even though these communes have changed the least electorally, they have undergone tremendous economic and social change. In Monsummano Terme an established agrarian radicalism, based on the class conflict inherent in the system of sharecropping dominant locally, was effectively harnessed by the local PCI, which also successfully recruited southern immigrants into the party.[54] The party was also active in promoting and supporting the local shoe industry and improving physical infrastructure and housing. Since 1992 the local electoral success of Rifondazione Comunista and its successors demonstrates how far a radical communism was not only rooted but reinforced in this context.

In Capannori the industrialization of the local economy has reinforced

Figure 6.3   A new Communist Manifesto? "The firm as labor," a meeting of small and medium entrepreneurs under PCI sponsorship, Palazzo dei Congressi, Florence, 4 February 1989. Source: Author.

the dispersed settlement pattern of a commune that still looks to Lucca as its center. Until 1978 the seat of the commune government was Lucca rather than within the commune itself. Many workers also still farm small family-owned plots even when they work full time at factory or workshop jobs. These peasant workers identify closely with the city of Lucca, which is the center for most social services.[55] The important social role of the local priest in everyday life reinforces the persistence of a social Catholicism that lent itself to support for the DC. Rather than breaking down DC dominance, therefore, social and economic changes in Capannori long supported it. This is somewhat different, however, from the myth of transcendental subcultures persisting autonomously to constantly recreate the politics of the past.

A different mix of processes, then, operated in different communes to produce the range of shifts in support for the two major political parties that characterize both of the provinces. Rather than the rise of a nationalized-individualized opinion voting or the workings of primordial subcultures, therefore, explanation has been sought in the fluid, constantly reworked cultural contexts of particular places.

CONCLUSION

My main purpose in this chapter has been to dispute dominant views of primordial territorial political subcultures in Italy and describe an alternative perspective that views local politics as socially constructed and changing but ever present rather than either residual or primordial. In other words, the creation and dissipation of red and white subcultures such as those associated with different places in Italy are inherent to the structuring of politics in all places rather than totally unique to these particular places.

The major advantages of the perspective informing this chapter are as follows:

1. It can deal with changes in the geography of electoral politics over time.

2. Political culture is not equated with tradition but is seen as the intersubjective framework of practices, ideas, and symbols in which political choices and activities are embedded and from which opinions and votes are drawn.

3. *All* people live in cultural worlds that are made and remade through their everyday activities, not just those who live in areas where specific political parties are said to have created systems of consensus or hegemony.

4. Cultural worlds are grounded geographically in the experience of place. Culture therefore is *inherently* geographical, defined in places and through the geographical sedimentation of practices, and thus is *internally related* to the geographical dynamics of politics.

The cases of Lucca and Pistoia help to identify some of the specific problems with the territorial-subculture model of local politics that are best dealt with by the alternative perspective. The first is that the territorial-subculture model presupposes that the two zones are "special" in having peculiar characteristics that set them totally apart from the rest of Italy and from each other. This claim is unsustainable on both counts. If these provinces are any guide, certain historical-geographical conjunctures produced a bias toward certain political parties that then became institutionalized. But even as the parties institutionalized themselves, conditions were changing to reduce single-party dominance. These zones differed only in the degree of their dominance by single-parties, *not* in the nature of voting or the developments that structure the political process. In particular, the widely accepted notion that voting in the two zones illustrates the hegemony of a vote of identity or belonging is questionable. Local accounts of voting across the period 1948–92 (and since) suggest that many voters in both Lucca and Pistoia have been weighing their options in tune with local patterns of political socialization and associated conceptions of political agency. The idea that there is a systematic set of differences between the two zones in the character of local political hegemony is also questionable. The case studies show how similar in many respects the provinces in the two zones have been, even down to the role of the same historical events, similar types of associationism, and other factors in producing single but different party dominance.

In the second place, identification with the locally dominant of the parties never involved more than a slim majority of voters in the two provinces. Many people remained either indifferent or opposed to the dominance of the single party in their local area. Indeed, a case can be made that, particularly in Pistoia, the political complexion of the provinces could have turned out quite differently. The die was not cast in the distant past, as most accounts of the red and white zones tend to assume. Rather, extralocal processes relating to the nature of the Italian polity and the shifting bases to Italian economic development conspired with local characteristics to produce patterns of party hegemony that were much more fragile than the logic of table 6.1 makes them seem.

Finally, there does not seem much basis for claiming, as the territorial-subculture model tends to do, that political change is entirely concentrated in certain historical bursts followed by long periods of stability in political affiliation and voting behavior. Though it is undoubtedly true that periods such as the late nineteenth century and the years after World Wars I and II were socially disruptive and gave rise to new movements with geographically differentiated patterns of support, the subsequent stability of this support can be exaggerated. In both Lucca and Pistoia, dominance by the DC and the PCI, respectively, rested on historically shifting ground. In particular, how far the parties could tap organizations oriented toward them varied historically and thus cannot be read as a permanent feature of party rule. The territorial-subculture model therefore merely replaces one territorial trap, nationalization, with another: primordial political cultures set in geographical stone. The geography of electoral politics is simply too historically dynamic to be successfully captured by it.

SOURCES OF INFORMATION

Interviews (Initial Interviews March–July 1989)

Vittorio Brachi, DC politician, Quarrata, Pistoia; active in the 1950s and 1960s
On. Gerardo Bianchi, DC politician, Pistoia; former DC deputy; active in the 1950s and 1960s
Vittorio Amadori, DC mayor of Quarrata, Pistoia, 1951–75
Pierluigi Bartolini, retired rural bank official, DC and Misericordia activist, Pistoia
Agostino Palazzo, president of the Faculty of Political Science, University of Pisa

(1990–96); specialist on local economic development in Pistoia from the 1940s to the 1970s

Vincenzo Menchise, secretary of DC Provincial Committee, Lucca

On. Sergio Dardini, former secretary of Lucca PCI Provincial Federation, 1959–70, former PCI deputy, and sharecropping union official in Altopascio (Lucca), 1955–57

Armando Carnini, secretary of PCI commune committee, Lucca

Ivo Lucchesi, secretary of PCI Provincial Federation, Pistoia

Giovanna Lombardi, local PCI activist, Pistoia

Local Newspapers and Magazines

La Voce (PCI, Pistoia), vol. 8, nos. 1, 5, 7 (1956); n.s., vol. 4, nos. 1–2 (1968); June 1976; March 1977.

La Bandiera del Popolo (DC, Pistoia), vol. 1, nos. 1–6 (1945); vol. 5, nos. 1–9 (1951); vol. 6, nos. 13–15 (1952–53); n.s., vol. 3, nos. 10, 12, 14–15 (1956); vol. 4, no. 1 (1958); vol. 8, no. 1 (1962); vol. 9, nos. 1, 3, 5 (1963); vol. 10, nos. 1–3 (1964); vol. 11, nos. 1–2 (1965); n.s., vol. 1 (1974); vol. 2, nos. 3–5 (1975).

La Vita Cattolica (Catholic, Pistoia), vol. 53, nos. 42, 45 (1975); vol. 54, nos. 5–9, 12–17, 19–20, 22, 24–44 (1976).

La Gazzetta di Quarrata (DC, Quarrata, Pistoia), June 1973–August 1973; vol. 1, nos. 1–3 (1975).

La Provincia di Lucca (Provincial Chamber of Commerce, Lucca), vols. 1 (1960) to 19 (1979).

CHAPTER 7

The Geography of Party Replacement in Northern Italy, 1987–96

Episodic and periodic realignments in the relative dominance of political parties in elections have long been interpreted in geographical terms. In electoral democracies it is political parties that knit together the disparate identities and interests of different places into national coalitions that contest elections and provide the ideologies and personnel for national and local governments. New political coalitions weaving together groups in different places are said to produce new national electoral alignments.

The disintegration of the Italian party system in 1992 provides a prime example of such a process. What happened in northern Italy is particularly interesting because one of the new or replacement parties is that of a regionalist movement, the Northern League (Lega Nord), committed to a radical restructuring of Italian government along federalist lines or possible secession of the North ("Padania" to the League) from Italy.

Walter Dean Burnham's famous study of American party politics over time reveals no fewer than five party systems based on different cross-regional coalitions.[1] This cyclical pattern of medium-term continuity interrupted by short periods of dramatic change has also been noted for other countries, although none has had either as long a series of elections or as limited a number of effective national political parties as the United States. In these other cases, such as Britain, France, and Italy, another scenario has been much more important than American-style realignment between regionally based coalitions of interests with two party names persisting over time. This is the replacement of one party by another, sometimes following the collapse of an entire system of parties or a long period of authoritarian rule.

Party systems can be expected to have distinctive geographies, given the differential appeal of different parties in different places, different densities of party organization across places, and the emergence of parties based on identification with particular regions and localities. How new parties replace old ones geographically, however, is largely unexplored.

The typical assumption is that there is straightforward substitution of new for old. In majoritarian electoral systems with a bias toward two parties (such as the United States and Britain) this may well often be the case. Elsewhere, however, this is much less likely, particularly when proportional representation sets the bar fairly low for translating votes for new parties into seats. Whatever the electoral system, however, new political parties must conquer or colonize places previously occupied by old ones. This is a dramatic way political change takes place geographically.

The replacement of one party by another can take a number of forms. In one situation, where several parties are close to a particular point on the political spectrum, one takes votes from the other and grows at its expense even as the other continues to exist. This is what happened to the Italian Socialist Party (PSI) in the 1950s as it lost votes to the Communist Party (PCI) and, in reverse, what happened in France in the 1970s when the Socialists came from oblivion, under the leadership of François Mitterrand, to marginalize the French Communist Party. In each of these cases the advancing party used a regional base to reach out into traditionally hostile territory. The most famous twentieth-century example in the English-speaking world is probably the emergence of the Labour Party in Britain in the 1920s at the expense of the Liberals.[2] This involved a march from urban-industrial outposts into marginal constituencies previously represented by Liberals, helped along by defections of sitting members to the insurgent party. In another situation an existing system of parties disintegrates and new ones pop up across the spectrum, defining a new party system. This happened in France in 1958 as many of the parties of the previous Fourth Republic, above all the Radicals, disappeared and were replaced by new ones, above all the party based on the patronage of the new president of the Fifth Republic, Charles de Gaulle. This is also what happened in Italy between 1987 and 1996 as the Communists split into Partito Democratico della Sinistra (PDS) and Rifondazione Comunista (RC) and the Christian Democrats and Socialists, which had together dominated Italian governments since the 1960s (and the DC even longer), disappeared along with many of the smaller parties of the center such as the Social Democrats (PSDI) and the Republicans (PRI).

This chapter concerns the process of party replacement in northern Italy, partly because it was different in different regions and should be studied so as to reflect this, but also because in the North it has involved a party restricted to the North (indeed, seeing itself as representing the North)—the Northern League. The geography of party replacement in central and southern Italy, though with reformulation and renaming of the parties, has left a less distinctive new party menu. Several parties, including offshoots from the Christian Democrats and the Communists, the new Forza Italia party of Silvio Berlusconi, the Italian media tycoon, and the reinvented Fascists (post-Fascists) of the National Alliance (Alleanza Nazionale), all vie to replace the old parties in a fluid and volatile situation in which party identifications are very low except in the areas of central Italy historically affiliated with the Communists and in southern strongholds of the old neo-Fascist party, the Movimento Sociale Italiano (MSI). In northern Italy the menu has changed: the other parties compete, but in a context where they must react to the provocations and ideology of a regionalist party that attacks existing political institutions and calls for either a dramatic federal reform or secession of the North from Italy.

After briefly reviewing some theoretical issues related to the geographical process of party replacement, I want to examine how the Northern League replaced the Christian Democrats as the dominant electoral party in many areas of northern Italy after 1992. This involves looking at the growth and spread of the Northern League in the North as a whole, particularly the Veneto, and in one city where it has had considerable success, the Lombard city of Varese. I then turn to how this occurred, suggesting that party replacement is not the same as either straightforward vote switching from the old party to the new one or political replacement, in the sense of the new party filling the same political role as the old one. Finally, the difficulties the League has faced in capturing the most important city of northern Italy, Milan, are discussed in terms of the distinctive place characteristics of that city and its surrounding hinterland. The general theme running across the chapter is the role of place-to-place similarities and differences in how one party replaced another electorally during a period of rapid political change. In other words, the chapter is about how the collapse of the Christian Democratic Party and the rise of the Northern League were mediated geographically.

THE GEOGRAPHICAL PROCESS OF PARTY REPLACEMENT

One party replacing another in electoral competition can be thought of in terms of a number of understandings of the term replacement. In one meaning replacement is akin to substitution, in which the new party takes over all or a large share of the votes of a previous one that has disappeared. This is the quantitative electoral sense used by most commentators. The electoral success of the Northern League has been viewed largely in terms of its replacing the Christian Democrats in this sense. Even Ilvo Diamanti, an astute student of the rise of the League, seems to suggest this.[3] In a related understanding, however, replacement involves a number of parties splitting the votes of an old one among them. This is the consensus position on what has happened to the Christian Democratic vote in central and southern Italy. In a third scenario, the collapse or disappearance of one party draws attention to a crisis in the social world that the old party had long represented. This allows an existing, opportunistic party to move in and colonize that world, not necessarily by taking over the old vote so much as by providing a voice for new voters and elements increasingly alienated from the old party even before its final disappearance. I would argue that this is much more what has happened in northern Italy over 1987–96 than a simple substitution of the Northern League for the Christian Democratic Party.

This third understanding of the term replacement draws attention to three important contingencies when thinking about how new parties arise as old ones disappear. One is that electoral choices can be understood only in relation to the discrete social-territorial settings or places where such choices are exercised. Old parties do not simply disappear without reason. They are often no longer in tune with local social mores. Their electoral persistence is more a matter of inertia than of persisting enthusiasm from a popular base. The two replacement parties for the Communists share much the same proportion of the total vote in central Italy as the Communists held before them, and between them they cover much the same ideological space as did the old PCI, suggesting a continuing match between the new parties and the social-territorial milieu of central Italy. Evidence of the erosion of DC support long before the final collapse indicates that the nature of replacement depends on local contingencies.

Second, parties are not simply electoral vehicles, although orthodox thinking in Anglo-American political science often regards them as such, perhaps because the American parties (as opposed to individual representatives) often seem unrelated to particular sectoral or sectional interests. Parties can be more or less effective intermediaries between state and society, channeling resources from center to periphery and rewarding some social and territorial interests at the expense of others. In this sense the distinction between mass and patronage parties is a false dichotomy: all parties are patronage parties. Judgments are made about how effective the party is in delivering the goods and whether we (in our place) are being rewarded more or less than they (in their place). Much of the geography of party politics is more a result of who gets what, when, and where than a reflection of underlying or foundational social cleavages that have a geographical bias. Certainly in Italy by the 1970s all the parties were more or less parts of a system of *partitocrazia,* a party-based political economy in which large parts of the private sector as well as the huge Italian public sector depended on party affiliations for jobs and financial rewards. This included the Communists in the regions they dominated in central Italy. Though largely excluded from the fruits of central government, and certainly less corrupted than the parties of national government, they were able to reproduce their own version of party-based political economy where they controlled local government.

Third, new parties can have totally different symbolic, interest, and strategy repertoires than the parties they replace. In particular, they can appeal to new territorial formulations of the dilemmas that the old party dealt with through allocations of public resources (see chapter 9). Ethnic and regionalist parties are the most obvious exponents of such a territorialized approach. Typically they focus on regional relative deprivation or a sense of resentment at the success of other regions in commanding state resources or acquiring more than an average per capita share of national revenues. But nationalist parties wanting to expel foreigners and put up protectionist barriers and liberal parties desiring to remove all limits on trade and investment are also engaged in territorial reframing. In contemporary northern Italy it is indeed a territorial reframing, in this case involving either large-scale devolution of powers to the North or secession by the North, that is the hub of the appeal of the Northern League to a northern electorate heretofore integrated into Italy by the mediating role of the Christian Democratic Party, the *balena bianca* (white whale) of the Northeast.

CHRISTIAN DEMOCRATIC DOMINANCE, CRISIS, AND REPLACEMENT

Though the immediate cause of the disappearance of the Christian Democratic Party from the electoral landscape was the aftermath of the corruption scandal that erupted in Milan in 1992, that party had already begun to suffer a rapid erosion of support to the Socialists and others in the South, and it had suffered a slower erosion of its base and affiliated institutions in the Northeast and Lombardy beginning in the 1970s. Indeed, where the League has achieved its highest and most consistent success since 1992, the Christian Democratic Party once reigned supreme. This was *la zona bianca* (the white zone) of the Northeast, in which the Christian Democrats tapped into a Catholic subculture that long predated the existence of the party (see chapter 6). In addition, as the main party of national and local government, the DC increasingly relied on its ability to direct state resources to its supporters as the older clerical structures (such as co-ops, unions, leisure-time organizations, and parish) faded in significance for social life under the pressures of modern work behavior and mass entertainment. In its areas of strength in the North the party had been one of the specialized structures of the Catholic movement, oriented toward parliamentary government and capture of the state. Elsewhere, but particularly in the South, the party had been based on capturing local notables and using them to channel state funds in return for votes. Slowly but surely this model spread throughout Italy. As Percy Allum describes this, "the DC turned itself into a simple power system founded on a series of local machines, controlled by a political boss (for example, the 'Organizzazione Bisaglia' in Vicenza)."[4]

If voting for the DC in *la zona bianca* had represented identification with the Church, Catholicism, and a way of life in the 1950s and 1960s, by the 1980s the DC was represented by many full-time local bosses controlling public-sector jobs (and influencing hiring in many private businesses) and a self-interested conception of politics in which votes were a commodity to be bought and sold. Allum argues that at this stage the only differences between North and South were the greater change from ideology to spoils in the North (spoils had always mattered in the South) and the nature of political influence networks at work in each, with northern machines relying on lieutenants with established social roles (teachers, influential businessmen, etc.) and southern ones on the rewards of state patronage and in some cases links to organized crime.[5] The DC had become a means for a new class of politicians to "impose themselves individually and get rich quickly. Political careers depended less and less on party organization (which, moreover, was losing its base in civil society) and were determined more and more by ability to insert oneself in 'business' circuits."[6] As long as the economy grew and the Cold War allowed the DC to present itself as the only alternative to the Communists ("Better thieves than reds," mused the ex-Communist philosopher Lucio Colletti in 1985), the alliance of local machines oiled by state resources that constituted the DC survived the decay of its social supports. But faced with the end of the Cold War, serious economic recession in the late 1980s and early 1990s, and the revelations of systematic corruption by its Socialist partners and many of its own in the Milan scandal of 1992, the party suddenly and unexpectedly collapsed in January 1994, some of its unindicted leaders starting a new Partito Popolare to ensure the continued presence of a Catholic party but without the negative associations that the DC now aroused, not least among many of its erstwhile supporters.

Two points from this story are of prime importance. First, the Christian Democrats were already beginning to fade in the 1980s before the final denouement of 1992.[7] Second, unhappiness with the clientelistic model was manifest in the high level of support in the Northeast in a 1991 referendum for reducing the number of preference votes for candidates to one. This reform was viewed as a blow against the localistic-particularism the DC machines depended on. Obviously this model was in trouble in the Northeast even as it still had considerable support in DC areas in the South. A revolt against the southernization of the DC was under way in its onetime heartland in the North.[8]

THE RISE OF THE NORTHERN LEAGUE AND THE
REPLACEMENT OF THE CHRISTIAN DEMOCRATS

The Northern League began as a series of regional leagues or autonomist parties in the early 1980s. The Lombard League achieved modest success in elections, both local and national, during the 1980s, as did its counterpart in the Veneto, the Venetian League (Liga Veneta). Emerging as a united political party in 1992, the Northern League has established itself as the major or second party in large parts of northern Italy. Moving from an autonomist to a federalist position in the late 1980s and then to a secessionist position in the aftermath of its experience of entering into national government coalition with the two main right-wing parties, Forza Italia and the National Alliance, the party's authoritarian leader, Umberto Bossi, put most of his energy from 1996 until 2000 into a project for the independence of northern Italy, or Padania as he calls it. In 2000 he abruptly returned to a federalist track and reentered into alliance with Forza Italia and the National Alliance. Perhaps the most important persisting themes of his appeal to the North are the interests of northern small businesses and artisans in a negative public economy (high taxes, poor services, too much northern tax money going to an indolent South) and an intense hostility to the old regime of *partitocrazia* or party-based political economy (see chapters 8 and 9).

Let me briefly draw attention to several elements to the electoral success of the Northern League. In the first place, and at the scale of the North as a whole, the League became the main party in a section of the North in which it gained most of its early support. In 1987 to 1992 it expanded its base by increasing its level of support in adjacent areas of the North, but then between 1992 and 1996, as its support deepened in its original strongholds, it retreated from a prominent into a secondary position in those areas it had moved into. This is analogous to a "swash" effect followed by a "backwash" in levels of support in contiguous areas.[9]

Second, by 1996 the League was strongest at a provincial scale in those areas where the DC had been strongest historically. This gave the impression that the former could be simply substituting electorally for the latter with straightforward vote switching between parties. Two maps Diamanti uses in his account of the transition leave this impression. Of the fifteen provinces where the Christian Democrats had their best results in 1948, twelve are ones where the League was at its strongest and was the major party in 1996.[10]

Examining electoral data for the DC and the League at the commune level within one of the regions, the Veneto, reveals a somewhat more complex story. The main local areas in which the League established its

strongest roots are *not* the ones where the DC was at its strongest historically. They are, rather, places where the DC had been successfully challenged by other parties, particularly the Socialists, to the north and scattered among the communes where the DC was hegemonic electorally and
politically (see figs. 7.1 and 7.2).[11] Moreover, the important expansion of
the League within the Veneto between 1987 and 1992 was somewhat
weaker in the areas of total DC dominance, where the DC also experienced
its largest declines (particularly Vicenza, where the DC lost a third of its
vote) than in the those areas where the DC had been either marginal or
weaker (e.g., Belluno, Treviso) but the parties of the left were also very
weak (see figs. 7.3 and 7.4).[12]

This conclusion based on visual inspection of maps is reinforced by
measures of spatial autocorrelation showing the degree of spatial dependence between where the old party was strong or weak and where the new
party is strong or weak. Similar levels of spatial autocorrelation between
the old and the new parties indicate that the new party inherited the old
one's constituency, whereas dissimilar levels suggest a colonization of a region from areas where the old party was relatively weak. Indicators of spatial autocorrelation, Moran's I statistics, calculated for the DC and the
Northern League across all elections from 1987 to 1996 suggest that the

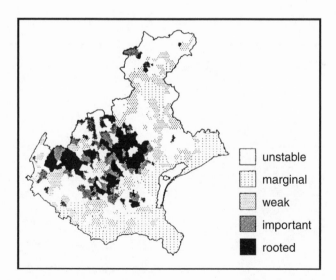

Figure 7.1   Map of communes in the Veneto using election results for the DC in
national elections (Chamber of Deputies) 1946–87, showing where the party was
more and less rooted. Source: redrawn from Ilvo Diamanti and Gianni Riccamboni,
La parabola del voto bianco: Elezioni e società in Veneto (1946–1992) (Vicenza: Neri
Pozza, 1992), 140.

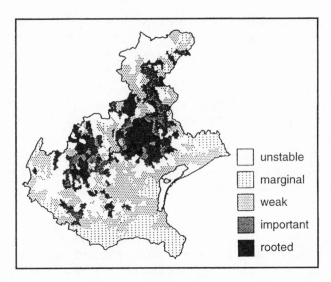

Figure 7.2 Map of communes in the Veneto showing where the Venetian League was more and less rooted over the period 1983–87, national elections (Chamber of Deputies). Source: redrawn from Diamanti and Riccamboni, *Parabola del voto bianco*, 142.

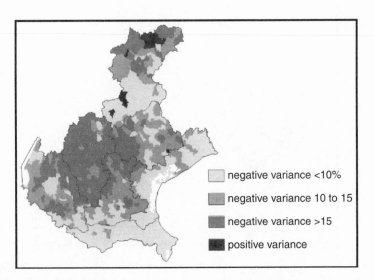

Figure 7.3 Variation in the vote for the DC by commune in the Veneto, national elections (Chamber of Deputies) 1987–92. Source: redrawn from Diamanti and Riccamboni, *Parabola del voto bianco*, 136.

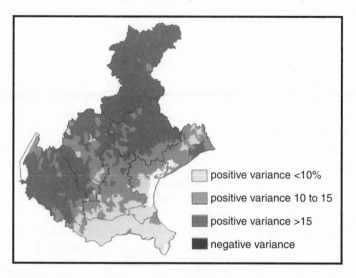

positive variance <10%

positive variance 10 to 15

positive variance >15

negative variance

Figure 7.4 Variation in the vote for the Northern League–Venetian League by commune in the Veneto, national elections (Chamber of Deputies), 1987–92. Source: redrawn from Diamanti and Riccamboni, *Parabola del voto bianco,* 138.

Table 7.1 Moran's I Statistics for the DC and the Northern League–Venetian League in the Veneto, National Elections (Chamber of Deputies), 1987–1996

Election	DC	Northern League
1987	0.651	0.588
1992	0.524	0.775
1994	—	0.837
1996	—	0.828

SOURCE: Michael Shin and author.

NOTE: A score of 1.0 equals perfect autocorrelation, meaning that each commune vote for a given party can be predicted by the average of surrounding observations.

support for the League was initially less concentrated in the Veneto than was the DC vote and that after the post-1992 disappearance of the DC, the League moved into the geographical vacuum left by the DC and its high votes clustered much more than they or the DC's had previously done (table 7.1).[13] In other words, between 1987 and 1992 the DC lost more of its votes in areas where the League had smaller relative gains than it did elsewhere in the region. It lost these largely both to the MSI (neo-Fascists) and to more localistic groupings and parties than the League, but once the DC was gone from the political scene the League began to penetrate the DC's former strongholds.

Third, the League has done well in some areas of the North traditionally on the margins of *la zona bianca*. Good examples are such Lombard provinces as Como and Varese. These are areas with historical ties to left-wing politics, in part reflecting early success in trade union organization in local factories, as well as much weaker connections to the Catholic associations that once characterized the Veneto and eastern Lombard provinces such as Bergamo and Brescia. Home to many of the leading figures in the Lombard League and the Northern League (such as Bossi, Leoni, Maroni, Pivetti, and Speroni) Varese had elected the first League deputy (Leoni) and senator (Bossi) in 1987. In the commune election in Varese in 1992 the League won seventeen out of forty seats on the municipal council and, with the support of one Republican and the "apology" of three PDS councillors, formed the municipal council. Present on the council since 1985, by 1990 the League had become the second party of the city after the DC. Arrests of leading DC and PSI politicians for corruption led to the premature demise of the council elected in 1990. The League's success in the subsequent election meant that for the first time the party controlled the main commune of a province and was able to appoint a mayor from its ranks (see chapter 8).

Analysis of the 1992 results reveals that the left did best in areas of the city with many workers in large firms, often with southern Italian origins, living in large housing projects (eastern sector areas: San Fermo, Belforte, and Valle Olona); that the League supplanted the DC in many parts of the periphery with scattered settlement and in areas with high levels of self-employment and pensioners, but the DC maintained its hold, if weakened, over the most historically white zones of the city, such as Casbeno, Bizzozero, and Capolago, because of support for its neighborhood candidates; and that other parties, particularly the so-called parties of opinion such as the Republicans and Liberals, shared the city center with the League.[14] Only certain sectors of the old DC vote, therefore, can be seen as going to the League during the crucial second half of 1992: the ones seemingly least affiliated with Catholic institutions. In fact, a flow-of-vote study using election districts (715 cases) shows that between the national election of April 1992 and the local election of December 1992 the League drew votes from a number of parties, above all *any* of those (including the DC) that had been in local government recently.[15] But the movement of votes to the League from the DC is not an overwhelming feature of this flow of votes between parties and within the electorate (fig. 7.5).

FROM VOTE SWITCHING TO PARTY REPLACEMENT

The picture of replacement, therefore, is more complex than one of simple substitution. In the critical years 1989 to 1992 the DC maintained a degree of support at local scales even as the party as a whole suffered erosion of its hegemony by the League and other parties. What accounts for this

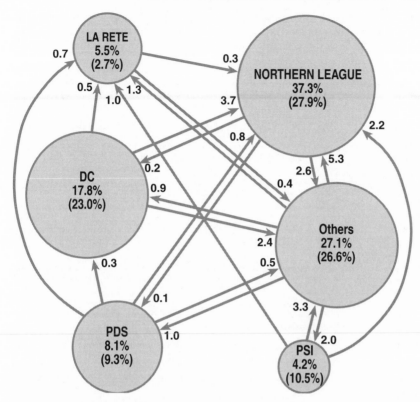

Figure 7.5 The flow of interparty votes between the national election (Chamber of Deputies) of April 1992 and the commune election of December 1992, Varese (Lombardy); April 1992 percentages are in parentheses. Source: Carlo Brusa, "Elezioni e territorio in una città media e in un momento critico: Varese," *Lombardia Nord-Ovest* 2 (1993): 28.

seeming disparity between substitution and replacement? One factor is that the League became strongest in those areas that have the highest levels of industrialization based on small firms and the highest percentages of workers employed in such firms.[16] This contextual predictor is much more important than are individual-level ones in a statistical analysis of the 1996 vote in the Veneto, though relative youth (new voters) and employment in a small business show up as significant in most studies (table 7.2). The DC was always strongest in the agricultural areas and the smallest towns, providing a link between one and the other. As the economy of small industries specializing in customized production of consumer and intermediate goods (metalworking, etc.) has taken off in the Northeast over the past twenty years, it has done so in areas marginal to the traditional economy of commercial agriculture in the countryside and

Table 7.2 The Veneto, 1996 National Election (Chamber of Deputies): The Political and Socioeconomic Characteristics of Communes in Which Different Parties Performed Best

	PDS	RC	PP	Dini	FI	CCD/ CDU	AN	League	Veneto Mean
Veneto mean	11.8	5.3	8.1	5.2	17.1	5.4	11.7	**29.3**	
Threshold (≥M + σ)	21.5	9.2	11.0	7.6	23.0	9.7	16.2	49.6	
Number of communes	72	92	79	75	70	82	94	107	
% in majoritarian contests in selected communes									
Center-left	43.4	42.3	36.6	36.4	34.0	28.4	35.1	24.4	33.8
Center-right	34.3	34.5	31.8	30.7	39.9	31.8	37.3	23.8	32.3
Center-right League	21.6	22.6	30.5	31.2	28.2	37.6	25.3	**51.6**	32.8

Indicators	PDS	RC	PP	Dini	FI	CCD/ CDU	AN	League	Veneto Mean
Mean residents	11,338	10,075	8,555	7,526	6,204	3,779	14,334	4,505	7,553
Population density	254	236	302	255	187	176	330	217	247
Old age index	146.7	126.2	112.5	125.3	117.0	101.3	125.4	**105.5**	118.5
% illiterate	1.2	1.3	0.7	0.6	1.5	0.8	0.6	0.6	0.8
% grad. sch./coll.	22.1	21.5	24.5	23.4	16.2	13.7	26.9	15.0	21.2
Unemployment rate	9.4	8.3	6.6	6.9	7.6	6.3	7.9	**5.5**	6.9
Youth unemployment rate	18.1	15.9	12.2	12.6	13.9	10.8	15.4	**9.7**	12.6
% employed agric.	5.7	6.0	4.5	4.3	10.4	11.3	4.9	7.1	5.8
% employed industry	37.0	37.4	42.5	41.5	42.9	53.3	34.47	**58.5**	44.0
% employed service	57.3	56.6	53.0	54.2	46.6	35.4	60.8	**34.4**	50.2
% owners/profess.	6.4	6.3	8.6	7.2	7.2	6.6	8.8	6.8	7.4
% self-employed	16.1	16.1	15.8	14.8	21.7	21.4	16.1	18.9	19.9
% self-employed agric.	2.9	3.1	2.6	2.3	5.2	6.9	2.4	4.5	3.8
% self-employed ind.	4.4	4.4	5.1	4.6	7.2	6.9	4.7	7.0	5.5
% self-employed serv.	8.8	8.5	8.1	7.9	9.3	7.5	9.0	7.3	8.4
% employees industry	5.2	5.2	6.6	6.3	3.8	4.5	6.1	5.7	5.8

Table 7.2   (continued)

Indicators	PDS	RC	PP	Dini	FI	CCD/ CDU	AN	League	Veneto Mean
% employees service	19.9	19.4	19.7	20.0	11.8	8.9	23.3	8.9	16.8
% other industry wkrs.	24.7	25.1	27.0	27.3	28.4	37.9	20.1	**41.6**	29.1
% other service wkrs.	20.8	21.1	16.2	18.7	18.2	13.8	18.7	12.6	17.4
% owned housing	69.5	70.0	70.5	72.1	74.1	80.0	65.2	80.2	72.1

SOURCE: Gianni Riccamboni, "Ritorno al futuro? La transizione nell'ex subcultura bianca," in *Le elezioni della transizione: Il sistema politico italiano alla prova del voto 1994–1996,* ed. Giuseppe Gangemi and Gianni Riccamboni (Turin: UTET, 1997), 293.

NOTE: Numbers in **bold** in League column signify particular differences between "League communes" in 1996 and others.

medium-large firms in the cities. It is in these places that the League has achieved its greatest strength, reflecting their dominant populations' alienation from the DC model of representation and increasing anger at the state's failure to provide what they perceive as necessary services to local industries at a time when international competition in their sectors is increasingly intense.

Of course the League is also a type of party very different from the Christian Democrats. Although at a local government level (communes and provinces) it offers the prospect of good government in place of the corrupt practices of the old regime, the weakness of these tiers relative to national government means that little can be accomplished without dramatic reform. The 1996–2000 ideological shift from federalism and involvement in national politics to secessionism and abandonment of reform within the context of Italy meant that the party was vulnerable to other groupings (such as Forza Italia) that offer practical solutions as opposed to the utopian promise of an enterprise such as an independent Padania. But as long as memory of the failure of the DC remains strong, there is still political mileage in running against the role of parties as political intermediaries. The antipolitical message of the League, however, though an understandable reaction against the old regime's politicizing everything, presumes that markets can operate independent of the role of parties as agents of transmission of values and demands between state and society and also contrasts with the call for self-government with adequate resources, which is something entirely different from the message of antigovernment the League has increasingly identified itself with.[17]

Finally, the League has introduced a geographical reframing of Italian politics that is much more than a simple substitution of one national party for another. If there was always an uneven pattern of support for Italian political parties, representing the geography of social cleavages and their historical rootedness in different places, there was at least agreement on a national focus for politics. The League represents a politicizing of the very territorial template Italian politics rests on. The question, How many Italys? is no longer a simple academic one; it has become political.[18] The politics of resentment that is at the heart of the League's appeal to its electorate takes an essentially geographical form, identifying the enemy as being outside the North but not outside Italy. It is associated closely with the old regime of parties and government in Rome. It is a purely territorial as opposed to an ethnic appeal, however much Bossi might invoke Mel Gibson and *Braveheart* to make his case, based on concocting a cultural identity for northern Italy to pursue the interests of the small businesses and their problems that the League increasingly identifies itself with (see chapters 8 and 9).

MILAN AND THE NORTHERN LEAGUE, 1987–96

In the 1992 national elections the Northern League demonstrated considerable inroads in Milan as well as in its hinterland. This was further demonstrated in the elections for mayor and council in 1993 and, to a much lesser extent, in the national elections of 1994. This led to some speculation that the League was a movement on behalf of the interests of Milan and its hinterland. The League's rhetoric in the early 1990s, representing itself as the agent of the North that produces against an Italian South that consumes at the North's expense, seemed to indicate that the erstwhile economic capital of Italy might be on its way to becoming a full-fledged capital of something else. Politically, Rome was to be exchanged for Milan, at least symbolically if not substantively, as the title of one book suggested (*Milano a Roma*, edited by Ilvo Diamanti and Renato Mannheimer, a title that also alludes to the 1994 national election success of both the League and the Milan-based Forza Italia of Silvio Berlusconi, the Italian Rupert Murdoch).[19] The editors of the book expressed the connection between Milan and the League thus: "At bottom, the League represents the Italy of producers, whose capital is Milan, in counterpoint to Rome, capital of the old party system [*partitocrazia*] and of state centralism."[20]

The Electoral Pattern

In fact, the connection between Milan and the League proved much more tenuous than first reports suggested. To illustrate this point, table 7.3 provides the average level of support obtained by the Northern League within each of the main provinces of the Milan metropolitan area for the three na-

Table 7.3   Provincial Average Percentage of Support for the Northern League, National Elections (Chamber of Deputies), 1992–96, Bergamo, Como, Lecco, Milan, Varese

	Bergamo	Como	Lecco	Milan	Varese
1992	27.45	30.57	28.64	22.01	30.55
1994	32.45	26.31	28.23	19.32	32.09
1996	47.51	38.26	37.50	25.93	36.11
		% increase			
1992–94	5.00	(4.26)	(0.41)	(2.69)	1.54
1994–96	15.06	11.95	9.27	6.61	4.02
1992–96	73.10	25.10	30.90	17.80	18.20

SOURCE: Michael Shin and author.

tional elections of 1992, 1994, and 1996.[21] Though there is a regionwide upward trend in support, the province of Milan consistently shows the lowest levels relative to the other provinces. The box-and-whisker plots in figure 7.6 provide a vivid display of this tendency. Looking more specifically at shifts in League support between elections, figure 7.6 reveals a retrenchment across the region in 1994, with a resurgence in 1996. Provinces have distinctive profiles: in Bergamo, League support increased on average by a remarkable 73.1 percent, whereas in Milan average support by commune went up by "only" 17.8 percent over the period 1992–96.

The 1994 election revealed the electoral emergence of "two Norths," as Ilvo Diamanti termed them in his chapter on the League; in the same book, he and Mannheimer had portrayed "Milan" as taking over Rome, in the persons of Bossi (of the League) and Berlusconi (of Forza Italia).[22] In 1992 the League was one of the few alternatives to the established parties as the old system of parties began to disintegrate under twin pressures: the end of the Cold War reduced the Communist threat that the Christian Democrats had always used to advantage and led to a reformulation of the old Communist Party into two new formations (PDS and RC); and the emerging corruption scandal centered in Milan (which became known in Italy as Tangentopoli, or Bribesville). In 1994, however, Berlusconi invented his Forza Italia party, which drew off a considerable proportion of the vote that the League obtained in 1992 and in the 1993 local elections. This was much more the case in Milan itself than in the hinterland of the city. The more conventional center-right ideology of Berlusconi, based primarily on his own celebrity and his reputation as a savvy businessman, was more attractive to the average Milanese voter than the localist-regionalist message of the League. But there was more to it than that. Using referendum turnout data showing that League strongholds tend to have more extreme participation rates (i.e., lower and higher) than the

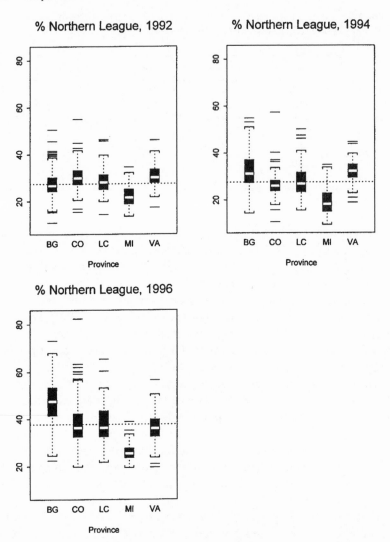

Figure 7.6 Box-and-whisker plots of Northern League support in the main provinces of the Milan metropolitan region, 1992–96. Source: Michael Shin and author.

"urban North," Luca Ricolfi suggests that the "territory of the League" in the "Deep North" is marked by much greater "concrete particularism" in political attitudes than the more "civic" and "universalistic" cities.[23] Be that as it may, the League has retreated across the board from the areas it had penetrated in the early 1990s (Milan and other metropolitan centers such as Genoa and Venice, traditionally leftist areas such as Mantua) while keeping considerable support in areas of historical strength such as Bergamo, Como, Varese, and some of the communes in the north of the province of Milan. The League's problem with Milan in particular, and urban centers in general, is evident when the percentage of League voters (y-axis) is plotted against the log of the number of voters for each commune for the urban region as a whole (x-axis) (fig. 7.7). The number of voters in a commune is used as an indicator of urbanization; high numbers of voters correspond to more urbanized areas. Because some heavily urban communes have far more voters than the average, the numbers of voters were converted to logarithms for graphing. Summary measures for pooled data, shown in table 7.4, are reported to give greater precision to interelection comparisons. Within each scatterplot, the areas within the dotted vertical and horizontal lines represent the interquartile range of the pooled, logged number of voters and the pooled vote share of the Northern League, respectively, and the solid lines mark the median values for each pooled variable. These lines and the scales on the y- and x-axes remain constant across the plots, so each interelection plot can be compared with the others and with the pooled plot (1992–96).

Two items of interest emerge from a visual perusal of the scatterplots in figure 7.7. First, there is a strong negative correlation or inverse relation between League support and urbanization. This is verified statistically using a simple correlation between the two variables across the Milan metropolitan region as represented by the five provinces of Bergamo, Como, Lecco, Milan, and Varese: across all elections (1992–96) it is −0.382 ($p < 0.001$). Second, there is significant provincial variation in the correlation between support for the League and degree of urbanization across the urban region. Figure 7.8 shows the plots of the relation with a regression line superimposed for the selected provinces of

Table 7.4 Summary Measures of the Northern League and Logged Voter Densities in the Milan Metropolitan Region, 1992–96

	Minimum	First Quartile	Median	Third Quartile	Maximum
%NL 1992	10.95	23.69	27.55	31.03	54.93
%NL 1994	9.58	22.94	27.70	32.49	57.32
%NL 1996	19.46	29.04	36.15	44.80	82.39
Pooled % 1992–96	9.58	24.67	29.38	35.76	82.39
Ln (voter dens. 1992)	3.18	6.74	7.62	8.36	13.85
Ln (voter dens. 1994)	3.22	6.75	7.66	8.39	13.84
Ln (voter dens. 1996)	3.37	6.73	7.65	8.38	13.77
Pooled 1992–96	3.18	6.74	7.64	8.38	13.85

SOURCE: Michael Shin and author.

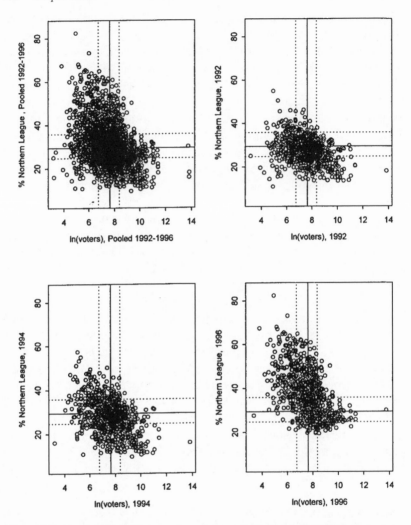

Figure 7.7 Scatterplots of the number of voters (logged) against Northern League support for all communes in the Milan metropolitan region, 1992–96. Source: Michael Shin and author.

Bergamo, Como, and Milan in 1996. The negative correlations between the two variables in the provinces of Bergamo and Como are –0.54 and –0.53, respectively (both statistically significant at the $p < 0.001$ level). Within the province of Milan, however, there is no statistically significant relation between support for the Northern League and the logged number of voters ($r = 0.007$, $p = 0.920$). Closer analysis suggests that the distribution of the data may account for this difference between the province of Milan and the others. For most communes in the province

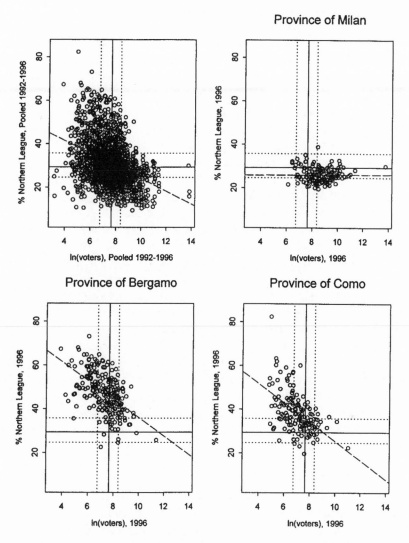

Figure 7.8   Scatterplots of the number of voters (logged) against Northern League support in the Milan metropolitan region (pooled 1992–96) and in the provinces of Milan, Bergamo, and Como (1996). Source: Michael Shin and author.

of Milan the logged number of voters is above the pooled regional median of 7.64 and League support is below the pooled region medium of 29.38. By contrast, in Bergamo and Como there are more communes with fewer voters (more data points to the left of the pooled median line), and League support tends to be above the pooled median. The more urbanized province of Milan therefore has a much lower prevalence of support for the Northern League than the less urbanized hinterland areas of Bergamo and Como.

Conventional wisdom in social science suggests that this division between city and hinterland is an unlikely outcome because the functional links between the two are often viewed as influencing, if not determining, electoral choice. It is also a major challenge for the League to claim to represent the whole of northern Italy rather than only the extreme or Deep North. Of course local populations are always split in electoral affiliations. Left-wing, center and right-wing parties have all garnered support historically in Milan and its surrounding area.[24] But not only was there a dominant consensus for many years between the two areas expressed in majority support for the two major parties of national government in postwar Italy—the Christian Democrats and the Socialists—there was, so to speak, a common menu of political choices, largely organized in left/right terms and oriented to national political goals. From the 1950s to the late 1980s the two parties of government dominated Milan and its environs, even though they were faced with effective opposition from the former Communists and other groupings, particularly in the areas of heavy industry in the inner northern suburbs. In the city, support for the Christian Democrats was also largely one of open choice among electoral rivals, whereas elsewhere, particularly in parts of the northern hinterland such as Bergamo and Brescia, the Christian Democrats were beneficiaries of a long-standing Catholic subculture reproduced by a dense network of associations and affinity groups.[25] Now there seems to have been a fundamental spatial break between the city and its hinterland in the menu of real political choices and the economic-cultural orientations associated with it.

The Difficulty of the Northern League in Milan

I identify four causes of the emerging political difference between Milan and its hinterland, particularly its historically important hinterland to the north. The first is the fundamentally different character of the economies of Milan and its periphery as they have evolved over the past twenty years. The second is the population composition of Milan, particularly the presence there of a substantial population of southern Italian immigrants and their offspring (plus more recent foreign-born immigrants) who cannot be expected to support the explicitly antisouthern, antiforeign, and anti-Italian agenda of the League. The third is the new symbolism of the League since 1995, which is increasingly oriented to the Venetian element in northern history and the heroic role of tiny businesses and artisans in economic growth, neither of which can have much positive resonance in Milan. Finally, the League has been undercut in Milan since 1994 by the emergence of a conventional national political right associated with the various parties of the so-called Pole of Liberty (particularly Forza Italia and the National Alliance).

The New Spatial Economy of a Polyarchic City-Region

Historically, Milan and its hinterland have been thought of as part of the famous industrial triangle of northwestern Italy, stretching between Milan, Turin, and Genoa, in which large firms led the industrialization of Italy in the late nineteenth and early twentieth centuries. This industrialization grew out of an older diffuse pattern in which factories emerged in the countryside and often employed people who lived nearby and still farmed part time. Beginning with Fascism and continuing during the 1950s and 1960s, agriculture and manufacturing became much more separated in the immediate region of Milan. Factory jobs in the cities, particularly Milan, grew faster than the urban population, indicating the concentration of manufacturing industry in city settings in relatively large units. In the 1950s and 1960s Milan grew in both manufacturing jobs and population at the highest rate of all cities in Lombardy as a whole. Since the 1970s this pattern has been reversed in that the internal economies of scale of large factories have lost much of their advantage and the accessibility and transportation advantages of large cities in industrial production have weakened considerably. These trends have had a number of decisive effects in dividing the large city from its hinterland.

In the first place, small-scale production that adjusts readily to rapid shifts in demand has found a new role. It is in the small cities and urbanized countryside to the north of Milan that the small-scale producers have come into their own.[26] In such settings, industrial districts have appeared, similar to those previously identified in central and northeastern Italy, in which local external economies of scale (local banking, labor pool, technological support, etc.) substitute for the internal economies enjoyed by larger businesses.[27] In other words, the Third Italy of industrial districts has invaded the First Italy of large-scale manufacturing industries linked functionally in a city-regional complex. Meanwhile, in the second place, Milan has gone through a massive restructuring with the destruction of many large factories and the emergence of a much shrunken large-firm sector.[28]

One important political consequence has been a large decrease in blue-collar workers and a significant increase in professional and managerial employees. This transformation has been particularly marked in the historical center of the city and the immediate suburban ring.[29] Business owners, professionals, and managers are concentrated there. But perhaps more important, a tertiary sector with relatively weak links to existing manufacturing industries in the region has become the main generator of jobs in the city. Involving such expanding markets as advertising, marketing, show business, computer software, health care, and finance, this sector is largely free of the social linkages of manager-worker that characterize the factory economy; but unlike the local horizons of the small businesses in the hinterland, the horizons of these businesses and their employees are national and international.[30] They connect to people in other cities daily, and in their own lives they partake of a social world that is without precise territorial limits. The old urban-industrial model of city-hinterland relations therefore is in crisis.

The Milan metropolitan region can be divided into three segments. First is the city itself and its traditional industrial and residential suburbs, forming an arc around the city but particularly extensive to the north in the direction of Como. In this zone the League is weakly based, challenged from both left and right by parties that can appeal to the cosmopolitan and traditional industrial interests of its economic sectors. Second is the zone in which small and medium manufacturing firms have largely displaced the large employers of yesterday and expanded production into entirely new products. The social character of these areas is very different from that of the first zone. There are high levels of self-employment and intensive local orientations in the supply of both labor and services. This zone stretches from Magenta through the southern communes of the province of Varese (e.g., Busto Arsizio, Gallarate, Saronno) to southern Como (e.g., Cantù), ending south of Bergamo in the vicinity of Treviglio and other communes to the west of the river Serio. The third zone is the most peripheral, stretching between the second zone and the Swiss border or the Trento region. This area has remnants of old industrialization, some new small-scale manufacturing, and tourism. Its dependence on regional-government expenditures and on infrastructure (road, rail) decisions emanating from Milan set it apart from the second zone in terms of confidence in its own devices.[31]

The political consequences are distinctive in the different zones. On one hand, the intense competitiveness of the small-firm sector in the central hinterland induces a strong identification with work as defining of life and a constant worry about next year's bottom line. Survey data suggest that in these areas voters typically are extremely provincial yet worry that global competition threatens their hard-won standard of living.[32] This generally produces support for a party such as the League, which appeals to the values and worries of the small business owner. On the other hand and in Milan, in place of the class relations of Fordism—large-scale industrial production—there is now a much more fragmentary social structure. This is already producing a fluid electoral politics in which no party can rely on permanent support and there are dramatic flows of votes between elections. Some voters, particularly male workers in traditionally working-class areas such as Sesto San Giovanni, remain attached to parties of the left, but others, particularly women, exhibit much more pragmatic political affiliations even in such areas.[33] Across both zones, however, it is women who show the greatest volatility in their political affiliations, suggesting that the collapse of the old dominant parties (the DC and the PCI) has had a greater impact on them than on men, who have shifted to the Northern League or remained affiliated with the PDS as the heir to the PCI.[34] The third zone has undoubtedly drifted toward the League, but its continuing dependence on the regional capital means that its residents must still look to Milan rather than seeing themselves in entirely localistic terms. Political affiliations in this zone remain more oriented to local candidates and their entrepreneurial capacities in dealing with the regional government in Milan than to particular political parties.

The Southern and Foreign-Born Populations in Milan

A second, and less noted, feature of Milan when compared with its hinterland is its more heterogeneous population. Not only is the population made up of migrants and their offspring from all over Italy, particularly the North, there is also a significant southern-origin population that arrived in large numbers in the late 1950s and early 1960s to work in the Fordist factories that were expanding at that time and, more recently, a mass immigration from Africa, Asia, and Latin America.[35] This is not to say that there is no southern or foreign-born population in the hinterland, only that there are sizable southern and foreign-born blocs in the population of Milan and its immediate vicinity, setting it apart from the outer hinterland where the League is so strong. The southern population was never as segregated residentially as the focus in the 1960s on certain inner suburbs tended to suggest.[36] So it is difficult to identify distinctive southern enclaves in which voters might vote alike. Furthermore, the increased number of foreign-born immigrants in recent years makes southerners even less obvious socially as a bloc. Since its arrival, the southern population, particularly the dominant working-class segment, has tended to support the parties of the left, in particular the Communists and their successor parties, even if other segments, especially those employed by the state, have tended to support the parties of government or the far right. Though hardly voluble in its criticisms of the League for demonizing the Italian South and southerners as the source of all that ails the North or speaking in one monolithic voice, this population does provide a core of support for the labor unions and the parties most critical of the League (from Rifondazione Comunista on the left through the Partito Popolare in the center-left to the National Alliance on the right). Leaders of the League sometimes claim that southerners are among the supporters of the party. But apart from Bossi's Sicilian-born wife, who is one of the founders, no leading figures are southern, and the rhetoric and policies of the League are certainly not designed to attract the votes of southerners or foreign-born citizens, however long they and their offspring have lived in the region.

The Northern League's Post-1994 Symbolism

After the failure in 1994 of its strategy of entering into alliance with other parties to pursue federal reform of the Italian state, the Northern League has tended to emphasize some new issues in which the identity and interests of contemporary Milan take on little if any significance in the ideology of the party (see chapter 9). One of these is the increasing role of the position and problems of small businesses, particularly the small businesses typical of the Veneto. The League has long seen itself as the voice of the small-business sector in the industrial districts of northern Italy. But as this sector has become increasingly differentiated between the organized networks of firms in the large and medium-sized cities of Lombardy and Piedmont and the much more localized and independent businesses of the Veneto and rural Lombardy, the League has identified more and more with the interests and problems of the latter. These businesses are particularly angry about the state's failure to provide needed services at the same time that they have lost the intermediary agent that once acted, if unreliably and intermittently, to represent them against Roman bureaucracy: the locally hegemonic Christian Democratic Party.

As if to reinforce this identification, the League has also turned toward a representation of northern history that resonates more with the past of the Veneto than with that of Lombardy. Much of the rhetoric about the new region of "Padania" invented since 1995 relies on symbols from the Venetian past, largely because Venice had a distinguished independent past when large sections of northern Italy were under foreign rule or were fragmented among small principalities of one type or another. The League's actions in setting up its shadow parliament in Mantua, organizing demonstrations along the river Po and in Venice itself, and returning to a logic of cultural separatism after flirting with macroregional federalism point to its symbolic withdrawal from the metropolitan North represented by Milan.

The Rise of the National New Right

Finally, since 1994 the Northern League has been challenged on such issues as foreign immigration, the need to liberate the economy from the shackles of state regulation, and the virtues of small business by the emergence of Berlusconi's Forza Italia party and the makeover of the neo-Fascist MSI into the post-Fascist National Alliance both of which have taken votes from the League in Milan and elsewhere in the North. In both the 1996 national election and the 1997 local elections these parties in alliance took over a significant proportion of the League's previous vote in Milan. In Milan, therefore, there is still support for a right-wing politics that frames issues in national more than in regional terms. As of early 2001, this new right was the main antagonist of the government. After the 2001 national election, the League's best hope for national political survival is to be its unwilling and sullen partner. The League's cultural responses to political dilemmas appear too simplistic to achieve a positive response in large cities such as Milan, where the everyday reality is too complex for a convinced reaction from a sufficiently large segment of the electorate.[37]

CONCLUSION

The Catholic Church may have represented a degree of universalism or commitment to universal values in an Italian context, but the form that its relation to the Italian state took after World War II—mediation by the Christian Democratic Party—led to a heavy emphasis on localism and particularistic attachments in the areas of that party's strength in northern Italy. The decay of the Church's ancillary organizations, under the pressures of secularization, the growth of a consumer society, and the development of an industrial sector heavily dependent on family labor and vulnerable to international markets, have allied with the powerful localism released into public view by the political scandals of the early 1990s to produce a new political regime in northern Italy in which a new party with regionalist, not national, ambitions has replaced the old perennial party of Italian national government.

The Northern League, therefore, though it has grown in ground long tilled by the Christian Democrats, is not a direct substitute for that party *in any sense of the term*. It grew separately as the DC declined, benefiting from this decline but hardly entirely dependent on it, as some maps and statistics demonstrate. But it is also a very different kind of party, oriented primarily toward a particular set of sectoral interests (that of small manufacturing firms and artisans) and a very different geographical imagination of an Italian North no longer dependent on power emanating from Rome, the demonized capital of a state whose dominance by a cabal of parties (*partitocrazia*) has now come back to haunt it. The League's exponents believe that the "small virtues" (honesty, efficiency, and merit) were shortchanged by the old system. Whether an independent North could develop them better alone than as part of Italy is a different matter entirely. The North has, after all, been part of Italy for a long time. The history of the DC and its association with corrupt practices are part of the North's history too.

Without Milan, however, the League would not have a geographically coherent North to govern. Yet without a more cosmopolitan or nationally oriented message, the League cannot expect to prosper there. Trapped between the heritage of the Christian Democrats and the contemporary spatial economy of northern Italy, the Northern League is hardly a suitable vehicle to replace the DC as a governing party even in the part of Italy it claims. Place differences set stringent limits on the geographical claims of a party that bases its appeal entirely on its identification with a specific region of Italy. The DC may have been localistic in its practices in northern Italy, but its national orientation and connection to the Catholic Church allowed it the possibility of putting together a wide range of group coalitions across a wide range of places at election time. The League does not have this option. Its localism does not travel well beyond a narrow geographical segment of northern Italy. Fulfilling its ambition is limited, therefore, by its place-based appeal. The next chapter attempts to explain more about why the League had the success it did in the 1990s and what its experience tells us about the geographical construction of political identities.

CHAPTER 8

The Northern League and Political Identity in Northern Italy

The Northern League is not just another political party oriented to obtaining national office and delivering the goods to its electorate in the fashion of the departed Christian Democrats. This is the source of both its appeal and its dilemma, as I argued in chapter 7. Originating in several localistic movements in the early 1980s, the League took on its present organizational form in 1992. Its leader, Umberto Bossi, has shifted back and forth between demanding a new federal Italy and proclaiming outright secession.[1] The second or first party in both national and local elections in many places in northern Lombardy and the Veneto region of the Northeast for most of the 1990s, the League currently stands for a federal Italy. From 1996 until 2000 the party followed a secessionist strategy based on an independent "Padania," a new state variously defined but usually claiming Italy from its northern alpine boundary as far south as a line running along the southern borders of the administrative regions of Tuscany, Umbria, and Marche. In 2001 the League reentered a national electoral alliance with two parties, Forza Italia and the National Alliance (Alleanza Nazionale), that it had abandoned in 1994 and whose visions of a future Italy differ significantly from its own (see chapter 9).

The League, as an explicitly northern-regional party, represents a novel departure from the nationally oriented, if rarely nationally successful, character of the two major postwar Italian political movements, with the ideologically universalistic Communists dominating central Italy and the equally (if distinctively) universalistic Catholics (in the Christian Democratic Party) dominating the Northeast and parts of the South. Variously explained as a protest movement or an antisystem party whose future survival was seen as unlikely by most orthodox political scientists, the League has had a remarkable staying power over the past ten years.[2] Part of this relates to the fertile period when it was planted and grew as the collapse of the old system of parties in 1992 in reaction to the great corruption scandal of Tangentopoli provided an opening to new parties running against the old system, its politicians, and their model of national integration.[3] But part of it also relates to the appeal of a regional party in conditions of economic globalization and increased European integration. The success of the League in changing the terms of Italian political debate says something meaningful about the current status of Italian national identity: the sense of place associated with Italy as a whole. So the Northern League is important in contemporary Italian politics not simply as the main electoral successor to the Christian Democratic Party in much of northern Italy in the 1990s, but also as the prime mover in creating a public debate about the geography of Italian political identity. This may be its most lasting contribution to Italian politics.

THE NORTHERN LEAGUE AND POLITICAL IDENTITY

National identities are often seen as the polar opposite of identities associated with other geographical scales of political identity, such as the local and the regional. In contemporary circumstances, however, including the globalization of economies and the questioning of the efficacy of existing states, national identity may no longer be best thought of as opposed to political identities at other geographical scales. Using the case of the Northern League in Italy, this chapter identifies three rules of political identity formation—the self-conscious invention of political units, the malleability of identities, and the multiplicity of identities—that suggest the mutual contingency of different geographical scales in the crafting of political identities, including national ones.

These rules are by no means unique to Italy. The success of the League in changing the terms of debate about the geography of political identity in Italy illustrates in focused form three developing aspects of the politics of identity in Europe and North America more generally: first, the explicit and self-conscious *design* of new territorial entities—in this case, known as Padania—where none had much more than the slightest existence before; second, the *malleability* of political identities after a period when these had seemed to take on a permanent cast, particularly in terms of the priority of established national identities over those associated with other geographical scales and the emergence of geographically differentiated class, gender, and religious identities that were supposedly invariant within existing national territories; and third, the *coexistence* of multiple political identities without one's necessarily replacing all others. It is these three aspects of place and political identity as manifested in the Northern League that I address in this chapter. First, however, I want to say a few words about the geography of support for the League and its territorial claim to a region called Padania and to briefly examine a general subtext running across the three aspects of the geography of political identity: the place and identity question in contemporary social science.

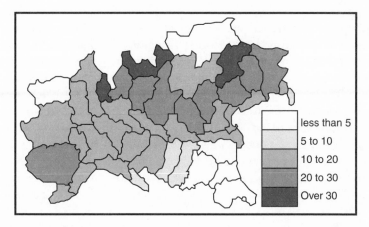

Figure 8.1 Percentage of the total vote for the Northern League by province, national election (Chamber of Deputies), 1994. Source: Author.

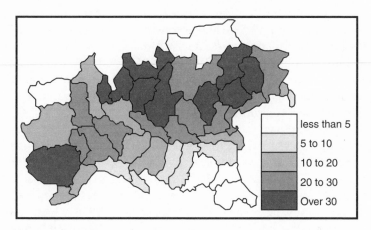

Figure 8.2 Percentage of the total vote for the Northern League by province, national election (Chamber of Deputies), 1996. Source: Author.

THE ELECTORAL GEOGRAPHY OF THE NORTHERN LEAGUE

From 1987 to 2001 the Northern League was the major or second party throughout large parts of northern Italy. Its main areas of support have been in the Veneto and Friuli in the Northeast, northern Lombardy, and Piedmont (figs. 8.1 and 8.2). Typically these are rural areas where small-scale manufacturing industries have become strongly rooted but where typical supporters are attached to certain traditional values relating to individual effort, strict gender roles, the unreliability of government, and the unfairness of taxes not returned in the form of superior public services and infrastructure for economic development.[4] The core supporters of the

League are younger male voters engaged in small-scale manufacturing as self-employed entrepreneurs. But in areas where the League is strongly rooted it also appeals to many others, including women and employees. So it is a mistake to reduce it solely to a movement of the lower-middle class, akin to old-style explanations of Fascist and shopkeeper movements (such as Poujadism in 1950s France). Its strongest roots have lain in areas or zones where the local economy is export driven and volatile and where the political props to local economic development provided by the Christian Democrats and Socialists before 1992 have collapsed.[5] It is a movement of such areas rather than of such-and-such a social group. It has had limited success elsewhere, with a retrenchment since 1994 in Liguria (around Genoa in particular), a substantial retreat in the largest cities such as Milan, Venice, and Turin, and trivial levels of support to the south of the river Po, in Emilia- Romagna and Tuscany. At the same time that its geographical reach has been contained, its level of support in its electoral fortresses such as Varese, Vicenza, and Treviso initially increased, although the October 1998 defection of leaders of the League in the Veneto to a new Venetian League (Liga Veneta) and everywhere to Forza Italia boded ill for the League's performance in the 2001 national election. Still, a so-called Deep North running along the southern edge of the Italian Alps has become the stronghold of the League in national and local elections in the way another famous region, the American Deep South, acquired a high degree of political consensus in its day.

Yet the geographical claim that the League's leaders put increasingly at the heart of their rhetoric in the 1990s—the claim of Padania—extends well beyond its areas of electoral strength into localities long dominated politically by support for the Italian Communist Party and its heirs. This is, of course, only the latest in a long series of federalist and other territorial plans put forward by the League.[6] Indeed, until 1996, when Umberto Bossi unveiled the concept of Padania, the League had been committed first, before 1990, to a loose sense of the North with Lombardy and the Veneto as the two main constitutive units; second, in the early 1990s, to a division of Italy into three macroregions; and third, from 1994 to 1996, to a federal plan with much smaller units.[7] Since 2000, federalism has been the chosen strategy once more.

One dilemma for the League, therefore, is its lack of much electoral support in large tracts of the "promised Padania." Another is whether its territorial designs can be expected to elicit much explicit commitment from its activists and supporters when they and associated political strategies have changed so often. In an interview given at Marina di Pietrasanta (Tuscany) on 2 August 1998, Bossi began to back away from secession by claiming that Padania could be created within existing institutions. He identified the presidents of the northern administrative regions as the agents for launching autonomy in the year 2000.[8] Finally, the term Padania itself is potentially a problem, referring conventionally to the region of the Po Valley rather than to the more expansive superregion Bossi now has in mind. This has encouraged him to work at creating a sense of the larger region by reorganizing his rhetoric and the policy goals of the League around Padania through symbolic acts such as a pilgrimage to the banks of the Po (on 13–15 September 1996), repeated visits to Venice to capture its history as an independent polity, and continuing use of provocative language and phrases to distinguish a "continental" or "European" Italy north of Rome from a "Mediterranean" or even "African" Italy to the south—represented, for example, by slogans such as "Africa begins at Rome" and repeated association of the South with Mafia criminality and the "Roman" political parties, particularly Berlusconi's Forza Italia, the League's main electoral competitor (see figs. 8.3 and 8.4).[9] This effectively racializes the territorial design of Padania as well as situating it in the familiar modern/backward pairing of, respectively, northern and southern Italy. It also ensures that a possibly separate Padania will be large enough economically to support the plans for a separate northern currency and an independent set of macroeconomic policies that Bossi has also proposed. Unfortunately for Bossi and the League, the mythology of Venice and its historical political independence are more readily appropriated by a local Venetian movement (such as the Venetian League), which can use them to present itself both as more culturally authentic and as true to the tolerant political heritage of the Venetian republic than the Lombard dictatorial style and extremist rhetoric of Bossi (a point made brilliantly in Michael Dibdin's 1994 detective novel *Dead Lagoon*).[10] Even more of a problem for the future of the idea of Padania, the admission of Italy into the European monetary system on 1 January 1999 makes the proposal of a new currency and associated monetary and fiscal policies, symbolically important as they would be for establishing northern "nationhood," totally redundant economically.[11]

MYTHS OF PLACE AND IDENTITY

Turning to the place and identity question, I would identify several dimensions of how considerations of political identity have been related explicitly and implicitly to understandings of place and territory. One of the commonplaces of mid-twentieth century social science has been that places (or the spaces of various sizes that people occupy and live in) have no *independent* role in political identity in the modern world. Class, religion, ideology, and gender are variously seen as primary. Even nationalism is deterritorialized as an ideological projection of the imagination of

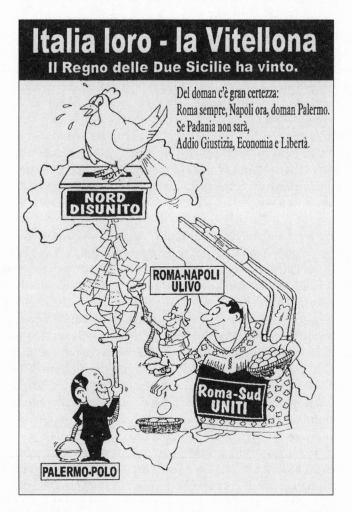

Figure 8.3 Northern League propaganda cartoon. A disunited but productive North lays the golden eggs for a united South, a corrupted Church, and a smiling Berlusconi. "Their Italy—the good-for-nothing," it commences: "The Kingdom of the Two Sicilies [the South] has won." Underneath it continues: "For tomorrow there is a great certainty: Rome always, Naples today, tomorrow Palermo. If Padania doesn't come about, goodbye to justice, economy [thrift, management] and liberty." Source: Lega Nord per L'Independenza della Padania (Northern League), September 1998, 1.

Figure 8.4 Northern League propaganda cartoon. A noble Bossi, held aloft by the balloons of fewer taxes, Europe, federalism, liberty, and more growth, wields a sword to cut the rope grasped by the Roman bosses, Berlusconi, D'Alema, and Fini. Source: Northern League, 1994.

groups that make no essential claims to specific bits of territory, only to "imagined communities."[12] Taking the existing boundaries between states as defining something akin to a territorial state of nature (as is common in political theory) allows discussion of political identity to ignore the geographical parameters of who is inside and who is outside a particular political project.[13] Social scientists simply presume that debate about political identities and actual contestation of them takes place within the territorial parameters of the existing state structure. This is not to say that this presumption is invariably false. Indeed, a case can be made that in Europe from the nineteenth century until the 1960s, the primary context of political identity formation was largely that of the established nation-states. In recent years this has changed, however, largely as a result of increased international communication, the development of the idea of an integrated Europe, the strengthening of regional economic disparities, and the flowering of regional movements. Today a hierarchy of territorial affiliations presents itself to the average citizen from Europe (or the world as a whole) through existing nation-states to regional nations (such as Catalonia, Scotland, and Corsica) and localisms. Social cleavages and economic dependencies cut across these place differences in complex ways to create multiple identities that include a range of intrinsic geographical definitions. For example, with respect to language a whole new cultural configuration is under construction in Europe, one more like that of India since 1947 than that of France after 1870. The emergence of regional languages and languages of wider currency, particularly English, portends a normalization of multicultural identities (perhaps even a Europewide one) rather than the establishment of mutually exclusive linguistic realms in which a single linguistic identity and associated political identity will prevail.[14]

A second dimension of conventional wisdom about place and identity is that acknowledgeable cultural and political differences that are local or on less than a national scale are seen as products of the long distant past rather than as constituted over time and potentially invented in the present. One of the dominant stories told about Italy, for example, by scholars as well as politicians, is that the North and South are politically different today either because of the forms of government they had in the Middle Ages or because of historical amoral familism (ethics that extend only to family members) in the South as opposed to the North. The other is that there is continuing powerful localism because Italy unified late (in the 1860s) or has experienced a peculiar kind of industrialization dependent on a family capitalism of a few large firms and millions of very small ones established in the distant past.[15] There is little or no place for considering the role of the contemporary institutional framework, the national economic structure as constituted since the 1960s, and the operations of political parties since World War II in not so much reproducing as *creating* the geographical differences that are so much a feature of contemporary Italy.[16] To the extent that generalizing about "Italy" remains questionable, therefore, commentators have available a stock of stories that put present-day geographical differences down to past social and political ones.[17]

Finally, insofar as one geographical scale is seen as emergent and threatening to the hegemony of the national scale, it is the local one. This is very much the sense one derives from the burgeoning literature on globalization, particularly in cultural studies and political sociology. Though rarely defined in other than the vaguest terms, the "local" is often sited at one end of a global-local dialectic to define a world where the national scale, as well as geographical scales other than the local and global, is in eclipse. Under conditions of globalization, as localities are inserted directly into the networks of global capitalism with diminished national state regulation, the local is seen as replacing or substituting for the national in the reproduction of uneven development. A spatial dialectic like this has room for only two geographical scales.[18] To the extent that a political identity is in crisis, therefore, it is seen as the national; and to the extent that a new scale is in the ascendancy it is the local (which usually seems to subsume the regional). In this view, political identities are invariably substitute rather than complementary "goods," and the local-regional is seen as increasingly substituting for the national. Yet as Alon Confino shows persuasively for Württemberg, Germany, in 1871–1918, national identity does not necessarily exclude other identities. Rather, it is constructed between the "intimate, immediate, and real local place and the distant, abstract, and not-less-real national world."[19] In the contemporary context of globalization, however—the unmediated insertion of localities and regions into world markets and the emergence of higher-tier governments such as the European Union—it is not simply the local and the existing national that are involved. The current trend is for a renegotiation of the relationships between various scales of political identity, including the national. As a result, a multiplicity of crosscutting territorial identities—local, regional, national, and so on—are available for stimulus and mobilization by political movements and populist politicians.

THE NORTHERN LEAGUE AND THE CONTEMPORARY POLITICS OF POLITICAL IDENTITY

It is in this theoretical context that the case of the Italian Northern League is interesting and important. From the League's recent experience, as interpreted by means of my fieldwork in Varese and elsewhere in northern Italy and the results of recent Italywide and northern opinion polls, I want to emphasize three rules relating to political identity formation that have consequences for theoretical debates about place and political identity. I chose Varese as the setting for interviewing League politicians because most of the important leaders of the League, including Bossi, come from the province, the League has become the main electoral force in the province since 1992, and the League has been strongly established in local government in Varese since the early 1990s.

Designing Padania

The first of the three rules involves the self-conscious invention of a new political entity, the Italian North or Padania, complete with its own myths, symbols, and rendering of history. Even though the League's leaders largely accept the view of pollsters that local, not regional, identities have lain behind much support for the movement, they nevertheless have come to believe that to achieve success in decentralizing power from Rome they must create a new territorial entity on which they can focus their aspirations. Having failed in a previous strategy of wresting power from Rome by participating in Roman (national) government (after the 1994 election) to promote some type of federalism, by 1996 they were investing their hopes in welding together an imagined community for northern Italy as an alternative to Italy as a whole.

The deliberate nature of this process shows how much has changed from the last great round of creating national units in the late nineteenth century, when nations were not so much designed or customized as off-the-shelf products of at least minimal ethnic distinctions. All nations may have founding moments, but these are usually the outcome of long periods of excitement, enthusiasm, and mobilization in which the symbols of nationhood, not least the claimed national boundaries, arise from widespread acceptance of their naturalness and rootedness in a common past, however mythic that past might be. The Northern League may be the first authentic European postmodernist territorial political movement in its *self-conscious* manipulation of territorial imagery to create a sense of cultural-economic difference within an existing state. Italy, of course, as League activists never tire of telling interviewers, was always the least natural of cultural units for European nationhood. Ironically, the nineteenth- and early twentieth-century attempts at unifying Italy under Liberal and Fascist regimes faced a continuing dilemma of creating Italians out of a disparate populace, not dissimilar to the task facing the League with Padania. The difference, however, is that there was a geographic entity called Italy that did have some prior history of political and economic unity, and there was no sudden, deliberate concoction of a territorial entity on which political hopes could be projected, such as has occurred with Bossi's invention of Padania. Italy may have been only a geographical expression in 1860, but it was at least that.

The League has had few if any primordial ethnic elements to play with except a set of dialects, many of them mutually unintelligible. The region and its history have had to be made from scratch, largely in terms of giving cultural dressing to resentments about the mismatch between the contemporary institutional structure of Italy and the economic trajectory of its northern part.[20] A geographical entity thus provides the basis for making a set of historical claims rather than historical claims' providing the basis for a geographical claim. This is a powerful example of how space is perhaps becoming the "everything" that Edward Soja has claimed for it.[21] First of all, Padania has had to be given a territorial definition. The League has felt the need to reify its cultural claims about northern cultural distinctiveness by giving the region definite borders, even when these seem to go well beyond the geographical limits of mass support or the understanding of militants who have tended to have a more geographically constrained definition of northern Italy than does Bossi. From the League's perspective, these borders do not involve a claim for a separate state so much as the secession of a cultural-economic region from an existing state in the context of an integrating Europe. Indeed, it is not always clear that the *precise* boundaries in themselves really matter that much to Bossi or the party militants.

The approach seems to be that the boundaries are better left somewhat fuzzy so as to keep one's opponents off guard. After all, in Bossi's world the territory of Padania works outward from the *leghistas'* (League supporters') local base as a phenomenological construct, with the South—sometimes beginning around Rome, sometimes farther north, but with Calabria and Sicily as its essential moments—defining what Padania is not. Rather more positively, when delegates to the February 1997 Congress of the League were asked how they would define Padania, it was the "moral values," "productive system," "customs," and "respect for rules" that distinguished Padania from the rest of Italy.[22] The radical "particularism"[23] of Bossi and the League's core supporters betrays itself in their lack of interest in articulating a rational geographical basis—a common past or natural boundaries—to the secession or the increased institutional autonomy they propose. What is more critical is the rigid differentiation drawn between a northern approach to politics based on efficiency and transparency and a southern (and Roman) approach based on clientelism and corruption. Territory matters crucially to the political imagination of the League, but from this point of view territory defines a culture associated with myriad northern localities rather than a homogeneous Padanian culture defining a Padanian territory. Padania has been invented first, and the cultural strands giving it expression are being selected and interwoven afterward to bring the disparate "Norths" together into one functional unit.

Corresponding to the invention of Padania in 1995–96, the League has also discovered a commitment to "Europe" as a component of its political project. Roberto Maroni, one of the League's leaders and the highest-ranking League minister in the Berlusconi coalition government of 1994, interviewed on 19 September 1997, sees a connection between the design of Padania and the new attitude toward European integration. He sees Padania as the

> packaging of everything the League stands for into one word. Padania is a region in Europe that does not aim for the same kind of independence as in the Czech, Yugoslav, and Baltic cases. It would be sufficient for Rome to allow autonomy to the northern regions under the umbrella of the EU. Padania is too big for a single identity. It is the objective conditions that the regions within Padania share that is the source of the idea. There is no historical or cultural identity to Padania in the sense that Catalonia or Scotland has. This is our weak point. But if an identity of Padania does not exist, then neither does that of Italy. Each is an invention, except that of Padania reflects the needs of northerners for self-government against the power of Rome.

Second, in the creation of Padania preexisting elements from the past have been put together in a pastiche of deliberate, explicit invention. Bossi has never claimed that he is simply recovering something that once existed but that faded away or was destroyed. His is a rather brazen attempt to invent a territorial entity as a vehicle for a set of local identities with little in common save a common hostility to the political institutions of contemporary Italy, represented by the single word Rome. Critical elements in the invention of Padania include the use of the unfamiliar word Padania itself (derived from imperial Rome's name for its province in the Po basin), around which more familiar cultural threads can be woven. These include reference to the political traditions of the Venetian republic as a precursor for the present enterprise, reminding potential Padanians of a past in which they were not subjugated either by foreign powers such as Austria or by more Italian forces such as the popes, Mussolini, and modern governments dominated by "southerners," as well as repeated reference to "northern values" of hard work, honesty, and responsibility that distinguish the citizens of Padania from other Italians.

Third, long before the invocation of Padania, Bossi had broken with the typical language and rhetorical style of the Italian political class. Partly this involved adopting a populist vocabulary associated with demonization of politicians and national political institutions—what Mino Martinazzoli, a leading politician in the old Christian Democratic Party, dubbed "the politics of the bar." This appealed to those who saw themselves on the margins of organized politics, alienated from the established parties and angry at the seeming indifference to local demands of the national bureaucracy and its local agents.[24] But it also involved restructuring political discourse around a new type of political polarization. Since World War II, Italian politics had been structured around such oppositions as left/right, Catholic/lay, workers/bosses, democratic/fascist, and a few others. The League has created a strong sense of "us" for its militants and supporters by breaking with the past and organizing a new political discourse against the other of Rome, southerners, and immigrants.

Roberto Biorcio, a political scientist, identifies two dimensions to this discourse.[25] One distinguishes populations and their territories, basically the North and the South, based on very strong normative distinctions between the two. In its strongest form this opposition is that of Europe (the North) versus Africa (the South), but it also includes the ordinary folk (of the North or Padania) versus the southerners and non-European foreigners. Along the other dimension is an opposition between the high and the low in a hierarchy of social groups, with southern elites identified with the power of Rome, the old political parties of government, and the Mafia but with northern big business, finance, and media conglomerates also conniving with Roman political power. In Bossi's rhetoric after 1994, the media baron and leader of Forza Italia, Silvio Berlusconi, became the main symbol of the system or the oppressor against which the League must mobilize the people of Padania. Thus the League has combined a set of classic populist themes about the small person exploited by the system with a strong sense of the homogeneously small-fry population of Padania embattled against entrenched interests within Italian political institutions. Padania therefore becomes a territorial means of "ignoring the religious fracture and trying to overcome in a populist key the fractures of class between workers, small businessmen, artisans, and shopkeepers so as to rediscover unity against big business and a colonizing state that dissipates the resources of northern regions in favor of the South."[26]

Finally, the leader of the party, Umberto Bossi, has been the key proponent of the secessionist strategy, in the face of considerable initial (and in some cases continuing) skepticism from other leading figures. The more sober and conventionally liberal of them often seem disturbed by Bossi's verbal extravagance, use of sexual innuendo about his opponents, and deliberate provocations such as his declarations of independence and creation of parallel institutions for Padania, such as a parliament and a national guard. But it is Bossi's style that propels the party into the daily newspapers and has led to public debate among his opponents about the prospects for secession. He even welcomes prosecution as a mechanism not only for publicity but also for "martyrdom."[27] His skinny, unkempt physical appearance and outrageous rhetoric convey an image of victimization by the powers that be that reinforces the idea of a northern Italy similarly victimized.[28] Padania has provided a powerful vehicle for Bossi's creativity, allowing him to bring together in one relatively concrete territorial concept all his favorite themes concerning the deficiencies of the present Italian state: in other words, a positive counterpoint to the relentless negativity that previously tended to be his stock-in-trade. Even as he has retreated from secession—partly, it seems, to respond to internal critics but also to find allies to prevent damaging changes in the electoral system, such as a shift to a completely majoritarian one—Bossi has maintained a focus on Padania as the alternative to Italy as it is.

Malleable Political Identities

The idea of Padania and its prospective autonomy-independence seems to have grown rapidly in acceptability among both the militants of the League and significant sections of its electorate. In a mere year and a half after Bossi's original declaration of independence on 15 September 1996, he carried most of his party with him on the secessionist path. Even such a moderate as Raimondo Fassa, the League mayor of the commune of Varese from 1992 to 1997, acknowledges (in an interview of 8 September 1997) that the "secession idea has met with success. An ignored North has discovered its political destiny because other political currents have not had specific responses to the fiscal and other problems of the region. National unification obviously has no real meaning." He goes on to add, though, that there is "limited possibility of independence" and "no cultural unity to Padania." Neither is there "a strong sense of being part of Europe. For example, Bossi is localistic, not European in outlook." Fassa expressed these views just ten days before he announced he would not be a candidate for mayor of Varese in the November 1997 election. He had obviously broken with Bossi. His relatively pure libertarianism allied to a strong sense of Europe acquired during his term as a member of the European Parliament was no longer compatible with the new secessionist strategy even as he could recognize its propaganda success.[29]

Where Fassa seems to underestimate the Padanian strategy is in assuming that cultural identities are strictly inherited from a distant past and that in the absence of such primordial roots new political identities are invariably inauthentic.[30] This, of course, is the "common sense" of much contemporary social science. What is remarkable in the case of northern Italy today is that we can see before our eyes the attempted invention of an identity that has had no previous existence. What the latest turn in the League's manipulation of territorial symbolism suggests, therefore, is that political identities are much more malleable or subject to revision than most social scientists and historians have tended to think, particularly when combined with powerful aversions to existing institutions and fear that these institutions no longer defend or further local interests.[31] The difficulty, as put by Gianfranco Miglio, a former adviser to Bossi, has been in turning such local interests into an identity that can effectively mobilize people politically.[32] In his detailed examination of opinion polls among League activists and northern voters, Roberto Biorcio claims that by 1997 "the invention of the nation of Padania, considered by many to be without any foundation whatever, has started to put down roots, if still among a minority, in the electoral sphere of the League, and in general in public opinion in the regions of northern Italy."[33]

How did this happen? It started as recently as the mid-1980s when Bossi and the Lombard League (as the League was then called) publicly challenged the Italian territorial status quo. In a 1984 study of political participation in Lombardy, sentiments of local and regional belonging or identity were much less important than other types of identity based on class, occupation, status, religion, and demographic characteristics such as age, generation, and marital status.[34] Only 18.3 percent of the respondents to a survey reported that any kind of territorial identity (national, regional, or local) was more important than others, whereas over half (53.1 percent) said that social positions of one sort or another were most important. Among the territorial identifiers the most widespread attachment was to the national level. The local and regional identifiers were widely seen at the time as exemplifying the localistic type in Robert Merton's famous distinction between locals and cosmopolitans: locals were people without much interest in politics, churchgoing, interested in local gossip, with the regionalists somewhat more sophisticated politically than the average localist.[35] In other words, they were the remnants of gemeinschaft, or community, in a world that was increasingly that of gesellschaft, or geographically wider-ranging society.

To track shifts in territorial identities. there is evidence from two Italy-wide surveys of young people aged fifteen to twenty-nine conducted in 1986 and 1991 and three general population surveys conducted in 1992, 1994, and 1996. From these surveys it is not possible to weigh territorial against social identities, only to see how much change has occurred in the nature of territorial attachments. In 1986, young people throughout Italy tended to privilege local attachments. Regional attachments were much lower. Somewhat ironic in the context of later changes, northern respondents were more likely to report an identity with Italy than were those in the Center and the South. By 1991 local identities had weakened considerably, with a commensurate rise in the importance of all others (nation, Europe, the world, region), with region having the largest increase in the North, going from 11.4 percent in 1986 to 15.1 percent in 1991. This trend was particularly noticeable among young people voting or intending to vote for the League. Close to one-third of them reported a priority attachment to region, with a similar number expressing local attachments and about 24 percent an attachment to Italy.

In a 1992 survey of northern residents fully 46.1 percent favored large-scale fiscal decentralization to the northern administrative regions, with shopkeepers, artisans, and workers giving it the strongest support. For these social groups a regional identity seemed to increasingly capture their social identities. This trend deepened in two more recent surveys in 1994 and 1996, in which a net majority of all residents expressed support for northern autonomy, far more than actually vote for the League. Although local attachments remain the most common, realizing these is seen as requiring regional autonomy. Among League supporters, however, the territorial sphere to which they feel most linked has shifted from the local to northern Italy as a whole. In 1996, 46.9 percent of League sympathizers reported a primary identification with northern Italy compared with 47.6 percent identifying with their local commune. Indeed, close to a quarter of the voters for the two main right-wing parties, Forza Italia and the National Alliance, also expressed this preference. A sizable proportion of the northern population, about 50 percent, picked a primary northern Italian or northern regional identity (Lombard, Venetian, etc.) as a first or second choice. This comes very close to challenging the dominance of local identities and is greater than the primary or secondary preference for an Italian political identity (44.1 percent).

The growing sense of attachment to northern Italy or Padania is reflected also in the changing levels of support for different institutional arrangements. In 1996, about 11 percent of the residents of northern Italy were in favor of a strong autonomy for Padania as part of confederation or as a macroregion within a federal state; 39.8 percent of the League's sympathizers and 29 percent of its voters expressed the same opinions; 36.4 percent of all respondents would have liked an Italian federation of administrative regions (34.6 percent of the League's sympathizers and 41.8 percent of its voters). Very few League supporters wanted enhanced powers for local entities, whereas among other political groupings this option tended to be much more popular. This conclusion is reinforced by comparing the findings of a survey of participants in the March to the Po in September 1996 with that of delegates to the League's Congress of February 1997. Not only did sentiments in favor of independence increase from

65.9 to 74.9 percent over the six months, the attachment was more strongly to Padania than to the other levels on offer, such as city, region, or Italy. There is a danger, however, in projecting such findings from activists onto the population of northern Italy at large. Most poll respondents in northern Italy neither wanted nor expected secession. At the same time, those respondents with the strongest identification with the North or Padania did see secession as a threat that could empower regional and local levels of government.[36]

At the very least, therefore, the proposal for Padania has pushed the general population and the other political parties toward favoring more powers for local government. For example, only 27.4 percent of respondents to the 1996 survey expressed support for the present system of government. Among many League supporters and an increasing number of other northerners without strong affiliations to the League, the substitution of the North for such administrative regions as Lombardy and the Veneto and the invention of Padania seem to have produced a veritable shift in dominant political identity from the local area to that of Padania. It remains to be seen, however, whether such sentiments will ever translate into the kind of vote that will be required for secession to achieve success, given that they seem largely confined to localities within the North that are already both strongly localistic and pro-League. Bossi's equivocation about secession beginning in August 1998 and the defection of many of the League's local leaders in the Veneto to the Venetian League and everywhere in the North to Forza Italia suggest that such a choice may never have to be made.[37]

Multiplicity of Identities

It is misleading, however, to give the impression that a new Padanian identity is simply replacing older ones in a parade or serial progression of political identities. In fact, each of the surveys I have referred to presents evidence that people have relatively complex political identities in which a number of territorial and social dimensions intersect. Of course this is not news to students of postcolonial societies, where national identities have been implanted into existing local identities and have had to coexist with long-standing religious and pan-national identities (e.g., pan-Arab). But in modern Europe the overriding political significance of national identities has long gone unquestioned.[38]

With respect to multiple identities, two aspects of the Padanian case are worth identifying. The first is the ease with which people maintain a number of political identities even as they shift the order of priority. In contemporary northern Italy (and Italy as a whole) local and national identities have long coexisted without any sense of mutual exclusion. Each of the surveys of Italian youth from 1986 through 1991 to that of 1997 demonstrates this. When people are asked to name in order of importance their two most important geographical units, there always arise not only a hierarchy of levels but also combinations of attachments. Although the local appears consistently in these surveys as the most important territorial identity everywhere in Italy, two-thirds of those who rank it so also consider "Italy" a complement to it rather than a competitor. In the words of Ilvo Diamanti, one of the most careful students of the League and its impact on Italian identities, this mixing of territorial identities is "a sort of frame that permits a country of localisms and localists like Italy to stay together, even if with conflicts and particularisms."[39]

In such a core area of the League as the Northeast, for example, in 1997 attachment to Italy did not register support above the national average as a primary affiliation, but it did have the highest affiliation of any major regional division of Italy as a secondary attachment. Indeed, it is among higher-status social groups and supporters of left-wing parties that there is the least "pride in being Italian" and higher commitment to the "world" or "Europe" or both. Most young Italians, including supporters of the League, manage to combine a high degree of municipalism-localism and regionalism with a significant sentiment of national pride (table 8.1). A preference for the League and for Padania can readily coexist with a significant, if hardly dominant, sense of national identity and other identities such as European. At least for younger Italians, therefore, the local and the cosmopolitan are not necessarily in opposition, as conventional sociological thinking might lead us to expect. Rather, "Italy continues to suggest," as Paolo Segatti has proposed, "a nation of *compaesani,* or fellow local dwellers, who look to Europe and the world with great attention, but with limited passion."[40] Passion is now far closer to home.[41]

The second aspect of the Padanian case in relation to a multiplicity of political-territorial identities is that the League's leaders appear conflicted about its primary territorial orientation. Its very success in local elections in northern Italy means that the League is institutionalizing itself. Many communes and not a few provinces are now dominated by League politicians. They tend to see the electoral future of the League, and their own retention of office, as lying in delivering "good government" at the local level or building a new northern Italy "from below." This inevitably seems to privilege the existing local government units at the expense of the vision of a northern macroregion such as Padania.[42] But rather like the Communists in central Italy in the 1970s, when exclusion from national governments led them to invest heavily in creating efficient and honest local government so as to advertise their qualifications for national office, the League can use its control over local administrations to tout the possibili-

Table 8.1 "To Which of the Following Units do You Have the Strongest Attachment? And In Second Place?"

	First Choice	Second Choice	Total
The city you live in	**40.2**	19.2	59.4
The region or province	10.5	23.2	35.7
Italy	32.2	31.8	**64.0**
Europe	3.1	13.1	16.2
The world in general	12.6	10.6	23.2
No reply	1.4	2.2	3.6
Total	100.0	100.0	

SOURCE: La Luce 7 December 1997, 4.

NOTE: Italian national survey of fifteen- to twenty-four-year-olds, December 1997, percentage responses. Totals of first and second choices do not add up to 100 percent.

ties for government throughout the North when the evils of Roman rule are finally removed. This is the point of view encountered most frequently in formal interviews with local politicians in Varese, in both September and December 1997.[43] Massimo Ferrario, at the time president of the province of Varese (interviewed on 11 September 1997), for example, is an important League politician who sees the local and the macroregional as complementary: "The institutionalization of the League in local agencies," he says, "allows for an active growth of federalism because it is impossible that the Italian state will reform itself to allow for a true federalism. Provincial autonomy is a goal shared by all presidents of provinces, but it can happen only under the threat of leaving Italy behind." In other words, Padania and increased autonomy for local institutions are seen as going hand in hand. The local and the regional therefore are complementary more than competing. This can lead to a technocratic or good-government ethos that actively undermines Bossi's confrontational strategy. This could happen through an absence of zeal for Bossi's latest example of political "performance art." It is more likely to happen, however, through the need to build local political coalitions. In the commune of Varese in 1992–97, for example, the shortage of qualified League representatives to serve as administrators led to the appointment of former Communists and others in an anomalous municipal government that aroused much comment and not a little ridicule among the League's opponents.

CONCLUSION

The Italian Northern League has a postmodern cast. It is not well organized as a political party, and it focuses on the experience of ordinary people more on than the thoughts or theories of famous intellectuals. It presents itself as economically liberal and beyond ideology (in the sense of left versus right). It represents areas with specific economic characteristics, in particular export-oriented small-scale manufacturing, formerly supported by the local political dominance of the now-defunct Christian Democrats and Socialists, more than it represents the interests of particular social strata. Its leader, Umberto Bossi, has created not so much an internally coherent political ideology as a series of powerful and evocative metaphors against centralized power that have focused on the idea of Padania, an independent or autonomous northern Italy, and increasingly autonomous local government.

The League's electoral success is a monument to the power of words in the service of localized interests. It has harnessed a long-standing localism, no more entrenched in the North than elsewhere in Italy, for a project of radical political devolution. In bringing this project into Italian politics, the League's strategy of inventing a new political discourse constructed around the geographical claim to "Padania" illustrates in extreme form three of the key rules now governing the relations between place and political identity: the willingness and ability to design a new political territoriality, the malleability of political identities, and the coexistence of multiple political identities. The idea of Padania has allowed the League to replace an Italian language of politics largely based on social divisions with a new language based on geographical ones. This in turn has required a manipulation of existing political identities that can prove remarkably plastic. In taking on a new or radically reworked identity, however, no one has had to sacrifice existing ones. New identities can be taken on without jettisoning the old. The three rules of political identity formation illustrated by the Northern League may well define the emerging realities of political identity at the outset of the twenty-first century elsewhere in Europe.

Gilles Ceron's satirical parable on the seventy-fifth anniversary of the declaration of the Italian Republic in 1946 provides an appropriate conclusion:

Bad News from Italy

Rome, late April 2021. As a result of the tragic events that have been occurring here, the seventy-fifth anniversary of the Italian Republic has been very soberly celebrated. It will be recalled that the Italians have never had a sense of the State, because of their long history of invasions and divisions, and that, in the climate of institutional disintegration, the days of the Italian Republic are numbered. On this occasion, the President of the Italian Republic received numerous messages of sympathy, notably from the Prime Minister of the XII

French Republic, the Presidents of California, Wyoming, and forty other American republics, from the Kings of Mercia and of Wales, and from the Grand Duke of Schleswig-Holstein.[44]

Formal Interviews with Politicians in Varese (September and December 1997)

Fabio Binelli, League councillor, commune of Varese, 8 September and 18 December 1997

Mauro Carabelli, secretary to League mayor Aldo Fumagalli, commune of Varese, 16 December 1997

Raimondo Fassa, League mayor of commune of Varese, 8 September 1997

Massimo Ferrario, League president of the province of Varese, 11 September 1997

Aldo Fumagalli, League mayor of commune of Varese (effective 2 December 1997), 17 December 1997

Sergio Ghiringelli, League councillor, commune of Varese, 8 September 1997

On. Giuseppe Leoni, League councillor, commune of Varese, 8 September 1997; one of the founders (with Umberto Bossi and two others) of the Lombard League, first League deputy, and first League councillor in Varese

On. Roberto Maroni, deputy leader, Northern League, minister of the interior in the 1994 Berlusconi government, 19 September 1997

Cesare Montalberti, Popular Party councillor, commune of Varese, 17 December 1997

Paolo Sassi, secretary to Robert Maroni in 1994 when Maroni was Italian minister of the interior, 3 September 1997

CHAPTER 9

Reimagining Italy after the Collapse of the Old Party System in 1992

The four major political parties in contemporary Italy after the collapse of the old party system in 1992 (Forza Italia, the Northern League, the Democratic Party of the Left, and the National Alliance) were brand new in name and ideology. The central claim of this chapter is that they have geographically structured their conceptions of "Italy" in ways that vary from the largely agreed-on geographical frame of reference of the parties in the old system. In particular, in its rhetoric and organization each of these parties has been constructing different conceptions of the geographical scales—international, national, regional, local—in terms of which they understand Italy. The collapse of the old system of parties in 1992–94 created an opening for a reorganization of parties more in line with recent trends toward a fragmented Italian political economy and society that are now also more open to non-Italian influences.

The Italian case, however, illustrates a more general point: political parties must organize themselves and their ideologies through the ways they divide, order, and organize space. There is an intrinsically geographical basis to the drama of organized politics even when all parties structure a national space in the same ways. This is all the more obvious at times of dramatic political change, when there are competing conceptions of how to organize potential constituencies and interests in different places. Geography therefore is not external to the operations of political parties, a Euclidean surface or a stage on which the drama of politics is played out. The drama of party politics is scripted in terms of the geographical horizons parties set for themselves and how these appeal in different places.

In contemporary political studies geographical scale is almost always treated in terms of either the fixed or the emerging dominance of one level over others in political organization and behavior. The national and the global in particular have achieved a privileged status as the geographical scales at which political activity is said to be determined. In the former case this is accomplished by invoking a set of typical national voters divided according to census categories rather than geographical subunits and by seeing political parties as essentially national in rhetoric, organization, and appeal. In the latter case, a country's position within a global division of labor is seen as automatically producing particular political outcomes at other geographical scales.

In this chapter I use the example of post-1992 Italian political parties with a focus on the 1994 national election to show the ways geographical scales (national, regional, local) are implicated in their rhetoric and organization. The major claim is that the political parties cannot be adequately understood without attending to how considerations of geographical scale are intertwined with their ideologies and organizational activities. Before turning to a general argument concerning the "geographical dramaturgy" of parties, the new Italian political parties themselves, and the historical situation in which they have sprung up, I briefly examine the concept of geographical scale as it is used here, expanding on the discussion in chapter 2.

GEOGRAPHICAL SCALE AND POLITICS

The first requirement is to identify precisely what the term geographical scale signifies. One important clarification involves distinguishing geographical scale from cartographic scale. Cartographic scale refers to the scale of representation or density of information found on a map. This can be enlarged or shrunk to convey more or less information about a given area. Geographical scale refers to the level of geographical resolution at which a given phenomenon is thought of, acted on, or studied. Conventionally, terms such as local, regional, national, and global are used to convey this meaning of scale. It is not, therefore, the amount of information on a map that matters, but the scale at which a particular phenomenon or question is framed geographically. In other words, geographical scale is the focal setting at which spatial boundaries are defined for a specific social claim, activity, or behavior.[1]

From one point of view this geographical meaning of scale is akin to the idea of levels of analysis, in which at each "higher" level a phenomenon takes on a different aspect and thus requires a different or more complex explanation. The doctrine of emergence in the philosophy of science is based on this understanding. In this construction there can never be one scale or level at which total explanation can be found. Phenomena are themselves scale specific with respect to how they occur and can be explained; no single scale can ever tell the full story.[2]

However, there is nothing very determinate about the terms typically used to convey a geographical scale of reference. "Local," for example, can in different cases refer to areas of vastly different sizes. Even "global" may mean not worldwide but, rather, a geographical scope extending beyond the continental. Relevance can be established only in relation to particular empirical cases and the usage that arises from the practices of specific groups and institutions. In social science there is an arbitrariness to the definition of geographical scale that in practice often conforms to the administrative divisions used by governments (municipalities and administrative regions are local, groups of administrative regions are regional, etc.) rather than to any coherent theoretical logic about the scales inherent in the nature of things. One scale, however, makes sense only in relation to others. Within this constraint, geographical scale is socially constructed rather than ontologically given.[3]

Finally, geographical scale provides an organizational framework for human perception and action.[4] For example, for many states in Western Europe immediately after World War II there was wide agreement among most commentators that the nation-state territory defined the geographical scale at which both political identity and political action operated. National industrial-economic organization, welfare states, and national cultures were seen as mutually reinforcing. But with globalization, as the scale at which the means of material production operates has shifted from the national to the supranational (e.g., Europe) and global, the spatial dimensions of effective action have also been redefined. However, the mass of people still remain locked into everyday routines and outlooks and have access to institutional opportunities that continue to produce much more limited perceptual horizons than may be appropriate to the new order.[5] As a result, there are disputes over the geographical scale at which political action can and should best be concentrated.

Of course, whether the postwar political-geographical consensus was ever so total as was often claimed is open to doubt. Certainly, all political parties and most social movements oriented themselves to the national-state territory with a single-mindedness that became less apparent in the 1990s. But even during that period (about 1948–76) there were all sorts of regional and local anomalies involving appeals to local or municipal identities and interests as much as class or other social-sectoral differences that contradicted the image of pervasive nationalization (e.g., the Democratic South in the United States, the northern bias in support for the Labour Party in Britain, the white, or Christian Democrat, and red, or Communist, zones in Italy).[6] Likewise, the meaning and extent of globalization and how to react to it remain a matter of contention among parties and movements. For example, the disputes in the United States over NAFTA and United States–Japan trade not only divide labor from capital but also divide regions from one another and split political parties internally. The geographical scale at which to focus political action—state versus federal, municipal or local versus coordinating internationally—therefore becomes the explicit subject of political dispute.

In a period of dramatic political and economic change, political actors can be expected to offer new and perhaps competing visions of the relevant geographical scales at which politics should best be organized. Much of the United States Republican Party's "Contract with America," on which the party campaigned in the 1994 congressional elections, concerned reducing the scope and reach of the federal government and reviving the powers of state and municipal governments. In Britain, the one country in Western Europe where local government was much diminished in autonomy and activity in the 1980s, there are now calls from the Labour and Liberal Democratic Parties to establish a tier of regional governments and to revive local government more generally. At the same time, the main crisis of the British Conservative Party involves internal controversy over the extent to which British national government should be subject to the authority of the institutions of the European Union.

Of course the intensity of dispute over the allocation of authority to and representation of different geographical levels of government varies widely. At one end of the continuum are fairly settled unitary and federal arrangements (as in Sweden and Germany), while at the other end are shattered states (such as the former Yugoslavia, the former Soviet Union, the former Czechoslovakia). Scattered in between are such cases as Canada, Italy, the United States, Britain, and France, ranked from greatest to least in intensity of controversy. Italy is a case of a heavily centralized state that has recently undergone a dramatic breakdown of its old system of managing severe geographical cleavages, particularly the North/South division, and the rise of contending visions among new political parties of how "Italy" can be reconstructed.

WRITING THE SCRIPTS OF GEOGRAPHICAL SCALE

The previous section can serve as the basis for a general argument about the connection between geographical scale and contemporary politics. The mix of geographical scales at which political action is directed and takes place at any time is the outcome of the decisions and behavior of three sets of actors:

1. Businesses and governments allocating and reallocating investments in infrastructure, human capital, factories, technology, and labor. The net effect of these activities is a shift in the spatial division of labor from one form (say, regional clustering) to another (say, localized concentrations). Patterns of local interests and seemingly permanent geographical clusters of political affiliation are likely to be disrupted by shifts in spatial divisions of labor.

2. Political movements producing in their manifestos and other rhetorical pronouncements various claims about region, locality, and nation as well as about social class, ethnic, and gender divisions. These generate different appeals in different places and can tie political movements to particular representations of scale.

3. Populations constrained by the spatial limits they set on their political horizons as they pursue their everyday interests and ideologies. Resources, available political movements, localized territorial representation within most systems of government, and political imagination limited by everyday experience all conspire to set the geographical scope of much mass politics linking populations to political parties.

Political parties are key actors in the politics of scale from which emanate the dominant geographical scales of political rhetoric and organization. Parties provide one important organizational link between individual citizens and collective action. They also articulate the political goals around which populations are mobilized. But the leaders of political parties must justify their rhetorical claims to their constituencies while also remaining available for negotiation with their political opponents, particularly in political systems where governments are usually created from coalitions of parties.[7] This cross-pressure can be expected to draw parties toward a national or common norm, at least in the long run, if they wish to gain political office within existing institutions.

Working against a simple binary vision of geographical scale (national versus local, for example), however, are political-economic trends, the history of national political attachments, and the growth of new social movements that frame politics in other than national terms (e.g., antiwar groups, feminist groups, ecology groups). These set the conditions for alternative conceptions of the best mix of geographical scales within party rhetoric and organization. First, in contemporary Western Europe and North America the whole process of economic development seems to have become progressively more focused at the regional and local scales. As David Harvey has pointed out, the increased connectedness of communication networks has had the effect of magnifying the significance of what local spaces contain.[8] The new flexibility of businesses encourages the exploitation of relatively small differences between localities and regions to great effect. In some economic sectors the clustering of firms within specialized industrial districts has also become a successful form of competition in emerging global markets. Regions without this kind of development must continue to rely on national governments for stimulative policies. However, national governments appear to have less commanding influence across a range of policy areas and have abandoned much of the influence they could still have for market-biased policy decisions.[9] In this context, set in motion in part by the emergence of such institutional innovations as the supranational European Union and in part by the globalization of competition in many economic sectors, the role of regional and local tiers of government in economic regulation takes on greater importance for political parties.[10] Not surprisingly, creating regional governments and devolving powers to lower-tier governments have become important topics of political debate.

Second, from their beginnings modern states have contained a diversity of social groups within their boundaries. Often they are concentrated geographically, in particular regions or urban districts. Creating a sense of national identity at the level of the state has entailed either eliminating this diversity or superseding it. In the social science literature the term ethnicity has come to signify the organization of cultural diversity within states. Ethnic groups, whether of ancient residents or recent immigrants, are not simply primordial groupings. They are differentiated and integrated through such mechanisms as a cultural division of labor, political favoritism, and bureaucratic recruitment. In recent years, conflicts between ethnic groups have increased in number and intensity.[11]

Among the possible causes for this explosion of intergroup conflict, four have acquired most acceptance among commentators. In particular instances one or more may be at work. One is increased income polarization between groups and regions, leading to a sense of relative deprivation among the poorer and resentment by the richer of subsidies paid to the poorer. A second is the demise of the strong central governments associated with state socialism and communist ideology, which has had the effect not only of stimulating ethnic conflict in Eastern Europe and the former Soviet Union but of discrediting central government per se by associating it everywhere with the failure of state socialism and the intellectual exhaustion of communism.

A third cause is the rejection of state bureaucracy and the increased intrusiveness of the state into private life. Ethnic and local identity can be the basis for collective action against the law enforcement, taxation, and other regulatory activities of existing states. This is a particularly important element of the revival of interest in federalist forms of government in countries both with (e.g., the United States) and without (e.g., Italy) federal constitutions. Finally, the increased flows of immigrants from distant parts and the emergence of supranational institutions (the EU) and compacts (NAFTA) have stimulated the xenophobia of long-resident ethnic groups and revived "great nation" nationalism among dominant groups. Politics in Western Europe and North America has been rocked by the growing challenge from populist movements appealing to either local identities or a renewal of national-state identities.

Third, throughout Western Europe and North America political parties have also come under increasing influence from social movements of one kind or another that have grown in response to the perception of problems not addressed adequately through existing institutional channels.[12] The proliferation of movements devoted to single issues since the 1960s has posed a major dilemma for both the ideologically defined and the catchall political parties that continue to dominate national electoral politics. How can they take positions on particular issues (abortion, tax limitation, immigration control, environmental protection, affirmative action, human rights abroad, etc.) that might garner new support without alienating traditional constituencies? When social movements acquire large constituencies, they both threaten parties and attract them with the prospect of mobilized activists and voters whose energies and commitments can be captured for the interests of one party or another. Often these movements address problems relating to the physical environment, women's issues, human rights, and war that transcend the boundaries of particular states. Just as frequently, new social movements are organized so as to avoid easy co-optation into the routines of national-state institutions. They do this by emphasizing local initiatives and loose confederal arrangements among activists rather than rigid national hierarchies. To capture social movement activists and supporters, political parties must concern themselves with issues that are not always easily squeezed into a singularly national context. As yet, however, parties provide an important part of the opportunity structure for political action that is largely still available for social movements only at the national scale. To apply pressure at an international scale (such as Europe), social movements often have recourse to the national resources (such as parties and national governments) that are more readily at hand.[13]

WRITING ITALY IN THE 1990S

Since 1970 Italy has experienced each of these trends, perhaps even more so than most other electoral democracies in Western Europe and North America. The persistence of specialized industrial districts, particularly in central and northeastern Italy, allowed for a ready adaptation to the new world economy favoring local adaptability and encouraged the demand for enhanced powers for regional-level government.[14] At the same time, however, the heavy industries of the Italian Northwest and South have experienced crisis and dramatic restructuring.[15] One effect was to divide labor as a political force by reducing the importance of large unionized workforces and elevating local wage bargaining at the expense of national.[16] The fiscal problems of the Italian state—based in large part on tax evasion by small businesses, the crisis of state-owned (mainly heavy) industries (in 1994 about 40 percent of the Italian economy was still state owned), and the use of subsidies and welfare programs (particularly in the South) to reward supporters of the long-dominant parties of government, the Christian Democrats and Socialists—have led to the near collapse of many government services and the subsequent rise of an ideology of economic liberalism critical of state economic activities.[17] The expansion of regional government after 1970 introduced the major opposition party, the Communists, to administrative power in its strongholds in central Italy and encouraged the devolution of many government functions, if initially without revenue-raising capability.[18]

To outsiders Italy often looks culturally homogeneous. Yet internal cultural-geographical divisions have long been of major significance and have undermined the achievement of a widely shared national identity equivalent to that of, say, the Germans or the English.[19] The best-known division is that between North and South, which is often put down to the different traditions of political participation in a North with a history of active citizenship and a South with a history of political clientelism (see chapter 4). Whatever the historical reality, the division of North and South has become an increasingly important theme in Italian politics, if only because a new political party, the Northern League, has used it to take issue with government policies seen as favoring the South and discriminating against the (Far) North. Much of the League's success, however, has lain in its leaders' ability to play off Rome, the capital of a "corrupt" national politics, against the virtuous character of small town life in the northern regions of Lombardy and the Veneto. In this vision, the agents of corruption are the southern-born employees of the state bureaucracy and foreign immigrants threatening the cultural identity of northerners.[20]

Economic and cultural differences overlap in Italy to reinforce the geographical definition of interests and identities.[21] Contrasting interests and distinctive opinions cumulate geographically to overwhelm sectoral differences, such as those of social class defined in national terms. Parties therefore must aggregate diverse geographical constituencies to achieve nationwide success by appealing to particularistic interests and using appeals that conform to local traditions and identities. Not surprisingly, this has proved exceedingly difficult. For example, the Communist Party, with a strong base in red central Italy, always had difficulty appealing to the heavily Catholic voters of the white Northeast, who shared many of the social class characteristics of staunch Communist voters in Emilia-Romagna or Tuscany. The party had to adapt itself to local social rules when it tried to expand in the South.[22] Recent political-economic and cultural trends therefore have only exacerbated already significant geographical divisions.

Beginning in the late 1960s, Italy also acquired the issue- group politics characteristic of other Western European countries and the United States. Student, worker, and women's groups were the first to emerge outside the established party system.[23] Many of these had an autonomous orientation: they looked to change society rather than the state. To do so they advocated local organizing and focused on specific issues, usually involving group solidarity against established institutional forms such as unions, state bureaucracies, and large firms. Some became violent, others faded. In the 1970s and 1980s feminist and environmental groups in particular became more active both generally and in relation to specific national referendum campaigns on positions they sponsored or opposed. Parties recruited from those mobilized by the new movements.[24] The dilemma was that this sometimes involved sacrificing established constituencies or espousing contradictory positions. For example, in supporting national restrictions on hunting to satisfy a segment of the environmental lobby they had recruited, the Communists had to abandon a regional peasant constituency (in Tuscany) committed to hunting (see chapter 6). Likewise, in supporting greater devolution of power to the regions, a party (such as the Communists) could find itself in difficulty when arguing in favor of a national standard for wage increases.

In the early 1990s the unique party-mediated political economy of Italy disintegrated. This was a system whereby various sectoral and geographical groups had been integrated into the national economy largely through the use of state resources mediated by the parties, including the opposition Communists by the 1970s. Stefano Guzzini calls this a "dualistic clientelistic system" because of its major geographical characteristic: "In an implicit contract, an externally oriented economic sector (in the North), and a domestically oriented sector, increasingly public and service oriented (mainly in the South) were accommodated. Clientelism managed domestic consent in a segmented society and buffered the effects of the necessary opening to the European and wider international system."[25]

This party-state system, or oligarchy of parties allied to networks of particularistic interests, had its roots in the permanent exclusion of the Communists from national government. The Christian Democrats, the dominant party of government from the late 1940s until 1992, could rule only in coalition with other parties. Permanence in office and the need to reward partners led to a systematic spoils system in which the state served as a source of favors to allies. With the growth of opinion voting and issue group politics in the 1960s (as opposed to the strong politics of identity that the Christian Democrats and the Communists initially enjoyed in the 1950s), the parties built their success on particularistic and localistic links.[26] Factions (*correnti*) within the main parties (particularly the Christian Democrats) served to integrate these fragmented interests into electoral support for the party as a whole.[27] In the 1970s the Communists, hitherto excluded from the system, also began to participate, as a result of their historic compromise with the DC and, if to nothing like the same extent, with the Christian Democrats and Socialists. But by gaining a share of the loot (for example, "their" television channel, RAI-3) and adopting a conciliatory attitude toward clientelism, the Communist Party became a consociational partner in the system rather than an opponent.[28]

Parties not only divided the spoils vertically, therefore, they also shared them horizontally (geographically). Different parties and factions of parties had dominant roles in mediating between Rome and the various regions and localities where they were most strongly embedded. This is how the country was drawn together in the presence of strong geographical cleavages and the absence of a strong national identity.

In this system, politicians succeeded insofar as they could mediate particularistic interests and generate financing for the party. Firms and parties rewarded one another in an organized and increasingly formalized cartel of covert political alliances, state contracts, and bribery. Many voters also participated by exchanging votes for (particularly in the South) personal assistance from the state (in the form of pensions and jobs) and (particularly in the North) the lack of enforcement of tax laws.[29] In the South the diversification of organized crime into a wide range of activities, especially building construction, allowed it to become a major provider of jobs and thus a source of guaranteed votes for those parties that rewarded Mafia enterprises with government contracts. This system as a whole required the critical services of the businessman-politician, loyal to the party but able to exploit networks of ties with private business by awarding personal favors.[30] Perhaps the two best examples of businessmen-politicians are Giulio Andreotti, leading Christian Democrat and seven times prime minister, and Bettino Craxi, Socialist leader and former prime minister.

The party-state system, evolving out of the particular Italian situation of blocked alternation between the two largest parties, the Christian Democrats and the Communists, is only an extreme version, however, of the intimate relationship between parties and government that has grown up in most electoral democracies. Strong parties, a proportional electoral system, and the consociational sharing of government resources combine in many cases to produce a pattern not unlike Italy's.[31] Exceptional to Italy were the extent of corruption, the involvement of organized crime, and the vast resources available to the parties because of the massive presence of the state in the economy.

Some commentators attributed the collapse of the Italian system to the end of the Cold War, whose bipolar division ran through Italian politics and served to polarize electoral politics and exclude the Communists from national government. There is certainly more to it than this. Guzzini shows that not only the main parties but also the other main interest groups involved in the system had reached an impasse with one another by the mid-1980s, some years before the destruction of the Berlin Wall. In particular, as clientelistic logic became more and more central to political consent through exchanges of votes for resources or favors, "the more it lost legitimacy, the more it needed to resort to covert exchanges, which in turn undermined legitimacy, and so on."[32] Of particular importance, as the national budget deficit grew ever greater, in large part because expenditures increased much faster than revenues under the dualistic-clientelistic system, governments came under pressure from both the European Union and businesses trading internationally to raise revenues and lower spending. This reduced the value of the system to many of its erstwhile beneficiaries and called into question the bargain struck between the parties and Italian society. Finally, the increased corruption of the regime, as it came to rely more on illegal transactions and links with organized crime, produced a break in the contract between rulers and ruled that gave rise to the criminal investigation of leading politicians and businessmen beginning in 1992 and the subsequent withdrawal of popular support for the main parties of government.[33] The boldness and ruthlessness of the "new" Mafia in the 1980s also drew attention to a negative feature of the system: the failure of leading government politicians to deal with a challenge to state authority that put in question the legitimacy of the system they had constructed.[34] A relatively new and explicitly anti-system party, the Northern League, was an important agent in dramatizing the corruption of the existing system and associating it with the "southernization" (spreading of clientelistic politics) of Italy as a whole. Mafia and tax themes were combined in one League campaign slogan in 1992: "Mafia from the South, money from the North."[35]

In a politically unstable situation such as Italy in 1994, contention over how to remake the political system broke into the open. The new parties that emerged from the wreckage of the old party system had to embark on defining themselves in relation to the new Italian reality in which the old mechanisms for national integration had largely broken down.[36] The rest of this chapter explores the ways the main political parties in 1994–95 Italy have undertaken to reconstruct a new Italy.

THE DRAMATURGY OF HORIZONS OF THE NEW ITALIAN PARTIES

Between 1992 and 1994, the old regime of parties that had dominated Italy after 1947 collapsed. A very good account of the details of the disintegration of the old order and the emergence of the disordered situation in the mid-1990s has been provided by Mark Gilbert.[37] During the old regime the main parties all campaigned nationally, but each tended to have different macroregional bases where their support was concentrated and to which they were tied through ancillary organizations and the networks of particular interests discussed previously. The Christian Democrats were especially strong in the Northeast (the white zone) and the South. The Communists were strongest in central Italy. Only during 1963–76 did the two largest parties, the Christian Democrats and the Communists, achieve significant nationalization in their levels of popular support (chapters 5 and 6). The other parties either remained bottled up in particular regions (the neo-Fascist MSI in the urban South) or switched regional bases in terms of their highest levels of support (the socialist PSI moved south from its original northwestern base). The smaller parties, largely at the center of the political spectrum, were (except for the Republicans) largely clientelistic and mainly reliant on local notables for their electoral success.

The 1994 national election presented the first robust information about how the new parties were proposing to replace the disgraced old system. A brief description of the election and its outcome sets the scene for discussion of how the main new parties presented their options for reconstructing Italian politics and of the critical role played by considerations of geographical scale.

The 1994 National Election

At the 27 March 1994 national election under a new party regime and electoral system, a totally new electoral map emerged. The major parties were the Democratic Party of the Left (PDS) and Refounded Communism (RC) (coming from the old Communist Party [PCI]), the National Alliance (AN) (an expanded "conservative" version of the old MSI), the Northern League (an alliance of northern leagues founded in 1991), and Forza Italia (Go Italy!), a brand new party founded in January 1994 by Silvio Berlusconi, media mogul and owner of the AC Milan soccer team. A new electoral system was in operation that replaced the previous proportional representation: 75 percent of the seats were now from single-member majority vote districts, and 25 percent were elected proportionally. Voters cast two votes, one for their single-district member and the other for a party list from which the proportional seats were allocated. The idea was to encourage preelection compacts between parties rather than postelection coalitions that had not received popular endorsement.[38]

By brilliant maneuvering Berlusconi negotiated two preelectoral pacts, one with the Northern League and the other with the National Alliance, creating an affiliation that reduced electoral competition on the right in the North and in the South, that allowed the League and the MSI core of the National Alliance to pretend they were not in alliance with one another, and that presented a common face (that of Berlusconi) to a Progressive alliance organized around the PDS. A centrist alliance around the Popular Party provided the third (and minor) of the poles around which most of the parties organized themselves for the majoritarian component of the election.

The final result was that the right-wing alliances won an overall majority of seats in the Chamber of Deputies and close to a majority in the Senate. The distribution of votes for the party lists in the proportional part of the election (Chamber of Deputies) by regional constituencies gives a good idea of the spectacularly heterogeneous political geography of the new electoral regime (see fig. 9.1 and table 9.1). There seems to have been very little split-ticket voting—votes for one alliance followed by votes for a party not in that alliance—so one can assume a high degree of parallelism between the two parts of the election.[39]

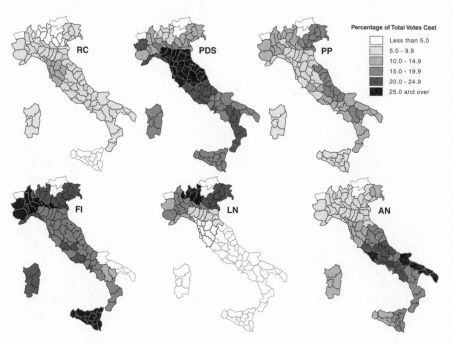

Figure 9.1   Percentage of the vote cast for the six parties in table 9.1 in the proportional part of the national election (Chamber of Deputies), 27 March 1994. Source: *Corriere della Sera,* 28 March 1994, 8–9.

Table 9.1   Percentage of Total Votes Cast for Major Parties on Party Lists (Proportional Component) in Regional Constituencies for the Italian Chamber of Deputies, 27 March 1994

Region	RC	PDS	PP	FI	LN	AN
Piedmont 1	5.9	20.0	10.2	25.8	11.9	9.0
Piedmont 2	5.8	13.0	13.8	27.4	19.8	7.5
Lombardy 1	5.6	14.9	8.3	28.2	17.4	6.4
Lombardy 2	4.0	9.0	13.2	23.6	28.3	5.1
Lombardy 3	6.5	18.4	13.6	26.7	18.7	5.9
Veneto 1	3.9	10.8	15.2	23.2	20.8	8.3
Veneto 2	5.2	14.1	16.2	24.3	22.9	6.9
Liguria	8.2	22.3	8.3	22.5	11.4	8.0
Friuli V.G.	6.0	12.0	15.6	24.3	22.9	14.2
Emilia-Romagna	6.6	36.6	8.3	16.5	6.4	9.0
Tuscany	10.1	33.7	8.3	16.4	2.2	10.9
Marche	8.7	28.9	17.2	19.7		15.7
Umbria	8.9	35.6	9.9	15.3		16.3
Abruzzo	7.4	20.2	15.4	17.7		20.8
Molise	5.5	17.5	15.8	15.4		19.1
Lazio 1	6.4	24.3	6.3	19.3		26.0
Lazio 2	7.3	20.4	14.6	24.2		23.2
Campania 1	8.2	23.3	6.7	20.2		19.1
Campania 2	5.5	15.7	13.0	19.8		21.6
Puglia	7.0	19.9	13.8	—[a]		26.5
Basilicata	7.5	23.2	19.6	11.6		17.0
Calabria	9.3	22.2	11.9	19.0		17.2
Sicily 1	—[b]	16.7	8.9	34.8		11.0
Sicily 2	—	16.2	7.8	32.4		16.7
Sardinia	5.9	19.3	9.2	21.8		12.1

SOURCE: *Corriere della Sera*, 28 March 1994, 8-9.

NOTE: RC = Rifondazione Comunista; PDS = Partito Democratico della Sinistra; PP = Partito Popolare; FI = Forza Italia; LN = Lega Nord (Northern League); AN = Alleanza Nazionale (National Alliance).

[a]Forza Italia did not present a proportional list in Puglia.

[b]RC presented a common list with the anti-Mafia Rete (Network) that polled, respectively, 12.2 and 10.7 in Sicily 1 and 2.

Only Forza Italia and the PDS, at the core of the alliances that restricted electoral choice in the majoritarian component of the election and thereby nationalized this element of representation, were truly nationwide political actors.[40] The electoral strength of the PDS (plus the RC) tended to weaken where Forza Italia was strong. Where one did relatively well, the other did relatively poorly. In the regions of central Italy the PDS and RC predominated, whereas in many northern regions and in the islands (Sardinia and Sicily) Forza Italia was the major party. The PDS did surprisingly well in parts of the South such as Basilicata and Calabria, hitherto strongholds of the Christian Democrats. The Northern League remained entirely confined to the North, particularly the Veneto and Lombardy. Forza Italia made considerable inroads into the League's 1992 support, pushing it into second or third place almost everywhere except in those areas where the League had been well established before 1990 (the small town and industrial districts of northern Italy). However, the majoritarian component of the electoral system helped the League gain far more seats than its share of the vote would have warranted in a true proportional representation system.[41] The AN was strongest in the South, but even there it experienced considerable variation in support, with much its strongest showing around Rome and in Puglia (where Forza Italia did not run candidates). The geographical pattern of support for the rump of the former Christian Democrats (the Popular Party) showed little in the way of a North-South dimension, perhaps reflecting the hold of notable politicians and the persistence of a solidly Catholic vote in some districts (e.g., Marche, Basilicata). A popular cartoonist's view of the April 1995 regional elections, with the leaders of the major parties associated with the regions where they predominated or struggled with one another, portrays the strong geographical interpretation that most commentators also gave to the results of the 1994 national election (fig. 9.2).

As a fresh system with largely new political parties competing with one another against the ghosts of the old regime (even though some, such as the PDS [since 2000, Democratici Sinistra or DS], RC, AN, and Popular Party, are repackaged versions of old ones), the ideological appeal of the parties (as opposed to organizational capacity or established pools of voters) appears to have been of particular importance in the outcome of the election.[42] This is not to say that older party attachments or clientelistic links were totally irrelevant. In central Italy affiliations with the old Communist Party, and by extension with its offspring the PDS and RC, died hard, and in Sicily the Mafia probably favored Berlusconi's Forza Italia, at any rate as the least of several evils from its very particular point of view. But the 1994 national election was much more overtly a wide-ranging ideological contest (as displayed in the content of the parties' rhetoric and their contrasting positions on a number of issues, including some allied with one another in single-member districts!) than any national election since that of 1948, the famous election in which voting decisions were widely interpreted by many Italians as involving a "civilizational" choice between a capitalist West and a communist East.

Each party in 1994 was proposing some sort of clean start for Italy after the debilitating corruption scandals exposed since 1992. Each claimed to represent a break with the *partitocrazia* or party-based system that much of Italy's economic and political life had been based on, even when the

Figure 9.2 Italy's new parties and Italy's regions: the cartoonist Giannelli's political cartography. The cartoon shows the leaders of five parties after the regional elections of 23 April 1995. Moving from North to South, Berlusconi (Forza Italia), with the microphone, is claiming victory, while straddling Bossi (the Northern League), also claiming victory, with Buttiglione, an ally from a small party of conservative former Christian Democrats, sitting on Berlusconi's shoulder; D'Alema (PDS) is claiming victory in central Italy and Fini (Alleanza Nazionale) is in the South breathing flames, the symbol of the old MSI, to the discomfort of D'Alema. Source: *Corriere della Sera,* 24 April 1995.

personnel seemed remarkably familiar.[43] But each also used appeals that structured "Italy" geographically in very different ways than their opponents did. In so doing, each actively worked with a logic that offered a distinctive conception of the geographical scales at which Italian politics is best conceptualized and should take place.

There is not scope in this chapter to cover all the new parties. I restrict attention to the major ones in terms of their shares of the total national vote: the PDS (later renamed DS), the Northern League, the National Alliance, and Forza Italia.

The PDS (DS)

The Democratic Party of the Left (Partito Democratico della Sinistra) or PDS was the main organizational heir to the PCI, having retained the bulk of the membership and the organizational resources of the older party. It is well organized throughout Italy and as of the 1994 had an important national media presence in its influence over RAI-3, the third state television channel. Since the institutionalizing of administrative regions throughout Italy in 1970, the PCI had been the dominant party in regional governments in Emilia-Romagna, Tuscany, and Umbria. The PDS inherited this role. Historically the PCI had a strong link to the largest trade union federation, the Italian General Confederation of Labor (CGIL), though this loosened in the 1970s and 1980s.[44] Nominally the party of the working class, the PCI had a strong appeal to other groups, especially in central Italy, so it is misleading to think of it as simply a working-class party (see chapter 6). However, the PDS (following the example of the PCI) represents those who have a strong commitment to the defense of welfare policies and government intervention to encourage industrial development. The regional governments it has controlled have also encouraged the development of the small firms and industrial districts that local economic development has counted on.[45]

As noted previously, the PDS was, with Forza Italia, one of only two truly nationwide parties in 1994 in terms of substantial levels of support throughout Italy. Its highest proportions of the vote, however, came in those regions of central Italy with which it has been historically associated since World War II. The red or socialist subculture of this region is usually invoked to explain the success of the PCI and now of the PDS (and RC). To David Kertzer, for example, writing about identification with the PCI in a neighborhood of Bologna in the 1970s, "allegiance to the Party is not generally perceived as calling for the subordination of allegiance to the family or friends. Indeed, membership in the Party is often identified with peer group and family solidarity; Party membership does not isolate the individual from his friends, it unites them with him."[46] But this subculture has long been in decline as the rural–small city lifestyles and dense networks of Communist-affiliated organizations it was based on have withered.[47] A final blow came with the fall of the Berlin Wall, the collapse of the Communist Party of the Soviet Union, and the disintegration of the Soviet Union itself.

One of the central myths of popular Communist ideology in central Italy (if not among Communist intellectuals) has been the identification of the Soviet Union as the "homeland of socialism." Not only had the PCI taken a social democratic path in response to changing international and national circumstances, not the least in its manifestation as the PDS after 1989, but the faithful now had to swallow the demise of the international connection to the Soviet Union and international socialism on which much of the party's official ideology had hung.[48] Notwithstanding efforts to define a new internationalism within the PCI in the 1980s (this took the form of a mild Third Worldism that never had concrete examples of what its successful employment entailed), the PDS has had to come to terms with the fact that to its core constituency internationalism had always meant privileging the Soviet connection. This was now gone.

At the same time, the history of socialism in central Italy is that of parties and movements, such as the cooperative movement, that always involved an appeal to local interests and local initiatives.[49] In part this was a rejection of the national state and its Jacobin ideals. But it was also a commitment to a municipal socialism that gave priority to local welfare over abstract entities such as the state or class. It was to this tradition that the PDS appealed in 1994, hoping to tap into the reserves of local collectivism so as to immunize its electorate against the siren songs of individualism and consumerism emanating from the Northern League and Forza Italia. It was probably Refounded Communism (Rifondazione Comunista) that was most successful in mobilizing the localistic vote, however, if only because it appealed to the rural population furious at the ecological turn of the PDS and its support for restrictions on hunting.[50]

The PDS did not endorse a pure localism, however. This would have played into the hands of the Northern League and the RC. Rather, it proposed a new regionalism, laying claim to the historical roots of autonomy, decentralization, and participation in Tuscany and other parts of central Italy but framing these in terms of a federal state for Italy as a whole. In this way the PDS could square the appeal to the local interests of its core constituency in central Italy as a return to a deep-seated (if hidden) past with the needs of voters elsewhere who have a less glorious past to celebrate but who can be convinced that in a post-Fordist era they too need strong regional economic regulation.[51] An abstract localism now provided an alternative throughout Italy to the national-corporatist construction of

Italy that the old Communist Party had come to share with elements of the Christian Democrats and the Socialists in the late 1970s. It was the local and administrative-regional scales (Tuscany, Emilia-Romagna, Basilicata, etc.) rather than the international or, certainly, the national that were at the center of PDS ideology. However, as Franco Ferraresi suggests, there was also a continuing attraction to the PDS and other progressive parties from those in the South and nationally among some groups, such as women, fearful that with the rise of the Northern League and the economic liberalism of Forza Italia state protection (pensions, unemployment benefits, nationwide wage rates, etc.) would be menaced.[52] How the PDS (now the Democratici Sinistra or DS) can square this with the new-found commitment to a municipalism that has its historical basis only in central Italy remains to be seen.

The Northern League

For the Northern League the construction of geographical scale has gone through a number of phases. Though obviously a party with an explicitly geographical agenda, over time it has shifted the basis for this agenda.[53] From 1983 to 1987, the various leagues (in particular the Lombard League and the Venetian League) appealed to ethnoregional differences (dialect, behavioral differences, etc.) to motivate a sense of regional territory (Lombardy, the Veneto, etc.) as the prime source of political identity. Unfortunately for the leagues, this proved difficult, particularly in Lombardy. Local identities proved to be much stronger than regional identities. As a result, in 1987–90 the rhetoric shifted away from regional cultural identity toward the negative economic impact on northern localities of an Italian state oriented to the problems of the South. This was paired with unrelenting hostility to southern migrants and foreign immigrants, who were seen as racially inferior and draining the assets of industrious northerners. The South was portrayed as a singular territory without geography, in which a culture of criminality and political clientelism preyed on an Italian state financed from the North. This stereotypical view of the South has remained of central importance in the ideology of the Northern League, even though the increased geographical differentiation within that macroregion in terms of economic development and political organization has become widely acknowledged among Italian social scientists, if less so among some foreign observers.[54]

From 1990 to 1992 a federal state based on three macroregions became the overriding subject of the newly integrated Northern League. All Italians were invited to partake of this. The argument was an economic one, as asserted in the League's program for the 1992 national election: "Competition today is no longer between states but between regions and macroregions."[55] The North was the geographical unit that had to look out for itself in global competition. The other macroregions had better look out for themselves if they were not to be left further behind the North in level of economic development.

After the 1992 election, however, there was a further shift in the construction of scale. This was the most dramatic of all. Now it was not southerners or the new global economy of regions but the southern-biased political economy of Italy as a whole that was accorded central importance. This fit neatly with the exposés coming from the corruption investigations of the established parties and their leaders that exploded in 1992 and 1993. Consequently the Northern League was positioning itself as a national party bringing to the rest of the country the values—entrepreneurship and hard work—that had produced success for the North. A macroregion now spoke to a nation through its political party. Speaking of his decision in December 1994 to remove the League's support from the national government formed between it, Forza Italia, and the National Alliance after the March 1994 election—over differences concerning antitrust, privatization, Berlusconi's business interests, and electoral reform—Bossi said publicly on 1 January 1995 that "the people understand. They understand that the League has saved democracy in Italy."[56] A national mission could hardly be more clearly stated.

The League has been the most dynamic of all of the parties in terms of its representations of scale. This has had some cost with respect to the ideological and organizational unanimity of the party. When the coalition government of the League, Forza Italia, and the National Alliance foundered in December 1994, there was a split in the League that saw Roberto Maroni, the highest-ranking *leghista* in the government (minister of the interior) and a group of supporters refusing to endorse Umberto Bossi's policy of leaving the government and supporting Berlusconi's call for early elections in the face of official League opposition to this.[57] This division undoubtedly owed something to Maroni's enjoyment of political office, a feature of the man apparent from his political biography.[58] Bossi, worried more than Maroni about maintaining the identity of the League separate from Forza Italia, was also encouraged to sever the connection with Berlusconi (ever more wounded by his interference in the judicial investigation into his own financial activities and those of his associates) by municipal election results in November and early December 1994 that showed the League doing better when allied with the Popular Party and the PDS in the two-stage French voting system used in that election than when teamed up with Forza Italia.[59]

But the division in the League also related to Maroni's suspicion of the latest (1992–94) metamorphosis of the League and his continuing commitment to the economic goals of the 1992 election campaign. He saw himself representing northern interests rather than northern values. In December 1994 Berlusconi appeared a better proponent of these interests than did Bossi and his opening to the left.[60] The main dilemma for the League is that it has limited electoral prospects, outside of the areas in the Deep or Far North where it gained strength in the 1980s, without beating back the challenge of Forza Italia, which has a national version of much of the League's political-economic message.[61] The Northern League's best electoral hope lies in a plurality electoral system with two "turns" (French system) in which Berlusconi has been removed from contention either through the collapse of Forza Italia or through limiting his control over television campaigning. Bossi's strategy between the 1994 election and his withdrawal from the government in December 1994 was precisely to weaken Berlusconi so as to gain a new electoral system and garner Berlusconi's voters in the metropolitan North. The Berlusconi government was replaced by a government of "technocrats" headed by Lamberto Dini, supported by the PDS, most League deputies, and many centrist representatives, to implement a number of fiscal reforms (particularly reform of Italy's generous pension system) and pave the way for new elections.

However, without electoral reform that does not require alliance with other parties, the Northern League is likely to find itself having to return to its original separatist program (see chapter 8). Bossi began heading in this direction in 1995, opposing alliances with other parties and setting up a parliament of the North in Mantua.[62] From 1996 until 2000 the League pursued a relentlessly separatist strategy focusing on the creation of a new northern Italian entity called Padania (see chapter 8). An alternative would be to go toward a federalism that orients the North toward Europe rather than Italy. This was the actual vision of the nineteenth-century Italian federal theorist Carlo Cattaneo, whose work has been appropriated by the League to justify its federalism. However, as journalist-editor Indro Montanelli has pointed out, Cattaneo's "dream was not national unity but a central European commonwealth guided by Austria, in which Lombardy and the Veneto took their place as a Land endowed with ample autonomy."[63] As of 2001 this vision was not yet on the League's horizon, the party having returned to the earlier federalist strategy of 1992–94.

The National Alliance

The National Alliance is the most obviously nationalist and statist of the new Italian parties. It is organized around the neo-Fascist MSI (Movimento Sociale Italiano), a party that had been excluded from sharing the spoils in the old system because of its historical associations, and many activists still venerate Mussolini and the strong Italy that they associate with the Fascist period in Italian history. Mussolini's speeches on compact disc were still hot items at AN rallies in Rome during the 1994 election campaign, as were T-shirts with Il Duce giving the Roman salute or showing maps of Italy with Istria and the Dalmatian coast of Croatia restored to Italian rule. Indeed, reviving territorial claims and restoring the reality of Fascism as an epoch in Italian history have been central to the ideology of the MSI. Sometimes portrayed as a protest party, the MSI had in fact built up a strong following among elements of the urban bourgeoisie in Rome, Naples, and other southern cities. It was never simply a party of the southern subproletariat, skinheads, or other urban toughs, even though they populated the ranks of its supporters.[64]

The AN, however, has positioned itself as a post-Fascist conservative party. Its telegenic leader, Gianfranco Fini, has used the British Conservative Party as a model. He wishes to restore a sense of communality or common purpose to Italians. He explicitly rejects the call for greater devolution to regional and local levels made by some of the other parties. In 1994 he publicly attacked the Northern League for its localism even while allied with it electorally. Within his party, however, there remains a Fascist current, resistant to its marginalization and attached to old Fascist themes such as the Italian territorial claim to the Istrian peninsula (split today between Slovenia and Croatia), the memory of Mussolini, and the demand that state pensions be given to the Italian veterans of the Republic of Salò, the puppet state established in northern Italy by Mussolini under German auspices after the surrender of the Italian government in 1943. Even though some of the most fervent elements left the AN in 1995, only attaching the rump of the AN to Forza Italia could create an authentic and totally non-Fascist Italian conservative party. At its 1995 Congress the party supported a much more authoritarian state for Italy: it was tough on crime, wanted immigrants sent back home, and favored abolishing abortion rights.[65] Some leaders of the French National Front talked admiringly of the MSI-AN as a model for themselves.[66] But in Italy the present AN sits uncomfortably on a political right whose innovative forces, the League and Forza Italia, stress economic liberalism rather than nationalism.

The AN is also trapped in expanding its constituency by its reliance on southern and urban voters and its popularity among civil servants in the central bureaucracy. It is not just nostalgia for the good old days of Fascism that attracts support (a much stronger sentiment in the South because Allied control in 1943–45 meant there was no civil war as in the North) but also the AN's commitment to an activist state and economic development projects in the South. In this respect the AN has inherited some of the southern support of the former Christian Democrats and Socialists. Yet to increase its support elsewhere it would need to temporize in its commitment to its core constituencies.[67] In parts of northern and central Italy there is also a continuing hostility to the normalization of the MSI as a respectable political party.[68] This finds its strongest representations in opposition to paying pensions to veterans of the Republic of Salò and in calls to resist the redefinition of the AN as the "post-Fascist" MSI. The idea of popular resistance to Fascism in northern and central Italy from 1943 to 1945 was a central element in postwar Communist propaganda about the possibilities of interparty and cross-class alliances. All those who had been anti-Fascist were potential allies after Fascism's demise. Though this myth of opposition has faded as the postwar generations have aged, suspicion of the MSI (and of its new manifestation the National Alliance) as a disreputable and untrustworthy political movement has not disappeared, particularly in central Italy.[69]

Forza Italia

The appeal of Silvio Berlusconi's Forza Italia in 1994 was overtly and immediately national. Founded only two months before the 1994 national election, this party was essentially an expansion of the national network of supporters' clubs for Berlusconi's AC Milan soccer team, one of the few club teams with scattered nationwide support, and the three major private television channels that Berlusconi also owned. Berlusconi was the prototypical postmodern politician: he was his party, using sound bites intermingled with television shows and product advertising to propose himself as the best manager for Italy. Recruiting neophyte politicians as well as established figures from the old parties (particularly the Christian Democrats and the Socialists, with whom he had long-standing business as well as political ties), Berlusconi tapped the only available instruments of national identification in Italy (the Catholic Church was off-limits for him): soccer and television.[70]

"Football [soccer] is the true civil religion in Italy; it alone reconciles the existence of strong local rivalries with a superior national institution, visible in the national team assembled for the World Cup."[71] As the national game, *calcio* (kick) may be the single vestige of the Fascist encouragement of physical and manly virtues that survives from a time when national pride was manifested more on the battlefield than on the playing field.[72] "Football serves as a common identity on any number of levels, an identity tied to familiarity and being 'at home.' If the nation is the homeland and the national team represents the nation, then the stadium they play in is 'home.'"[73] Berlusconi tapped this sentiment through his use of fan clubs and the language of soccer (including the name of his party, which is the cheer for the national team) and the anticipated success of the *azzurri* (the blues, the color of the shirts of the national team) in the 1994 World Cup in the United States.

The role of soccer can be overplayed. Major support for Forza Italia in March 1994 came from self-employed workers and housewives, although the young men to whom soccer has the greatest appeal also showed up as strong supporters.[74] But the success in attracting these other voters directs attention to Berlusconi's other major asset: television. Television has been the main medium in the creation of a national mass culture in Italy. Only with the penetration of television into every valley and hilltop town has a standard Italian become the everyday speech of most Italians. National standards of consumption and taste have been one very important by-product of the medium, particularly given the centrality of advertising to the economics of Italian television. More than television itself, it was the cultural model propagated by Berlusconi's three private channels that turned an audience into a constituency. Berlusconi used the example of himself, the self-made man, to sell the idea of hope in a new economic miracle that would follow from a government in which he was a central figure.[75] He was thus in a unique position to exploit both available instruments of nationwide influence.

Berlusconi's ownership of AC Milan, the premier club in Italy in the early 1990s, and his control of the three main private television networks gave him unique "advantages as a 'new' politician. Not only did he use the model of the national network of Milan supporters' clubs to organize his party, Berlusconi had an audience available in all those addicted to the diet of quiz shows, soap operas, and advertising his TV channels had provided them with over the previous ten years. His appeal to them as individual entrepreneurs or consumers fell on receptive ears."[76]

Berlusconi's main negative message was an old-fashioned anti-Communist one: vote for me or the Communists will get in. So much for the end of the Cold War. This was not simply a scare tactic. Berlusconi himself had reason to fear that left-wing success would lead to restrictions on his media and other business activities (in his firm Fininvest), many of which were in financial trouble. A multitude of other Italians had reason to fear a government that might crack down on tax evasion or redistribute wealth. Other than this negative appeal, Forza Italia adopted a political message redolent of Thatcherism in Britain or Reaganism in the United States. Business should be left to its own devices: a rising tide raises all ships, government is the enemy, and so on. Government austerity was packaged with personal consumption. The positive message was "cut back on the former and the latter will grow." This message was directed particularly to the small-scale businessmen and entrepreneurs of northern Italy with whom it could be expected to resonate. Forza Italia reached its maximum level of support in Lombardy. At the same time a more generic appeal to social order and promised consumption was packaged in a glamorous television presentation that explicitly drew on the celebrity and familiarity of the leader. Of course the small-business constituency in the North was one that the League had previously captured with some success. The alliance between Forza Italia and the League in March 1994 (and again in May 2001) was a product of each party's fear that the other would steal its potential voters.

The collapse of the coalition government in December 1994, when Bossi withdrew the Northern League from supporting the government in a series of no-confidence motions, was due to the essential conflict of vision between the League and Forza Italia on such issues as control over the media, Berlusconi's failure to divest himself of his business interests after becoming prime minister, and the lack of progress in decentralizing government from Rome. To Bossi and the League Berlusconi represented the centralization of power in national networks organized from above rather than from below. This was manifested by the few links that Forza Italia deputies and senators had with the constituencies by which they were elected in 1994, either in local interests or in place of residence.[77] Berlusconi also advocated a powerful presidency for Italy, based on a false if self-serving reading of the American political system as vesting enormous powers in the hands of the president, which was at odds with the League's decentralist vision. As a result of the collapse of the alliance with the League, Forza Italia was forced toward relying for support on its other partner, the National Alliance—a worrisome prospect for the more liberal members of Berlusconi's party. Polls taken at the time of the late 1994 municipal elections showed its remaining supporters as much more right or center-right in self-designation than previously, evidence for the erosion of the center in Italian politics and Forza Italia's role in bringing this about.[78]

Forza Italia's construction of scale is the most effectively nationalized among all of the main parties. Alone of all of the four parties, it combines a national-level rhetoric (national interest, national fiscal crisis, national celebrity, national consumption model) with a nationwide organizational capability (if with shallow territorial roots) and a wide geographical spread of support among a largely middle-class constituency throughout Italy. Its control over a key national symbol (soccer) in the run-up to the World Cup of 1994 and the ruthless exploitation of the airwaves that Berlusconi controlled gave it national advantages over the other parties in 1994. These had evaporated by 1996. What remains to be seen is how robust the nationalization of Forza Italia's electorate turns out to be.

On one side, Berlusconi has proved himself a cunning user of his vast media holdings to advertise his virtues as a leader and a wily exploiter of differences in the center-left governments that ruled Italy from 1996 to 2001. In particular, he totally outwitted Massimo D'Alema, the secretary of the PDS, in negotiations over a new electoral system.[79] In May 2001 he reaped a major victory at the polls, winning significant votes all over the country and simultaneously eclipsing his alliance partners in their regions of strength, the AN in the South and the League in the North, as well as the center-left opposition of the DS and La Margherita (an electoral party founded by Romano Prodi and based on the Partito Popolare) everywhere except in central Italy. On the other side, not only is Forza Italia really the invention of one man ("Forza Italia is me," says Berlusconi), it has no organization to speak of save the football clubs and the television channels.[80] Its essentially negative message is also a problem when there are two other right-wing parties with much clearer ideological (and scale) commitments available to potential voters. Forza Italia could disappear as fast as it was invented if Berlusconi is ever charged and found guilty of crimes (principally tax evasion) committed under the old regime or if the emperor is finally seen to have no ideological clothes save those that mask his personal business interests.

In many ways Berlusconi is a throwback to the politics of his erstwhile mentor Bettino Craxi rather than the augury of a new Italian politics. He is a businessman-politician par excellence. His own business holdings are in large part the result of government patronage in the early 1980s. But comparisons to Mussolini, such as appeared during the 2001 election campaign, are far-fetched. Even if Berlusconi's dalliance with some degree of fiscal decentralization since 1998 has not yet been put to governmental test, it is a step away from the discourse of centralized statehood long associated with the Italian right. The electoral reform of 1992 has also produced the possibility of both responsible opposition and alternation in national office between coalitions on the center-left and on the center-right. Italy seems to have moved beyond the *trasformismo* versus dictatorship alternation, therefore, but to quite what yet remains to be seen.

CONCLUSION

The four main political parties in the Italy of 1994 after the collapse of the old regime of parties each structured Italy in distinctive if not always incompatible ways through their constitution of geographical scale. None of them can be understood satisfactorily without understanding how they construct scale and how that affects their politics. Designating specific parties as self-evidently national (e.g., the PDS, now DS) or regional (the Northern League) misses precisely what must be explained: the way understandings of geography enter into the ideology, organization, and possible support bases of parties.

A period of political restructuring such as that under way in Italy in the 1990s provides an unusual opportunity for identifying what becomes less obvious when ordinary politics prevails, with widely shared presumptions about the optimal geographical horizons of political focus and organization. Although only one party, the Northern League, has called into question (on occasion) the inherited scale of the nation itself, all the new parties have had to struggle with how to replace the geographical compact the old system relied on. They have provided very different responses, all based to one degree or another on reactions to the League. The PDS (DS) has proposed a mix of municipalism and national welfarism. The AN offers a return to strong national government. Forza Italia sells a mix of national consumerism and strong personal leadership with some sympathy for the League's goal of fiscal decentralization. The League plans for a strong federalism with the "Republic of the North" as a prototype, after a detour through threatening secession. None of the parties makes much if anything of European unification as a political project, in relation either to a Europe of the regions or to a potential federation of states. The mix of scales is still very much defined by the boundaries of Italy. As Sidney Tarrow argues for social movements, so it is for Italy's new parties: "National social movements cannot easily escape from the structure of political opportunities and constraints of their respective nation-states."[81]

This case also illustrates a theoretical point. In a political context, geographical scale is not external to political activity, a dimension on which abstract forces and ideas are inscribed. It is internally related to party or movement imagination and competition. Each of the new Italian parties structures Italy in distinctive ways. This affects both the political messages they transmit and the constituencies they can attract. It also affects the possibility of creating national governments when potential coalition partners with particular national, local, or regional takes on the country (such as the League and Forza Italia in the North and Forza Italia and the National Alliance in the South) prove incompatible. But competing visions do not a system make. As yet, the conflict of geographical visions among the parties is such that nothing comparable in single spatial scope to the old system has yet emerged.

Political parties organize themselves and their messages through the ways they divide and order space. The boundaries they draw, tentative and contingent as they may be, define the geographical scales that channel and limit their political horizons. This was the case with the old Italian system before 1992, even though it produced a brokered compromise of visions around a dualistic national framework: the DC and its allies versus the PCI. The extraordinary character of the Italian situation since 1992 draws attention to the mundane spatiality basic to ordinary national politics. Party politics is inherently a spatialized activity. Parties always have to deal with the identities and interests of people in places, and they have a powerful role in designing the ways places are configured together or apart.

CHAPTER 10

Place and Understanding Italian Politics

Mapping politics can be done in a number of ways. Typically it is thought of either in purely national terms or with respect to largely fixed regional patterns within countries. I urge a break with these modes of representation. The conception of territoriality that lies behind both of them is deficient. It sees geographical space as inert, a surface on which active social processes are inscribed, rather than as being invariably implicated in those processes. But it is difficult to theorize abstractly about how geographical space does count in politics. Indeed, abstract political theorizing requires that space and time be held constant so as to better examine how differences in power arise between this and that group or how institutions of this or that type come into existence. Unfortunately, doing so makes what is found less relevant for the real world such theories are applied to. Inherent in the real world are significant geographical differences and historical changes in power and institutional forms that must be incorporated into any adequate account of their origins and persistence. It seems advisable to address time-space variation rather than to ignore it, depreciate it, or imperiously sweep it aside.

This book uses a frequently neglected or taken-for-granted feature of politics—its place-to-place differences—as a way of examining many features of Italian politics over the past 130 years, particularly those apparent since World War II. I take one case as a means of demonstrating the usefulness of the theoretical framework. A totally abstract argument for place would be something of a contradiction in terms. Only when applied to a specific empirical case does the theory come to life. Its success must be judged, then, by how well it helps us understand particular cases.

The approach to geography I adopt here openly questions the understandings of space and place typical among students of politics. I challenge two assumptions about place that have long guided political analysis. One, the idea that place, understood as national territory, is such an obvious feature of politics that it merits little or no critical scrutiny misses the fact that territoriality, as expressed in the concept of place rather than limited to the spatial dimensions of statehood, can provide a remarkably clear lens for examining a range of political issues—from voting to party organization and political identity. Another assumption, that territory is always tied to statehood, is equally questionable. The crucial issue is to weigh historical and recent changes in economic and political relations to see how these translate into shifts in the geographical organization of political power. Two inclinations in particular must be avoided. The first is the tendency to give states power over the places within their territories that they rarely have. The second is the tendency to see politics as invariably derivative of the workings of statehood, as if all politics simply devolves from states rather than having autonomous sources in society both within and across national boundaries.

This book suggests a largely new way of thinking about politics. Specifically, I question the adequacy of doing so in purely national-territorial terms. In its stead I suggest a multiscalar concept of place as offering greater insight into how politics works. People are place makers—they construct their lives out of the material that places provide. Grounded in the locales of everyday life, places are also parts of webs connecting different locales; people endow places with meaning and construct their identities in relation to them. Particular places are rarely if ever isolated, yet modernity has seen them increasingly organized in contiguous territorial blocs of national space. This could be thought of as the essential feature of modernity. Intensified globalization, however, suggests that places need not be singularly identified with national territorial spaces, now or in the past. Politics is structured through the places people make in their transactions with one another—local, regional, national, and wider.

This perspective offers an exit from the impasse between the currently dominant perspectives in political studies: the rational actor, political culture, and multicultural models of political action. As shown in chapter 2, elements of these models can be brought together under the rubric "active socialization" to produce a synthetic position that avoids many of the pitfalls of each taken separately. This understanding of socialization is quite different from the conventional one of individuals subjected to pressure from an external cultural environment. Here it means a constantly reworked sociability emanating from the concrete social networks that envelop us every day. As a result, people act as agents with identities and interests garnered from their interactions with groups they choose to associate with and from the political dispositions they develop in their daily lives. In this understanding the networks people are enmeshed in have a necessary territorial rootedness. Even as their transactions are more and more spatially extensive, people remain anchored in the familiar practices of physical places. In other words, it is by means of the social experiences and institutional opportunities of the places they inhabit that people construct the reasons and emotions that either encourage or inhibit particular identities and interests.

This book is organized around a set of analytic narratives that examine various facets of how to think about politics in terms of a theory that highlights the role of active socialization in place. The common subject matter is politics in modern Italy. Most chapters analyze a specific aspect of this politics but also tell a story about Italian national identity. They think about geographical differences in Italy and how they are typically represented, trends in the geographical structuring of national election results, the formation and dissolution of local political hegemonies in central Italy, the electoral replacement of the Christian Democrats by the Northern League in northern Italy during the collapse of the established party system between the late 1980s and early 1990s, the ways the Northern League has helped to reorganize popular self-understandings of geographical levels of political identity in northern Italy, and how the post-1992 political parties have been reorienting themselves geographically. In the end, the main contribution of the book must be judged in terms of the new light it casts on the long course of Italian politics, particularly since World War II.

Italian politics has long been understood in terms of what Italy *lacks* compared with more exemplary polities. It has lacked a widely accepted sense of common national identity. It has lacked alternation in national government office between opposing conservative and progressive political parties, veering between a personalized patronage politics (*trasformismo*) and dictatorship (under Fascism). It has lacked a history of responsible political opposition—an opposition political party with the possibility of acquiring national office. It has lacked a sense of public service separate from the pursuit of private interests in public office. It has lacked an effective tier of local government to match the degree of local attachments and identities. Finally, it has lacked political parties with a combination of national vision and nationwide electoral support.

What has been equally lacking, however, is an effective explanation of why Italian politics has exhibited *all* of these attributes. Of course other countries have their very own shortcomings of one sort or another—a lack of formal voice for minority political opinions (as in the United States), heavy-handed political centralization (as in France), a lack of alternation between political parties on left and right (as in Japan)—that have institutional and geographical correlates. Electoral systems that either dampen or encourage minority currents of opinion are particularly important. But a major claim of this book is that in Italy, and probably elsewhere, the process of national unification and the dynamics of place-based politics are of primary significance in accounting for all the particular features of national politics.

Four themes bind the chapters together. The first is that of *place and scale*. A fundamental tenet is that rather than being a metric space, place is a topological space in which diverse geographical scales intersect through local and external networks to produce the milieus of everyday life in which people invest meaning as a source of their political identity. Place in this conception is definitely not isolated community in the sense of old-fashioned community studies. Existing geographical variation in characteristics such as votes for parties and sense of political identity responds to changes in the interaction of networks that interweave the local and the extralocal to produce new variation over time.

The second theme of *historical contingency* addresses the importance of putting places in a historical frame of reference: the dynamic mapping of shifts in political identities and actions is approached in various ways. Political life is constituted out of the covariation of time and space in places, not the privileging of one at the expense of the other in exclusively national or regional accounts that fix space to allow for historical change or see chunks of space like national territories or regions as essentially unchanging historically. As the main alternative account, the idea of a linear model of history in which "backward" nations such as Italy and regions such as the Italian South are compared negatively to quintessential modern cases such as England or the United States is subjected to specific criticism. The success of the analytic narratives should be judged in terms of their ability to offer a more convincing understanding.

The third theme is that political action is not solely the result of the volition of autonomous individuals or the group memberships to which observers allocate them but that individuals never exist apart from the *historical-geographical contexts* of their lives. All chapters share in the view that adequate explanation is about discovering the mix of reasons and causes of political action in different places, not generalizing about persons independent of time and space. The attempt to create a social science independent of time-space variation just does not work; it ends up privileging ideal type individuals or groups that may well be the projection of certain cultural archetypes (usually that of their social scientist inventor) rather than representative in any way of real-world people engaged in social networks in which their agency is embedded.

Finally, an important theme running through the book is that there is evidence, from Italy at any rate, of an increasing disjuncture between the political spaces that are relevant to contemporary practical interests and identities and the state-based territories to which politics has been largely directed over the past several centuries (*the search for normative political space*). This is not to predict the imminent demise of the state. It is to argue that the either/or of state centrism is misleading. States have never monopolized politics in the way that many theorists have often claimed or presumed, and a range of political identities are potentially available other than singularly national ones. The contemporary rescaling of political identities suggests that instead of a rampant deterritorializing of states, recent globalization seems to prefigure the emergence of multiple identities that coexist rather than conflict with one another. It is time for political scholarship to catch up with the emerging world of politics—to abandon the obsession with state-based territory for a richer and potentially more rewarding concern with place.

NOTES

Chapter 1

1. For a useful attempt at integrating networks and territories into a single account of globalization see Peter Dicken et al., "Chains and Networks, Territories and Scales: Towards a Relational Framework for Analysing the Global Economy," *Global Networks* 1 (2001): 89–112.

2. For one interesting account of some features of the recent "eruption" of place-based social and political analysis in a range of fields, see Arif Dirlik, "Place-Based Imagination: Globalism and the Politics of Place," in *Places and Politics in an Age of Globalization,* ed. Roxann Prazniak and Arif Dirlik (Lanham, Md.: Rowman and Littlefield, 2001).

3. I have previously explored this approach in studies of American and Scottish politics in John Agnew, *Place and Politics: The Geographical Mediation of State and Society* (London: Allen and Unwin, 1987).

4. For an interesting discussion of how the territorial state has been given a particularly powerful foundational status in modern social science see John G. Ruggie, "Territoriality and Beyond: Problematizing Modernity in International Relations," *International Organization* 47 (1993): 139–74.

5. John Agnew, "Representing Space: Space, Scale and Culture in Social Science," in *Place/Culture/Representation,* ed. James Duncan and David Ley (London: Routledge, 1993).

6. John Agnew, "The Devaluation of Place in Social Science," in *The Power of Place: Bringing Together Sociological and Geographical Imaginations,* ed. John Agnew and James Duncan (London: Unwin Hyman, 1989); John Agnew, "The Territorial Trap: The Geographical Assumptions of International Relations Theory," *Review of International Political Economy,* 1 (1994): 53–80.

7. James C. Scott, *Seeing Like a State: How Certain Schemes to Improve the Human Condition Have Failed* (New Haven: Yale University Press, 1996).

8. See, for example, Immanuel Wallerstein, *Unthinking Social Science: The Limits of Nineteenth-Century Paradigms* (Cambridge, Mass.: Polity Press, 1991), and Terrence J. McDonald, *The Historic Turn in the Human Sciences* (Ann Arbor: University of Michigan Press, 1996).

9. Some feminist writing has much to offer in this regard, challenging the naturalness of fixed social-spatial boundaries and emphasizing historical shifts in geographical barriers to political participation in everyday life for women and other subordinated groups. See, for example, Kathleen M. Kirby, "Re: Mapping

Subjectivity: Cartographic Vision and the Limits of Politics," in *BodySpace: Desta-bilizing Geographies of Gender and Sexuality*, ed. Nancy Duncan (London: Rout-ledge, 1996).

10. Charles Taylor, *Sources of the Self* (Cambridge: Harvard University Press, 1989).

11. Charles Taylor, *Philosophical Arguments* (Cambridge: Harvard University Press, 1995), 230.

12. Agnew, *Place and Politics;* Margaret Somers, "Citizenship and the Public Sphere," *American Sociological Review* 58 (1993): 587–620.

13. For two very different ways of making this point see, for example, Yale H. Ferguson and Richard W. Mansbach, *Polities: Authorities, Identities and Change* (Columbia: University of South Carolina Press, 1996), and Warren Magnusson, *The Search for Political Space: Globalization, Social Movements, and the Urban Politi-cal Experience* (Toronto: University of Toronto Press, 1996).

Chapter 2

1. The extent to which nationalization of voting behavior came to be pre-sumed in Anglo-American political studies is detailed in John Agnew, *Place and Politics: The Geographical Mediation of State and Society* (London: Allen and Unwin, 1987), chap. 6.

2. Agnew, *Place and Politics*, chaps. 2 and 3.

3. Geographically sensitive discussions of globalization and its effects in-clude Aihwa Ong, *Flexible Citizenship: The Cultural Logics of Transnationality* (Durham, N.C.: Duke University Press, 1999), and Roxann Prazniak and Arif Dir-lik, eds., *Places and Politics in an Age of Globalization* (Lanham, Md.: Rowman and Littlefield, 2001).

4. On the first see, e.g., Carlo Trigilia, *Grandi partiti e piccole imprese: Comunisti e democristiani nelle regioni a economia diffusa* (Bologna: Il Mulino, 1986); on the second see, e.g., Carlo Tullio-Altan, *La nostra Italia: Arretratezza socioculturale, clientelismo, trasformismo e ribellismo dall'Unità ad oggi* (Milan: Feltrinelli, 1986). For more detail on these understandings and their commonalities see this book, chapters 4 and 6.

5. This is one of their similarities. I realize there is more to the differences be-tween these perspectives. In particular, they differ on a wide range of epistemo-logical, ontological, and methodological issues. As Rudra Sil argues, however, it is possible to "blunt the sharpness of the present debate by recognizing the *dif-ferent* kinds of insights each approach has to offer, and by considering the epis-temological foundations upon which some scholars can pursue what Eckstein has referred to as 'eclecticism of theoretical languages.'" See Rudra Sil, "The Foundations of Eclecticism: The Epistemological Status of Agency, Culture, and Structure in Social Theory," *Journal of Theoretical Politics* 12 (2000): 354.

6. I thus share the view of Pierre Bourdieu as expressed by Löic Wacquant that "accomplished theory, for the author of *Distinction*, takes after the chameleon more than the peacock: far from seeking to attract the eye to itself, it blends in with its empirical habitat; it borrows the colours, shades, and shapes of the con-crete object, located in time and place, onto which it seems merely to hang but which it in fact produces" (Löic Wacquant, "Durkheim and Bourdieu: The Com-mon Plinth and Its Cracks," in *Reading Bourdieu on Culture and Society*, ed. Bridget Fowler [Oxford: Blackwell, 2000], 109).

7. See, among others, Edward S. Casey, *The Fate of Place: A Philosophical History*

(Berkeley and Los Angeles: University of California Press, 1997); Yi-Fu Tuan, *Space and Place: The Perspective of Experience* (Minneapolis: University of Minnesota Press, 1977); Robert D. Sack, *Homo Geographicus: A Framework for Action, Awareness, and Moral Concern* (Baltimore: Johns Hopkins University Press, 1997); J. Nicholas Entrikin, *The Betweenness of Place: Towards a Geography of Modernity* (Baltimore: Johns Hopkins University Press, 1991); and Edward Soja, *Postmodern Geographies: The Reassertion of Space in Critical Social Theory* (London: Verso, 1989).

8. John Agnew, "Mapping Political Power beyond State Boundaries: Territory, Identity, and Movement in World Politics," *Millennium* 28 (1999): 499–521. See chapters 5 and 9 of this book for more detailed discussions of this understanding of scale and politics.

9. Herminio Martins, "Time and Theory in Sociology," in *Approaches to Sociology: An Introduction to Major Trends in British Sociology,* ed. John Rex (London: Routledge and Kegan Paul, 1974), 276–77. In Agnew, *Place and Politics,* 74, and John Agnew and Stuart Corbridge, *Mastering Space: Hegemony, Territory, and International Political Economy* (London: Routledge, 1995), 92, the first use of this phrase is mistakenly attributed to Anthony D. Smith, *Nationalism in the Twentieth Century* (London: Martin Robertson, 1979), 191.

10. Agnew, "Mapping Political Power beyond State Boundaries," and Philip Cerny, "Globalization and the Changing Logic of Collective Action," *International Organization* 49 (1995): 595–625.

11. Ilana F. Silber, "Space, Fields, Boundaries: The Rise of Spatial Metaphors in Contemporary Sociological Theory," *Social Research* 62 (1995): 323–55.

12. E.g., Pierre Bourdieu, "Social Space and Symbolic Power," *Sociological Theory* 7 (1989): 14–25; Harrison C. White, *Identity and Control: A Structural Theory of Social Action* (Princeton: Princeton University Press, 1992); Anthony Giddens, *The Constitution of Society: Outline of the Theory of Structuration* (Berkeley and Los Angeles: University of California Press, 1984).

13. Luciano Gallino, *Della ingovernabilità: La società italiana tra premoderno e neo-industriale* (Milan: Comunità, 1987); Arnaldo Bagnasco, *La costruzione sociale del mercato: Studi sullo sviluppo di piccola impresa in Italia* (Bologna: Il Mulino, 1988).

14. Robert D. Putnam, with Robert Leonardi and Raffaella Y. Nanetti, *Making Democracy Work: Civic Traditions in Modern Italy* (Princeton: Princeton University Press, 1993).

15. Ellis Goldberg, "Thinking about How Democracy Works," *Politics and Society* 24 (1996): 7–18.

16. Agnew, *Place and Politics,* chap. 3.

17. Bernard Lahire, "La variation des contextes en sciences sociales: Remarques épistémologiques," *Annales: Histoires, Sciences Sociales* 51 (1996): 381–407; Mustafa Emirbayer and Ann Mische, "What Is Agency?" *American Journal of Sociology* 103 (1998): 962–1023. In the narrower field of electoral studies see Helena Catt, *Voting Behaviour: A Radical Critique* (London: Pinter, 1996), 120–25, and Roberto Biorcio and Ilvo Diamanti, "La scelta di voto: Dal risultato all'attore sociale. Appunti per una rilettura del comportamento elettorale in Italia," *Quaderni dell'Osservatorio Elettorale* 19 (1987): 43–85.

18. This term is adapted from the usage in psychology that distinguishes explanation in terms of a configuration of traits from a simple aggregation of components. See, e.g., D. T. Lykken et al., "Emergenesis: Genetic Traits That May Not Run in Families," *American Psychologist* 47 (1992): 1565–77.

19. P. Corbetta and A. Parisi, "Smobilitazione partitica e astensionismo elettorale," *Polis* 8 (1994): 423–43.

20. For an example of all three, see Gary King, "Why Context Should Not Count," *Political Geography* 15 (1996): 159–64, and the reply in John Agnew, "Maps and Models in Political Studies: A Reply to Comments," *Political Geography* 15 (1996): 165–67.

21. John Agnew, "Mapping Politics: How Context Counts in Electoral Geography," *Political Geography* 15 (1996): 129–46.

22. The term "communities of fate" was coined in somewhat different usage by Arthur Stinchcombe, "Social Structures and Organizations," in *Handbook of Organizations,* ed. James G. March (New York: Rand McNally, 1965).

23. A brilliant case study of class formation within this frame of reference is provided by Edward C. Hansen, "The Great Bambi War: Tocquevillians versus Keynesians in an Upstate New York County," in *Articulating Hidden Histories: Exploring the Influence of Eric R. Wolf,* ed. Jane Schneider and Rayna Rapp (Berkeley and Los Angeles: University of California Press, 1995).

24. Nicholas J. Spykman, *The Social Theory of Georg Simmel* (New York: Russell and Russell, 1925), 147.

25. Lahire, "Variation des contextes en sciences sociales," 393–95. This, of course, is an important tenet of nonnaturalistic social theories such as those influenced by Wittgenstein, Husserl, and Habermas, surveyed in Richard J. Bernstein, *The Restructuring of Social and Political Theory* (Philadelphia: University of Pennsylvania Press, 1978). See the later section of this chapter on socialization. Chapters 5, 6, and 8 of this book have a particular emphasis on trying to show how the microgeography of everyday life relates to political outlooks and choices.

26. See, e.g., Eric R. Wolf, *Europe and the People without History* (Berkeley and Los Angeles: University of California Press, 1982); Doreen Massey, *Spatial Divisions of Labour* (London: Macmillan, 1984); Kevin R. Cox, ed., *Spaces of Globalization: Reasserting the Power of the Local* (New York: Guilford Press, 1997); and David Harvey, *The Condition of Postmodernity* (Oxford: Blackwell, 1989).

27. D. Gerstein, "To Unpack Micro and Macro: Link Small with Large and Part with Whole," in *The Micro-Macro Link,* ed. Jeffrey Alexander et al. (Berkeley and Los Angeles: University of California Press, 1987).

28. Fausto Anderlini, "Grandi metropoli, piccole province," in *L'urbanistica dell'aree metropolitane,* ed. Rino Rosini (Florence: Alinea, 1992).

29. See, e.g., Sidney Tarrow, Peter J. Katzenstein, and Luigi Graziano, eds., *Territorial Politics in Industrial Nations* (New York: Praeger, 1978).

30. On Britain, for example, see Jon Lawrence and Miles Taylor, eds., *Party, State and Society: Electoral Behaviour in Britain since 1820* (Brookfield, Vt.: Ashgate, 1997).

31. Celia Applegate, *A Nation of Provincials: The German Idea of "Heimat"* (Berkeley and Los Angeles: University of California Press, 1990); Jacques Lévy, *Europe: Une géographie* (Paris: Hachette, 1997), 53–79; Jost Hermand and James Steakley, eds., *"Heimat," Nation, Fatherland: The German Sense of Belonging* (New York: Peter Lang, 1996); Elizabeth Boa and Rachel Palfreyman, *"Heimat"—a German Dream: Regional Loyalties and National Identity in German Culture, 1890–1990* (Oxford: Oxford University Press, 2000). Also see chapters 3, 8, and 9 of this book. The idea of *Heimat,* however, has often, if not always, had a connotation of a mystical union with the land that goes in a different ontological and political direction from the sense of milieu associated with place.

32. Craig Calhoun, "The Problem of Identity in Collective Action," in *Macro-Micro Linkages in Sociology,* ed. Joan Huber (Thousand Oaks, Calif.: Sage, 1991), 51.

33. R. J. Johnston, *A Question of Place: Exploring the Practice of Human Geography* (Oxford: Blackwell, 1991), 102–33.

34. See, in particular, chapters 7, 8, and 9 of this book.

35. Chapters 5, 6, and 7 of this book are designed to address this issue.

36. Karl-Dieter Opp, "Contending Conceptions of the Theory of Rational Action," *Journal of Theoretical Politics* 11 (1999): 171–202.

37. Amartya K. Sen, "Rational Fools: A Critique of the Behavioral Foundations of Economic Theory," in *Beyond Self-Interest,* ed. Jane J. Mansbridge (Chicago: University of Chicago Press, 1990), 25–43.

38. Steven K. Vogel, "When Interests Are Not Preferences: The Cautionary Tale of Japanese Consumers," *Comparative Politics* 31 (1999): 187–207.

39. Milan Zafirovski, "What Is Really Rational Choice? Beyond the Utilitarian Concept of Rationality," *Current Sociology* 47 (1999): 47–113.

40. A writer such as Michael Oakeshott, *Rationalism in Politics and Other Essays* (London: Methuen, 1962), 109, would go much further, claiming that "an impulsive action, a 'spontaneous outburst,' activity in obedience to a custom or to a rule, and an action which is preceded by a long reflective process may, alike, be 'rational.'"

41. Debra Satz and John Ferejohn, "Rational Choice and Social Theory," *Journal of Philosophy* 91 (1994): 71–87.

42. One of the most persuasive accounts of why this need not be the case is in Iris Marion Young, *Inclusion and Democracy* (Oxford: Oxford University Press, 2000), chap. 3.

43. James Tully, *Strange Multiplicity: Constitutionalism in an Age of Diversity* (New York: Cambridge University Press, 1995), 66.

44. For powerful critiques of the way "identity" can be misleading as an analytical concept see C. Kukathas, "Liberalism and Multiculturalism: The Politics of Indifference," *Political Theory,* 26 (1998): 686–99, and Rogers Brubaker and Frederick Cooper, "Beyond 'Identity,'" *Theory and Society* 29 (2000): 1–47.

45. Kevin Hetherington and Rolland Munro, eds., *Ideas of Difference: Social Spaces and the Labour of Division* (Oxford: Blackwell, 1997). Also see Kevin Hetherington, *Expressions of Identity: Space, Performance, Politics* (London: Sage, 1998).

46. See, for example, William E. Connolly, "Speed, Concentric Cultures, and Cosmopolitanism," *Political Theory* 28 (2000): 596–618.

47. For example, Stephen Whitefield and Geoffrey Evans, "Political Culture versus Rational Choice: Explaining Responses to Transition in the Czech Republic and Slovakia," *British Journal of Political Science* 29 (1999): 129–55.

48. Filippo Sabetti, "Path Dependency and Civic Culture: Some Lessons from Italy about Interpreting Social Experiments," *Politics and Society* 24 (1996): 19–44.

49. Michael W. Foley and Bob Edwards, "Beyond Tocqueville: Civil Society and Social Capital in Comparative Perspective," *American Behavioral Scientist* 42 (1998): 5–20.

50. Pierre Bourdieu, *The Logic of Practice* (Stanford: Stanford University Press, 1990); James S. Coleman, "Social Capital in the Creation of Human Capital," *American Journal of Sociology* 93 (1988): 95–1120.

51. The best known is the work of Robert D. Putnam on Italy and the United States. See, for example, Putnam, *Making Democracy Work,* and Putnam, "The Strange Disappearance of Civic America," *American Prospect* 24 (1996): 34–48.

52. Michael Shapiro, "Bowling Blind: Post Liberal Civil Society and the Worlds of Neo-Tocquevillean Social Theory," *Theory and Event* 1 (1997): 2.

53. Theda Skocpol, "The Tocqueville Problem: Civic Engagement in American Democracy," *Social Science History* 21 (1997): 463.

54. Stephen Baron, John Field, and Tom Schuller, eds., *Social Capital: Critical Perspectives* (Oxford: Oxford University Press, 2000).

55. Nancy L. Rosenblum, *Membership and Morals: The Personal Uses of Pluralism in America* (Princeton: Princeton University Press, 1998).

56. See, e.g., Mark Bevir, "Foucault and Critique: Deploying Agency against Autonomy," *Political Theory* 27 (1999): 65–84.

57. This is close to the understanding of *structure* as a metaphor for the duality of cultural schemas and accumulation of resources in the reproduction and transformation of social life advocated by William H. Sewell Jr., "A Theory of Structure: Duality, Agency, and Transformation," *American Journal of Sociology* 98 (1992): 1–29.

58. Georg Simmel, *Sociologie et épistémologie* (1917; Paris: Presses Universitaires de France, 1981); Claire Bidart, "Sociabilités: Quelque variables," *Revue Française de Sociologie* 29 (1988): 621–48.

59. Eviatar Zerubavel, *The Fine Line: Making Distinctions in Everyday Life* (New York: Free Press, 1991), 15.

60. Zerubavel, *Fine Line,* 16.

61. E.g., William Mitchell, *City of Bits: Space, Place, and Infobahn* (Cambridge: MIT Press, 1995).

62. Even in the United States, according to Robert D. Putnam, *Bowling Alone: The Collapse and Revival of American Community* (New York: Simon and Schuster, 2000).

63. Boa and Palfreyman, *"Heimat"—a German Dream,* 205.

64. Joshua Meyrowitz, *No Sense of Place: The Impact of Electronic Media on Social Behavior* (New York: Oxford University Press, 1985); Marc Augé, *Non-places: Introduction to the Anthropology of Supermodernity* (London: Verso, 1995).

65. Eric R. Wolf, "Aspects of Group Relations in a Complex Society: Mexico," *American Anthropologist* 58 (1956): 1065–1078, made this point in his critique of the idea of community as a closed system.

66. Anthony Giddens, *The Consequences of Modernity* (Stanford: Stanford University Press, 1990).

67. Ulf Hannerz, *Transnational Connections: Culture, People, Places* (London: Routledge, 1996), 25–26. "In the meeting of the alien and the familiar," Hannerz maintains, "it is the familiar that wins out." A glass of cold milk, it seems, is the essence of familiarity to a Swede, even if produced by non-Swedish cows!

68. Charles Taylor, *Sources of the Self* (Cambridge: Harvard University Press, 1989).

69. Jane Schneider and Rayna Rapp, eds., *Articulating Hidden Histories: Exploring the Influence of Eric R. Wolf* (Berkeley and Los Angeles: University of California Press, 1995); Ann Swidler, "Culture in Action: Symbols and Strategies," *American Sociological Review* 51 (1986): 273–286.

70. Stephen Turner, *The Social Theory of Practices: Tradition, Tacit Knowledge, and Presuppositions* (Chicago: University of Chicago Press, 1994), 123.

Chapter 3

1. Benedict Anderson, *Imagined Communities: Reflections on the Origins and Spread of Nationalism* (London: Verso, 1983); Eric Hobsbawm and Terence

Ranger, eds., *The Invention of Tradition* (Cambridge: Cambridge University Press, 1983). The English case, however, challenges this modernist view, as detailed in Adrian Hastings, *The Construction of Nationhood: Ethnicity, Religion and Nationalism* (Cambridge: Cambridge University Press, 1997). But the fact that English nationalism goes back before the eighteenth century makes it more questionable as a model for understanding other European cases than if its experience paralleled theirs.

2. Raymond Williams, *The Country and the City* (New York: Oxford University Press, 1973).

3. See, for example, Pierre Nora, "Between Memory and History: Les Lieux de Mémoire," *Representations* 26 (1989): 7–25; Nuala Johnson, "Cast in Stone: Monuments, Geography, and Nationalism," *Environment and Planning D: Society and Space* 13 (1995): 51–65; and Ilaria Porciani, *La festa della nazione: Rappresentazione dello Stato e spazi sociali nell'Italia unita* (Bologna: Il Mulino, 1997).

4. But on the former see Michael Biggs, "Putting the State on the Map: Cartography, Territory, and European State Formation," *Comparative Studies in Society and History* 41 (1999): 374–405; on the latter see, for example, Malcolm Andrews, *Landscape Imagery and Urban Culture in Early Nineteenth Century England* (Cambridge: Cambridge University Press, 1992); Elizabeth K. Helsinger, *Rural Scenes and National Representation: Britain, 1815–1850* (Princeton: Princeton University Press, 1997); Mark Bassin, "Geopolitics in the *Historikerstreit:* The Strange Return of *Mitellage,*" in *"Heimat," Nation, Fatherland: The German Sense of Belonging,* ed. Jost Hermand and James Steakley (New York: Peter Lang, 1996), 187–228; and Maunu Häyrynen, "The Kaleidoscopic View: The Finnish National Landscape Imagery," *National Identities* 2 (2000): 5–19.

5. Nadia Urbinati, "From the Periphery of Modernity: Antonio Gramsci's Theory of Subordination and Hegemony," *Political Theory* 26 (1998): 370–91.

6. Brian J. Graham, "No Place of Mind: Contested Protestant Representations of Ulster," *Ecumene* 1 (1994): 258.

7. This is what social psychologist Michael Billig refers to memorably as "banal nationalism" with respect to all the little signs of nationhood that surround us every day, from the symbols on currency to flags, uniforms, and other reminders of "who we are." See Michael Billig, *Banal Nationalism* (London: Sage, 1995).

8. David Lowenthal, "British National Identity and the English Landscape," *Rural History* 2 (1991): 213.

9. Gillian Rose, "Place and Identity: A Sense of Place," in *A Place in the World? Place, Cultures and Globalization,* ed. Doreen Massey and Pat Jess (Oxford: Open University/Oxford University Press, 1994).

10. For example, Peter Bishop, *An Archetypal Constable: National Identity and the Geography of Nostalgia* (Cranbury, N.J.: Fairleigh Dickinson University Press, 1995).

11. Although England was certainly a "prototype" for nationalist movements elsewhere.

12. In general, see Stephen Daniels, *Fields of Vision: Landscape Imagery and National Identity in England and the United States* (Princeton: Princeton University Press, 1993); on the depredations of agribusiness see Andrew O'Hagan, "The End of British Farming," *London Review of Books,* 22 March 2001, 3–16.

13. See, for example, Martin Thom, "City, Region and Nation: Carlo Cattaneo and the Making of Italy," *Citizenship Studies* 3 (1999): 187–201.

14. Ian Baucom, *Out of Place: Englishness, Empire, and the Locations of Identity* (Princeton: Princeton University Press, 1999).

15. John R. Gillis, "Memory and Identity: The History of a Relationship," in *Commemorations: The Politics of National Identity,* ed. John R. Gillis (Princeton: Princeton University Press, 1994), 7.

16. Celia Applegate, *A Nation of Provincials: The German Idea of "Heimat"* (Berkeley and Los Angeles: University of California Press, 1990).

17. John Agnew, "Liminal Travellers: Hebrideans at Home and Away," *Scotlands* 3 (1996): 31–42.

18. Stefano Cavazza, *Piccole patrie: Feste popolari tra regione e nazione durante il fascismo* (Bologna: Il Mulino, 1997).

19. Daniele Conversi, "Reassessing Current Theories of Nationalism: Nationalism as Boundary Maintenance and Control," *Nationalism and Ethnic Politics* 1 (1995): 73–85.

20. Gillis, "Memory and Identity."

21. Richard Handler, "Is 'Identity' a Useful Cross-Cultural Concept?" in *Commemorations: The Politics of National Identity,* ed. John R. Gillis (Princeton: Princeton University Press, 1994).

22. Rogers Brubaker and Frederick Cooper, "Beyond 'Identity,'" *Theory and Society* 29 (2000): 1–47.

23. See, for example, Daniels, *Fields of Vision,* and Lowenthal, "British National Identity and the English Landscape."

24. Giorgio Chittolini, "Cities, 'City-States,' and Regional States in North-Central Italy," in *Cities and the Rise of New States in Europe, A.D.* 1000–1800, ed. Charles Tilly and Wim P. Blockmans (Boulder, Colo.: Westview Press, 1994), 28. Also see Stuart Woolf, *A History of Italy, 1700–1860: The Social Constraints of Political Change* (London: Routledge, 1979).

25. Chittolini, "Cities, 'City-States,' and Regional States in North-Central Italy," 40.

26. See this book, chapter 4.

27. Kenneth Churchill, *Italy and English Literature, 1764–1930* (Totowa, N.J.: Barnes and Noble, 1980); W. M. Johnston, *In Search of Italy: Foreign Writers in Northern Italy since 1800* (University Park: Penn State University Press, 1987).

28. Albert Boime, "The Macchiaioli and the Risorgimento," in *The Macchiaioli: Painters of Italian Life, 1850–1900,* ed. E. Tonelli and K. Hart (Los Angeles: Wight Art Gallery, UCLA, 1986), 38.

29. Boime, "Macchiaioli and the Risorgimento," 36.

30. Boime, "Macchiaioli and the Risorgimento," 34–36.

31. Telemaco Signorini, *Caricaturisti e caricaturati al Caffè Michelangiolo* (1893; Florence: Le Monnier, 1952).

32. Alessandro Manzoni, *I Promessi Sposi/The Betrothed,* trans. Bruce Penman (London: Penguin, 1972).

33. Bruce Penman, "Introduction," in *I Promessi Sposi/The Betrothed,* by Alessandro Manzoni, trans. Bruce Penman (London: Penguin, 1972), 11.

34. Massimo D'Azeglio, *Things I Remember,* trans. E. R. Vincent (1867; London: Oxford University Press, 1966), 164.

35. Signorini, *Caricaturisti e caricaturati al Caffè Michelangiolo,* 186–87.

36. Boime, "Macchiaioli and the Risorgimento," 70.

37. Albert Boime, *The Art of the Macchia and the Risorgimento: Representing Culture and Nationalism in Nineteenth-Century Italy* (Chicago: University of Chicago Press, 1994).

38. This was characteristic of the so-called Strapaese or ultracountryside Fas-

cists, who were particularly well established in Florence in the 1920s and 1930s. The polemical quality of Signorini's writing and the emphasis on making a complete break with the past to establish a truly Italian art can be seen, however, as a forerunner of Futurism and the modernist strand in Fascism, even though Futurism's enthusiasm for technology and speed contrasts markedly with the pastoral and everyday focus of the Macchiaioli painters. Turn-of-the-century Futurism was also a product of the industrialized urban North with powerful international connections that created a greater sense of the need to establish an Italian national art. See Caroline Tisdall and Angelo Bozzolla, *Futurism* (London: Thames and Hudson, 1977), 22–23.

39. Cited in P. Treves, *L'idea di Roma e la cultura italiana del secolo XIX* (Milan: Ricciardi, 1962), 78.

40. Alberto Caraccioli, *Roma capitale: Dal Risorgimento alla crisi dello stato liberale* (Rome: Rinascita, 1956), 16.

41. Massimo Birindelli, *Roma italiana: Come fare una capitale e disfare una città* (Rome: Savelli, 1978), 23.

42. M. Scattareggia, "Roma capitale: Arretratezza e modernizzazione (1870–1914)," *Storia Urbana* 42 (1988): 43.

43. Giovanni Belardelli, "La terza Roma," in *Miti e storia dell'Italia unita,* ed. Giovanni Belardelli et al. (Bologna: Il Mulino, 1999).

44. Bruno Tobia, "Urban Space and Monuments in the 'Nationalization of the Masses': The Italian case," in *Nationalism in Europe, 1815 to the Present: A Reader,* ed. Stuart J. Woolf (London: Routledge, 1996), 180.

45. John Agnew, *Rome* (New York: Wiley, 1995), chap. 3.

46. Bruno Tobia, *Una Patria per gli italiani: Spazi, itinerari, monumenti nell'Italia unita (1870–1900)* (Rome: Laterza, 1991).

47. Tobia, "Urban Space and Monuments in the 'Nationalization of the Masses,'" 182.

48. Denis Cosgrove and David Atkinson, "Embodied Identities: City, Nation and Empire at the Vittorio-Emmanuele II Monument in Rome," *Annals of the Association of American Geographers* 88 (1998): 28–49.

49. Cosgrove and Atkinson, "Embodied Identities." More generally, for a range of interpretations of Fascism's aesthetic manipulations, see Emilio Gentile, *The Sacralization of Politics in Fascist Italy* (Cambridge: Harvard University Press, 1996); Simonetta Falasca Zamponi, *Fascist Spectacle: The Aesthetics of Power in Mussolini's Italy* (Berkeley and Los Angeles: University of California Press, 1997); and Mabel Berezin, *Making the Fascist Self: The Political Culture of Interwar Italy* (Ithaca: Cornell University Press, 1997). For an incisive critique of this literature for taking the claims of the Fascist regime too much at face value see R. J. B. Bosworth, *"Per Necessità Famigliare:* Hypocrisy and Corruption in Fascist Italy," *European History Quarterly* 30 (2000): 357–87.

50. John Agnew, "The Impossible Capital: Monumental Rome under Liberal and Fascist Regimes, 1870–1943," *Geografiska Annaler B* 80 (1998): 229–40.

51. Agnew, *Rome,* chaps. 2, 3, and 4.

52. As against, perhaps, the France described in Fernand Braudel, *The Identity of France,* vol. 1, *History and Environment* (London: Collins, 1988).

53. Simon Schama, *Landscape and Memory* (London: HarperCollins, 1995), 263.

54. Enrico Castelnuovo and Carlo Ginzburg, "Centre and Periphery," in *History of Italian Art,* vol. 1 (Cambridge: Polity Press, 1994), 101. Parenthetically,

these authors also note (30) that "even today, it is easier to go by train from Turin to Dijon than from Grosseto to Urbino."

55. See, for example, Paola Filipucci, "Anthropological Perspectives on Culture in Italy," in *Italian Cultural Studies,* ed. David Forgacs and Robert Lumley (Oxford: Oxford University Press, 1996); Jeff Pratt, "Catholic Culture," in *Italian Cultural Studies,* ed. David Forgacs and Robert Lumley (Oxford: Oxford University Press, 1996); and Roberto Cartocci, *Fra Lega e Chiesa: L'Italia in cerca di integrazione* (Bologna: Il Mulino, 1994).

56. See, e.g., Carl Levi, ed., *Italian Regionalism: History, Identity and Politics* (Oxford: Berg, 1996).

57. John Agnew, "The Rhetoric of Regionalism: The Northern League in Italian Politics, 1983–1994," *Transactions of the Institute of British Geographers* 20 (1995): 156–72. See also this book, chapter 9.

58. Stefano Guzzini, "The 'Long Night of the First Republic': Years of Clientelistic Implosion in Italy," *Review of International Political Economy* 2 (1995): 27–61; see also this book, chapters 5, 7, and 9. Many of the practices of *partitocrazia,* such as awarding government contracts based on patronage rather then free bidding, persisted even as the parties that were its main anchors, the DC and the PSI, disappeared.

59. See, for example, Adrian Lyttelton, "Italy: The Triumph of TV," *New York Review of Books* 41 (11 August 1994): 25–29; Silvio Lanaro, *L'Italia nuova: Identità e sviluppo, 1861–1988* (Turin: Einaudi, 1989); Stefano Pivato, "Sport," in *Italy since 1945,* ed. Patrick McCarthy (Oxford: Oxford University Press, 2000); and Stephen Gundle, "Feminine Beauty, National Identity and Political Conflict in Postwar Italy, 1945–1954," *Contemporary European History* 8 (1999): 359–78.

60. Emilio Gentile, *La grande Italia: Ascesa e declino del mito della nazione nel ventesimo secolo* (Milan: Mondadori, 1997).

61. John Agnew, "La città nel contesto culturale e i valori ambientali," in *Natura e cultura nella città del futuro,* ed. Calogero Muscarà and Lelio Pagani (Bergamo: Consorzio del Parco dei Colli di Bergamo, 1988).

62. See chapter 4 of this book.

63. Angela Dalle Vacche, *The Body in the Mirror: Shapes of History in Italian Cinema* (Princeton: Princeton University Press, 1992). By way of example, the uncertain symbolism of the Italian national flag is emphasized in Fiorenza Tarozzi and Giorgio Vecchio, eds., *Gli italiani e il Tricolore: Patriottismo, identità nazionale e fratture sociali lungo due secoli di storia* (Bologna: Il Mulino, 1999).

64. Gregorio Penco, *Storia della Chiesa in Italia* (Milan: Jaca, 1977); David I. Kertzer, "Religion and Society, 1789–1892," in *Italy in the Nineteenth Century,* ed. John A. Davis (Oxford: Oxford University Press, 2000); Patrick McCarthy, "The Church in Post-war Italy," in *Italy since 1945,* ed. Patrick McCarthy (Oxford: Oxford University Press, 2000). A powerful argument for the pivotal role of religion in often encouraging but sometimes discouraging nationalism and national identities is made by Hastings, *Construction of Nationhood.*

65. Raimondo Strassoldo, "Globalism and Localism: Theoretical Reflections and Some Evidence," in *Globalization and Territorial Identities,* ed. Zdravko Mlinar (Brookfield, Vt.: Avebury, 1992).

66. Kirsten Hastrup, ed., *Other Histories* (London: Routledge, 1992); Warren Magnusson, *The Search for Political Space: Globalization, Social Movements, and the Urban Political Experience* (Toronto: University of Toronto Press, 1996); Neal Ascherson, "Reflections on International Space," *London Review of Books,* 24 May 2001, 7–11.

Chapter 4

1. Both in the weekly magazine *L'Espresso,* 15 December 1991, 20.
2. See, in particular, Johannes Fabian, *Time and the Other: How Anthropology Makes Its Object* (New York: Columbia University Press, 1983).
3. John Agnew, *Geopolitics: Re-visioning World Politics* (London: Routledge, 1998), chap. 3.
4. Arjun Appadurai, "Putting Hierarchy in Its Place," *Cultural Anthropology* 3 (1988): 36–49; Akhil Gupta and James Ferguson, "Beyond 'Culture': Space, Identity, and the Politics of Difference," *Cultural Anthropology* 7 (1992): 6–23.
5. Tim Mason, "Italy and Modernization: A Montage," *History Workshop* 25–26 (1988): 127–47.
6. Nicola Rossi and Gianni Tonioli, "Catching up or Falling Behind? Italy's Economic Growth, 1895–1947," *Economic History Review* 45 (1992): 537–63.
7. Paul Ginsborg, *Storia d'Italia dal dopoguerra a oggi, 1943–1988* (Turin: Einaudi, 1989), 1. Translated as *A History of Contemporary Italy, 1943–1988* (London: Penguin, 1990).
8. Domenico Settembrini, *Storia dell'idea antiborghese, 1860–1989* (Rome: Laterza, 1991).
9. Roberto Vivarelli, "L'anomalia italiana," *La Rivista dei Libri,* November 1991, 13–16.
10. Carlo Tullio-Altan, *La nostra Italia: Arretratezza socioculturale, clientelismo, trasformismo e ribellismo dall'Unità ad oggi* (Milan: Feltrinelli, 1986).
11. Luciano Gallino, *Della ingovernabilità: La società italiana tra premoderno e neo-industriale* (Milan: Comunità, 1987), 76.
12. Elisabetta Rasy, Interview with Alberto Asor Rosa, *Panorama,* 8 December 1985, 185–86.
13. Renato Curcio, Interview, *L'Espresso,* 18 January 1987, 28.
14. John Agnew, "'Better Thieves Than Reds'? The Nationalization Thesis and the Possibility of a Geography of Italian Politics," *Political Geography Quarterly* 7 (1988): 307–21, and this book, chapter 5.
15. Robert D. Putnam, with Robert Leonardi and Raffaella Y. Nanetti, *Making Democracy Work: Civic Traditions in Modern Italy* (Princeton: Princeton University Press, 1993). An excellent critique of Putnam's analysis, suggesting that an overbearing national state promising more than it could deliver has more to do with the difficulties of Italian politics than Putnam's idea of "path dependent" regional political cultures endlessly reproducing themselves, is provided in Filippo Sabetti, *The Search for Good Government: Understanding the Paradox of Italian Democracy* (Montreal: McGill-Queen's University Press, 2000).
16. Ginsborg, *Storia d'Italia dal dopoguerra a oggi,* 421, 418, 417.
17. Mason, "Italy and Modernization," 131.
18. Edward C. Banfield, *The Moral Basis of a Backward Society* (New York: Free Press, 1958).
19. Edward C. Banfield, *The Unheavenly City* (Boston: Little, Brown, 1972).
20. Tullio-Altan, *Nostra Italia,* 16.
21. The constant search for a "grand center" in national politics (akin to the American idea of "bipartisan consensus") based on bargains struck between local and regional notables and bosses because of serious regional social and economic differences could be indicted as a more likely source of *trasformismo* than a pervasive pursuit of personal and family advantage at public expense. For this argument see, in particular, the especially fine book by Sandro Rogari, *Alle origini del trasformismo: Partiti e sistema politico nell'Italia liberale* (Rome: Laterza,

1998). The backroom dealings of *trasformismo* can also be indicted as a source of the widespread Italian attachment to conspiracy theories of politics. *Dietrologia* (literally "behindology") prevails because no one in public authority seems to have a clue about mysterious disappearances, surprising events, and rumors of coups d'état. See, for example, Giovanni Sabbatucci, "Il golpe in agguato e il doppio stato," in *Miti e storia dell'Italia unita,* ed. Giovanni Belardelli et al. (Bologna: Il Mulino, 1999).

22. David Blackbourn and Geoff Eley, *The Peculiarities of German History: Bourgeois Society and Politics in Nineteenth Century Germany* (New York: Oxford University Press, 1984).

23. Amalia Signorelli, Review of *La nostra Italia, L'Indice* 8 (1986): 45.

24. Mason, "Italy and Modernization," and Rosario Lembo, "Il Mezzogiorno tra storia e antropologia," *Studi Storici* 29 (1988): 1051–68.

25. Mason, "Italy and Modernization," 44.

26. Sabetti, *Search for Good Government,* chap. 8. For discussion of the role of family "types" in local mediation between large-scale social change and local political-economic effects that is more compelling than that of Banfield, Tullio-Altan, and Putnam, see, for example, Paolo Macry, "Rethinking a Stereotype: Territorial Differences and Family Models in the Modernization of Italy," *Journal of Modern Italian Studies* 2 (1997): 188–214; Francesco Benigno, "The Southern Family: A Comment on Paolo Macry," *Journal of Modern Italian Studies* 2 (1997): 215–17; and Paul Corner, "Thumbs down for the Family? A Comment on Paolo Macry," *Journal of Modern Italian Studies* 2 (1997): 218–20.

27. This has been one of the main arguments of Italian political theorists from Machiavelli to Antonio Gramsci and Piero Gobetti. For the crucial years in the late nineteenth century see David I. Kertzer, "Religion and Society, 1789–1892," in *Italy in the Nineteenth Century,* ed. John A. Davis (Oxford: Oxford University Press, 2000).

28. Frank Kermode, *The Sense of an Ending* (New York: Oxford University Press, 1967), 112–13, as represented by Terry Eagleton, *Ideology: An Introduction* (London: Verso, 1991), 191.

29. Sheldon Wolin, "Postmodern Society and the Absence of Myth," *Social Research* 52 (1985): 217–39.

30. See, for example, Mary Louise Pratt, *Imperial Eyes: Travel Writing and Transculturation* (London: Routledge, 1992).

31. Mary W. Helms, *Ulysses' Sail: An Ethnographic Odyssey of Power, Knowledge, and Geographical Discourse* (Princeton: Princeton University Press, 1988).

32. Michael T. Ryan, "Assimilating New Worlds in the Sixteenth and Seventeenth Centuries," *Comparative Studies in Society and History* 23 (1981): 537.

33. Anthony Pagden, *European Encounters with the New World: From Renaissance to Romanticism* (New Haven: Yale University Press, 1992).

34. Agnew, *Geopolitics,* chaps. 1 and 2.

35. Robert Mandrou, *From Humanism to Science, 1480–1700* (London: Penguin, 1978), 17.

36. Mandrou, *From Humanism to Science,* 23. This point is made tellingly and amusingly, if for a somewhat too early period than is historically convincing, in Umberto Eco's novel *The Name of the Rose* (New York: Vintage, 1983).

37. Edward W. Said, *Orientalism* (New York: Random House, 1978), 57.

38. Patricia Springborg, *Western Republicanism and the Oriental Prince* (Austin: University of Texas Press, 1992).

39. Springborg, *Western Republicanism and the Oriental Prince,* 20. Also see Yves Schemeil, "Democracy before Democracy?" *International Political Science Review* 21 (2000): 99–120.

40. Robert Schwoebel, *The Shadow of the Crescent: The Renaissance Image of the Turk (1453–1517)* (Nieuwkoop, Netherlands: De Graaf, 1967), 23.

41. Frederick John Dealtry Lugard, *The Dual Mandate in British Tropical Africa,* 3d ed. (Edinburgh: Blackwood, 1926), 618.

42. G. W. F. Hegel, *Philosophy of Right* (1821; Oxford: Oxford University Press, 1967).

43. John Agnew, "The Territorial Trap: The Geographical Assumptions of International Relations Theory," *Review of International Political Economy* 1 (1994): 53–80.

44. Gustavo Esteva, "Development," in *The Development Dictionary: A Guide to Knowledge as Power,* ed. Wolfgang Sachs (London: Zed Books, 1992).

45. Larry Wolff, *Inventing Eastern Europe: The Map of Civilization in the Mind of the Enlightenment* (Stanford: Stanford University Press, 1994), 9, plausibly claims that the invention of "Eastern Europe" was particularly important in the history of the language of backward and modern: "It was Eastern Europe's ambiguous location, within Europe but not fully European, that called for such notions as backwardness and development to mediate between the poles of civilization and barbarism. In fact, Eastern Europe in the eighteenth century provided Western Europe with its first model of underdevelopment, a concept that we now apply all over the globe."

46. Ranajit Guha, "Dominance without Hegemony and Its Historiography," *Subaltern Studies* 6 (1989): 287.

47. Dean Tipps, "Modernization Theory and the Comparative Study of Societies: A Critical Perspective," *Comparative Studies in Society and History* 15 (1973): 199–226.

48. Jürgen Habermas, *The Philosophical Discourse of Modernity* (Cambridge: Polity Press, 1987), 2.

49. Within the broad conception of a Western modernity, therefore, have appeared more specific "modernities" associated with the states politically dominant within particular epochs. Italy has been compared unfavorably to each in turn.

50. Carl E. Pletsch, "The Three Worlds, or The Division of Social Scientific Labor, circa 1950–1975," *Comparative Studies in Society and History* 23 (1981): 565–90.

51. Celia Applegate, *A Nation of Provincials: The German Idea of "Heimat"* (Berkeley and Los Angeles: University of California Press, 1990).

52. Silvio Lanaro, *L'Italia nuova: Identità e sviluppo, 1861–1988* (Turin: Einaudi, 1989), 28.

53. Although, as pointed out by Charles S. Maier, *Recasting Bourgeois Europe* (Princeton: Princeton University Press, 1975), 62, newly unified Italy had a more "compact" elite than "the wider and less defined French bourgeoisie."

54. Lanaro, *Italia nuova;* David Forgacs, *Italian Culture in the Industrial Era, 1880–1980: Cultural Industries, Politics and the Public* (Manchester: Manchester University Press, 1990).

55. See, for example, Christopher Duggan, *Fascism and the Mafia* (New Haven: Yale University Press, 1989), and Denis Mack Smith, *Modern Italy: A Political History* (Ann Arbor: University of Michigan Press, 1997).

56. A recent literature suggests that the development of *mafia* depended on a peculiar combination of excessively centralized and illegitimate national government in which commercial opportunities could be exploited by rational "entrepreneurs of violence." See, for example, Paolo Pezzino, *Una certa reciprocità di favori: Mafia e modernizzazione violenta nella Sicilia postunitaria* (Milan: Franco Angeli, 1990); Diego Gambetta, "Fragments of an Economic Theory of the Mafia," *European Journal of Sociology* 29 (1988): 127–45; and Salvatore Lupo, "The Mafia," in *Italy since 1945*, ed. Patrick McCarthy (Oxford: Oxford University Press, 2000). More generally on the "new" history of the Italian South, arguing for its internal differentiation and the rationality of its social and political life, see Robert Lumley and Jonathan Morris, eds., *The New History of the Italian South* (Exeter: University of Exeter Press, 1997).

57. On these points, see, respectively, Francesco Barbagallo, *La modernità squilibrata del Mezzogiorno d'Italia* (Turin: Einaudi, 1994), and Ivano Granata, "Storia nazionale e storia locale: Alcune considerazioni sulla problematica del fascismo delle origini (1919–1922)," *Storia Contemporanea* 11 (1980): 503–44.

58. J. T. Scott and V. B. Sullivan, "Patricide and the Plot of the Prince: Cesare Borgia and Machiavelli's Italy," *American Political Science Review* 8 (1994): 898.

59. Alessandro Manzoni, *I Promessi Sposi/The Betrothed*, trans. Bruce Penman (London: Penguin, 1972).

60. Angela Dalle Vacche, *The Body in the Mirror: Shapes of History in Italian Cinema* (Princeton: Princeton University Press, 1992).

61. Albert Boime, "The Macchiaioli and the Risorgimento," in *The Macchiaioli: Painters of Italian Life, 1850–1900*, ed. E. Tonelli and K. Hart (Los Angeles: Wight Art Gallery, UCLA, 1986), 68.

62. Lanaro, *Italia nuova*, 212. The famous writer and poet Giacomo Leopardi wrote a book in 1824 that set the scene for later interpretations by offering a denigrating account of the customs of Italians compared with those of more exemplary Europeans such as the English and the French: *Discorso sopra lo stato presente dei costumi degl'italiani* (Venice: Marsilio, 1989). Tim Parks has recently invoked Leopardi in justifying the view that Italians have a low opinion of themselves and hence treat one another with disrespect. This recycling helps perpetuate the image of Italian collective failure. See Tim Parks, "The Non-conformist," *New York Review of Books* 47 (21 September 2000): 30–35.

63. Christopher Duggan, "Francesco Crispi, 'Political Education' and the Problem of Italian National Consciousness, 1860–1896," *Journal of Modern Italian Studies* 2 (1997): 141–66. More generally, see Christopher Duggan, "Politics in the Era of Depretis and Crispi, 1870–96," in *Italy in the Nineteenth Century*, ed. John A. Davis (Oxford: Oxford University Press, 2000).

64. Lanaro, *Italia nuova*, 55.

65. Giovanni Sartori, *Stato e politica nel pensiero di Benedetto Croce* (Naples: Morano, 1966).

66. Alessandro Mantino, *La formazione della filosofia politica di Benedetto Croce* (Rome: Laterza, 1953); Carlo Carini, *Benedetto Croce e il partito politico* (Florence: Olschki, 1975).

67. Edmund E. Jacobitti, *Revolutionary Humanism and Historicism in Modern Italy* (New Haven: Yale University Press, 1981), 7, 162.

68. Talcott Parsons, *The Social System* (New York: Free Press, 1951).

69. Paul Veyne, *Bread and Circuses: Historical Sociology and Political Pluralism* (London: Allen Lane, 1990).

70. Lanaro, *Italia nuova.*
71. Maurizio Ferrera, "Il mercato politico-assistenziale," in *La società italiana degli anni ottanta,* ed. Ugo Ascoli and Raimondo Catanzaro (Rome: Laterza, 1989).
72. Marshall Sahlins, "Goodbye to Tristes Tropes: Ethnography in the Context of Modern World History," Ryerson Lecture, University of Chicago, 29 April 1992, 36.
73. Lanaro, *Italia nuova,* 81.
74. Agnew, "'Better Thieves Than Reds'?"
75. Hans Magnus Enzensberger, *Europe, Europe: Forays into a Continent* (London: Hutchinson, 1989), 40.
76. Sicily, for example. See John Agnew, "Italy's Island Other: Sicily's History in the Modern Italian Body Politic," *Emergences* 10 (2000): 301–11.

Chapter 5
1. Charles Tilly, *The Contentious French* (Cambridge: Belknap Press of Harvard University Press, 1986).
2. John Agnew, *Place and Politics: The Geographical Mediation of State and Society* (London: Allen and Unwin, 1987), chap. 6.
3. Perhaps more was made of nationalization than empirical evidence justified because of the increasing influence of American political science and its bias toward privileging the idea of nationalization as a facet of political modernization; the increased importance of national media in political communication and the assumption that nationwide messages elicit similar responses everywhere; the slow erosion of traditional values (and subcultures) under the onslaught of secularization and consumerism; and the tradition in Italian political theory of seeing any evidence for nationalization of behavior as signaling the "final" emergence of an Italian nation. For discussion of these influences, see John Agnew, "'Better Thieves Than Reds'? The Nationalization Thesis and the Possibility of a Geography of Italian Politics," *Political Geography Quarterly* 7 (1988): 307–21.
4. Giorgio Galli and Alfonso Prandi, eds., *Patterns of Political Participation in Italy* (New Haven: Yale University Press, 1970).
5. Arturo Parisi and Gianfranco Pasquino, "Relazioni partiti-elettori e tipi di voto," in *Il sistema politico italiano,* ed. Gianfranco Pasquino (Rome: Laterza, 1985); Piergiorgio Corbetta and Arturo Parisi, "Struttura e tipologia delle elezioni in Italia: 1946–1983," in *Il sistema politico italiano,* ed. Gianfranco Pasquino (Rome: Laterza, 1985). More generally, see Piergiorgio Corbetta, Arturo Parisi, and Hans Schadee, *Elezioni in Italia: Struttura e tipologia delle consultazioni politiche* (Bologna: Il Mulino, 1988).
6. See, e.g., Celso Ghini, *L'Italia che cambia: Il voto degli italiani, 1946–1976* (Rome: Riuniti, 1976).
7. John Agnew, "Mapping Politics: How Context Counts in Electoral Geography," *Political Geography* 15 (1996): 129–46; see also R. J. Johnston and C. J. Pattie, "Composition and Context: Region and Voting in Britain Revisited during Labour's 1990s' Revival," *Geoforum* 29 (1998): 309–29, and their "'People Who Talk Together Vote Together': An Exploration of Contextual Effects in Britain," *Annals of the Association of American Geographers* 90 (2000): 41–66.
8. See, e.g., Munroe Eagles, ed., *Spatial and Contextual Models in Political Research* (London: Taylor and Francis, 1995).

9. Parisi and Pasquino, "Relazioni partiti-elettori e tipi di voto."

10. Agnew, "'Better Thieves than Reds'?" and Rita Pavsić,"Esiste una ten-denza all'omogeneizzazione territoriale nei partiti italiani?" *Rivista Italiana di Scienza Politica* 15 (1985): 69–97.

11. See, for example, Carlo Trigilia, *Le subculture politiche territoriali* (Milan: Feltrinelli, 1981); Giorgio Galli, *Il bipartitismo imperfetto: Comunisti e democristiani in Italia* (Milan: Mondadori, 1984); Roberto Cartocci, "Differenze territoriali e tipi di voto: Le consultazioni del maggio-giugno 1985," *Rivista Italiana di Scienza Politica* 15 (1985): 421–54; and Mario Caciagli, "Quante Italie? Persistenza e trasformazione delle culture politiche subnazionali," *Polis* 2 (1988): 429–57. A much more sophisticated argument for the cross-regional diffusion of opinion and exchange voting leading to a restructuring of Italian electoral geography is provided in Roberto Cartocci, *Elettori in Italia: Riflessioni sulle vicende elettorali degli anni ottanta* (Bologna: Il Mulino, 1990). Also see Carlo Brusa, *Geografia del potere politico in Italia* (Milan: Unicopli, 1984), chap. 2.

12. This section is based mainly on Percy A. Allum, *Italy: Republic without Government?* (New York: Norton, 1973), and Stuart J. Woolf, ed., *The Rebirth of Italy, 1943–1950* (London: Longman, 1972).

13. David I. Kertzer, "Urban Research in Italy," in *Urban Life in Mediterranean Europe: Anthropological Perspectives,* ed. Michael Kenny and David I. Kertzer (Urbana: University of Illinois Press, 1983).

14. Whether this is adequate in detail is open to question. See, for example, John A. Davis, "The South, the Risorgimento and the Origins of the 'Southern Problem,'" in *Gramsci and Italy's Passive Revolution,* ed. John A. Davis (London: St. Martin's Press, 1979), and John A. Davis, "Remapping Italy's Path to the Twentieth Century," *Journal of Modern History* 66 (1994): 291–320.

15. See, for example, Sabino S. Acquaviva and Mario Santuccio, *Social Structure in Italy: Crisis of a System* (Boulder, Colo.: Westview Press, 1976).

16. Particularly important in making this point is P. A. Allum, "The South and National Politics, 1945–50," in *The Rebirth of Italy, 1943–1950,* ed. Stuart J. Woolf (London: Longman, 1972).

17. The most important contributions to the new historical balance sheet on the impact of the Resistance are Claudio Pavone, *Una guerra civile: Saggio storico sulla moralità della Resistenza* (Turin: Bollati Boringhieri, 1991); Pietro Scoppola, *25 aprile: Liberazione* (Turin: Einaudi, 1995); and Ernesto della Loggia, *La morte della patria: La crisi dell'idea di nazione tra Resistenza, antifascismo e Repubblica* (Rome: Laterza, 1996). For a range of views, also see, e.g., James E. Miller, "Who Chopped Down the Cherry Tree? The Italian Resistance in History and Politics, 1945–1998," *Journal of Modern Italian Studies* 4 (1999): 37–54; Spencer Di Scala, "Resistance Mythology," *Journal of Modern Italian Studies* 4 (1999): 67–72; Roy P. Domenico, *Italian Fascists on Trial, 1943–1948* (Chapel Hill: University of North Carolina Press, 1991); and Simone Neri Serneri, "A Past to Be Thrown Away? Politics and History in the Italian Resistance," *Contemporary European History* 4 (1995): 367–81.

18. Rosario Romeo, *Breve storia della grande industria in Italia* (Bologna: Il Mulino, 1963), 188.

19. See, for example, Paul Corner, *Fascism in Ferrara, 1915–1922* (Oxford: Clarendon Press, 1975); Roberto Vivarelli, "Revolution and Reaction in Italy, 1918–1922," *Journal of Italian History* 1 (1979): 235–63; and Donald H. Bell, *Sesto San Giovanni: Workers, Culture, and Politics in an Italian Town* (New Brunswick: Rutgers University Press, 1986).

20. Shepard Bancroft Clough, *The Economic History of Modern Italy* (New York: Columbia University Press, 1964), 290.

21. Russell King, *The Industrial Geography of Italy* (New York: St. Martin's Press, 1985), 69.

22. King, *Industrial Geography of Italy*, 69.

23. Arnaldo Bagnasco, *Tre Italie: La problematica territoriale dello sviluppo italiano* (Bologna: Il Mulino, 1987); Giulio Sapelli, *L'Italia inafferrabile: Conflitti, sviluppo, dissociazione dagli anni cinquanta a oggi* (Venice: Marsilio, 1989); King, *Industrial Geography of Italy*, 136–211; Marino Regini, "Social Institutions and Production Structure of Italian Capitalism in the 1980s," in *Political Economy of Modern Capitalism: Mapping Convergence and Diversity*, ed. Colin Crouch and Wolfgang Streeck (London: Sage, 1997).

24. Francesco Barbagallo, *La modernità squilibrata del Mezzogiorno d'Italia* (Turin: Einaudi, 1994).

25. Roberto Mainardi, *Le grandi città italiane* (Milan: Franco Angeli, 1973).

26. A. Mori and B. Cori, "L'area di attrazione delle maggiori città italiane," *Rivista Geografica Italiana* 76 (1969): 3–14.

27. Russell King, *Italy* (London: Harper and Row, 1987), 60–65.

28. The "special statute regions" of Sicily, Friuli-Venezia-Giulia, Valle D'Aosta, and Alto Adige already existed. The rest of the country should have been divided into regions under the terms of the 1946 constitution but was not until 1970. On Italian local government see Bruno Dente, *Governare la frammentazione: Stato, regioni e enti locali in Italia* (Bologna: Il Mulino, 1985), and John Agnew, "Political Decentralization and Urban Policy in Italy," *Policy Studies Journal* 18 (1990): 768–84. On the recent expansion of the powers and autonomy of local governments see Bruno Dente, "Sub-national Governments in the Long Italian Transition," *West European Politics* 20 (1997): 176–93.

29. For example, Robert D. Putnam, Robert Leonardi, Raffaella Y. Nanetti, and Franco Pavoncello, "Il rendimento dei governi regionali," in *Il sistema politico italiano*, ed. Gianfranco Pasquino (Rome: Laterza, 1985).

30. Alan S. Zuckerman, *The Politics of Faction* (New Haven: Yale University Press, 1979); Carol Mershon, "Expectations and Informal Rules in Coalition Formation," *Comparative Political Studies* 27 (1994): 40–79; and Carol Mershon, "The Costs of Coalition: Coalition Theories and Italian Governments," *American Political Science Review* 90 (1996): 534–54. Italy had six governments before the Constituent Assembly of 1946, three in 1946–48, forty-eight governments in the twelve parliaments from 1948 to 1995, and three governments from 1996 to 2000. Many of the same politicians, however, were recycled across governments in the years before 1992, so there was much greater stability than the number of government reshufflings might suggest. See Elvio Paolini and Alberto Douglas Scotti, *Da Badoglio a Berlusconi* (Milan: Sugarco, 1995).

31. Percy Allum, "'From Two into One': The Faces of the Italian Christian Democratic Party," *Party Politics* 3 (1997): 23–52. Also see the important study of Luigi Graziano, *Clientelismo e sistema politico* (Milan: Franco Angeli, 1980).

32. Mario Caciagli, *Democrazia Cristiana e potere nel Mezzogiorno* (Florence: Guaraldi, 1975); Mario Caciagli, "Il resistibile declino della Democrazia Cristiana," in *Il sistema politico italiano*, ed. Gianfranco Pasquino (Rome: Laterza, 1985).

33. Gianfranco Pasquino, "Il Partito Comunista nel sistema politico italiano," in *Il sistema politico italiano*, ed. Gianfranco Pasquino (Rome: Laterza, 1985); Franco Cazzola, "Struttura e potere del Partito Socialista Italiano," in *Il sis-*

tema politico italiano, ed. Gianfranco Pasquino (Rome: Laterza, 1985). More generally, see Alexander De Grand, *The Italian Left in the Twentieth Century: A History of the Socialist and Communist Parties* (Bloomington: Indiana University Press, 1989).

34. A case can be made that it is the high degree of division on the left and the choice of PSI leaders to move to the center rather than see themselves potentially subordinated in coalition with the PCI that failed to produce alternation in government of the right/left variety as experienced in many other European countries. In other words, continuing DC dominance of Italian governments depended on the split between the PCI and the PSI. See Donald Sassoon, "La sinistra in Italia e in Europa: Elezioni e governi 1945–1988," *Italia Contemporanea* 175 (1989): 5–23. More generally, see Giuseppe Tamburrano, "The Italian Socialist Party: Its Policies and Failure to Unite with the Italian Communist Party," in *The Formation of the Italian Republic,* ed. Frank J. Coppa and Margherita Repetto-Alaia (New York: Peter Lang, 1993); Spencer M. Di Scala, ed., *Italian Socialism: Between Politics and History* (Amherst: University of Massachusetts Press, 1996); and Ilaria Favretto, "1956 and the PSI: The End of 'Ten Winters,'" *Modern Italy* 5 (2000): 25–45.

35. See, for example, Robert Lumley, *States of Emergency: Cultures of Revolt in Italy from 1968 to 1978* (London: Verso, 1990), and Gianni Statera et al., *Violenza sociale e violenza politica nell'Italia degli anni '70: Analisi e interpretazioni sociopolitiche, giuridiche, della stampa quotidiana* (Milan: Franco Angeli, 1983).

36. See, for example, Yasmine Ergas, "Allargamento della cittadinanza e governo del conflitto," in *Il sistema politico italiano,* ed. Gianfranco Pasquino (Rome: Laterza, 1985); Donatella della Porta and Maurizio Rossi, "I terrorismi in Italia tra il 1969 e il 1982," in *Il sistema politico italiano,* ed. Gianfranco Pasquino (Rome: Laterza, 1985).

37. Stefano Guzzini, "The 'Long Night of the First Republic': Years of Clientelistic Implosion in Italy," *Review of International Political Economy* 2 (1995): 27–61. The role of Bettino Craxi, secretary of the PSI after 1976, in the creation of a more systematically corrupt system of parties is often emphasized. See, e.g., Wolfgang Merkel, *Prima e dopo Craxi: Le trasformazioni del PSI* (Padua: Liviana, 1987), and Mario Caciagli, "Italie 1993: Vers la Seconde Republique?" *Revue Française de Science Politique* 43 (1993): 244.

38. Franco Cazzola, *Della corruzione: Fisiologia e patologia di un sistema politico* (Bologna: Il Mulino, 1988); Donatella della Porta, "Risorse e attori nella corruzione politica: Appunti su tre casi di governo locale in Italia," *Polis* 4 (1990): 499–532; Miriam Golden, "Competitive Corruption: Factional Conflict and Political Corruption in Postwar Italian Christian Democracy," unpublished manuscript, Department of Political Science, UCLA, September 1999.

39. On the post-1992 electoral rules see this book, chapters 7 and 9.

40. Samuel H. Barnes, *Representation in Italy: Institutionalized Tradition and Electoral Choice* (Chicago: University of Chicago Press, 1977); Luigi D'Amato, *Il voto di preferenza in Italia, 1946–1963* (Milan: Giuffrè, 1964); and Renato D'Amico, "Voto di preferenza, movimento dell'elettorato e modelli di partito: L'andamento delle preferenze nelle elezioni politiche italiane del quindicennio, 1968–1983," *Quaderni dell'Osservatorio Elettorale* 18 (1987): 89–138. The nature of clientelism with respect to its connections to criminality, effectiveness, and legitimacy has varied much more between different parts of the South than conventional accounts suggest. See Simona Piattoni, "Clientelism Revisited: Clien-

telistic Politics and Economic Development in Postwar Italy," *Italian Politics and Society* 49 (1998): 44–62, and Simona Piattoni, "Politica locale e sviluppo economico nel Mezzogiorno," *Stato e Mercato* 55 (1999): 117–49.

41. The most thorough study of Italian turnouts and their decline beginning in the 1980s is Piergiorgio Corbetta and Arturo Parisi, "Smobilitazione partitica e astensionismo elettorale," *Polis* 8 (1994): 423–43.

42. Arturo Parisi, "Mobilità senza movimento," in *Mobilità senza movemento: Le elezioni del 3 giugno 1979,* ed. Arturo Parisi (Bologna: Il Mulino, 1980); Renato Mannheimer and François Zajczyk, "L'astensionismo elettorale, elementi di analisi a partire dai risultati del referendum 1981," *Quaderni di Sociologia* 2–4 (1982): 399–436; Arturo Parisi, *Luoghi e misure della politica* (Bologna: Il Mulino, 1984).

43. The most important of these are Corbetta and Parisi, "Struttura e tipologia delle elezioni"; Cartocci, *Elettori in Italia;* Guido Martinotti, "Le tendenze dell'elettorato italiano," in *La politica nell'Italia che cambia,* ed. Alberto Martinelli and Gianfranco Pasquino (Milan: Feltrinelli, 1978); Guido Martinotti, "Electoral Trends in Italy," *West European Politics* 6 (1986): 253–81; and Carlo Brusa, *Geografia elettorale nell'Italia del dopoguerra* (Milan: Unicopli, 1983).

44. Martinotti, "Electoral Trends in Italy," 261.

45. Peter Mair, "Myths of Electoral Change and the Survival of Traditional Parties: The 1992 Stein Rokkan Lecture," *European Journal of Political Research* 24 (1993): 121–33.

46. This method for measuring nationalization is suggested by William Claggett et al., "Nationalization of the American Electorate," *American Political Science Review* 78 (1984): 77–91.

47. Pavsić, "Esiste una tendenza all'omogeneizzazione territoriale nei partiti italiani?" Martinotti, "Electoral Trends in Italy."

48. For an impressive visual display of the electoral geography of Italy over the period 1946 to 1983, see the colored province-level maps in Emilio Rizzi, *Atlante geo-storico—1946–1983: Le elezioni politiche e il Parlamento nell'Italia Repubblicana* (Milan: Edizioni Geografia Storica Illustrata, 1986).

49. Galli and Prandi, *Patterns of Political Participation in Italy.* The original Italian study was published as Vittorio Capecchi et al., *Il comportamento elettorale in Italia* (Bologna: Il Mulino, 1968). The question of the adequacy of the classic electoral regionalization of Italy and alternatives to it are raised, inter alia, in Fausto Anderlini, "Una modellizazzione per zone sociopolitiche dell'Italia repubblicana," *Polis* 1 (1987): 443–79; Roberto Cartocci, "Otto risposte a un problema: La divisione dell'Italia in zone politicamente omogenee," *Polis* 1 (1987): 481–514; and Ferenc Csillag and John Agnew, "How Many Italies? A Strategy for Spatial Analysis of Regionalizations of Italian Election Results, 1953–87," in *Spatial and Contextual Models in Political Research,* ed. Munroe Eagles (London: Taylor and Francis, 1995).

50. Carlo Brusa, *Geografia elettorale nell'Italia del dopoguerra: Edizione aggiornata ai risultati delle elezioni politiche 1983* (Milan: Unicopli, 1984), 23.

51. Ilvo Diamanti and Giovanni Riccamboni, *La parabola del voto bianco: Elezioni e società in Veneto (1946–1992)* (Vicenza: Neri Pozza, 1992); Cartocci, *Elettori in Italia.*

52. On the economic changes, see King, *Industrial Geography of Italy,* 69–72, 238–39; on the political ones, see, for example, Mattei Dogan and O. M. Petrarca, eds., *Partiti politici e strutture sociali in Italia* (Milan: Comunità, 1968), and Sidney

Tarrow et al., *Sociologie du communisme en Italie* (Paris: Presses Universitaires de France, 1974).

53. King, *Industrial Geography of Italy*, 67–97.

54. Della Porta and Rossi, "Terrorismi in Italia tra il 1969 and il 1982," and Lumley, *States of Emergency.*

55. See, e.g., Sonia Stefanizzi, "Alle origini del nuovi movimenti sociali: Gli ecologisti e le donne in Italia (1966–1973)," *Quaderni di Sociologia* 34 (1988): 99–131.

56. Arturo Parisi, "Il matrice socio-religioso del dissenso cattolico in Italia," *Il Mulino* 21 (1971): 637–57; Giacomo Sani, "Le elezioni degli anni settanta: Terremoto o evoluzione?" in *Continuità e mutamento elettorale in Italia*, ed. Arturo Parisi and Gianfranco Pasquino (Bologna: Il Mulino, 1977); Caciagli, "Resistibile declino della Democrazia Cristiana"; and Judith Chubb, "The Christian Democratic Party: Reviving or Surviving?" in *Italian Politics: A Review*, vol. 1, ed. Robert Leonardi and Rafaella Y. Nanetti (London: Pinter, 1986).

57. Piergiorgio Cobetta and Arturo Parisi, "Struttura e tipologia delle elezioni in Italia: 1946–1983," in *Il sistema politico italiano*, ed. Gianfranco Pasquino (Rome: Laterza, 1985).

58. Brusa, *Geografia elettorale nell'Italia del dopoguerra: Edizione aggiornata;* Robert Leonardi, "The Changing Balance: The Rise of Small Parties in the 1983 Election," in *Italy at the Polls, 1983: A Study of the National Elections*, ed. H. R. Penniman (Durham, N.C.: Duke University Press, 1987); Roberto Biorcio and Paolo Natale, "Mobilità e fedeltà elettorale negli anni ottanta," *Quaderni dell'Osservatorio Elettorale* 18 (1987): 41–88; Geneviève Bibes and Jean Besson, "The Resurgence of Christian Democracy and the Search for New 'Rules' of the Game," in *Italian Politics: A Review*, vol. 3, ed. Robert Leonardi and Piergiorgio Corbetta (London: Pinter, 1989).

59. Brusa, *Geografia elettorale nell'Italia del dopoguerra: Edizione aggiornata*, 75, 139; Carlo Brusa, *Cambiamenti nella geografia elettorale italiana dopo le consultazioni politiche del 1987* (Milan: Unicopli, 1988).

60. See, for example, Bagnasco, *Tre Italie.*

61. Philip Cooke and A. de Rosa Pires, "Productive Decentralization in Three European Regions," *Environment and Planning A* 17 (1985): 527–54.

62. See in general Arnaldo Bagnasco, *L'Italia in tempi di cambiamento politico* (Bologna: Il Mulino, 1996); more specifically in relation to unionization during the critical years, Ettore Santi, "Un decennio di sindacalizzazione (1977–1986)," *Quaderni di Sociologia* 34 (1988): 61–96; and for an interesting case study, Giovanni Contini, "The Rise and Fall of Shop-Floor Bargaining at Fiat, 1945–1980," in *Between Fordism and Flexibility: The Automobile Industry and Its Workers*, ed. Steven Tolliday and Jonathan Zeitlin (Oxford: Berg, 1992), 144–67.

63. See, for example, Roberto Cartocci, *Fra Lega e Chiesa: L'Italia in cerca di integrazione* (Bologna: Il Mulino, 1994), chap. 4; Anna Cento Bull and Paul Corner, *From Peasant to Entrepreneur: The Survival of the Family Economy in Italy* (Oxford: Berg, 1995); Richard M. Locke, *Remaking the Italian Economy* (Ithaca: Cornell University Press, 1995); Aldo Bonomi, *Il capitalismo molecolare: La società al lavoro nel Nord Italia* (Turin: Einaudi, 1997); Arnaldo Bagnasco, "Geografia elettorale e basi sociali della politica," *Rassegna Italiana di Sociologia* 37 (1996): 279–85. Also see this book, chapter 7.

64. Guglielmo Tagliacarne, *Il reddito nelle province italiane nel 1983 e confronti con gli anni 1951, 1981 e 1982* (Milan: Franco Angeli, 1985).

65. Cartocci, *Elettori in Italia,* 125–89.

66. Donald Sassoon, *The Strategy of the Italian Communist Party* (New York: St. Martin's Press, 1981); Caciagli, "Resistibile declino della Democrazia Cristiana"; and Pasquino, "Partito Comunista nel sistema politico italiano."

67. Putnam et al., "Rendimento dei governi regionali."

68. P. Weitz, "The CGIL and the PCI: From Subordination to Independent Political Force," in *Communism in Italy and France,* ed. in D. L. M. Blackmer and S. Tarrow (Princeton: Princeton University Press, 1975); Judith A. Hellman, *Journeys among Women: Feminism in Five Italian Cities* (New York: Oxford University Press, 1987); Carol A. Mershon, "Unions and Politics in Italy," in *Italy at the Polls, 1983: A Study of the National Elections,* ed. H. R. Penniman (Durham, N.C.: Duke University Press, 1987).

69. Sidney Tarrow, *Peasant Communism in Southern Italy* (New Haven: Yale University Press, 1967); Grant Amyot, *The Italian Communist Party: The Crisis of the Popular Front Strategy* (New York: St Martin's Press, 1981).

70. Alan Stern, "Political Legitimacy in Local Politics: The Communist Party in Northeastern Italy," in *Communism in Italy and France,* ed. D. L. M. Blackmer and Sidney Tarrow (Princeton: Princeton University Press, 1975), 223.

71. Mario Tesini, *Oltre la città rossa: L'alternativa mancata di Dossetti a Bologna (1956–1958)* (Bologna: Il Mulino, 1986).

72. John Agnew, "The Rhetoric of Regionalism: The Northern League in Italian Politics, 1983–1994," *Transactions of the Institute of British Geographers* 20 (1995): 156–72.

73. Renato Mannheimer, "Un'analisi territoriale del calo comunista," in *Mobilità senza movimento: Le elezioni del 3 giugno 1979,* ed. Arturo Parisi (Bologna: Il Mulino, 1980).

74. The source of this analysis is Mannheimer, "Analisi territoriale del calo comunista."

75. Mannheimer, "Analisi territoriale del calo comunista," 93.

76. Sidney Tarrow, *Between Center and Periphery: Grassroots Politicians in Italy and France* (New Haven: Yale University Press, 1977), 63.

77. Giovanni Sartori, *La teoria dei partiti e caso italiano* (Milan: Feltrinelli, 1982).

78. Galli, *Bipartitismo imperfetto.*

79. Carlo Donolo, *Mutamento o transizione? Politica e società nella crisi italiana* (Bologna: Il Mulino, 1977).

Chapter 6

1. Catching the flavor of local football fanaticism in Italy is the main purpose of the exciting tale by Joe McGinness, *The Miracle of Castel di Sangro* (New York: Little, Brown, 1999).

2. Mattei Dogan, "Political Cleavages and Social Stratification in France and Italy," in *Party Systems and Voter Alignments,* ed. Seymour M. Lipset and Stein Rokkan (New York: Free Press, 1967); Vittorio Capecchi et al., *Il comportamento elettorale in Italia* (Bologna: Il Mulino, 1968); Roberto Cartocci, "Otto risposte a un problema: La divisione dell'Italia in zona politicamente omogenee," *Polis* 1 (1987): 481–514; Fausto Anderlini, "Una modellizzazione per zone sociopolitiche dell'Italia repubblicana," *Polis* 1 (1987): 443–79.

3. Cartocci, "Otto risposte a un problema," and Anderlini, "Modellizzazione per zone sociopolitiche dell'Italia repubblicana."

4. For example, Arnaldo Bagnasco and Carlo Trigilia, *Società e politica nelle*

aree di piccola impresa:Il caso di Valdelsa (Milan: Franco Angeli, 1985); Carlo Baccetti, "Memoria storica e continuità elettorale: Una zona rossa nella Toscana
rossa," *Italia Contemporanea* 167 (1988): 7–30; Mario Caciagli, "Approssimazione
alle culture politiche locali: Problemi di analisi ed esperienze di ricerca," *Il Politico*
53 (1988): 269–92.

5. For example, Arnaldo Bagnasco and Carlo Trigilia, *Società e politica nelle
aree di piccola impresa: Il caso di Bassano* (Venice: Arsenale, 1984); Patrizia
Messina, "Persistenza e mutamento nelle subculture politiche territoriali," in *Le
elezioni della transizione: Il sistema politico italiano alla prova del voto, 1994–1996,*
ed. Giuseppe Gangemi and Gianni Riccamboni (Turin: UTET, 1997).

6. For example, Carlo Tullio-Altan, *La nostra Italia: Arretratezza socioculturale,
clientelismo, trasformismo e ribellismo dall'Unità ad oggi* (Milan: Feltrinelli, 1986);
Robert D. Putnam, with Robert Leonardi and Raffaella Y. Nanetti, *Making Democracy Work: Civic Traditions in Modern Italy* (Princeton: Princeton University Press,
1993).

7. The American classic is Gabriel Almond and Sidney Verba, *The Civic Culture* (Boston: Little, Brown, 1963). On the Italian view, see Caciagli, "Approssimazione alle culture politiche locali."

8. For example, Sidney Tarrow, *Between Center and Periphery: Grassroots Politicians in Italy and France* (New Haven: Yale University Press, 1977); Giorgio Galli,
Il bipartitismo imperfetto: Comunisti e democristiani in Italia (Milan: Mondadori,
1984).

9. Carlo Trigilia, *Grandi partiti e piccole imprese: Comunisti e democristiani nelle
regioni a economia diffusa* (Bologna: Il Mulino, 1986); Arnaldo Bagnasco, *La
costruzione sociale del mercato* (Bologna: Il Mulino, 1988).

10. For detailed critiques see N. Bellini, "Il socialismo in una regione sola: Il
PCI e il governo dell'industria in Emilia-Romagna," *Il Mulino* 325 (1989): 707–32;
Michael L. Blim, "Economic Development and Decline in the Emerging Global
Factory," *Politics and Society* 18 (1990): 143–63; and Ash Amin and Kevin Robins,
"The Re-emergence of Regional Economies: The Mythical Geography of Flexible
Accumulation," *Society and Space* 8 (1990): 7–34.

11. See, for example, Trigilia, *Grandi partiti e piccole imprese.*

12. David C. Kertzer, *Comrades and Christians: Religion and Political Struggle in
Communist Italy* (Cambridge: Cambridge University Press, 1980), 252–55. Also
see Paolo Feltrin, "Le culture politiche locali: Alcune osservazioni critiche sugli
studi condotti in Italia," *Il Politico* 53 (1988): 296–306.

13. Raymond Williams, *Culture* (London: Fontana, 1981); Percy Allum, "Cultura o opinione? Su alcune dubbi epistemologici," *Il Politico* 53 (1988): 261–68.

14. Charles Taylor, "Interpretation and the Sciences of Man," in *Philosophy
and the Human Sciences,* Philosophical Papers 2 (Cambridge: Cambridge University Press, 1985), 15–57.

15. Allum, "Cultura o opinione?" 265.

16. Philip Cooke, "Locality, Structure, and Agency: A Theoretical Analysis,"
Cultural Anthropology 5 (1990): 3–15.

17. Carlo Trigilia, *Le subculture politiche territoriali* (Milan: Feltrinelli, 1981);
Trigilia, *Grandi partiti e piccole imprese.* Also see Roberto Cartocci, *Fra Lega e
Chiesa: L'Italia in cerca di integrazione* (Bologna: Il Mulino, 1994).

18. Mario Caciagli, "Quante Italie? Persistenza e trasformazioni delle culture
politiche subnazionali," *Polis* 3 (1988): 429–57.

19. Messina, "Persistenza e mutamento nelle subculture politiche territoriali," 23.

20. Giordano Sivini, "Socialisti e cattolici in Italia dalla società allo stato," in *Sociologia dei partiti politici,* ed. Giordano Sivini (Bologna: Il Mulino, 1971); also see Messina, "Persistenza e mutamento nelle subculture politiche territoriali," 27, and Valentino Zaghi, *L'eroica viltà: Socialismo e fascismo nelle campagne del Polesine, 1919–1926* (Milan: Franco Angeli, 1989). Other commentators, in particular Emmanuel Todd, *L'invention de l'Europe* (Paris: Seuil, 1990), 239–40, distinguish between an "anarchic" Piedmont and Lombard socialism and an "authoritarian" Emilian socialism. It was this latter that proved fertile ground for the PCI.

21. Trigilia, *Grandi partiti e piccole imprese;* Paolo Farneti, *Sistema politico, società civile* (Turin: Giappichelli, 1971); Messina, "Persistenza e mutamento nelle subculture politiche territoriali"; Sivini, "Socialisti e cattolici in Italia dalla società allo stato."

22. See, for example, Giorgio Candeloro, *Il movimento cattolico in Italia* (Rome: Riuniti, 1974); Silvio Lanaro, *Società e ideologia nel Veneto rurale (1866–1898)* (Rome: Edizioni Storia e Letteratura, 1976); and Percy A. Allum et al., "Le trasformazioni del mondo cattolico e della società rurale nel voto del 1946 in provincia di Vicenza," *Quaderni dell'Osservatorio Elettorale* 21 (1988): 33–85. The terms aggregative and integrative in this and later paragraphs are adopted from J. G. March and J. P. Olsen, *Rediscovering Institutions: The Organizational Basis of Politics* (New York: Free Press, 1989).

23. Sivini, "Socialisti e cattolici in Italia dalla società allo stato"; Trigilia, *Grandi partiti e piccole imprese.*

24. Sivini, "Socialisti e cattolici in Italia dalla società allo stato," 83.

25. Messina, "Persistenza e mutamento nelle subculture politiche territoriali," 30–34, particularly table 1, p. 31.

26. See this book, chapter 5. Also see, for example, Mario Caciagli, "Toscana: Il declino della subcultura rossa," in *Elezioni regionali del '90: Un punto di svolta,* ed. Paolo Feltrin and Andrea Politi (Venice: Fondazione Corazzin, 1990); Renato Mannheimer and Giacomo Sani, *La rivoluzione elettorale: L'Italia tra la Prima e la Seconda Repubblica* (Milan: Anabasi, 1994); Gianni Riccamboni, "Ritorno al futuro? La transizione nell'ex subcultura bianca," in *Le elezioni della transizione: Il sistema politico italiano alla prova del voto, 1994–1996,* ed. Giuseppe Gangemi and Gianni Riccamboni (Turin: UTET, 1997).

27. The following account draws these sources together. Persons interviewed and local newspapers and magazines are listed at the end of the chapter. That Pistoia produced competitive PCI and DC newspapers and Lucca did not suggests how much more open and contentious politics has been in the former province than in the latter. Other written sources are cited where most appropriate.

28. Paolo Bellandi, *Alle origini del movimento cattolico—Pistoia, 1892–1904* (Rome: Cinque Lune, 1976); Marco Francini, *Primo dopoguerra e origini del fascismo a Pistoia* (Milan: Feltrinelli, 1976).

29. Francini, *Primo dopoguerra e origini del fascismo a Pistoia;* Andrea Ottanelli, "Le officine meccaniche S. Giorgio: Capitalismo e classe operaia a Pistoia (1905–1925)," *Farestoria* 1 (1981): 55–56. Andrea Ottanelli, *Auto, treni, aerei: Le officine meccaniche San Giorgio di Pistoia. Un'industria genovese in Toscana tra Giolitti e la Resistenza (1905–1949)* (Pistoia: Amministrazione Comunale, 1987); V. Pieruccini, "La Cantoni di Lucca," *Politica e Società* 2 (1982): 16.

30. Gerardo Bianchi, "La Resistenza a Pistoia," *La Bandiero del Popolo* (Pistoia), March–April 1975, 7.

31. Renzo Bardelli, *Le mani degli amici* (Pistoia: Tellini, 1985); On. Gerardo Bianchi, interview, 13 June 1989, Pistoia; Renzo Bardelli and Marco Francini, *Pis-*

toia e la Resistenza (Pistoia: Tellini, 1980); R. Risaliti, *Antifascismo e Resistenza nel pistoiese* (Pistoia: Tellini, 1976).

32. The social confusion and political polarization of this time in Tuscany is captured beautifully in the Taviani Brothers film *La notte di San Lorenzo* (rendered in English as *Night of the Shooting Stars*). The selective interpretation of the past in collective memory is brought to light in Luisa Passerini's brilliant study of workers' memories of Fascism in Turin, *Fascism in Popular Memory: The Cultural Experience of the Turin Working Class* (Cambridge: Cambridge University Press, 1987). For a best estimate of what public opinion was probably like under Fascism, based on secret police archives, see Simona Colarizi, *L'opinione degli italiani sotto il regime, 1929–1943* (Rome: Laterza, 1991). This makes depressing reading for those who might like to think there was much opposition to the regime.

33. The foundations for the later success of the PCI in Tuscany are explored geographically in an important but often overlooked article by Carlo Baccetti, "Il triplice voto del 1946 in Toscana: La fondazione del predominio del PCI," *Quaderni dell'Osservatorio Elettorale* 20 (1988): 7–86.

34. Mario Pellegrini, "La Resistenza oggi," *La Provincia di Lucca* 13 (1973): 27–41. Another issue of the magazine celebrates the role of Catholic priests in the Resistance in Lucca: "Trent' anni della Resistenza e liberazione—contributi del clero," *La Provincia di Lucca* 14 (1974): 1–21. For a fascinating article that largely justifies the pluralistic conception of the Resistance, in this case based on a German army intelligence report, see Giovanni Verni, "Toscana autunno 1943: Un rapporto dei servizi di sicurezza della Wehrmacht," *Italia Contemporanea* 196 (1994): 545–60.

35. Piergiorgio Camaiani, *Dallo stato cittadino alla città bianca: La "società cristiana" lucchese e la rivoluzione toscana* (Florence: La Nuova Italia, 1979); Maurizio Tazartes, *Una città allo specchio: Lucca fra cronaca e storia* (Lucca: Maria Pacini Fazzi, 1987). That this identity has medieval roots is apparent from the intriguing discussion of the settlement patterns of the Plain of Lucca and surrounding areas in Chris Wickham, *Community and Clientele in Twelfth-Century Tuscany: The Origins of the Rural Commune in the Plain of Lucca* (Oxford: Clarendon Press, 1998).

36. On. Sergio Dardini, interview, 4 July 1989, S. Maria del Giudice, Lucca.

37. Noted in Geoffrey Pridham, *The Nature of the Italian Party System: A Regional Case Study* (London: St. Martin's Press, 1981), 132–33.

38. See, e.g., *La Voce* (Periodico della Federazione Comunista Pistoiese), 15 January 1956, 29 April 1956, and 1 March 1968. Note that by 1987 Pistoia was eleventh and Lucca thirty-first out of ninety-five provinces on a synthetic measure of economic development: Confindustria, *Indicatori economici provinciali* (Rome: SIPI, 1989), 11. Pistoia is a classic example of the high growth associated with the "Third Italy" type of economic development since the 1970s.

39. This lack of anticlericalism was more or less universal across all interviews. This undoubtedly reflects a certain rewriting of local history, however. The 1948 national election, for example, was marked by quite open anticlericalism from local PCI politicians and activists, notwithstanding a genuine "popular Catholicism" among the Communist electorate. See Valentino Baldacci, "Il 18 aprile 1948: La campagna di Toscana," *Quaderni dell'Osservatorio Elettorale* 20 (1988): 89–197. Of course, this election was also characterized by a high degree of red baiting from the other side. In Lucca this not only had local sources in the form of statements by the higher clergy as to the terrible consequences for Italy of a left-wing victory but also outside stimulus from the American relatives of

Lucchese emigrants (the mountains of northern Lucca had sent more emigrants abroad than had other parts of Tuscany), who engaged in a letter-writing campaign against the left, including threatening to cut off the food parcels they were sending and to leave Italy out of the proposed Marshall Plan (reported by On. Sergio Dardini, interview, 4 July 1989, S. Maria del Giudice, Lucca). More generally, see Wendy L. Wall, "America's 'Best Propagandists': Italian Americans and the 1948 'Letters to Italy' Campaign," in *Cold War Constructions: The Political Culture of United States Imperialism, 1945–1966,* ed. Christian G. Appy (Amherst: University of Massachusetts Press, 2000).

40. Marco Francini, *Pistoia 1927: Nascita di una provincia* (Pistoia: Amministrazione Provinciale, 1987). The deep historical roots of the city-rural connection in Lucca are stressed in Wickham, *Community and Clientele in Twelfth-Century Tuscany,* 47–81.

41. Marco Francini, *Cooperazione pistoiesi: Fra storia e memoria: La Federazione Provinciale di Pistoia della Lega delle Cooperative (1945–1987)* (Florence: GE9, 1988).

42. That this is now the case more generally in Italy is the theme of Mario Caciagli, ed., *Governo locale, associazionismo e politico culturale* (Padua: Liviana, 1986). With the decline of the "myths" of the Resistance and the Soviet Union, however, only a local tradition of solidarity might remain to underpin an increasingly thin red subculture in Tuscany. This is the conclusion drawn from a survey of PCI supporters at local *feste dell'Unità* in areas along the river Arno in the provinces of Pisa and Florence in 1991. The more traditional-militant had already drifted into the orbit of Rifondazione Comunista; the modernizers were in the PDS camp. See Carlo Baccetti and Mario Caciagli, "Dopo il PCI e dopo l'URSS: Una subcultura rossa rivisitata," *Polis* 6 (1992): 537–68. The aging of militants may have been one of the sources of the decay of commitment to the PCI. See in particular Carlo Baccetti, "L'ultima svolta: Il XIX Congresso Straordinario del PCI in Toscana," *Polis* 5 (1991): 519–51. This is so even though the electoral dominance of the left as a whole within Tuscany has not changed substantially since the disintegration of the PCI and the collapse of the Soviet Union (Carlo Baccetti, "La Toscana: Le nuove vesti di un'antica egemonia," in *Le elezioni della transizione: Il sistema politico italiano alla prova del voto 1994–1996,* ed. Giuseppe Gangemi and Gianni Riccamboni [Turin: UTET, 1997]).

43. Marco Francini, "Il travaglio ideologico e politico (1957–1968)," unpublished manuscript, Pistoia, 1988; Ivo Lucchesi, interview, 21 June 1989, Pistoia; "Luci e ombri: Il partito [PCI] in cifre," *Politica e Società* 5 (1980): 73–74.

44. Francini, "Travaglio ideologico e politico (1957–1968)"; Vannino Chiti, "La DC in Toscana: Economia, cultura, istituzioni," *Critica Marxista* 3 (1981): 153–174.

45. The DC and PCI politicians in Pistoia and Lucca during the 1950s and 1960s were of equally humble origins, coming largely from peasant, working-class, and lower-middle-class backgrounds. In the 1970s, however, the DC seems to have become more middle class and business oriented in the social background of its activists, particularly in Lucca.

46. René Nouat, "La société paysanne," in *Tradition et changement en Toscane,* ed. Anne-Marie Seronde et al. (Paris: Armand Colin, 1970), 60–66, reports that 49.7 percent of agricultural land in Lucca was owner-occupied in 1951 compared with 43.2 percent in Pistoia, and 20.4 percent was in sharecropping in Lucca compared with 27.1 percent in Pistoia. Both are above the Tuscan average for

owner occupation and below the regional average for sharecropping. In this respect at least Pistoia is more like Lucca than other Tuscan provinces, particularly Florence, Siena, and Pisa. Also see Geneviève Bibes, "Les mouvements de pensée," and Jean Besson, "Comportements électoraux et politiques," both in *Tradition et changement en Toscane,* ed. Seronde et al.

47. Gerardo Bianchi, "Lettera aperta a un oratore comunista," *La Bandiera del Popolo* (Pistoia), 2 March 1945; On. Gerardo Bianchi, interview, 13 June 1989, Pistoia. Also see Marco Francini and Aldo Morelli, *La Breda di Pistoia, 1944/1962* (Florence: La Nuova Italia, 1984), and Vittorio Magni, *Palmiro Foresi: L'uomo, il cristiano, l'educatore politico* (Rome: Città Nuova, 1987). This should not leave the impression that the DC in Pistoia in particular or in Tuscany in general was reactionary. Indeed, left factions of the DC were always relatively strong in Tuscany and Emilia-Romagna, as were those, such as the longtime DC mayor of Florence, Giorgio La Pira, who counseled open communication and collaboration (if not alliance) with the PCI. This is brought out in Pridham, *Nature of the Italian Party System,* and can be seen as reciprocated, inter alia, in the biography of Florence's first postwar Communist mayor, Mario Fabiani: Serena Innamorati, *Mario Fabiani, il sindaco della ricostruzione: Appunti per una storia* (Florence: Comune di Firenze, 1984).

48. Agostino Palazzo, *Programmazione e unità locali di decisione* (Milan: Giuffrè, 1966); Agostino Palazzo, interview, 29 March 1989, Florence; Olivo Ghilarducci, "Industrializzazione nella provincia di Lucca," *La Provincia di Lucca* 13 (1973): 7–15; A. Cecchella, *Lo sviluppo dell'economia lucchese dalla fine del secondo conflitto mondiale* (Pisa: ETS, 1975); Giacomo Becattini, ed., *Lo sviluppo economico della Toscana* (Florence: IRPET, 1975); Georges Reyne, "L'industrie en Toscane: Étude d'une région confrontée à la crise" (Ph.D. thesis, University of Nice, 1983); On. Sergio Dardini, interview, 4 July 1989, S. Maria del Giudice, Lucca.

49. Pierluigi Ballini, "La Democrazia Cristiana," in *La ricostruzione in Toscana: Dal CLN ai partiti,* vol. 2, *I partiti politici,* ed. E. Rotelli (Bologna: Il Mulino, 1981).

50. Ghilarducci, "Industrializzazione nella provincia di Lucca."

51. Tazartes, *Città allo specchio.*

52. Camaiani, *Dallo stato cittadino alla città bianca.*

53. Risaliti, *Antifascismo e Resistenza nel pistoiese.*

54. M. G. Rossi and G. Santomassimo, "Il Partito Comunista Italiano," in *La ricostruzione in Toscana: Dal CLN ai partiti,* vol. 2, *I partiti politici,* ed. E. Rotelli (Bologna: Il Mulino, 1981).

55. The long-standing character of this connection is strongly endorsed by Wickham, *Community and Clientele in Twelfth-Century Tuscany,* 69–71.

Chapter 7

1. Walter Dean Burnham, "Party Systems and Political Process," in *The American Party Systems: Stages of Political Development,* ed. W. N. Chambers and W. D. Burnham (New York: Oxford University Press, 1967).

2. See, e.g., Henry Pelling, *Social Geography of British Elections, 1895–1970* (London: Macmillan, 1967); Ross McKibbin, *The Evolution of the Labour Party, 1910–1924* (Oxford: Clarendon Press, 1974); Roy Douglas, *The History of the Liberal Party, 1895–1970* (London: Sidgwick and Jackson, 1971).

3. Ilvo Diamanti, *Il male del Nord: Lega, localismo, secessione* (Rome: Donzelli, 1996), 24–27.

4. Percy Allum, "'From Two into One': The Faces of the Italian Christian Democratic Party," *Party Politics* 3 (1997): 30–31.

5. Allum, "'From Two into One,'" 46.

6. Allum, "'From Two into One,'" 44.

7. Ilvo Diamanti and Gianni Riccamboni, *La parabola del voto bianco: Elezioni e società in Veneto (1946–1992)* (Vicenza: Neri Pozzi, 1992); Pietro Scoppola, "The Christian Democrats and the Political Crisis," *Modern Italy* 1 (1995) 18–29.

8. Diamanti and Riccamboni, *Parabola del voto bianco,* 167–87; Roberto Cartocci, *Fra Lega e Chiesa: L'Italia in cerca di integrazione* (Bologna: Il Mulino, 1994).

9. Roberto Biorcio, *La Padania promessa: La storia, le idee e la logica d'azione della Lega Nord* (Milan: Il Saggiatore, 1997), 51, 63, 80, 92.

10. Diamanti, *Male del Nord,* 24–25. Also see Giacomo Sani, "Il verdetto del 1992," in *La rivoluzione elettorale: L'Italia tra la Prima e la Seconda Repubblica,* ed. Renato Mannheimer and Giacomo Sani (Milan: Anabasi, 1994).

11. Diamanti and Riccamboni, *Parabola del voto bianco,* 136, 142.

12. Diamanti and Ricaamboni, *Parabola del voto bianco,* figs. 2 and 19.

13. Michael Shin and John Agnew, "The Geography of Party Replacement in Italy, 1987–1996," *Political Geography* 21 (2002): 221–42.

14. Carlo Brusa, "Elezioni e territorio in una città media in un momento critico: Varese," *Lombardia Nord-Ovest* 2 (1993): 9–35.

15. Brusa, "Elezioni e territorio in una città media in un momento critico," 22. In the 1997 commune elections the mayor was elected directly for the first time and with ballots on successive Sundays if no candidate achieved an absolute majority in the first round. The League candidate for mayor (Aldo Fumagalli) won easily in much of the periphery but lost in both rounds in the historical center, suggesting much the same microgeography of the vote as that of 1992 except that now, in the form of Forza Italia, there was a single plausible alternative to the League ("L'analisi del voto," *La Prealpina* [Varese], 3 December 1997, 13).

16. Diamanti and Riccamboni, *Parabola del voto bianco,* 167–87; Diamanti, *Male del Nord,* 88; Gianni Riccamboni, "Ritorno al futuro? La transizione nell'ex subcultura 'bianca,'" in *Le elezioni della transizione: Il sistema politico italiano alla prova del voto, 1994–1996,* ed. Giuseppe Gangemi and Gianni Riccamboni (Turin: UTET, 1997), 293.

17. Ilvo Diamanti, "Nordest: Si puo crescere senza politica?" *Il Mulino* 46 (1997): 1061–73.

18. Roberto Cartocci, "Indizi di un inverno precoce: Il voto proporzionale tra equilibrio e continuità," *Rivista Italiana di Scienza Politica* 26 (1996): 609–53.

19. Ilvo Diamanti and Renato Mannheimer, eds., *Milano a Roma: Guida all'Italia elettorale del 1994* (Rome: Donzelli, 1994).

20. Diamanti and Mannheimer, *Milano a Roma,* ix.

21. In 2001 the League vote decreased by about one-half compared with 1996 throughout northern Italy. This means, of course, that the party still has considerable support in places such as Varese, but its vote in the city of Milan has all but disappeared. This is largely a continuing story of a theft of votes from the League by Forza Italia. The League's own construction of the losses of 2001 is that the party sacrificed itself for the good of the electoral coalition with Forza Italia and Alleanza Nazionale, of which it was a part. See, for example, Giuseppe Baiocchi, "Da Berlusconi e CDL una prova di lealtà," *La Padania,* 15 May 2001.

22. Ilvo Diamanti, "La Lega," in *Milano a Roma: Guida all'Italia elettorale del 1994,* ed. Ilvo Diamanti and Renato Mannheimer (Rome: Donzelli, 1994).

23. Luca Ricolfi, "Quali Italie? Vecchie e nuove fratture territoriali," *Rassegna Italiana di Sociologia* 37 (1996): 275.

24. Franco Goio, Guido Maggioni, and Mario Stoppino, *Il comportamento elettorale in Lomabardia (1946–1980): Specificità regionali e vincoli sistemici* (Florence: Le Monnier, 1983).

25. See, for example, Carlo Brusa, *Geografia elettorale nell'Italia del dopoguerra: Edizione aggiornata ai risultati delle elezioni politiche 1983* (Milan: Unicopli, 1984).

26. Anna Cento Bull and Paul Corner, *From Peasant to Entrepreneur: The Survival of the Family Economy in Italy* (Oxford: Berg, 1993): Aldo Bonomi, *Il capitalismo molecolare: La società al lavoro nel Nord Italia* (Turin: Einaudi, 1997).

27. Arnaldo Bagnasco, "Geografia elettorale e basi sociali della politica," *Rassegna Italiana di Sociologia* 37 (1996): 279–85; Richard M. Locke, "The Composite Economy: Local Politics and Industrial Change in Contemporary Italy," *Economy and Society* 25 (1996): 483–510.

28. Carlo Carozzi, "Il caso Milano," in *La città prossima ventura,* ed. Jean Gottmann and Calogero Muscarà (Rome: Laterza, 1991).

29. P. Petsimeris, "Urban Decline and the New Social and Ethnic Divisions in the Core Cities of the Italian Industrial Triangle," *Urban Studies* 35 (1998): 449–65.

30. F. Bianchini, "Milan," in *European Cities towards 2000: Profiles, Policies, and Prospects,* ed. Alan Harding, J. Dawson, R. Evans, and M. Parkinson (Manchester: Manchester University Press, 1994).

31. The province of Varese is the only one to contain parts of all three "faces." See Giuseppe Bettoni, "Una provincia travagliata con tre 'facce' diverse," *La Prealpina* (Varese), 11 October 1998, 8, and Guglielmo Scaramellini and Gian Paolo Torricelli, "Attività industriali e di servizio in un'area transfrontaliera: L'indagine dell'*Atlante socioeconomico delle Regione Insubrica,*" *Lombardia Nord-Ovest* 1 (2001): 35–52.

32. See, in particular, Ludovico Gardani, "'Tutti a casa': La globalizzazione vista dalla Padania," *LiMes* 1 (1997): 310–13, and Heidi Beirich and Dwayne Woods, "Globalisation, Workers and the Northern League," *West European Politics* 23 (2000): 130–43.

33. Anna Cento Bull, "Class, Gender and Voting in Italy," *West European Politics* 20 (1997): 73–92.

34. Cento Bull, "Class, Gender and Voting in Italy," makes this point in her intriguing comparison of survey data from Erba (Como) in the second zone with those from Sesto San Giovanni in the first zone.

35. On the former see, e.g., Franco Alasio and Danilo Montaldi, *Milano, Corea: Inchiesta sugli immigrati* (Milan: Feltrinelli, 1975), and Ugo Ascoli, *Movimento migratori in Italia* (Bologna: Il Mulino, 1979); on the latter see John Foot, "Immigration and the City: Milan and Mass Immigration, 1958–1998," *Modern Italy* 4 (1999): 159–72.

36. John Foot, "Migration and the 'Miracle' at Milan: The Neighbourhoods of Baggio, Barona, Bovisa, and Comasina in the 1950s and 1960s," *Journal of Historical Sociology* 10 (1997): 184–212.

37. Ilvo Diamanti, "Un bipolarismo ancora imperfetto," *Il Sole/24 Ore,* 29 April 1997, 3.

Chapter 8

1. John A. Agnew, "The Rhetoric of Regionalism: The Northern League in Italian Politics, 1983–1994," *Transactions of the Institute of British Geographers* 20

(1995): 156–72; Ilvo Diamanti, *Il male del Nord: Lega, localismo, secessione* (Rome: Donzelli, 1996); Ilvo Diamanti, "The Northern League: From Regional Party to Party of Government," in *The New Italian Republic: From the Fall of the Berlin Wall to Berlusconi*, ed. Stephen Gundle and Simon Parker (London: Routledge, 1996), 113–29; Oliver Schmidtke, *Politics of Identity: Ethnicity, Territories, and the Political Opportunity Structure in Modern Italian Society* (Sinzheim, Germany: Pro Universitate, 1996).

2. Roberto Cartocci, *Fra Lega e Chiesa: L'Italia in cerca di integrazione* (Bologna: Il Mulino, 1994); William Brierley and Luca Giacometti, "Italian National Identity and the Failure of Regionalism," in *Nation and Identity in Contemporary Europe*, ed. Brian Jenkins and Spyros A. Sofos (London: Routledge, 1996), 172–97; Mario Diani, "Linking Mobilization Frames and Political Opportunities: Insights from Regional Populism in Italy," *American Sociological Review* 61 (1996): 1053–69.

3. Agnew, "Rhetoric of Regionalism"; Daniela Gobetti, "La Lega: Regularities and Innovation in Italian Politics," *Politics and Society* 24 (1996): 57–82.

4. See, e.g., Gobetti, "Lega"; Gian Antonio Stella, *"Schei": Dal boom alla rivolta: Il mitico Nordest* (Milan: Baldini and Castoldi, 1996); Aldo Bonomi, *Il capitalismo molecolare: La società al lavoro nel Nord Italia* (Turin: Einaudi, 1997).

5. See, e.g., Anna Cento Bull and Paul Corner, *From Peasant to Entrepreneur: The Survival of the Family Economy in Italy* (Oxford: Berg, 1993); Vincenzo Guarrasi, "Tempi della società, luoghi della politica e immagini della cultura," in *Geografia politica delle regioni italiane*, ed. Pasquale Coppola (Turin: Einaudi, 1997); Heidi Beirich and Dwayne Woods, "Globalisation, Workers and the Northern League," *West European Politics* 23 (2000): 130–43; and Renato Mannheimer, "Mannheimer: Il Carroccio non è più un fenomeno di massa," *Il Messaggero*, 28 June 1999, 4.

6. Ilvo Diamanti, *La Lega: Geografia, storia e sociologia di un nuovo soggetto politico* (Rome: Donzelli, 1993); Gianni D'Amato and Siegfried Schieder, "Italy's Northern League: Between Ethnic Citizenship and a Federal State," in *Rethinking Nationalism and Ethnicity: The Struggle for Meaning and Order in Europe*, ed. Hans-Rudolf Wicker (Oxford: Berg, 1997), 273–86. The Northern League's lack of success in areas with a similar type of economy but historical association with left-wing dominance in local politics, such as most of Emilia-Romagna and Tuscany, can be put down to the persisting entrenchment of the parties that replaced the Communists, the strong popular affiliations with local government, and the absence of the antistatalist localism that characterized the areas where the League is now strong even when they were represented by the Christian Democrats and Socialists. The best discussion of this situation and the problem it poses for the Padanian strategy of the Northern League is in Patrizia Messina, "Opposition in Italy in the 1990s: Local Political Cultures and the Northern League," *Government and Opposition* 33 (1998): 462–78.

7. Agnew, "Rhetoric of Regionalism"; D'Amato and Schieder, "Italy's Northern League."

8. "Bossi: 'Padania può arrivare anche senza secessione,'" *La Padania*, 3 August 1998. *La Padania* is the official daily newspaper of the Northern League.

9. Gian Antonio Stella, *Dio Po: Gli uomini che fecero la Padania* (Milan: Baldini and Castoldi, 1996); Roberto Biorcio, *La Padania promessa: La storia, le idee e la logica d'azione della Lega Nord* (Milan: Il Saggiatore, 1997). On the historically more modest concept of Padania, see Roberto Mainardi, *L'Italia delle regioni: Il Nord e la Padania* (Milan: Mondadori, 1998), 110.

10. Michael Dibdin, *Dead Lagoon* (New York: Vintage, 1994). In his Venetian adventure, Dibdin's detective, Aurelio Zen, encounters a Venetian separatist, Ferdinando Dal Maschio, who declares in a speech (94–95) that "we Venetians must take control of our own destiny." He later continues: "For over a century we have let ourselves be beguiled by the chimera of nationalism. We freed ourselves from the shackles of the Austrian empire only to hand ourselves over to the hegemony of Rome. And now that regime has been exposed as the rotten sham it is, there are those who urge us to deliver ourselves meekly into the power of Milan." As the crowd murmurs in response to this reference to the Northern League, Dal Maschio gets to the point: "That may make sense for others, for those regions which have historically acknowledged the supremacy of the Lombards, or those who have insufficient resources to support pretensions to independence. But we are different! Venice has always been different! Istria and the Dalmatian coast have always been closer to us than Verona, Corfu and the Aegean more familiar than Milan, Constantinople no more foreign than Rome. Where others look inward, we have always looked outward. That difference is our heritage and our glory. The New Venetian Republic will revive both." The 1998 rebellion against Bossi by League leaders in the Veneto suggests that Dibdin's story has a prophetic quality. See, e.g., Sergio Romano, "La Lega divisa, il caso Veneto," *Corriere della Sera*, 18 September 1998, 1; Mariano Maugeri, "La Liga Veneta dà l'addio al Carroccio," *Il Sole/24 Ore*, 28 September 1998, 2; Enrico Caiano, "I ribelli a Bossi: Faremo noi la vera Lega," *Corriere della Sera*, 27 July 1999, 7. More generally on the Northeast versus the North as a whole in Italian regionalism, see Ilvo Diamanti, ed., *Idee del Nordest: Mappe, rappresentazioni, progetti* (Turin: Fondazione Giovanni Agnelli, 1998).

11. Roberto Biorcio, "L'Unione in Italia: Chi ha paura dell'Euro?" *Il Mulino* 47 (1998): 535–45.

12. Benedict Anderson, *Imagined Communities: Reflections on the Origins and Spread of Nationalism* (London: Verso, 1983).

13. Beverly Allen and Mary Russo, eds., *Revisioning Italy: National Identity and Global Culture* (Minneapolis: University of Minnesota Press, 1997), and Sharon Macdonald, ed., *Inside European Identities: Ethnography in Western Europe* (Oxford: Berg, 1997).

14. David Laitin, "The Cultural Identities of a European State," *Politics and Society* 25 (1997): 277–302.

15. See chapter 4 of this book. For reviews of a range of views on North/South differences, see, for example, John Dickie, "Imagined Italies," in *Italian Cultural Studies*, ed. David Forgacs and Robert Lumley (Oxford: Oxford University Press, 1996), 19–33; Gabriella Gribaudi, "Images of the South," in *Italian Cultural Studies*, ed. Forgacs and Lumley, 72–87; Loredana Sciolla, *Italiani: Stereotipi di casa nostra* (Bologna: Il Mulino, 1997).

16. Carlo Brusa, *Geografia del potere politico in Italia* (Milan: Unicopli, 1984); Giulio Sapelli, *L'Italia inafferrabile: Conflitti, sviluppo, dissociazione dagli anni cinquanta a oggi* (Venice: Marsilio, 1989); Francesco Barbagallo, *La modernità squilibrata del Mezzogiorno d'Italia* (Turin: Einaudi, 1994); Filippo Sabetti, "Path Dependency and Civic Culture: Some Lessons from Italy about Interpreting Social Experiments," *Politics and Society* 24 (1996): 19–44.

17. The best-known recent example in English is Robert D. Putnam, with Robert Leonardi and Raffaella Y. Nanetti, *Making Democracy Work: Civic Traditions in Modern Italy* (Princeton: Princeton University Press, 1993). This book revives

the amoral familism thesis to explain the relative success of regional governments in northern and southern Italy. Bossi would find this book supportive of much of what he claims, notwithstanding its self-consciously neutral political tone (see chapter 4 of this book).

18. Edward W. Soja, *Postmodern Geographies: The Reassertion of Space in Critical Social Theory* (London: Verso, 1989).

19. Alon Confino, *The Nation as a Local Metaphor: Württemberg, Imperial Germany, and National Memory, 1871–1918* (Chapel Hill: University of North Carolina Press, 1997), 23. Stressing somewhat more the "variable appropriations" of *Heimat* in Germany is Rudy Koshar, "The Antinomies of *Heimat:* Homeland, History, Nazism," in *"Heimat," Nation, Fatherland: The German Sense of Belonging,* ed. Jost Hermand and James Steakley (New York: Peter Lang, 1996), 113–36.

20. Adriana Destro, "A New Era and New Themes in Italian Politics: The Case of Padania," *Journal of Modern Italian Studies* 2 (1997): 358–77; Luigi Ambrosoli, emeritus professor of history, University of Verona, interviewed at Varese, 12 September 1997; Carlo Lacaita, professor of contemporary history, University of Milan, interviewed at Varese, 9 September 1997.

21. Soja, *Postmodern Geographies.*

22. Biorcio, *Padania promessa,* 204. In League discourse "Padanians" are associated with a large number of civic virtues, whereas southerners are defined almost exclusively in terms of various ethnic traits. Indeed, Padania is seen very much in relation to the future, as a land of promise blessed by a virtuous population, dragged down by an Italy mired in fatalism, criminality, and dependency. On the civic-ethnic character of League discourse and opposing ones, see Giuseppe Sciortino, "'Just before the Fall': The Northern League and the Cultural Construction of a Secessionist Claim," *International Sociology* 14 (1999): 321–36.

23. Professor Carlo Lacaita, interview, 9 September 1997.

24. Professor Carlo Lacaita, interview, 9 September 1997.

25. Biorcio, *Padania promessa,* 207.

26. Biorcio, *Padania promessa,* 208.

27. "La Padania ha bisogno di martiri," *Corriere della Sera,* 29 June 1998, 5.

28. Richard Barraclough, "Umberto Bossi: Charisma, Personality and Leadership," *Modern Italy* 3 (1998): 263–69. More generally on changes in the language of Italian politics, see Patrick McCarthy, "Italy: A New Language for a New Politics?" *Journal of Modern Italian Studies* 2 (1997): 337–57.

29. A. Biglia, "Fassa: Il mio è un addio a tempo," *Corriere della Sera,* 17 November 1997, 7; Raimondo Fassa, *Le prospettive liberal del Paese in Europa: Federalismo? Presidenzialismo? Secessionismo?* (Varese: Gruppo dei Liberali Democratici e Riformatori Europei, 1997).

30. This assumption is apparent also in Fassa's books: Fassa, *Prospettive liberal;* Raimondo Fassa, *Dalla Lega di Stato alla Lega di Città: Riflessioni tra il Municipio di Varese e l'Europarlamento di Strasburgo* (Varese: ELDR, 1998).

31. Ilvo Diamanti, "La Lega fa finite elezioni," *Il Sole/24 Ore,* 26 October 1997, 2; "La Lega va in corner: Il Carroccio perde terreno ma difende fortini importanti," *La Prealpina* (Varese), 18 November 1997, 1.

32. Gianfranco Miglio and Augusto Barbera, *Federalismo e secessione: Un dialogo* (Milan: Mondadori, 1997), 168–69.

33. Biorcio, *Padania promessa,* 131.

34. Biorcio, *Padania promessa.*

35. Robert K. Merton, *Social Theory and Social Structure* (New York: Free Press, 1957). For critiques of this intellectually popular opposition and its negative effects on social theory and political practice in the twentieth century see John A. Agnew, *Place and Politics: The Geographical Mediation of State and Society* (London: Allen and Unwin, 1987), chaps. 3 and 4; also, and specifically in relation to Italian localism and the community/society opposition, see Raimondo Strassoldo and Nicoletta Tessarin, *Le radici del localismo: Indagine sociologica sull'appartenza territoriale in Friuli* (Trento: Reverdito, 1992), chap. 1.

36. Biorcio, *Padania promessa,* 121–25, 202–3; Ilvo Diamanti and Paolo Segatti, "Orgogliosi di essere italiani," *LiMes* 4 (1994): 15–36; Renato Mannheimer, "Ma solo 5 padani su 100 sono secessionisti," *Corriere della Sera,* 3 June 1996, 2; M. Chiara Barlucchi, "Quale secessione in Italia?" *Rivista Italiana di Scienza Politica* 27 (1997): 345–71.

37. This conclusion is reinforced by the decision to enter once again into electoral alliance with Berlusconi's Polo of Forza Italia and Alleanza Nazionale in January 2001 and by the return to the pre-1994 strategy of emphasizing federalism over secession. This was a direct response to the drift of League voters in the Veneto to either Forza Italia or the revived Liga Veneta as a result of Berlusconi's commitment to giving the Veneto the same special status as Friuli and Alto Adige and to disenchantment with Bossi's Padanian strategy. See, e.g., on the alliance, Gian Antonio Stella, "Cosi parla il senatur," *Corriere della Sera,* 26 January 2001, 1, 9, and Fabio Cavalero, "Patto con il Polo, 'si' dei capi leghisti," *Corriere della Sera,* 26 January 2001, 9; and, on the drift of the Veneto and the large cities away from the League, Roberto Biorcio, "Per il Polo una vittorio sola a metà," *Il Sole/24 Ore,* 29 April 1997, 3; Ilvo Diamanti, "Il vento del Nord porta bufere," *Il Sole/24 Ore,* 28 September 1998; and this book, chapter 7.

38. This has begun to change with the proliferation of regionalist movements in Western Europe since the 1970s. See, e.g., David McCrone, "Being British: Changing National and State Identities in Scotland and Wales," *Journal for the Study of British Cultures* 7 (2000): 39–49, and André Lecours, "Political Institutions, Elites, and Territorial Identity Formation in Belgium," *National Identities* 3 (2001): 51–68.

39. Ilvo Diamanti, "Nuove generazioni: L'Europa è lontana, l'Italia un po' meno," *Il Mulino* 46 (1997): 49.

40. Diamanti, "Nuove generazioni," 53.

41. The relative importance of local and national identites therefore is bad news for the League's strategy of emphasizing a northern regional identity. It also can be interpreted as suggesting the "possible reunification" of Italy around joint local-national identities. See Enzo Nocifora, *Italia: La riunificazione possibile. Differenziazione territoriale e regionalismo nella società degli anni novanta* (Rome: SEAM, 1994).

42. The fact is that local governments have increased their powers and autonomy in recent years, giving them greater political importance than under the old regime before 1992. In particular, city mayors are now elected directly. This gives mayors an importance in local politics independent of party, allows for a greater local authority, and gives city governments greater legitimacy in struggles with national governments. See, in particular, the important article by Bruno Dente, "Sub-national Governments in the Long Italian Transition," *West European Politics* 20 (1997): 176–93.

43. Politicians interviewed in Varese are listed at the end of the chapter.

44. Quoted in Michele Salvati, "Muddling Through: Economics and Politics in Italy, 1969–1979," in *Italy in Transition: Conflict and Consensus,* ed. Peter Lange and Sidney Tarrow (London: Pinter, 1980).

Chapter 9

1. J. B. Racine, C. Raffestin, and V. Ruffy, "Scala e azione, contributi per una interpretazione del meccanismo della scala nella pratica della geografia," in *Esistere e abitare: Prospettive umanistiche nella geografia francofona,* ed. Clara Copeta (Milan: Franco Angeli, 1986).

2. T. Valkonen, "Individual and Structural Effects in Ecological Research," in *Social Ecology,* ed. Mattei Dogan and Stein Rokkan (Cambridge: MIT Press, 1969).

3. Neil Smith, "Geography, Difference and the Politics of Scale," in *Postmodernism and the Social Sciences,* ed. Joe Doherty, Elspeth Graham, and Mo Malek (New York: St. Martin's Press, 1992).

4. Racine, Raffestin, and Ruffy, "Scala e azione."

5. See chapter 2 of this book and, for example, Byron Miller, "Political Action and the Geography of Defense Investment: Geographical Scale and the Representation of the Massachusetts Miracle," *Political Geography* 16 (1997): 171–85.

6. John Agnew, *Place and Politics: The Geographical Mediation of State and Society* (London: Allen and Unwin, 1987).

7. Angelo Panebianco, *Political Parties: Organization and Power* (Cambridge: Cambridge University Press, 1988).

8. David Harvey, "The Geographical and Geopolitical Consequences of the Transition from Fordist to Flexible Accumulation," in *America's New Market Geography,* ed. George Sternlieb and James W. Hughes (New Brunswick, N.J.: Center for Urban Policy Research Press, 1988).

9. Jeffry A. Frieden, "Invested Interests: The Politics of National Economic Policies in a World of Global Finance," *International Organization* 45 (1991): 425–51.

10. For example, Paul C. Cheshire et al., "Purpose Built for Failure: Local, Regional and National Government in Britain," *Environment and Planning C: Government and Policy* 10 (1992): 355–69; A. Knapp and P. Le Galès, "Top-Down to Bottom-Up? Centre-Periphery Relations and Power Structures in France's Gaullist party," *West European Politics* 16 (1993): 271–94.

11. Zdravko Mlinar, ed., *Globalization and Territorial Identities* (Brookfield, Vt.: Avebury, 1992).

12. For example, Claus Offe, "New Social Movements: Challenging the Boundaries of Institutional Politics," *Social Research* 52 (1985): 817–68; Sidney Tarrow, *Struggle, Politics, and Reform: Collective Action, Social Movements, and Cycles of Protest* (Ithaca: Center for International Studies, Cornell University, 1989); Donatella della Porta and Hanspeter Kriesi, "Movimenti sociali e globalizzazione," *Rivista Italiana di Scienza Politica* 28 (1998): 451–82.

13. Sidney Tarrow, "The Europeanisation of Conflict: Reflections from a Social Movement Perspective," *West European Politics* 18 (1995): 223–51.

14. Carlo Trigilia, *Grandi partiti e piccole imprese: Comunisti e democristiani nelle regioni di economia diffusa* (Bologna: Il Mulino, 1986); Carlo Trigilia, "The Paradox of the Region: Economic Regulation and the Representation of Interests," *Economy and Society* 20 (1991): 306–27.

15. Arnaldo Bagnasco, *La città dopo Ford: Il caso di Torino* (Turin: Bollati Boringhieri, 1990); Attilio Celant, "Regional Development, International Division

of Labour and the Italian Mezzogiorno," in *Italian Geography in the Eighties*, ed. Berardo Cori et al. (Pisa: Giardini, 1988).

16. Miriam Golden, *Labor Divided: Austerity and Working Class Politics in Contemporary Italy* (Ithaca: Cornell University Press, 1988); M. Kreile, "The Crisis of Italian Trade Unionism in the 1980s," *West European Politics* 11 (1988): 54–67; Richard M. Locke, "The Resurgence of the Local Union: Industrial Restructuring and Industrial Relations in Italy," *Politics and Society* 18 (1990): 327–79.

17. Stefano Guzzini, "The 'Long Night of the First Republic': Years of Clientelistic Implosion in Italy," *Review of International Political Economy* 2 (1995): 27–61.

18. John A. Agnew, "Political Decentralization and Urban Policy in Italy," *Policy Studies Journal* 18 (1990): 768–84. In the 1990s local authorities did acquire more revenue-raising powers. See Bruno Dente, "Sub-national Governments in the Long Italian Transition," *West European Politics* 20 (1997): 176–93.

19. Silvio Lanaro, *L'Italia nuova: Identità e sviluppo, 1861–1988* (Turin: Einaudi, 1988); Adrian Lyttelton, "The National Question in Italy," in *The National Question in Europe in Historical Context*, ed. Mikulás Teich and Roy Porter (Cambridge: Cambridge University Press, 1993).

20. John Agnew, "The Rhetoric of Regionalism: The Northern League in Italian Politics, 1983–1994," *Transactions of the Institute of British Geographers* 20 (1995): 156–72.

21. F. Ramella, "L'area rossa," in *Milano a Roma: Guida all'Italia elettorale del 1994*, ed. Ilvo Diamanti and Renato Mannheimer (Rome: Donzelli, 1994), 107; Giovanna Zincone, *U.S.A. con cautela: Il sistema politico italiano e il modello americano* (Rome: Donzelli, 1995), 34.

22. Sidney Tarrow, *Peasant Communism in Southern Italy* (New Haven: Yale University Press, 1967).

23. Sidney Tarrow, *Democracy and Disorder: Protest and Politics in Italy, 1965–1975* (New York: Oxford University Press, 1989); Robert Lumley, *States of Emergency: Cultures of Revolt in Italy, from 1968 to 1978* (London: Verso, 1990).

24. See, in particular, Peter Lange, Cynthia Irvin, and Sidney Tarrow, "Mobilization, Social Movements and Party Recruitment: The Italian Communist Party since the 1960s," *British Journal of Political Science* 20 (1990): 15–42.

25. Guzzini, "'Long Night of the First Republic,'" 31.

26. Alessandro Pizzorno, "Per un'analisi teorica dei partiti politici in Italia," in *I soggetti del pluralismo: Classi, partiti e sindacati*, by Alessandro Pizzorno (Bologna: Il Mulino, 1980), 39–42.

27. Alessandro Pizzorno, "I due poteri dei partiti," in *I soggetti del pluralismo: Classi, partiti e sindacati*, by Alessandro Pizzorno (Bologna: Il Mulino, 1980), 53–54.

28. Alessandro Pizzorno, "Categorie per una crisi," *MicroMega* 3 (June–July 1993): 81–96.

29. Pizzorno, "Categorie per una crisi," 95–96.

30. Guzzini, "'Long Night of the First Republic,'" 35–36.

31. Rudolf Wildenmann, "The Problematic of Party Government," in *Visions and Realities of Party Government*, ed. Francis G. Castles and Rudolf Wildenmann (Berlin: De Gruyter, 1986), 2; Zincone, *U.S.A. con cautela*, 23.

32. Guzzini, "'Long Night of the First Republic,'" 54.

33. The decline in bipolarity between left and right and the ascendancy of a new generation of magistrates with less commitment to *partitocrazia* were also

important in setting the scene for the corruption investigations. See, e.g., for various views on the role of the judiciary, Stanton H. Burnett and Luca Mantovani, *The Italian Guillotine:. Operation Clean Hands and the Overthrow of the First Republic* (Lanham, Md.: Rowman and Littlefield, 1998); Sarah Waters, "'Tangentopoli' and the Emergence of a New Political Order in Italy," *West European Politics* 17 (1994): 169–82; and Patrizia Pederzoli and Carlo Guarnieri, "The Judicialization of Politics, Italian Style," *Journal of Modern Italian Studies* 2 (1997): 321–36.

34. The Sicilian side of this is explored in Alexander Stille, *Excellent Cadavers: The Mafia and the Death of the First Italian Republic* (New York: Pantheon, 1995); the Neapolitan side is examined in Percy Allum, "La DC a Napoli: L'ultima fase. Il trionfo della macchina politico-criminale," *Nord e Sud* 45 (1998): 67–87, and Francesco Barbagallo, *Il potere della camorra (1973–1988)* (Turin: Einaudi, 1999).

35. See Agnew, "Rhetoric of Regionalism."

36. Since then there has hardly been a clean institutional break with the past. As Sergio Fabbrini has convincingly argued, "the crisis in the old party system did not generate an institutional transformation of Italian democracy" (Sergio Fabbrini, "Political Change without Institutional Transformation: What Can We Learn from the Italian Crisis of the 1990s?" *International Political Science Review* 21 [2000]: 174).

37. Mark Gilbert, *The Italian Revolution: The End of Politics, Italian Style?* (Boulder Colo.: Westview Press, 1995).

38. R. D'Alimonte and A. Chiaramonte, "Il nuovo sistema elettorale italiano: Quali opportunità?" *Rivista Italiana di Scienza Politica* 23 (1993): 513–47; Richard S. Katz, "Electoral Reform and the Transformation of Party Politics in Italy," *Party Politics* 2 (1996): 31–53.

39. Percy Allum, "Il Mezzogiorno," in *Milano a Roma: Guida all'Italia elettorale del 1994,* ed. Ilvo Diamanti and Renato Mannheimer (Rome: Donzelli, 1994).

40. A. Agosta, "Maggioritario e proporzionale," in *Milano a Roma: Guida all'Italia elettorale del 1994,* ed. Ilvo Diamanti and Renato Mannheimer (Rome: Donzelli, 1994).

41. It is important to note, however, that the League is not a fan of a fully majoritarian system because this would reduce its coalition bargaining power relative to parties such as Forza Italia. The unsuccessful 18 April 1999 referendum to create a fully majoritarian system was defeated in part because of this kind of opposition from the League and small parties across the political spectrum, but also because of very low turnout by voters of all persuasions. Indeed, the vote failed not because of the size of the "no" vote (only 8.9 percent) but because the turnout was under the 50 percent plus one required to make the result stand (49.6 percent). Ironically, given the League's position, the lowest turnouts were in the South. If only the South had voted a little more, the referendum would have succeeded and given Italy a simple majority electoral system (Daria Gorodisky, "L'Italia no va a votare, referendum nullo," *Corriere della Sera,* 19 April 1999, 2).

42. Martin J. Bull and James L. Newell, "Italy Changes Course? The 1994 Elections and the Victory of the Right," *Parliamentary Affairs* 48 (1995): 72–99.

43. Piergiorgio Corbetta and Arturo M. L. Parisi, eds., *Cavalieri e Fanti: Proposte e proponenti nelle elezioni del 1994 e del 1996* (Bologna: Il Mulino, 1997).

44. Golden, *Labour Divided.*

45. Trigilia, *Grandi partiti e piccole imprese.*

46. David I. Kertzer, *Comrades and Christians: Religion and Political Struggle in*

Communist Italy (Cambridge: Cambridge University Press, 1980), 63; also see Carlo Baccetti, "Memoria storica e continuità elettorale: Una zona rossa nella Toscana rossa," *Italia Contemporanea* 167 (1987): 7–30.

47. See Mario Caciagli, "Toscana: Il declino della subcultura rossa," in *Elezioni regionali del '90: Un punto di svolta?* ed. Paolo Feltrin and Andrea Politi (Venice: Marsilio, 1990).

48. Piero Ignazi, *Dal PCI al PDS* (Bologna: Il Mulino, 1992); Mario Caciagli, "Tra internazionalismo e localismo: L'area rossa," *Meridiana* 16 (1993): 93; Carlo Baccetti and Mario Caciagli, "Dopo il PCI e dopo l'URSS: Una subcultura rossa rivisitata," *Polis* 6 (1992): 537–68.

49. See, for example, Maurizio Degl'Innocenti, *Geografia e istituzioni del socialismo italiano* (Naples: Guida, 1983); Giulio Sapelli, *Comunità e mercato:. Socialisti, cattolici e governo municipale agli inizi del XX secolo* (Bologna: Il Mulino, 1986).

50. Caciagli, "Tra internazionalismo e localismo," 93–96.

51. See Trigilia, "Paradox of the Region." The appeal is more than economic, however. President Ciampi's attempt at making the Festa della Repubblica on 4 June 2000 a truly national event rather than a purely Roman one by privileging the role of regional and other local leaders represents a recognition of the political weight of renewed decentralist thinking in center-left circles. See Marzio Breda, "Ciampi invita le Regioni alla parata," *Corriere della Sera,* 30 May 2000, 2.

52. Franco Ferraresi, "Nord-Sud, destra-sinistra: La disunità del Bel Paese," *Corriere della Sera,* 16 June 1994, 1–2. Also see Bianca Beccalli, "The Modern Women's Movement in Italy," *New Left Review* 204 (1994): 86–112.

53. Ilvo Diamanti, *La Lega: Geografia, storia e sociologia di un nuovo soggetto politico* (Rome: Donzelli, 1993); Agnew, "Rhetoric of Regionalism."

54. For the former see, for example, Carlo Trigilia, *Sviluppo senza autonomia: Effetti perversi delle politiche nel Mezzogiorno* (Bologna: Il Mulino, 1992), and Simona Piattoni, "Clientelism Revisited: Clientelistic Politics and Economic Development in Postwar Italy," *Italian Politics and Society* 49 (1998): 44–62. For the latter see Robert D. Putnam, with Robert Leonardi and Raffaella Y. Nanetti, *Making Democracy Work: Civic Traditions in Modern Italy* (Princeton: Princeton University Press, 1993).

55. Stefano Allievi, *Le parole della Lega: Il movimento politico che vuole un'altra Italia* (Milan: Garzanti, 1992), 60.

56. N. Sunseri, "'E ora un governo di lunga durata': Bossi esulta e annuncia il suo programma, 'Subito l'antitrust,'" *La Repubblica,* 25 January 1995, 5.

57. Paul Ginsborg, "Italy Takes Its Time to Solve Latest Crisis," *Independent,* 30 December 1994, 9.

58. Carlo Zanzi, *Maroni l'arciere* (Varese: Lativa, 1994).

59. G. Credazzi, "Segni: La Lega vince solo con noi," *Corriere della Sera,* 5 December 1994, 2; D. Williams, "For Italians, It's Back to the Bad Old Days," *Washington Post National Weekly Edition,* 9–15 January 1995, 19–20.

60. Hints to this appear in G. Fre, "I ribelli lumbard: Solo con Forza Italia," *Corriere della Sera,* 5 January 1995, 4.

61. Giorgio Galli, *Diario politico 1994: L'imbroglio del 28 marzo e il governo* (Milan: Kaos, 1994), 46–47.

62. A. Padellaro, "Verrano a cercarmi di nuovo," *L'Espresso,* 14 July 1995, 58–60.

63. Indro Montanelli, "Un certo Cattaneo (norme per l'uso)," *Corriere della Sera,* 24 July 1995, 1.

64. Piero Ignazi, *Il polo escluso: Profilo del Movimento Sociale Italiano* (Bologna: Il Mulino, 1989).

65. G. Perna, "Fascisti, addio per sempre," *Epoca,* 29 January 1995, 28–33.

66. J. Fenby, "Les gages de la peur," *London Review of Books,* 3 August 1995, 24.

67. Cesare Mattina, "Il MSI-AN tra tradizione e modernità: Il voto e l'identità di un partito in trasformazione," *Nord e Sud* 45 (1998): 142–65.

68. R. Chiarini, "La destra italiana: Il paradosso di un'identità illegitima," *Italia Contemporanea* 185 (1991): 581–600. Notwithstanding the failure of the MSI-AN to really come to terms with its past and the authoritarian cast of its activists, the deradicalization of Italian politics since the late 1980s and the new tendency among intellectuals and the general public to look at the history of Fascism as more than a prelude to anti-Fascism and the Resistance (a part of the myth of the Resistance noted in chapters 5 and 6 of this book) have helped to remove the party from the political ghetto in which it was trapped for much of the postwar period. This has undoubtedly helped its normalization and enhanced its possibilities as a party of government. The closest analysis of these features of the MSI to AN transition is provided in Piero Ignazi, *Postfascisti? Dal Movimento Sociale Italiano ad Alleanza Nazionale* (Bologna: Il Mulino, 1994).

69. Recurring charges of MSI and far right involvement in attempts at destabilizing the national government throughout the postwar period, but particularly during the 1970s and early 1980s, receive their most convincing support in Franco Ferraresi, *Threats to Democracy: The Radical Right in Italy after the War* (Princeton: Princeton University Press, 1996).

70. Roberto Cartocci, *Fra Lega e Chiesa: L'Italia in cerca di integrazione* (Bologna: Il Mulino, 1994), 84–87.

71. Adrian Lyttelton, "Italy: The Triumph of TV," *New York Review of Books* 41 (11 August 1994): 25–29.

72. P. Milza, "Il football italiano: Una storia lunga un secolo," *Italia Contemporanea* 183 (1991): 245–55.

73. Euan Hague, "Uniting Italy, Fragmenting Italy: Football as Italy's Cultural Form," unpublished manuscript, Department of Geography, Syracuse University, 1994, 4.

74. Renato Mannheimer, "Forza Italia," in *Milano a Roma: Guida all'Italia elettorale del 1994,* ed. Ilvo Diamanti and Renato Mannheimer (Rome: Donzelli, 1994).

75. Mannheimer, "Forza Italia." More generally, on the role of the personalization and commercialization of Italian politics before the emergence of Berlusconi see, e.g., Gianfranco Pasquino, "Personae non gratae? Personalizzazione e spettacolarizzazione della politica," *Polis* 4 (1990): 203–16, and Gianpietro Mazzoleni, "Dal partito al candidato: Come cambia la comunicazione elettorale in Italia," *Polis* 4 (1990): 249–47. A large literature has now developed on Berlusconi as the progenitor of a new personalized national politics. See, e.g., Mauro Calise, *Il partito personale* (Rome: Laterza, 2000); Emanuela Poli, "Silvio Berlusconi and the Myth of the Creative Entrepreneur," *Modern Italy* 3 (1998): 153–57; and Gianni Statera, *Il volto seduttivo del potere: Berlusconi, i media, il consenso* (Rome: SEAM, 1994). This has made its way into the United States press. See, e.g., Alessandra Stanley, "Of TV and Soccer: The Power of Celebrity Hits Italian Politics," *New York Times,* Week in Review, 20 May 2001, 3.

76. Agnew, "Rhetoric of Regionalism," 20.

77. L. Verzichelli, "Gli eletti," *Rivista Italiana di Scienza Politica* 24 (1994): 713–39.

78. Renato Mannheimer, "E se fossero politiche? Azzurri più a destra," *Corriere della Sera,* 5 December 1994, 2.

79. Alexander Stille, "Making Way for Berlusconi," *New York Review of Books* 48 (21 June 2001): 73–74.

80. M. Latella, "Berlusconi: 'Forza Italia sono io,'" *Corriere della Sera,* 22 November 1994, 3.

81. Tarrow, "Europeanisation of Conflict," 231.

BIBLIOGRAPHY

Acquaviva, Sabino S., and Mario Santuccio. *Social Structure in Italy: Crisis of a System.* Boulder, Colo.: Westview Press, 1976.

Agnew, John A. *Place and Politics: The Geographical Mediation of State and Society.* London: Allen and Unwin, 1987.

———. "'Better Thieves Than Reds'? The Nationalization Thesis and the Possibility of a Geography of Italian Politics." *Political Geography Quarterly* 7 (1988): 307–21.

———. "La città nel contesto culturale e i valori ambientali." In *Natura e cultura nella città del futuro,* ed. Calogero Muscarà and Lelio Pagani. Bergamo: Consorzio del Parco dei Colli di Bergamo, 1988.

———. "The Devaluation of Place in Social Science." In *The Power of Place: Bringing Together Sociological and Geographical Imaginations,* ed. John Agnew and James Duncan. London: Unwin Hyman, 1989.

———. "Political Decentralization and Urban Policy in Italy." *Policy Studies Journal* 18 (1990): 768–84.

———. "Representing Space: Space, Scale and Culture in Social Science." In *Place/Culture/Representation,* ed. James Duncan and David Ley. London: Routledge, 1993.

———. "The Territorial Trap: The Geographical Assumptions of International Relations Theory." *Review of International Political Economy* 1 (1994): 53–80.

———. "The Rhetoric of Regionalism: The Northern League in Italian Politics, 1983–1994." *Transactions of the Institute of British Geographers* 20 (1995): 156–72.

———. *Rome.* New York: Wiley, 1995.

———. "Liminal Travellers: Hebrideans at Home and Away." *Scotlands* 3 (1996): 31–42.

———. "Mapping Politics: How Context Counts in Electoral Geography." *Political Geography* 15 (1996): 129–46.

———. "Maps and Models in Political Studies: A Reply to Comments." *Political Geography* 15 (1996): 165–67.

———. *Geopolitics: Re-visioning World Politics.* London: Routledge, 1998.

———. "The Impossible Capital: Monumental Rome under Liberal and Fascist Regimes, 1870–1943." *Geografiska Annaler B* 80 (1998): 229–40.

———. "Mapping Political Power beyond State Boundaries: Territory, Identity, and Movement in World Politics." *Millennium* 28 (1999): 499–521.

————. "Italy's Island Other: Sicily's History in the Modern Italian Body Politic." *Emergences* 10 (2000): 301–11.

Agnew, John A., and Stuart Corbridge. *Mastering Space: Hegemony, Territory, and International Political Economy.* London: Routledge, 1995.

Agosta, A. "Maggioritario e proporzionale." In *Milano a Roma: Guida all'Italia elettorale del 1994,* ed. Ilvo Dimanati and Renato Mannheimer. Rome: Donzelli, 1994.

Alasio, Franco, and Montaldi, Danilo. *Milano, Corea: Inchiesta sugli immigrati.* Milan: Feltrinelli, 1975.

Allen, Beverly, and Mary Russo, eds. *Revisioning Italy: National Identity and Global Culture.* Minneapolis: University of Minnesota Press, 1997.

Allievi, Stefano. *Le parole della Lega: Il movimento politico che vuole un'altra Italia.* Milan: Garzanti, 1992.

Allum, Percy A. "The South and National Politics, 1945–50." In *The Rebirth of Italy, 1943–50,* ed. Stuart J. Woolf. London: Longman, 1972.

————. *Italy: Republic without Government?* New York: Norton, 1973.

————. "Cultura o opinione? Su alcune dubbi epistemologici." *Il Politico* 53 (1988): 261–68.

————. "Il Mezzogiorno." In *Milano a Roma: Guida all'Italia elettorale del 1994,* ed. Ilvo Diamanti and Renato Mannheimer. Rome: Donzelli, 1994.

————. "'From Two into One': The Faces of the Italian Christian Democratic Party." *Party Politics* 3 (1997): 23–52.

————. "La DC a Napoli: L'ultima fase. Il trionfo della macchina politica-criminale." *Nord e Sud* 45 (1998): 67–87.

Allum, Percy A., et al. "Le trasformazioni del mondo cattolico e della società rurale nel voto del 1946 in provincia di Vicenza." *Quaderni dell'Osservatorio Elettorale* 21 (1988): 33–85.

Almond, Gabriel, and Sidney Verba. *The Civic Culture.* Boston: Little, Brown, 1963.

Amin, Ash, and Kevin Robins. "The Re-emergence of Regional Economies: The Mythical Geography of Flexible Accumulation." *Society and Space* 8 (1990): 7–34.

Amyot, Grant. *The Italian Communist Party: The Crisis of the Popular Front Strategy.* New York: St. Martin's Press, 1981.

"L'analisi del voto." *La Prealpina* (Varese), 3 December 1997, 13.

Anderlini, Fausto. "Una modellizzazione per zone sociopolitiche dell'Italia repubblicana." *Polis* 1 (1987): 443–79.

————. "Grandi metropoli, piccole province." In *L'urbanistica dell'aree metropolitane,* ed. Rino Rosini. Florence: Alinea, 1992.

Anderson, Benedict. *Imagined Communities: Reflections on the Origins and Spread of Nationalism.* London: Verso, 1983.

Andrews, Malcolm. *Landscape Imagery and Urban Culture in Early Nineteenth Century England.* Cambridge: Cambridge University Press, 1992.

Appadurai, Arjun. "Putting Hierarchy in Its Place." *Cultural Anthropology* 3 (1988): 36–49.

Applegate, Celia. *A Nation of Provincials: The German Idea of "Heimat."* Berkeley and Los Angeles: University of California Press, 1990.

Ascherson, Neal. "Reflections on International Space." *London Review of Books,* 24 May 2001, 7–11.

Ascoli, Ugo. *Movimento migratori in Italia.* Bologna: Il Mulino, 1979.

Augé, Marc. *Non-places: Introduction to the Anthropology of Supermodernity.* London: Verso, 1995.

Baccetti, Carlo. "Memoria storica e continuità elettorale: Una zona rossa nella Toscana rossa." *Italia Contemporanea* 167 (1987): 7–30.

———. "Il triplice voto del 1946 in Toscana: La fondazione del predominio del PCI." *Quaderni dell'Osservatorio Elettorale* 20 (1988): 7–86.

———. "L'ultima svolta: Il XIX Congresso Straordinario del PCI in Toscana." *Polis* 5 (1991): 519–51.

———. "La Toscana: Le nuove vesti di un'antica egemonia." In *Le elezioni della transizione: Il sistema politico italiano alla prova del voto 1994–1996,* ed. Giuseppe Gangemi and Gianni Riccamboni. Turin: UTET, 1997.

Baccetti, Carlo, and Mario Caciagli. "Dopo il PCI e dopo l'URSS: Una subcultura rossa rivisitata." *Polis* 6 (1992): 537–68.

Bagnasco, Arnaldo. *Tre Italie: La problematica territoriale dello sviluppo italiano.* Bologna: Il Mulino, 1987.

———. *La costruzione sociale del mercato: Studi sullo sviluppo di piccola impresa in Italia.* Bologna: Il Mulino, 1988.

———. *La città dopo Ford: Il caso di Torino.* Turin: Bollati Boringhieri, 1990.

———. "Geografia elettorale e basi sociali della politica." *Rassegna Italiana di Sociologia* 37 (1996): 279–85.

———. *L'Italia in tempi di cambiamento politico.* Bologna: Il Mulino, 1996.

Bagnasco, Arnaldo, and Carlo Trigilia. *Società e politica nelle aree di piccola impresa: Il caso di Bassano.* Venice: Arsenale, 1984.

———. *Società e politica nelle aree di piccola impresa: Il caso di Valdelsa.* Milan: Franco Angeli, 1985.

Baiocchi, Giuseppe. "Da Berlusconi e CDL una prova di lealtà." *La Padania* 15 May 2001.

Baldacci, Valentino. "Il 18 aprile 1948: La campagna di Toscana." *Quaderni dell'Osservatorio Elettorale* 20 (1988): 89–197.

Ballini, Pierluigi. "La Democrazia Cristiana." In *La ricostruzione in Toscana: Dal CLN ai partiti,* vol. 2, *I partiti politici,* ed. E. Rotelli. Bologna: Il Mulino, 1981.

Banfield, Edward C. *The Moral Basis of a Backward Society.* New York: Free Press, 1958.

———. *The Unheavenly City.* Boston: Little, Brown, 1972.

Barbagallo, Francesco. *La modernità squilibrata del Mezzogiorno d'Italia.* Turin: Einaudi, 1994.

———. *Il potere della camorra (1973–1988).* Turin: Einaudi, 1999.

Bardelli, Renzo. *Le mani degli amici.* Pistoia: Tellini, 1985.

Bardelli, Renzo, and Marco Francini. *Pistoia e la Resistenza.* Pistoia: Tellini, 1980.

Barlucchi, M. Chiara. "Quale secessione in Italia?" *Rivista Italiana di Scienza Politica* 27 (1997): 345–71.

Barnes, Samuel H. *Representation in Italy: Institutionalized Tradition and Electoral Choice.* Chicago: University of Chicago Press, 1977.

Baron, Stephen, John Field, and Tom Schuller, eds. *Social Capital: Critical Perspectives.* Oxford: Oxford University Press, 2000.

Barraclough, Richard. "Umberto Bossi: Charisma, Personality and Leadership." *Modern Italy* 3 (1998): 263–69.

Bassin, Mark. "Geopolitics in the *Historikerstreit:* The Strange Return of *Mitellage.*" In *"Heimat," Nation, Fatherland: The German Sense of Belonging,* ed. Jost Hermand and James Steakley. New York: Peter Lang, 1996.

Baucom, Ian. *Out of Place: Englishness, Empire, and the Locations of Identity.* Princeton: Princeton University Press, 1999.

Beccalli, Bianca. "The Modern Women's Movement in Italy." *New Left Review* 204 (1994): 86–112.

Becattini, Giacomo, ed. *Lo sviluppo economico della Toscana.* Florence: IRPET, 1975.

Beirich, Heidi, and Dwayne Woods. "Globalisation, Workers and the Northern League." *West European Politics* 23 (2000): 130–43.

Belardelli, Giovanni. "La terza Roma." In *Miti e storia dell'Italia unita,* ed. Giovanni Belardelli et al. Bologna: Il Mulino, 1999.

Bell, Donald H. *Sesto San Giovanni: Workers, Culture, and Politics in an Italian Town.* New Brunswick: Rutgers University Press, 1986.

Bellandi, Paolo. *Alle origini del movimento cattolico—Pistoia, 1892–1904.* Rome: Cinque Lune, 1976.

Bellini, N. "Il socialismo in una regione sola: Il PCI e il governo dell'industria in Emilia-Romagna." *Il Mulino* 325 (1989): 707–32.

Benigno, Francesco. "The Southern Family: A Comment on Paolo Macry." *Journal of Modern Italian Studies* 2 (1997): 215–17.

Berezin, Mabel. *Making the Fascist Self: The Political Culture of Interwar Italy.* Ithaca: Cornell University Press, 1997.

Bernstein, Richard J. *The Restructuring of Social and Political Theory.* Philadelphia: University of Pennsylvania Press, 1978.

Besson, Jean. "Comportements électoraux et politiques." In *Tradition et changement en Toscane,* ed. Anne-Marie Seronde et al. Paris: Armand Colin, 1970.

Bettoni, Giuseppe. "Una provincia travalgiata con tre 'facce' diverse." *La Prealpina* (Varese), 11 October 1998, 8.

Bevir, Mark. "Foucault and Critique: Deploying Agency against Autonomy." *Political Theory* 27 (1999): 65–84.

Bianchi, Gerardo. "Lettera aperta a un oratore comunista." *La Bandiera del Popolo* (Pistoia), 2 March 1945.

———. "La Resistenza a Pistoia." *La Bandiero del Popolo* (Pistoia), March–April 1975, 7.

Bianchini, F. "Milan." In *European Cities towards 2000: Profiles, Policies and Prospects,* ed. A. Harding, J. Dawson, R. Evans, and M. Parkinson. Manchester: Manchester University Press, 1994.

Bibes, Geneviève. "Les mouvements de pensée." In *Tradition et changement en Toscane,* ed. Anne-Marie Seronde et al. Paris: Armand Colin, 1970.

Bibes, Geneviève, and Jean Besson. "The Resurgence of Christian Democracy and the Search for New 'Rules' of the Game." In *Italian Politics: A Review,* vol. 3, ed. Robert Leonardi and Piergiorgio Corbetta. London: Pinter, 1989.

Bidart, Claire. "Sociabilités: Quelque variables." *Revue Française de Sociologie* 29 (1988): 621–48.

Biglia, A. "Fassa: Il mio è un addio a tempo." *Corriere della Sera,* 17 November 1997, 7.

Biggs, Michael. "Putting the State on the Map: Cartography, Territory, and European State Formation." *Comparative Studies in Society and History* 41 (1999): 374–505.

Billig, Michael. *Banal Nationalism.* London: Sage, 1995.

Biorcio, Roberto. *La Padania promessa: La storia, le idee e la logica d'azione della Lega Nord.* Milan: Il Saggiatore, 1997.

—————. "Per il Polo una vittoria sola a metà." *Il Sole/24 Ore,* 29 April 1997, 3.

—————. "L'Unione in Italia: Chi ha paura dell'Euro?" *Il Mulino* 47 (1998): 535–45.

Biorcio, Roberto, and Ilvo Diamanti, "La scelta del voto: Dal risultato all'attore sociale. Appunti per una rilettura del comportamento elettorale in Italia." *Quaderni dell'Osservatorio Elettorale* 19 (1987): 43–85.

Biorcio, Roberto, and Paolo Natale. "Mobilità e fedeltà elettorale negli anni ottanta." *Quaderni dell'Osservatorio Elettorale* 18 (1987): 41–88.

Birindelli, Massimo. *Roma italiana: Come fare una capitale e disfare una città.* Rome: Savelli, 1978.

Bishop, Peter. *An Archetypal Constable: National Identity and the Geography of Nostalgia.* Cranbury, N.J.: Fairleigh Dickinson University Press, 1995.

Blackbourn, David, and Geoff Eley. *The Peculiarities of German History: Bourgeois Society and Politics in Nineteenth Century Germany.* New York: Oxford University Press, 1984.

Blim, Michael L. "Economic Development and Decline in the Emerging Global Factory." *Politics and Society* 18 (1990): 143–63.

Boa, Elizabeth, and Rachel Palfreyman. *"Heimat"—a German Dream: Regional Loyalties and National Identity in German Culture, 1890–1990.* Oxford: Oxford University Press, 2000.

Boime, Albert. "The Macchiaioli and the Risorgimento." In *The Macchiaioli: Painters of Italian Life, 1850–1900,* ed. E. Tonelli and K. Hart. Los Angeles: Wight Art Gallery, UCLA, 1986.

—————. *The Art of the Macchia and the Risorgimento: Representing Culture and Nationalism in Nineteenth-Century Italy.* Chicago: University of Chicago Press, 1994.

Bonomi, Aldo. *Il capitalismo molecolare: La società al lavoro nel Nord Italia.* Turin: Einaudi, 1997.

"Bossi: Padania può arrivare anche senza secessione." *La Padania,* 3 August 1998.

Bosworth, R. J. B. *"Per Necessità Famigliare:* Hypocrisy and Corruption in Fascist Italy." *European History Quarterly* 30 (2000): 357–87.

Bourdieu, Pierre. "Social Space and Symbolic Power." *Sociological Theory* 7 (1989): 14–25.

—————. *The Logic of Practice.* Stanford: Stanford University Press, 1990.

Braudel, Fernand. *The Identity of France.*Vol. 1. *History and Environment.* London: Collins, 1988.

Breda, Marzio. "Ciampi invita le Regioni alla parata." *Corriere della Sera,* 30 May 2000, 2.

Brierley, William, and Luca Giancometti. "Italian National Identity and the Failure of Regionalism." In *Nation and Identity in Contemporary Europe,* ed. Brian Jenkins and Spyros A. Sofos. London: Routledge, 1996.

Brubaker, Rogers, and Frederick Cooper. "Beyond 'Identity.'" *Theory and Society* 29 (2000): 1–47.

Brusa, Carlo. *Geografia elettorale nell'Italia del dopoguerra.* Milan: Unicopli, 1983.

—————. *Geografia del potere politico in Italia.* Milan: Unicopli, 1984.

—————. *Geografia elettorale nell'Italia del dopoguerra: Edizione aggiornata ai risultati delle elezioni politiche 1983.* Milan: Unicopli, 1984.

—————. *Cambiamenti nella geografia elettorale italiana dopo le consultazioni politiche del 1987.* Milan: Unicopli, 1988.

—————. "Elezioni e territorio in una città media in un momento critico: Varese." *Lombardia Nord-Ovest* 2 (1993): 9–35.

Bull, Martin J., and James L. Newell. "Italy Changes Course? The 1994 Elections and the Victory of the Right." *Parliamentary Affairs* 48 (1995): 72–99.

Burnett, Stanton H., and Luca Mantovani. *The Italian Guillotine: Operation Clean Hands and the Overthrow of the First Republic.* Lanham, Md.: Rowman and Littlefield, 1998.

Burnham, Walter Dean. "Party Systems and Political Process." In *The American Party Systems: Stages of Political Development,* ed. W. N. Chambers and W. D. Burnham. New York: Oxford University Press, 1967.

Caciagli, Mario. *Democrazia Cristiana e potere nel Mezzogiorno.* Florence: Guaraldi, 1975.

———. "Il resistibile declino della Democrazia Cristiana." In *Il sistema politico italiano,* ed. Gianfranco Pasquino. Rome: Laterza, 1985.

———, ed. *Governo locale, associazionismo e politico culturale.* Padua: Liviana, 1986.

———. "Approssimazione alle culture politiche locali: Problemi di analisi ed esperienze di ricerca." *Il Politico* 53 (1988): 269–92.

———. "Quante Italie? Persistenza e trasformazione delle culture politiche subnazionali." *Polis* 2 (1988): 429–57.

———. "Toscana: Il declino della subcultura rossa." In *Elezioni regionali del '90: Un punto di svolta?* ed. Paolo Feltrin and Andrea Politi. Venice: Marsilio, 1990.

———. "Italie 1993: Vers la Seconde Republique?" *Revue Française de Science Politique* 43 (1993): 235–248.

———. "Tra internazionalismo e localismo: L'area rossa." *Meridiana* 16 (1993): 81–98.

Caiano, Enrico. "I ribelli a Bossi: Faremo noi la vera Lega." *Corriere della Sera,* 27 July 1999, 7.

Calhoun, Craig. "The Problem of Identity in Collective Action." In *Macro-Micro Linkages in Sociology,* ed. Joan Huber. Thousand Oaks, Calif.: Sage, 1991.

Calise, Mauro. *Il partito personale.* Rome: Laterza, 2000.

Camaiani, Piergiorgio. *Dallo stato cittadino alla città bianca: La "società cristiana" lucchese e la rivoluzione toscana.* Florence: La Nuova Italia, 1979.

Candeloro, Giorgio. *Il movimento cattolico in Italia.* Rome: Riuniti, 1974.

Capecchi, Vittorio, et al. *Il comportamento elettorale in Italia.* Bologna: Il Mulino, 1968.

Caraccioli, Alberto. *Roma capitale: Dal Risorgimento alla crisi dello stato liberale.* Rome: Rinascita, 1956.

Carini, Carlo. *Benedetto Croce e il partito politico.* Florence: Olschki, 1975.

Carozzi, Carlo. "Il caso Milano." In *La città prossima ventura,* ed. Jean Gottmann and Calogero Muscarà. Rome: Laterza, 1991.

Cartocci, Roberto. "Differenze territoriali e tipi di voto: Le consultazioni del maggio-giugno 1985." *Rivista Italiana di Scienza Politica* 15 (1985): 421–54.

———. "Otto risposte a un problema: La divisione dell'Italia in zona politicamente omogenee." *Polis* 1 (1987): 481–514.

———. *Elettori in Italia: Riflessioni sulle vicende elettorali degli anni ottanta.* Bologna: Il Mulino, 1990.

———. *Fra Lega e Chiesa: L'Italia in cerca di integrazione.* Bologna: Il Mulino, 1994.

———. "Indizi di un inverno precoce: Il voto proporzionale tra equilibrio e continuità." *Rivista Italiana di Scienza Politica* 26 (1996): 609–53.

Casey, Edward S. *The Fate of Place: A Philosophical History.* Berkeley and Los Angeles: University of California Press, 1997.

Castelnuovo, Enrico, and Carlo Ginzburg. "Centre and Periphery." In *History of Italian Art*, vol. 1, ed. Peter Burke. Cambridge: Polity Press, 1994.

Catt, Helena. *Voting Behaviour: A Radical Critique*. London: Pinter, 1996.

Cavalero, Fabio. "Patto con il Polo, 'si' dei capi leghisti." *Corriere della Sera*, 26 January 2001, 9.

Cavazza, Stefano. *Piccole patrie: Feste popolari tra regione e nazione durante il fascismo*. Bologna: Il Mulino, 1997.

Cazzola, Franco. "Struttura e potere del Partito Socialista Italiano." In *Il sistema politico italiano*, ed. Gianfranco Pasquino. Rome: Laterza, 1985.

———. *Della corruzione: Fisiologia e patologia di un sistema politico*. Bologna: Il Mulino, 1988.

Cecchella, A. *Lo sviluppo dell'economia lucchese dalla fine del secondo conflitto mondiale*. Pisa: ETS, 1975.

Celant, Attilio. "Regional Development, International Division of Labour and the Italian Mezzogiorno." In *Italian Geography in the Eighties*, ed. Berardo Cori et al. Pisa: Giardini, 1988.

Cento Bull, Anna. "Class, Gender and Voting in Italy." *West European Politics* 20 (1997): 73–92.

Cento Bull, Anna, and Paul Corner. *From Peasant to Entrepreneur: The Survival of the Family Economy in Italy*. Oxford: Berg, 1995.

Cerny, Philip. "Globalization and the Changing Logic of Collective Action." *International Organization* 49 (1995): 595–625.

Cheshire, Paul C., et al. "Purpose Built for Failure: Local, Regional and National Government in Britain." *Environment and Planning C: Government and Policy* 10 (1992): 355–69.

Chiarini, R. "La destra italiana: Il paradosso di un'identità illegitima." *Italia Contemporanea* 185 (1991): 581–600.

Chiti, Vannino. "La DC in Toscana: Economia, cultura, istituzioni." *Critica Marxista* 3 (1981): 153–74.

Chittolini, Giorgio. "Cities, 'City-States,' and Regional States in North-Central Italy." In *Cities and the Rise of New States in Europe, A.D. 1000–1800*, ed. Charles Tilly and Wim Blockmans. Boulder, Colo: Westview Press, 1994.

Chubb, Judith. "The Christian Democratic Party: Reviving or Surviving?" In *Italian Politics: A Review*, vol. 1, ed. Robert Leonardi and Raffaella Y. Nanetti. London: Pinter, 1989.

Churchill, Kenneth. *Italy and English Literature, 1764–1930*. Totowa, N.J.: Barnes and Noble, 1980.

Claggett, William, et al. "Nationalization of the American Electorate." *American Political Science Review* 78 (1984): 77–91.

Clough, Shepard Bancroft *The Economic History of Modern Italy*. New York: Columbia University Press, 1964.

Colarizi, Simona. *L'opinione degli italiani sotto il regime, 1929–1943*. Rome: Laterza, 1991.

Coleman, James S. "Social Capital in the Creation of Human Capital." *American Journal of Sociology* 93 (1988): 1095–1120.

Confindustria. *Indicatori economici provinciali*. Rome: SIPI, 1989.

Confino, Alon. *The Nation as a Local Metaphor: Württemburg, Imperial Germany, and National Memory, 1871–1918*. Chapel Hill: University of North Carolina Press, 1997.

Connolly, William E. "Speed, Concentric Cultures, and Cosmopolitanism." *Political Theory* 28 (2000): 596–618.

Contini, Giovanni. "The Rise and Fall of Shop-Floor Bargaining at Fiat, 1945–1980." In *Between Fordism and Flexibility: The Automobile Industry and Its Workers*, ed. Steven Tolliday and Jonathan Zeitlin. Oxford: Berg, 1992.

Conversi, Daniele. "Reassessing Current Theories of Nationalism: Nationalism as Boundary Maintenance and Control." *Nationalism and Ethnic Politics* 1 (1995): 73–85.

Cooke, Philip. "Locality, Structure, and Agency: A Theoretical Analysis." *Cultural Anthropology* 5 (1990): 3–15.

Cooke, Philip, and A. de Rosa Pires. "Productive Decentralization in Three European Regions." *Environment and Planning A* 17 (1985): 527–54.

Corbetta, Piergiorgio, and Arturo Parisi. "Struttura e tipologia delle elezioni in Italia: 1946–1983." In *Il sistema politico italiano*, ed. Gianfranco Pasquino. Rome: Laterza, 1985.

————. "Smobilitazione partitica e astensionismo elettorale." *Polis* 8 (1994): 423–43.

————, eds. *Cavalieri e Fanti: Proposte e proponenti nelle elezioni del 1994 e del 1996.* Bologna: Il Mulino, 1997.

Corbetta, Piergiorgio, Arturo Parisi, and Hans Schadee. *Elezioni in Italia: Struttura e tipologia delle consultazioni politiche.* Bologna: Il Mulino, 1988.

Corner, Paul. *Fascism in Ferrara, 1915–1922.* Oxford: Clarendon Press, 1975.

————. "Thumbs down for the Family? A Comment on Paolo Macry." *Journal of Modern Italian Studies* 2 (1997): 218–20.

Cosgrove, Denis, and David Atkinson. "Embodied Identities: City, Nation, and Empire at the Vittorio-Emanuele II Monument in Rome." *Annals of the Association of American Geographers* 88 (1998): 28–49.

Cox, Kevin R., ed. *Spaces of Globalization: Reasserting the Power of the Local.* New York: Guilford Press, 1997.

Credazzi, G. "Segni: La Lega vince solo con noi." *Corriere della Sera*, 5 December 1994, 2.

Csillag, Ferenc, and John Agnew. "How Many Italies? A Strategy for Spatial Analysis of Regionalizations of Italian Election Results, 1953–1987." In *Spatial and Contextual Models in Political Research*, ed. Munroe Eagles. London: Taylor and Francis, 1995.

Curcio, Renato. Interview. *L'Espresso*, 18 January 1987, 28.

D'Alimonte, R., and A. Chiaramonte. "Il nuova sistema elettorale italiano: Quali opportunità?" *Rivista Italiana di Scienza Politica* 23 (1993): 513–47.

Dalle Vacche, Angela. *The Body in the Mirror: Shapes of History in Italian Cinema.* Princeton: Princeton University Press, 1992.

D'Amato, Gianni, and Siegfried Schieder. "Italy's Northern League: Between Ethnic Citizenship and a Federal State." In *Rethinking Nationalism and Ethnicity: The Struggle for Meaning and Order in Europe*, ed. Hans-Rudolf Wicker. Oxford: Berg, 1997.

D'Amato, Luigi. *Il voto di preferenza in Italia, 1946–1963.* Milan: Giuffrè, 1964.

D'Amico, Renato. "Voto di preferenza, movimento dell'elettorato e modelli di partito: L'andamento delle preferenze nelle elezioni politiche italiane del quindicennio, 1968–1983." *Quaderni dell'Osservatorio Elettorale* 18 (1987): 89–138.

Daniels, Stephen. *Fields of Vision: Landscape Imagery and National Identity in England and the United States.* Princeton: Princeton University Press, 1993.

Davis, John A. "The South, the Risorgimento and the Origins of the 'Southern

Problem.'" In *Gramsci and Italy's Passive Revolution*, ed. John A. Davis. London: St. Martin's Press, 1979.

———. "Remapping Italy's Path to the Twentieth Century." *Journal of Modern History* 66 (1994): 291–320.

———, ed. *Italy in the Nineteenth Century*. Oxford: Oxford University Press, 2000.

D'Azeglio, Massimo. *Things I Remember*. 1967. Trans. E. R. Vincent. London: Oxford University Press, 1966.

Degl'Innocenti, Maurizio. *Geografia e istituzioni del socialismo italiano*. Naples: Guida, 1983.

De Grand, Alexander. *The Italian Left in the Twentieth Century: A History of the Socialist and Communist Parties*. Bloomington: Indiana University Press, 1989.

Dente, Bruno. *Governare la frammentazione: Stato, regioni e enti locali in Italia*. Bologna: Il Mulino, 1985.

———. "Sub-national Governments in the Long Italian Transition." *West European Politics* 20 (1997): 176–93.

Derivry, D., and Mattei Dogan. "Religion, classe et politique en France: Six types des relations causales." *Revue Française de Science Politique* 36 (1986): 157–81.

Destro, Adriana. "A New Era and New Themes in Italian Politics: The Case of Padania." *Journal of Modern Italian Studies* 2 (1997): 358–77.

Diamanti, Ilvo. *La Lega: Geografia, storia e sociologia di un nuovo soggetto politico*. Rome: Donzelli, 1993.

———. "La Lega." In *Milano a Roma: Guida all'Italia elettorale del 1994*, ed. Ilvo Diamanti and Renato Mannheimer. Rome: Donzelli, 1994.

———. *Il male del Nord: Lega, localismo, secessione*. Rome: Donzelli, 1996.

———. "The Northern League: From Regional Party to Party of Government." In *The New Italian Republic: From the Fall of the Berlin Wall to Berlusconi*, ed. Stephen Gundle and Simon Parker. London: Routledge, 1996.

———. "Un bipolarismo ancora imperfetto." *Il Sole/24 Ore*, 29 April 1997, 3.

———. "La Lega fa finite elezioni." *Il Sole/24 Ore*, 26 October 1997, 2.

———. "Nordest: Si puo crescere senza politica?" *Il Mulino* 46 (1997): 1061–73.

———. "Nuove generazioni: L'Europa è lontana, l'Italia un po' meno." *Il Mulino* 46 (1997): 46–54.

———, ed. *Idee del Nordest: Mappe, rappresentazioni, progetti*. Turin: Fondazione Giovanni Agnelli, 1998.

———. "Il vento del Nord porta bufere." *Il Sole/24 Ore*, 28 September 1998, 2.

Diamanti, Ilvo, and Renato Mannheimer, eds. *Milano a Roma: Guida all'Italia elettorale del 1994*. Rome: Donzelli, 1994.

Diamanti, Ilvo, and Gianni Riccamboni. *La parabola del voto bianco: Elezioni e società in Veneto (1946–1992)*. Vicenza: Neri Pozzi, 1992.

Diamanti, Ilvo, and Paolo Segatti. "Orgogliosi di essere italiani." *LiMes* 4 (1994): 15–36.

Diani, Mario. "Linking Mobilization Frames and Political Opportunities: Insights from Regional Populism in Italy." *American Sociological Review* 61 (1996): 1053–69.

Dibdin, Michael. *Dead Lagoon*. New York: Vintage, 1994.

Dicken, Peter, Philip F. Kelly, Kris Olds, and Henry Wai-Chung Yeung. "Chains and Networks, Territories and Scales: Towards a Relational Framework for Analysing the Global Economy." *Global Networks* 1 (2001): 89–112.

Dickie, John. "Imagined Italies." In *Italian Cultural Studies*, ed. David Forgacs and Robert Lumley. Oxford: Oxford University Press, 1996.

Dirlik, Arif. "Place-Based Imagination: Globalism and the Politics of Place." *In Places and Politics in an Age of Globalization*, ed. Roxann Prazniak and Arif Dirlik. Lanham, Md.: Rowman and Littlefield, 2001.

Di Scala, Spencer, ed. *Italian Socialism: Between Politics and History*. Amherst: University of Massachusetts Press, 1996.

———. "Resistance Mythology." *Journal of Modern Italian Studies* 4 (1999): 67–72.

Dogan, Mattei. "Political Cleavages and Social Stratification in France and Italy." In *Party Systems and Voter Alignments*, ed. Seymour M. Lipset and Stein Rokkan. New York: Free Press, 1967.

Dogan, Mattei, and O. M. Petrarca, eds. *Partiti politici e strutture sociali in Italia*. Milan: Comunità, 1968.

Domenico, Roy P. *Italian Fascists on Trial, 1943–1948*. Chapel Hill: University of North Carolina Press, 1991.

Donolo, Carlo. *Mutamento o transizione? Politica e società nella crisi italiana*. Bologna: Il Mulino, 1977.

Douglas, Roy. *The History of the Liberal Party, 1895–1970*. London: Sidgwick and Jackson, 1971.

Duggan, Christopher. *Fascism and the Mafia*. New Haven: Yale University Press, 1989.

———. "Francesco Crispi, 'Political Education' and the Problem of Italian National Consciousness, 1860–1896." *Journal of Modern Italian Studies* 2 (1997): 141–66.

———. "Politics in the Era of Depretis and Crispi, 1870–96." In *Italy in the Nineteenth Century*, ed. John A. Davis. Oxford: Oxford University Press, 2000.

Eagles, Munroe, ed. *Spatial and Contextual Models in Political Research*. London: Taylor and Francis, 1995.

Eagleton, Terry. *Ideology: An Introduction*. London: Verso, 1991.

Eco, Umberto. *The Name of the Rose*. New York: Vintage, 1983.

Emirbayer, Mustafa, and Ann Mische. "What Is Agency?" *American Journal of Sociology* 103 (1998): 962–1023.

Entrikin, J. Nicholas. *The Betweenness of Place: Towards a Geography of Modernity*. Baltimore: Johns Hopkins University Press, 1991.

Enzensberger, Hans M. *Europe, Europe: Forays into a Continent*. London: Hutchinson, 1989.

Ergas, Yasmine. "Allargamento della cittadinanza e governo del conflitto." In *Il sistema politico italiano*, ed. Gianfranco Pasquino. Rome: Laterza, 1985.

Esteva, Gustavo. "Development." In *The Development Dictionary: A Guide to Knowledge as Power*, ed. Wofgang Sachs. London: Zed Books, 1992.

Fabbrini, Sergio. "Political Change without Institutional Transformation: What Can We Learn from the Italian Crisis of the 1990s?" *International Political Science Review* 21 (2000): 158–75.

Fabian, Johannes. *Time and the Other: How Anthropology Makes Its Object*. New York: Columbia University Press, 1983.

Farneti, Paolo. *Sistema politico, società civile*. Turin: Giappichelli, 1971.

Fassa, Raimondo. *Le prospettive liberal del Paese in Europa: Federalismo? Presidenzialismo? Secessionismo?* Varese: Gruppo dei Liberal Democratici e Riformatori Europei, 1997.

———. *Dalla Lega di Stato alla Lega di Città: Riflessioni tra il Municipio di Varese e l'Europarlamento di Strasburgo*. Varese: ELDR, 1998.

Favretto, Ilaria. "1956 and the PSI: the End of 'Ten Winters.'" *Modern Italy* 5 (2000): 25–45.

Feltrin, Paolo. "Le culture politiche locali: Alcune osservazioni critiche sugli studi condotti in Italia." *Il Politico* 53 (1988): 296–306.

Fenby, J. "Les gages de la peur." *London Review of Books*, 3 August 1995, 24.

Ferguson, Yale H., and Richard W. Mansbach. *Polities: Authorities, Identities and Change*. Columbia: University of South Carolina Press, 1996.

Ferraresi, Franco. "Nord-Sud, destra-sinistra: La disunità del Bel Paese." *Corriere della Sera*, 16 June 1994, 1–2.

———. *Threats to Democracy: The Radical Right in Italy after the War*. Princeton: Princeton University Press, 1996.

Ferrera, Maurizio. "Il mercato politico-assistenziale." In *La società italiana degli anni ottanta*, ed. Ugo Ascoli and Raimondo Catanzaro. Rome: Laterza, 1989.

Filipucci, Paola. "Anthropological Perspectives on Culture in Italy." In *Italian Cultural Studies*, ed. David Forgacs and Robert Lumley. Oxford: Oxford University Press, 1996.

Foley, Michael W., and Bob Edwards. "Beyond Tocqueville: Civil Society and Social Capital in Comparative Perspective." *American Behavioral Scientist* 42 (1998): 5–20.

Foot, John. "Migration and the 'Miracle' at Milan. The Neighbourhoods of Baggio, Barona, Bovisa, and Comasina in the 1950s and 1960s." *Journal of Historical Sociology* 10 (1997): 184–212.

———. "Immigration and the City: Milan and Mass Immigration, 1958–1998." *Modern Italy* 4 (1999): 159–72.

Forgacs, David. *Italian Culture in the Industrial Era, 1880–1980: Cultural Industries, Politics and the Public*. Manchester: Manchester University Press, 1990.

Francini, Marco. *Primo dopoguerra e origini del fascismo a Pistoia*. Milan: Feltrinelli, 1976.

———. *Pistoia 1927: Nascita di una provincia*. Pistoia: Amministrazione Provinciale, 1987.

———. *Cooperazione pistoiesi: Fra storia e memoria: La Federazione Provinciale di Pistoia della Lega delle Cooperative (1945–1987)*. Florence: GE9, 1988.

———. "Il travaglio ideologico e politico (1957–1968)." Unpublished manuscript, Pistoia, 1988.

Francini, Marco, and Aldo Morelli. *La Breda di Pistoia, 1944/1962*. Florence: La Nuova Italia, 1984.

Fre, G. "I ribelli lumbard: Solo con Forza Italia." *Corriere della Sera*, 5 January 1995, 4.

Frieden, Jeffry A. "Invested Interests: The Politics of National Economic Policies in a World of Global Finance." *International Organization* 45 (1991): 425–51.

Galli, Giorgio. *Il bipartitismo imperfetto: Comunisti e democristiani in Italia*. Milan: Mondadori, 1984.

———. *Diario politico 1994: L'imbroglio del 28 marzo e il governo*. Milan: Kaos, 1994.

Galli, Giorgio, and Alfonso Prandi, eds. *Patterns of Political Participation in Italy*. New Haven: Yale University Press, 1970.

Gallino, Luciano. *Della ingovernabilità: La società italiana tra premoderno e neo-industriale*. Milan: Comunità, 1987.

Gambetta, Diego. "Fragments of an Economic Theory of Mafia." *European Journal of Sociology* 29 (1988): 127–45.

Gardani, Ludovico. "'Tutti a casa': La globalizzazione vista dalla Padania." *LiMes* 1 (1997): 310–13.

Gentile, Emilio. *The Sacralization of Politics in Fascist Italy.* Cambridge Harvard University Press, 1996.

———. *La grande Italia: Ascesa e declino del mito della nazione nel ventesimo secolo.* Milan: Mondadori, 1997.

Gerstein, D. "To Unpack Micro and Macro: Link Small with Large and Part with Whole." In *The Micro-Macro Link,* ed. Jeffrey Alexander et al. Berkeley and Los Angeles: University of California Press, 1987.

Ghilarducci, Olivo. "Industrializzazione nella provincia di Lucca." *La Provincia di Lucca* 13 (1973): 7–15.

Ghini, Celso. *L'Italia che cambia: Il voto degli italiani, 1946–1976.* Rome: Riuniti, 1976.

Giddens, Anthony. *The Constitution of Society: Outline of the Theory of Structuration.* Berkeley and Los Angeles: University of California Press, 1984.

———. *The Consequences of Modernity.* Stanford: Stanford University Press, 1990.

Gilbert, Mark. *The Italian Revolution: The End of Politics, Italian Style?* Boulder Colo.: Westview Press, 1995.

Gillis, John R. "Memory and Identity: The History of a Relationship." In *Commemorations: The Politics of National Identity,* ed. John R. Gillis. Princeton: Princeton University Press, 1994.

Ginsborg, Paul. *Storia d'Italia dal dopoguerra a oggi, 1943–1988.* Turin: Einaudi, 1989. Translated as *A History of Contemporary Italy, 1943–1988.* London: Penguin, 1990.

———. "Italy Takes Its Time to Solve Latest Crisis." *Independent,* 30 December 1994, 9.

Gobetti, Daniela. "La Lega: Regularities and Innovation in Italian Politics." *Politics and Society* 24 (1996): 57–82.

Goio, Franco, Guido Maggioni, and Mario Stoppino. *Il comportamento elettorale in Lombardia (1946–1980): Specificità regionali e vincoli sistemici.* Florence: Le Monnier, 1983.

Goldberg, Ellis. "Thinking about How Democracy Works." *Politics and Society* 24 (1996): 7–18.

Golden, Miriam. *Labor Divided: Austerity and Working Class Politics in Contemporary Italy.* Ithaca: Cornell University Press, 1988.

———. "Competitive Corruption: Factional Conflict and Political Corruption in Postwar Italian Christian Democracy." Unpublished manuscript, Department of Political Science, UCLA, September 1999.

Gorodisky, Daria. "L'Italia non va a votare, referendum nullo." *Corriere della Sera,* 19 April 1999, 2.

Graham, Brian J. "No Place of Mind: Contested Protestant Representations of Ulster." *Ecumene* 1 (1994), 257–81.

Granata, Ivano. "Storia nazionale e storia locale: Alcune considerazioni sulla problematica del fascismo delle origini (1919–1922)." *Storia Contemporanea* 11 (1980): 503–44.

Graziano, Luigi. *Clientelismo e sistema politico.* Milan: Franco Angeli, 1980.

Gribaudi, Gabriella. "Images of the South." In *Italian Cultural Studies,* ed. David Forgacs and Robert Lumley. Oxford: Oxford University Press, 1996.

Guarrasi, Vincenzo. "Tempi della società, luoghi della politica e immagini della cultura." In *Geografia politica delle regioni italiane,* ed. Pasquale Coppola. Turin: Einaudi, 1997.

Guha, Ranajit. "Dominance without Hegemony and Its Historiography." *Subaltern Studies* 6 (1989): 210–309.

Gundle, Stephen. "Feminine Beauty, National Identity and Political Conflict in Postwar Italy, 1945–1954." *Contemporary European History* 8 (1999): 359–78.

Gupta, Akhil, and James Ferguson. "Beyond 'Culture': Space, Identity, and the Politics of Difference." *Cultural Anthropology* 7 (1992): 6–23.

Guzzini, Stefano. "The 'Long Night of the First Republic': Years of Clientelistic Implosion in Italy." *Review of International Political Economy* 2 (1995): 27–61.

Habermas, Jürgen. *The Philosophical Discourse of Modernity.* Cambridge: Polity Press, 1987.

Hague, Euan. "Uniting Italy, Fragmenting Italy: Football as Italy's Cultural Form." Unpublished manuscript, Department of Geography, Syracuse University, 1994.

Handler, Richard. "Is 'Identity' a Useful Cross-Cultural Concept?" In *Commemorations: The Politics of National Identity,* ed. John R. Gillis. Princeton: Princeton University Press, 1994.

Hannerz, Ulf. *Transnational Connections: Culture, People, Places.* London: Routledge, 1996.

Hansen, Edward C. "The Great Bambi War: Tocquevillians versus Keynesians in an Upstate New York County." In *Articulating Hidden Histories: Exploring the Influence of Eric R. Wolf,* ed. Jane Schneider and Rayna Rapp. Berkeley and Los Angeles: University of California Press, 1995.

Harvey, David. "The Geographical and Geopolitical Consequences of the Transition from Fordist to Flexible Accumulation." In *America's New Market Geography,* ed. George Sternlieb and James W. Hughes. New Brunswick, N.J.: Center for Urban Policy Research Press, 1988.

———. *The Condition of Postmodernity.* Oxford: Blackwell, 1989.

Hastings, Adrian. *The Construction of Nationhood: Ethnicity, Religion and Nationalism.* Cambridge: Cambridge University Press, 1997.

Hastrup, Kirsten, ed. *Other Histories.* London: Routledge, 1992.

Häyrynen, Maunu. "The Kaleidoscopic View: The Finnish National Landscape Imagery." *National Identities* 2 (2000): 5–19.

Hegel, G. W. F. *Philosophy of Right.* 1821. Oxford: Oxford University Press, 1967.

Hellman, Judith A. *Journeys among Women: Feminism in Five Italian Cities.* New York: Oxford University Press, 1987.

Helms, Mary W. *Ulysses' Sail: An Ethnographic Odyssey of Power, Knowledge, and Geographical Discourse.* Princeton: Princeton University Press, 1988.

Helsinger Elizabeth K. *Rural Scenes and National Representation: Britain, 1815–1850.* Princeton: Princeton University Press, 1997.

Hermand, Jost, and James Steakley, eds. *"Heimat," Nation, Fatherland: The German Sense of Belonging.* New York: Peter Lang, 1996.

Hetherington, Kevin. *Expressions of Identity: Space, Performance, Politics.* London: Sage, 1998.

Hetherington, Kevin, and Rolland Munro, eds. *Ideas of Difference: Social Spaces and the Labour of Division.* Oxford: Blackwell, 1997.

Hobsbawm, Eric, and Ranger, Terence, eds. *The Invention of Tradition.* Cambridge: Cambridge University Press, 1983.

Ignazi, Piero. *Il polo escluso: Profilo del Movimento Sociale Italiano.* Bologna: Il Mulino, 1989.

———. *Dal PCI al PDS.* Bologna: Il Mulino, 1992.

———. *Postfascisti? Dal Movimento Sociale Italiano ad Alleanza Nazionale.* Bologna: Il Mulino, 1994.

Innamorati, Serena. *Mario Fabiani, il sindaco della ricostruzione: Appunti per una storia.* Florence: Comune di Firenze, 1984.

Jacobitti, Edmund E. *Revolutionary Humanism and Historicism in Modern Italy.* New Haven: Yale University Press, 1981.

Johnson, Nuala. "Cast in Stone: Monuments, Geography, and Nationalism." *Environment and Planning D: Society and Space* 13 (1995): 51–65.

Johnston, R. J. *A Question of Place: Exploring the Practice of Human Geography.* Oxford: Blackwell, 1991.

Johnston, R. J., and C. J. Pattie. "Composition and Context: Region and Voting in Britain Revisited during Labour's 1990s' Revival." *Geoforum* 29 (1998): 309–29.

———. "People Who Talk Together Vote Together: An Exploration of Contextual Effects in Britain." *Annals of the Association of American Geographers* 90 (2000): 41–66.

Johnston, W. M. *In Search of Italy: Foreign Writers in Northern Italy since 1800.* University Park: Penn State University Press.

Katz, Richard S. "Electoral Reform and the Transformation of Party Politics in Italy." *Party Politics* 2 (1996): 31–53.

Kermode, Frank. *The Sense of an Ending.* New York: Oxford University Press, 1967.

Kertzer, David I. *Comrades and Christians: Religion and Political Struggle in Communist Italy.* Cambridge: Cambridge University Press, 1980.

———. "Urban Research in Italy." In *Urban Life in Mediterranean Europe: Anthropological Perspectives,* ed. Michael Kenny and David I. Kertzer. Urbana: University of Illinois Press, 1983.

———. "Religion and Society, 1789–1892." In *Italy in the Nineteenth Century,* ed. John A. Davis. Oxford: Oxford University Press, 2000.

King, Gary. "Why Context Should Not Count." *Political Geography* 15 (1996): 159–64.

King, Russell. *The Industrial Geography of Italy.* New York: St. Martin's Press, 1985.

———. *Italy.* London: Harper and Row, 1987.

Kirby, Kathleen M. "Re: Mapping Subjectivity: Cartographic Vision and the Limits of Politics." In *BodySpace: Destabilizing Geographies of Gender and Sexuality,* ed. Nancy Duncan. London: Routledge, 1996.

Knapp, A., and P. Le Galès. "Top-Down to Bottom-Up? Centre-Periphery Relations and Power Structures in France's Gaullist Party." *West European Politics* 16 (1993): 271–94.

Koshar, Rudy. "The Antinomies of *Heimat:* Homeland, History, Nazism." In *"Heimat," Nation, Fatherland: The German Sense of Belonging,* ed. Jost Hermand and James Steakley. New York: Peter Lang, 1996.

Kreile, M. "The Crisis of Italian Trade Unionism in the 1980s." *West European Politics* 11 (1988): 54–67.

Kukathas, C. "Liberalism and Multiculturalism: The Politics of Indifference," *Political Theory* 26 (1998): 686–99.

Lahire, Bernard. "La variation des contextes en sciences sociales: Remarques épistémologiques." *Annales: Histoires, Sciences Sociales* 51 (1996): 381–407.

Laitin, David. "The Cultural Identities of a European State." *Politics and Society* 25 (1997): 277–302.

Lanaro, Silvio. *Società e ideologia nel Veneto rurale (1866–1898).* Rome: Edizioni Storia e Letteratura, 1976.

————. *L'Italia nuova: Identità e sviluppo, 1861–1988*. Turin: Einaudi, 1988.

Lange, Peter, Cynthia Irvin, and Sidney Tarrow. "Mobilization, Social Movements and Party Recruitment: The Italian Communist Party since the 1960s." *British Journal of Political Science* 20 (1990): 15–42.

Latella, M. "Berlusconi: 'Forza Italia sono io.'" *Corriere della Sera*, 22 November 1994, 3.

Lawrence, Jon, and Miles Taylor, eds. *Party, State, and Society: Electoral Behaviour in Britain since 1820*. Brookfield, Vt.: Ashgate, 1997.

Lecours, André. "Political Institutions, Elites, and Territorial Identity Formation in Belgium." *National Identities* 3 (2001): 51–68.

"La Lega va in corner: Il Carroccio perde terreno ma difende fortini importanti." *La Prealpina* (Varese), 18 November 1997, 1.

Lembo, Rosario. "Il Mezzogiorno tra storia e antropologia." *Studi Storici* 29 (1988): 1051–68.

Leonardi, Robert. "The Changing Balance: The Rise of Small Parties in the 1983 Election." In *Italy at the Polls, 1983: A Study of the National Elections*, ed. H. R. Penniman. Durham, N.C.: Duke University Press, 1987.

Leopardi, Giacomo. *Discorso sopra lo stato presente dei costumi degl'italiani*. 1824. Venice: Marsilio, 1989.

Levi, Carl, ed. *Italian Regionalism: History, Identity and Politics*. Oxford: Berg, 1996.

Lévy, Jacques. *Europe: Une géographie*. Paris: Hachette, 1997.

Locke, Richard M. "The Resurgence of the Local Union: Industrial Restructuring and Industrial Relations in Italy." *Politics and Society* 18 (1990): 327–79.

————. *Remaking the Italian Economy*. Ithaca: Cornell University Press, 1995.

————. "The Composite Economy: Local Politics and Industrial Change in Contemporary Italy." *Economy and Society* 25 (1996): 483–510.

Loggia, Ernesto della. *La morte della patria: La crisi dell'idea di nazione tra Resistenza, antifascismo e Repubblica*. Rome: Laterza, 1996.

Lowenthal, David. "British National Identity and the English Landscape." *Rural History* 2 (1991): 205–30.

Lugard, Frederick John Dealtry. *The Dual Mandate in British Tropical Africa*. 3d ed. Edinburgh: Blackwood, 1926.

Lumley, Robert. *States of Emergency: Cultures of Revolt in Italy from 1968 to 1978*. London: Verso, 1990.

Lumley, Robert, and Jonathan Morris, eds., *The New History of the Italian South*. Exeter: University of Exeter Press, 1997.

Lupo, Salvatore. "The Mafia." In *Italy since 1945*, ed. Patrick McCarthy. Oxford: Oxford University Press, 2000.

Lykken, D. T., et al. "Emergenesis: Genetic Traits That May Not Run in Families." *American Psychologist* 47 (1992): 1565–77.

Lyttelton, Adrian. "The National Question in Italy." In *The National Question in Europe in Historical Context*, ed. Mikulás Teich and Roy Porter. Cambridge: Cambridge University Press, 1993.

————. "Italy: The Triumph of TV." *New York Review of Books* 41 (11 August 1994): 25–29.

Macdonald, Sharon, ed. *Inside European Identities: Ethnography in Western Europe*. Oxford: Berg, 1997.

Macry, Paolo. "Rethinking a Stereotype: Territorial Differences and Family Models in the Modernization of Italy." *Journal of Modern Italian Studies* 2 (1997): 188–214.

Magni, Vittorio. *Palmiro Foresi: L'uomo, il cristiano, l'educatore politico*. Rome: Città Nuova, 1987.

Magnusson, Warren. *The Search for Political Space: Globalization, Social Movements, and the Urban Political Experience*. Toronto: University of Toronto Press, 1996.

Maier, Charles S. *Recasting Bourgeois Europe*. Princeton: Princeton University Press, 1975.

Mainardi, Roberto. *Le grandi città italiane*. Milan: Franco Angeli, 1973.

———. *L'Italia delle regioni: Il Nord e la Padania*. Milan: Mondadori, 1998.

Mair, Peter. "Myths of Electoral Change and the Survival of Traditional Parties: The 1992 Stein Rokkan Lecture." *European Journal of Political Research* 24 (1993): 121–33.

Mandrou, Robert. *From Humanism to Science, 1480–1700*. London: Penguin, 1978.

Mannheimer, Renato. "Un'analisi territoriale del calo comunista." In *Mobilità senza movimento: Le elezioni del 3 giugno 1979*, ed. Arturo Parisi. Bologna: Il Mulino, 1980.

———. "E se fossero politiche? Azzurri più a destra." *Corriere della Sera*, 5 December 1994, 2.

———. "Forza Italia." In *Milano a Roma: Guida all'Italia elettorale del 1994*, ed. Ilvo Diamanti and Renato Mannheimer. Rome: Donzelli, 1994.

———. "Ma solo 5 padani su 100 sono secessionisti." *Corriere della Sera*, 3 June 1996, 2.

———. "Mannheimer: Il Carroccio non è più un fenomeno di massa." *Il Messaggero*, 28 June 1999, 4.

Mannheimer, Renato, and Giacomo Sani, eds. *La rivoluzione elettorale: L'Italia tra la Prima e la Seconda Repubblica*. Milan: Anabasi, 1994.

Mannheimer, Renato, and François Zajczyk. "L'astensionismo elettorale, elementi di analisi a partire dai risultati del referendum 1981." *Quaderni di Sociologia* 2–4 (1982): 399–436.

Mantino, Alessandro. *La formazione della filosofia politica di Benedetto Croce*. Rome: Laterza, 1953.

Manzoni, Alessandro. *I Promessi Sposi/The Betrothed*. Trans. Bruce Penman. London: Penguin, 1972.

March, J. G., and J. P. Olsen. *Rediscovering Institutions: The Organizational Basis of Politics*. New York: Free Press, 1989.

Martinotti, Guido. "Le tendenze dell'elettorato italiano." In *La politica nell'Italia che cambia*, ed. Alberto Martinelli and Gianfranco Pasquino. Milan: Feltrinelli, 1978.

———. "Electoral Trends in Italy." *West European Politics* 6 (1986): 253–81.

Martins, Herminio. "Time and Theory in Sociology." In *Approaches to Sociology: An Introduction to Major Trends in British Sociology*, ed. John Rex. London: Routledge and Kegan Paul, 1974.

Mason, Tim. "Italy and Modernization: A Montage." *History Workshop* 25–26 (1988): 127–47.

Massey, Doreen. *Spatial Divisions of Labour*. London: Macmillan, 1984.

Mattina, Cesare. "Il MSI-AN tra tradizione e modernità: Il voto e l'identità di un partito in trasformazione." *Nord e Sud* 45 (1998): 142–65.

Maugeri, Mariano. "La Liga Veneta dà l'addio al Carroccio." *Il Sole/24 Ore*, 28 September 1998, 2.

Mazzoleni, Gianpietro. "Dal partito al candidato: Come cambia la comunicazione elettorale in Italia." *Polis* 4 (1990): 249–73.

McCarthy, Patrick. "Italy: A New Language for a New Politics?" *Journal of Modern Italian Studies* 2 (1997): 337–57.

———. "The Church in Post-war Italy." In *Italy since 1945,* ed. Patrick McCarthy. Oxford: Oxford University Press, 2000.

McCrone, David. "Being British: Changing National and State Identities in Scotland and Wales." *Journal for the Study of British Cultures* 7 (2000): 39–49.

McDonald, Terrence J., ed. *The Historic Turn in the Human Sciences.* Ann Arbor: University of Michigan Press, 1996.

McGinness, Joe. *The Miracle of Castel di Sangro.* New York: Little, Brown, 1999.

McKibbin, Ross. *The Evolution of the Labour Party, 1910–1924.* Oxford: Clarendon Press, 1974.

Merkel, Wolfgang. *Prima e dopo Craxi: Le trasformazioni del PSI.* Padua: Liviana, 1987.

Mershon, Carol A. "Unions and Politics in Italy." In *Italy at the Polls, 1983: A Study of the National Elections,* ed. H. R. Penniman. Durham, N.C.: Duke University Press, 1987.

———. "Expectations and Informal Rules in Coalition Formation." *Comparative Political Studies* 27 (1994): 40–79.

———. "The Costs of Coalition: Coalition Theories and Italian Governments." *American Political Science Review* 90 (1996): 534–54.

Merton, Robert K. *Social Theory and Social Structure.* New York: Free Press, 1957.

Messina, Patrizia. "Persistenza e mutamento nelle subculture politiche territoriali." In *Le elezioni della transizione: Il sistema politico italiano alla prova del voto, 1994–1996,* ed. Giuseppe Gangemi and Gianni Riccamboni. Turin: UTET, 1997.

———. "Opposition in Italy in the 1990s: Local Political Cultures and the Northern League." *Government and Opposition* 33, (1998): 462–78.

Meyrowitz, Joshua. *No Sense of Place: The Impact of Electronic Media on Social Behavior.* New York: Oxford University Press, 1985.

Miglio, Gianfranco, and Augusto Barbera. *Federalismo e secessione: Un dialogo.* Milan: Mondadori, 1997.

Miller, Byron. "Political Action and the Geography of Defense Investment: Geographical Scale and the Representation of the Massachusetts Miracle." *Political Geography* 16 (1997): 171–85.

Miller, James E. "Who Chopped Down the Cherry Tree? The Italian Resistance in History and Politics, 1945–1998." *Journal of Modern Italian Studies* 4 (1999): 37–54.

Milza, P. "Il football italiano: Una storia lunga un secolo." *Italia Contemporanea* 183 (1991): 245–55.

Mitchell, William. *City of Bits: Space, Place, and Infobahn.* Cambridge: MIT Press, 1995.

Mlinar, Zdravko, ed. *Globalization and Territorial Identities.* Brookfield, Vt.: Avebury, 1992.

Montanelli, Indro. "Un certo Cattaneo (norme per l'uso)." *Corriere della Sera,* 24 July 1995, 1.

Mori, A., and B. Cori. "L'area di attrazione delle maggiori città italiane." *Rivista Geografica Italiana* 76 (1969): 3–14.

Nocifora, Enzo. *Italia: La riunificazione possibile. Differenziazione territoriale e regionalismo nella società italiana degli anni novanta.* Rome: SEAM, 1994.

Nora, Pierre. "Between Memory and History: Les Lieux de Mémoire." *Representations* 26 (1989): 7–25.

Nouat, René. "La société paysanne." In *Tradition et changement en Toscane,* ed. Anne-Marie Seronde et al. Paris: Armand Colin, 1970.

Oakeshott, Michael. *Rationalism in Politics and Other Essays.* London: Methuen, 1962.

Offe, Claus. "New Social Movements: Challenging the Boundaries of Institutional Politics." *Social Research* 52 (1985): 817–68.

O'Hagan, Andrew. "The End of British Farming." *London Review of Books,* 22 March 2001, 3–16.

Ong, Aihwa. *Flexible Citizenship: The Cultural Logics of Transnationality.* Durham, N.C.: Duke University Press, 1999.

Opp, Karl-Dieter. "Contending Conceptions of the Theory of Rational Action." *Journal of Theoretical Politics* 11 (1999): 171–202.

Ottanelli, Andrea. "Le officine mecchaniche S. Giorgio: Capitalismo e classe operai a Pistoia (1905–1925)." *Farestoria* 1 (1981): 55–56.

———. *Auto, treni, aerei: Le officine mecchaniche San Giorgio di Pistoia. Un'industria genovese in Toscana tra Giolitti e la Resistenza (1905–1949).* Pistoia: Amministrazione Comunale, 1987.

"La Padania ha bisogno di martiri." *Corriere della Sera,* 29 June 1998, 5.

Padellaro, A. "Verrano a cercarmi di nuovo." *L'Espresso* 14 July 1995, 58–60.

Pagden, Anthony. *European Encounters with the New World: From Renaissance to Romanticism.* New Haven: Yale University Press, 1992.

Palazzo, Agostino. *Programmazione e unità locali di decisione.* Milan: Giuffrè, 1966.

Panebianco, Angelo. *Political Parties: Organization and Power.* Cambridge: Cambridge University Press, 1988.

Paolini, Elvio, and Alberto Douglas Scotti. *Da Badoglio a Berlusconi.* Milan: Sugarco, 1995.

Parisi, Arturo. "Il matrice socio-religioso del dissenso cattolico in Italia." *Il Mulino* 21 (1971): 637–57.

———. "Mobilità senza movimento." In *Mobilità senza movimento: Le elezioni del 3 giugno 1979,* ed. Arturo Parisi. Bologna: Il Mulino, 1980.

———. *Luoghi e misure della politica.* Bologna: Il Mulino, 1984.

Parisi, Arturo, and Gianfranco Pasquino. "Relazioni partiti-elettori e tipi di voto." In *Il sistema politico italiano,* ed. Gianfranco Pasquino. Rome: Laterza, 1985.

Parks, Tim. "The Non-conformist." *New York Review of Books* 47 (21 September 2000): 30–35.

Parsons, Talcott. *The Social System.* New York: Free Press, 1951.

Pasquino, Gianfranco. "Il Partito Comunista Italiano nel sistema politico italiano." In *Il sistema politico italiano,* ed. Gianfranco Pasquino. Rome: Laterza, 1985.

———. "Personae non gratae? Personalizzazione e spettacolarizzazione della politica." *Polis* 4 (1990): 203–16.

Passerini, Luisa. *Fascism in Popular Memory: The Cultural Experience of the Turin Working Class.* Cambridge: Cambridge University Press, 1987.

Pavsić, Rita. "Esiste una tendenza all'omogeneizzazione territoriale nei partiti italiani." *Rivista Italiana di Scienza Politica* 15 (1985): 69–97.

Pavone, Claudio. *Una guerra civile: Saggio storico sulla moralità della Resistenza.* Turin: Bollati Boringhieri, 1991.

Pederzoli, Patrizia, and Carlo Guarnieri. "The Judicialization of Politics, Italian Style." *Journal of Modern Italian Studies* 2 (1997): 321–36.

Pellegrini, Mario. "La Resistenza oggi." *La Provincia di Lucca* 13 (1973): 27–41.

Pelling, Henry. *Social Geography of British Elections, 1895–1970.* London: Macmillan, 1967.

Penco, Gregorio. *Storia della Chiesa in Italia.* Milan: Jaca, 1977.

Penman, Bruce. "Introduction." In *I Promessi Sposi/The Betrothed,* by Alessandro Manzoni, trans. Bruce Penman. London: Penguin, 1972.

Perna, G. "Fascisti, addio per sempre." *Epoca,* 29 January 1995 28–33.

Petsimeris, P. "Urban Decline and the New Social and Ethnic Divisions in the Core Cities of the Italian Industrial Triangle." *Urban Studies* 35 (1998): 449–65.

Pezzino, Paolo. *Una certo reciprocità di favori: Mafia e modernizzazione violenta nella Sicilia postunitaria.* Milan: Franco Angeli, 1990.

Piattoni, Simona. "Clientelism Revisited: Clientelistic Politics and Economic Development in Postwar Italy." *Italian Politics and Society* 49 (1998): 44–62.

———. "Politica locale e sviluppo economico nel Mezzogiorno." *Stato e Mercato* 55 (1999): 117–49.

Pieruccini, V. "La Cantoni di Lucca." *Politica e Società* 2 (1982): 16.

Pivato, Stefano. "Sport." In *Italy since 1945,* ed. Patrick McCarthy. Oxford: Oxford University Press, 2000.

Pizzorno, Alessandro. "I due poteri dei partiti." In *I soggetti del pluralismo: Classi, partiti e sindacati,* by Alessandro Pizzorno. Bologna: Il Mulino, 1980.

———. "Per un'analisi teorica dei partiti politici in Italia." In *I soggetti del pluralismo: Classi, partiti e sindacati,* by Alessandro Pizzorno. Bologna: Il Mulino, 1980.

———. "Categorie per una crisi." *MicroMega* 3 (June–July 1993): 81–96.

Pletsch, Carl E. "The Three Worlds, or The Division of Social Scientific Labor, circa 1950–1975." *Comparative Studies in Society and History,* 23 (1981): 565–90.

Poli, Emanuela. "Silvio Berlusconi and the Myth of the Creative Entrepreneur." *Modern Italy* 3 (1998): 153–57.

Politica e Società. "Luci e ombri: Il partito [PCI] in cifre." 5 (1980): 73–74.

Porciani, Ilaria. *La festa della nazione: Rappresentazione dello Stato e spazi sociali nell'Italia unita.* Bologna: Il Mulino, 1997.

Porta, Donatella della. "Risorse e attori nella corruzione politica: Appunti su tre casi di governo locale in Italia." *Polis* 4 (1990): 499–532.

Porta, Donatella della, and Hanspeter Kriesi. "Movimenti sociali e globalizzazione." *Rivista Italiana di Scienza Politica* 28 (1998): 451–82.

Porta, Donatella della, and Maurizio Rossi. "I terrorismi in Italia tra il 1969 and il 1982." In *Il sistema politico italiano,* ed. Gianfranco Pasquino. Rome: Laterza, 1985.

Pratt, Jeff. "Catholic Culture." In *Italian Cultural Studies,* ed. David Forgacs and Robert Lumley. Oxford: Oxford University Press, 1996.

Pratt, Mary Louise. *Imperial Eyes: Travel Writing and Transculturation.* London: Routledge, 1992.

Prazniak, Roxann, and Arif Dirlik, ed. *Places and Politics in an Age of Globalization.* Lanham, Md.: Rowman and Littlefield, 2001.

Pridham, Geoffrey. *The Nature of the Italian Party System: A Regional Case Study.* London: St. Martin's Press, 1981.

Putnam, Robert D., with Robert Leonardi and Raffaella Y. Nanetti. *Making Democracy Work: Civic Traditions in Modern Italy.* Princeton: Princeton University Press, 1993.

———. "The Strange Disappearance of Civic America." *American Prospect* 24 (1996): 34–48.

———. *Bowling Alone: The Collapse and Revival of American Community.* New York: Simon and Schuster, 2000.

Putnam, Robert D., Robert Leonardi, Raffaella Y. Nanetti, and Franco Pavoncello. "Il rendimento dei governi regionali." In *Il sistema politico italiano,* ed. Gianfranco Pasquino. Rome: Laterza, 1985.

Racine, J. B., C. Raffestin, and V. Ruffy. "Scala e azione, contributi per una interpretazione del meccanismo della scala nella pratica della geografia." In *Esistere e abitare: Prospettive umanistiche nella geografia francofona,* ed. Clara Copeta. Milan: Franco Angeli, 1986.

Ramella, F. "L'area rossa." In *Milano a Roma: Guida all'Italia elettorale del 1994,* ed. Ilvo Diamanti and Renato Mannheimer. Rome: Donzelli, 1994.

Rasy, Elisabetta. Interview with Albert Asor Rosa. *Panorama,* 8 December 1985, 185–86.

Regini, Marino. "Social Institutions and Production Structure of Italian Capitalism in the 1980s." In *Political Economy of Modern Capitalism: Mapping Convergence and Diversity,* ed. Colin Crouch and Wolfgang Streeck. London: Sage, 1997.

Reyne, Georges. "L'industrie en Toscane: Étude d'une région confrontée à la crise." Ph.D. thesis, University of Nice, 1983.

Riccamboni, Gianni. "Ritorno al futuro? La transizione nell'ex subcultura bianca." In *Le elezioni della transizione: Il sistema politico italiano alla prova del voto, 1994–1996,* ed. Giuseppe Gangemi and Gianni Riccamboni. Turin: UTET, 1997.

Ricolfi, Luca. "Quali Italie? Vecchie e nuove fratture territoriali." *Rassegna Italiana di Sociologia* 37 (1996): 267–77.

Risaliti, R. *Antifascismo e Resistenza nel pistoiese.* Pistoia: Tellini, 1976.

Rizzi, Emilio. *Atlante geo-storico—1946–1983: Le elezioni politiche e il Parlamento nell'Italia Repubblicana.* Milan: Edizioni Geografia Storica Illustrata, 1986.

Rogari, Sandro. *Alle origini del trasformismo: Partiti e sistema politico nell'Italia liberale.* Rome: Laterza, 1998.

Romano, Sergio. "La Lega divisa, il caso Veneto." *Corriere della Sera,* 18 September 1998, 1.

Romeo, Rosario. *Breve storia della grande industria in Italia.* Bologna: Il Mulino, 1963.

Rose, Gillian. "Place and Identity: A Sense of Place." In *A Place in the World? Place, Cultures and Globalization,* ed. Doreen Massey and Pat Jess. Oxford: Open University/Oxford University Press, 1994.

Rosenblum, Nancy L. *Membership and Morals: The Personal Uses of Pluralism in America.* Princeton: Princeton University Press, 1998.

Rossi, M. G., and G. Santomassimo. "Il Partito Comunista Italiano." In *La ricostruzione in Toscana: Dal CLN ai partiti,* vol. 2, *I partiti politici,* ed. E. Rotelli. Bologna: Il Mulino, 1981.

Rossi, Nicola, and Gianni Tonioli. "Catching up or Falling Behind? Italy's Economic Growth, 1895–1947." *Economic History Review* 45 (1992): 537–63.

Ruggie, John G. "Territoriality and Beyond: Problematizing Modernity in International Relations." *International Organization* 47 (1993): 139–74.

Ryan, Michael T. "Assimilating New Worlds in the Sixteenth and Seventeenth Centuries." *Comparative Studies in Society and History* 23 (1981): 519–38.

Sabbatucci, Giovanni. "Il golpe in agguato e il doppio stato." In *Miti e storia dell'Italia unita,* ed. Giovanni Belardelli et al. Bologna: Il Mulino, 1999.

Sabetti, Filippo. "Path Dependency and Civic Culture: Some Lessons from Italy about Interpreting Social Experiments." *Politics and Society* 24 (1996): 19–44.

———. *The Search for Good Government: Understanding the Paradox of Italian Democracy.* Montreal: McGill-Queen's University Press, 2000.

Sack, Robert D. *Homo Geographicus: A Framework for Action, Awareness, and Moral Concern.* Baltimore: Johns Hopkins University Press, 1997.

Sahlins, Marshall. "Goodbye to Tristes Tropes: Ethnography in the Context of Modern World History." Ryerson Lecture, University of Chicago, 29 April 1992.

Said, Edward W. *Orientalism.* New York: Random House, 1978.

Salvati, Michele. "Muddling Through: Economics and Politics in Italy, 1969–1979." In *Italy in Transition: Conflict and Consensus,* ed. Peter Lange and Sidney Tarrow. London: Pinter, 1980.

Sani, Giacomo. "Le elezioni degli anni settanta: Terremoto o evoluzione?" In *Continuità e mutamento elettorale in Italia,* ed. Arturo Parisi and Gianfranco Pasquino. Bologna: Il Mulino, 1977.

———. "Il verdetto del 1992." In *La rivoluzione elettorale: L'Italia tra la Prima e la Seconda Repubblica,* ed. Renato Mannheimer and Giacomo Sani. Milan: Anabasi, 1994.

Santi, Ettore. "Un decennio di sindacalizzazione (1977–1986)." *Quaderni di Sociologia* 34 (1988): 61–96.

Sapelli, Giulio. *Comunità e mercato: Socialisti, cattolici e governo municipale agli inizi del XX secolo.* Bologna: Il Mulino, 1986.

———. *L'Italia inafferrabile: Conflitti, sviluppo, dissociazione dagli anni cinquanta a oggi.* Venice: Marsilio, 1989.

Sartori, Giovanni. *Stato e politica nel pensiero di Benedetto Croce.* Naples: Morano, 1966.

———. *La teoria dei partiti e caso italiano.* Milan: Feltrinelli, 1982.

Sassoon, Donald. *The Strategy of the Italian Communist Party.* New York: St. Martin's Press, 1981.

———. "La sinistra in Italia e in Europa: Elezioni e governi 1945–1988." *Italia Contemporanea* 175 (1989): 5–23.

Satz, Debra, and John Ferejohn. "Rational Choice and Social Theory." *Journal of Philosophy* 91 (1994): 71–87.

Scaramellini, Guglielmo, and Gian Paolo Torricelli. "Attività industriali e di servizio in un'area transfrontaliera: L'indagine dell'*Atlante socioeconomico della Regione Insubrica.*" *Lombardia Nord-Ovest* 1 (2001): 35–52.

Scattareggia, M. "Roma capitale: Arretratezza e modernizzazione (1870–1914)." *Storia Urbana* 42 (1988): 30–62.

Schama, Simon. *Landscape and Memory.* London: HarperCollins, 1995.

Schemeil, Yves. "Democracy before Democracy?" *International Political Science Review* 21 (2000): 99–120.

Schmidtke, Oliver. *Politics of Identity: Ethnicity, Territories, and the Political Opportunity Structure in Modern Italian Society.* Sinzheim, Germany: Pro Universitate, 1996.

Schneider, Jane, and Rayna Rapp, eds. *Articulating Hidden Histories: Exploring the Influence of Eric R. Wolf.* Berkeley and Los Angeles: University of California Press, 1995.

Schwoebel, Robert. *The Shadow of the Crescent: The Renaissance Image of the Turk (1453–1517).* Nieuwkoop, Netherlands: De Graaf, 1967.

Sciolla, Loredana. *Italiani: Stereotipi di casa nostra.* Bologna: Il Mulino, 1997.

Sciortino, Giuseppe. "'Just before the Fall': The Northern League and the Cultural Construction of a Secessionist Claim." *International Sociology* 14 (1999): 321–36.

Scoppola, Pietro. "The Christian Democrats and the Political Crisis." *Modern Italy* 1 (1995): 18–29.

———. *25 aprile: Liberazione.* Turin: Einaudi, 1995.

Scott, J. T., and V. B. Sullivan. "Patricide and the Plot of the Prince: Cesare Borgia and Machiavelli's Italy." *American Political Science Review* 8 (1994): 887–900.

Scott, James C. *Seeing Like a State: How Certain Schemes to Improve the Human Condition Have Failed.* New Haven: Yale University Press, 1996.

Sen, Amartya K. "Rational Fools: A Critique of the Behavioral Foundations of Economic Theory." In *Beyond Self-Interest,* ed. Jane J. Mansbridge. Chicago: University of Chicago Press, 1990.

Serneri, Simone Neri. "A Past to Be Thrown Away? Politics and the History of the Italian Resistance." *Contemporary European History* 4 (1995): 367–81.

Settembrini, Domenico. *Storia dell'idea antiborghese, 1860–1989.* Bari: Laterza, 1991.

Sewell, William H., Jr. "A Theory of Structure: Duality, Agency, and Transformation." *American Journal of Sociology* 98 (1992): 1–29.

Shapiro, Michael. "Bowling Blind: Post Liberal Civil Society and the Worlds of Neo-Tocquevillian Social Theory." *Theory and Event* 1 (1997): 2–12.

Shin, Michael, and John Agnew. "The Geography of Party Replacement in Italy, 1987–1996." *Political Geography* 21 (2002): 221–42.

Signorelli, Amalia. Review of *La Nostra Italia. L'Indice* 8 (1986): 45.

Signorini, Telemaco. *Caricaturisti e caricaturati al Caffè Michelangiolo.* 1893. Florence: Le Monnier, 1952.

Sil, Rudra. "The Foundations of Eclecticism: The Epistemological Status of Agency, Culture, and Structure in Social Theory." *Journal of Theoretical Politics* 12 (2000): 353–87.

Silber, Ilana F. "Space, Fields, Boundaries: The Rise of Spatial Metaphors in Contemporary Sociological Theory." *Social Research* 62 (1995): 323–55.

Simmel, Georg. *Sociologie et épistémologie.* 1917. Paris: Presses Universitaires de France, 1981.

Sivini, Giordano. "Socialisti e cattolici in Italia dalla società allo stato." In *Sociologia dei partiti politici,* ed. Giordano Sivini. Bologna: Il Mulino, 1971.

Skocpol, Theda. "The Tocqueville Problem: Civic Engagement in American Democracy." *Social Science History* 21 (1997): 455–79.

Smith, Anthony D. *Nationalism in the Twentieth Century.* London: Martin Robertson, 1979.

Smith, Denis Mack. *Modern Italy: A Political History.* Ann Arbor: University of Michigan Press, 1997.

Smith, Neil. "Geography, Difference and the Politics of Scale." In *Postmodernism and the Social Sciences,* ed. Joe Doherty, Elspeth Graham, and Mo Malek. New York: St. Martin's Press, 1992.

Soja, Edward W. *Postmodern Geographies: The Reassertion of Space in Critical Social Theory.* London: Verso, 1989.

Somers, Margaret. "Citizenship and the Public Sphere." *American Sociological Review* 58 (1993): 587–620.

Springborg, Patricia. *Western Republicanism and the Oriental Prince.* Austin: University of Texas Press, 1992.

Spykman, Nicholas J. *The Social Theory of Georg Simmel.* New York: Russell and Russell, 1925.

Stanley, Alessandra. "Of TV and Soccer: The Power of Celebrity Hits Italian Politics." *New York Times,* Week in Review, 20 May 2001, 3.

Statera, Gianni. *Il volto seduttivo del potere: Berlusconi, i media, il consenso.* Rome: SEAM, 1994.

Statera, Gianni, et al. *Violenza sociale e violenza politica nell'Italia degli anni '70: Analisi e interpretazioni sociopolitiche, giuridiche, della stampa quotidiana.* Milan: Franco Angeli, 1983.

Stefanizzi, Sonia. "Alle origini del nuovi movimenti sociali: Gli ecologisti e le donne in Italia (1966–1973)." *Quaderni di Sociologia* 34 (1988): 99–131.

Stella, Gian Antonio. *Dio Po: Gli uomini che fecero la Padania.* Milan: Baldini and Castaldi, 1996.

———. *"Schei": Dal boom alla rivolta: Il mitico Nordest.* Milan: Baldini and Castoldi, 1996.

———. "Cosi parla il senatur." *Corriere della Sera,* 26 January 2001, 1, 9.

Stern, Alan. "Political Legitimacy in Local Politics: The Communist Party in Northeastern Italy." In *Communism in Italy and France,* ed. D. L. M. Blackmer and Sidney Tarrow. Princeton: Princeton University Press, 1975.

Stille, Alexander. *Excellent Cadavers: The Mafia and the Death of the Italian First Republic.* New York: Pantheon, 1995.

———. "Making Way for Berlusconi." *New York Review of Books* 48 (21 June 2001): 73–74.

Stinchcombe, Arthur. "Social Structures and Organizations." In *Handbook of Organizations,* ed. James G. March. New York: Rand McNally, 1965.

Strassoldo, Raimondo. "Globalism and Localism: Theoretical Reflections and Some Evidence." In *Globalization and Territorial Identities,* ed. Zdravko Mlnar. Brookfield, Vt.: Avebury, 1992.

Strassoldo, Raimondo, and Nicoletta Tessarin. *Le radici del localismo: Indagine sociologica sull'appartenza territoriale in Friuli.* Trento: Reverdito, 1992.

Sunseri, N. "'E ora un governo di lunga durata': Bossi esulta e annuncia il suo programma, 'Subito l'antitrust.'" *La Repubblica,* 25 January 1995, 5.

Swidler, Ann. "Culture in Action: Symbols and Strategies." *American Sociological Review* 51 (1986): 273–86.

Tagliacarne, Guglielmo. *Il reddito nelle province italiane nel 1983 e confronti con gli anni 1951, 1981 e 1982.* Milan: Franco Angeli, 1985.

Tamburrano, Giuseppe. "The Italian Socialist Party: Its Policies and Failure to Unite with the Italian Communist Party." In *The Formation of the Italian Republic,* ed. Frank J. Coppa and Margherita Repetto-Alaia. New York: Peter Lang, 1993.

Tarozzi, Fiorenza, and Giorgio Vecchio, eds. *Gli italiani e il Tricolore: Patriottismo, identità nazionale e fratture sociali lungo due secoli di storia.* Bologna: Il Mulino, 1999.

Tarrow, Sidney. *Peasant Communism in Southern Italy.* New Haven: Yale University Press, 1967.

————. *Between Center and Periphery: Grassroots Politicians in Italy and France.* New Haven: Yale University Press, 1977.

————. *Democracy and Disorder: Protest and Politics in Italy, 1965–1975.* New York: Oxford University Press, 1989.

————. *Struggle, Politics, and Reform: Collective Action, Social Movements, and Cycles of Protest.* Ithaca: Center for International Studies, Cornell University, 1989.

————. "The Europeanisation of Conflict: Reflections from a Social Movement Perspective." *West European Politics* 18 (1995): 223–51.

Tarrow, Sidney, Peter J. Katzenstein, and Luigi Graziano, eds. *Territorial Politics In Industrial Nations.* New York: Praeger, 1978.

Tarrow, Sidney, et al. *Sociologie du communisme en Italie.* Paris: Presses Universitaires de France, 1974.

Taylor, Charles. "Interpretation and the Sciences of Man." In *Philosophy and the Human Sciences.* Philosophical Papers 2. Cambridge: Cambridge University Press, 1985.

————. *Sources of the Self.* Cambridge: Harvard University Press, 1989.

————. *Philosophical Arguments.* Cambridge: Harvard University Press, 1995.

Tazartes, Maurizio. *Una città allo specchio: Lucca fra cronaca e storia.* Lucca: Maria Pacini Fazzi, 1987.

Tesini, Mario. *Oltre la città rossa: L'alternative mancata di Dossetti a Bologna (1956–1958).* Bologna: Il Mulino, 1986.

Thom, Martin. "City, Region and Nation: Carlo Cattaneo and the Making of Italy." *Citizenship Studies* 3 (1999): 187–201.

Tilly, Charles. *The Contentious French.* Cambridge: Belknap Press of the Harvard University Press, 1986.

Tipps, Dean. "Modernization Theory and the Comparative Study of Societies: A Critical Perspective." *Comparative Studies in Society and History* 15 (1973): 199–226.

Tisdall, Caroline, and Angelo Bozzola. *Futurism.* London: Thames and Hudson, 1977.

Tobia, Bruno. *Una Patria per gli italiani: Spazi, itinerari, monumenti nell'Italia unita (1870–1900).* Rome: Laterza, 1991.

————. "Urban Space and Monuments in the 'Nationalization of the Masses': The Italian case." In *Nationalism in Europe, 1815-Present: A Reader,* ed. Stuart Woolf. London: Routledge, 1996.

Todd, Emmanuel. *L'invention de l'Europe.* Paris: Seuil, 1990.

"Trent' anni della resistenza e liberazione—contributi del clero." *La Provincia di Lucca* 14 (1974): 1–21.

Treves, P. *L'idea di Roma e la cultura italiana del secolo XIX.* Milan: Ricciardi, 1962.

Trigilia, Carlo. *Le subculture politiche territoriali.* Milan: Feltrinelli, 1981.

————. *Grandi partiti e piccole imprese: Comunisti e democristiani nelle regioni a economia diffusa.* Bologna: Il Mulino, 1986.

————. "The Paradox of the Region: Economic Regulation and the Representation of Interests." *Economy and Society* 20 (1991): 306–27.

————. *Sviluppo senza autonomia: Effetti perversi delle politiche nel Mezzogiorno.* Bologna: Il Mulino, 1992.

Tuan, Yi-Fu. *Space and Place: The Perspective of Experience.* Minneapolis: University of Minnesota Press, 1977.

Tullio-Altan, Carlo. *La nostra Italia: Arretratezza socioculturale, clientelismo, trasformismo e ribellismo dall'Unità ad oggi.* Milan: Feltrinelli, 1986.

Tully, James. *Strange Multiplicity: Constitutionalism in an Age of Diversity.* New York: Cambridge University Press, 1995.

Turner, Stephen. *The Social Theory of Practices: Tradition, Tacit Knowledge, and Presuppositions.* Chicago: University of Chicago Press, 1994.

Urbinati, Nadia. "From the Periphery of Modernity: Antonio Gramsci's Theory of Subordination and Hegemony." *Political Theory* 26 (1998): 370–91.

Valkonen, T. "Individual and Structural Effects in Ecological Research." In *Social Ecology,* ed. Mattei Dogan and Stein Rokkan. Cambridge: MIT Press, 1969.

Verni, Giovanni. "Toscana autunno 1943: Un rapporto dei servizi di sicurezza della Wehrmacht." *Italia Contemporanea* 196 (1994): 545–60.

Verzichelli, L. "Gli eletti." *Rivista Italiana di Scienza Politica* 24 (1994): 713–39.

Veyne, Paul. *Bread and Circuses: Historical Sociology and Political Pluralism.* London: Allen Lane, 1990.

Vivarelli, Roberto. "Revolution and Reaction in Italy, 1918–1922." *Journal of Italian History* 1 (1979): 235–63.

———. "L'anomalia italiana," *La Rivista dei Libri,* November 1991, 13–16.

Vogel, Steven K. "When Interests Are Not Preferences: The Cautionary Tale of Japanese Consumers." *Comparative Politics* 31 (1999): 187–207.

Wacquant, Löic. "Durkheim and Bourdieu: The Common Plinth and Its Cracks." In *Reading Bourdieu on Culture and Society,* ed. Bridget Fowler. Oxford: Blackwell, 2000.

Wall, Wendy L. "America's 'Best Propagandists': Italian Americans and the 1948 'Letters to Italy' Campaign." In *Cold War Constructions: The Political Culture of United States Imperialism, 1945–1966,* ed. Christian G. Appy. Amherst: University of Massachusetts Press, 2000.

Wallerstein, Immanuel. *Unthinking Social Science: The Limits of Nineteenth-Century Paradigms.* Cambridge, Mass.: Polity Press, 1991.

Waters, Sarah. "'Tangentopoli' and the Emergence of a New Political Order in Italy." *West European Politics* 17 (1994): 169–82.

Weitz, P. "The CGIL and the PCI: From Subordination to Independent Political Force." In *Communism in Italy and France,* ed. D. L. M. Blackmer and Sidney Tarrow. Princeton: Princeton University Press, 1975.

White, Harrison C. *Identity and Control: A Structural Theory of Social Action.* Princeton: Princeton University Press, 1992.

Whitefield, Stephen, and Geoffrey Evans. "Political Culture versus Rational Choice: Explaining Responses to Transition in the Czech Republic and Slovakia." *British Journal of Political Science* 29 (1999): 129–55.

Wickham, Chris. *Community and Clientele in Twelfth-Century Tuscany: The Origins of the Rural Commune in the Plain of Lucca.* Oxford: Clarendon Press, 1998.

Wildenmann, Rudolf. "The Problematic of Party Government." In *Visions and Realities of Party Government,* ed. Francis G. Castles and Rudolf Wildenmann. Berlin: De Gruyter, 1986.

Williams, D. "For Italians, It's Back to the Bad Old Days." *Washington Post National Weekly Edition,* 9–15 January 1995, 19–20.

Williams, Raymond. *The Country and the City.* New York: Oxford University Press, 1973.

———. *Culture.* London: Fontana, 1981.

Wolf, Eric R. "Aspects of Group Relations in a Complex Society: Mexico." *American Anthropologist* 58 (1956): 1065–78.

———. *Europe and the People without History.* Berkeley and Los Angeles: University of California Press, 1982.

Wolff, Larry. *Inventing Eastern Europe: The Map of Civilization in the Mind of the Enlightenment.* Stanford: Stanford University Press, 1994.

Wolin, Sheldon. "Postmodern Society and the Absence of Myth." *Social Research* 52 (1985): 217–39.

Woolf, Stuart, ed. *The Rebirth of Italy, 1943–1950.* London: Longman, 1972.

———. *A History of Italy, 1700–1860: The Social Constraints of Political Change.* London: Routledge, 1979.

Young, Iris Marion. *Inclusion and Democracy.* Oxford: Oxford University Press, 2000.

Zafirovski, Milan. "What Is Really Rational Choice? Beyond the Utilitarian Concept of Rationality." *Current Sociology* 47 (1999): 47–113.

Zaghi, Valentino. *L'eroica viltà: Socialismo e fascismo nelle campagne del Polesine, 1919–1926.* Milan: Franco Angeli, 1989.

Zamponi, Simonetta Falasca. *Fascist Spectacle: The Aesthetics of Power in Mussolini's Italy.* Berkeley and Los Angeles: University of California Press, 1997.

Zanzi, Carlo. *Maroni l'arciere.* Varese: Lativa, 1994.

Zerubavel, Eviatar. *The Fine Line: Making Distinctions in Everyday Life.* New York: Free Press, 1991.

Zincone, Giovanna. *U.S.A. con cautela: Il sistema politico italiano e il modello americano.* Rome: Donzelli, 1995.

Zuckerman, Alan S. *The Politics of Faction: Christian Democratic Rule in Italy.* New Haven: Yale University Press, 1979.

The University of Chicago
GEOGRAPHY RESEARCH PAPERS

Titles in Print

127. **PETER G. GOHEEN,** *Victorian Toronto, 1850 to 1900: Pattern and Process of Growth,* 1970

132. **NORMAN T. MOLINE,** *Mobility and the Small Town, 1900–1930,* 1971

152. **MARVIN W. MIKESELL, ed.,** *Geographers Abroad: Essays on the Problems and Prospects of Research in Foreign Areas,* 1973

186. **KARL W. BUTZER,** *Recent History of an Ethiopian Delta: The Omo River and the Level of Lake Rudolf,* 1971

194. **CHAUNCY D. HARRIS,** *Annotated World List of Selected Current Geographical Serials,* 4th ed., 1980

206. **CHAUNCY D. HARRIS,** *Bibliography of Geography,* part 2, *Regional,* volume 1, *The United States of America,* 1984

207–8. **PAUL WHEATLEY,** *Nagara and Commandery: Origins of the Southeast Asian Urban Traditions,* 1983

209. **THOMAS F. SAARINEN, DAVID SEAMON, and JAMES L. SELL, eds.,** *Environmental Perception and Behavior: An Inventory and Prospect,* 1984

210. **JAMES L. WESCOAT JR.,** *Integrated Water Development: Water Use and Conservation Practice in Western Colorado,* 1984

213. **RICHARD LOUIS EDMONDS,** *Northern Frontiers of Qing China and Tokugawa Japan: A Comparative Study of Frontier Policy,* 1985

216. **NANCY J. OBERMEYER,** *Bureaucrats, Clients, and Geography: The Bailly Nuclear Power Plant Battle in Northern Indiana,* 1989

217–18. **MICHAEL P. CONZEN, ed.,** *World Patterns of Modern Urban Change: Essays in Honor of Chauncy D. Harris,* 1986

222. **MARILYN APRIL DORN,** *The Administrative Partitioning of Costa Rica: Politics and Planners in the 1970s,* 1989

223. **JOSEPH H. ASTROTH JR.,** *Understanding Peasant Agriculture: An Integrated Land-Use Model for the Punjab,* 1990

224. **RUTHERFORD H. PLATT, SHEILA G. PELCZARSKI, and BARBARA K. BURBANK, eds.,** *Cities on the Beach: Management Issues of Developed Coastal Barriers,* 1987

225. **GIL LATZ,** *Agricultural Development in Japan: The Land Improvement District in Concept and Practice,* 1989

226. **JEFFREY A. GRITZNER,** *The West African Sahel: Human Agency and Environmental Change,* 1988

228–29. **BARRY C. BISHOP,** *Karnali under Stress: Livelihood Strategies and Seasonal Rhythms in a Changing Nepal Himalaya,* 1990

230. **CHRISTOPHER MUELLER-WILLE,** *Natural Landscape Amenities and Suburban Growth: Metropolitan Chicago, 1970–1980,* 1900

233. **RISA PALM and MICHAEL E. HODGSON,** *After a California Earthquake: Attitude and Behavior Change,* 1992

234. **DAVID M. KUMMER,** *Deforestation in the Postwar Philippines,* 1992

235. **MICHAEL P. CONZEN,** Thomas A. Rumney, and Graeme Wynn, *A Scholar's Guide to Geographical Writing on the American and Canadian Past,* 1993

236. **SHAUL EPHRAIM COHEN,** *The Politics of Planting: Israeli-Palestinian Competition for Control of Land in the Jerusalem Periphery,* 1993

237. **CHAD F. EMMETT,** *Beyond the Basilica: Christians and Muslims in Nazareth,* 1995

238. **EDWARD T. PRICE,** *Dividing the Land: Early American Beginnings of Our Private Property Mosaic,* 1995
239. **ALEX G. PAPADOPOULOS,** *Urban Regimes and Strategies: Building Europe's Central Executive District in Brussels,* 1996
240. **ANNE KELLY KNOWLES,** *Calvinists Incorporated: Welsh Immigrants on Ohio's Industrial Frontier,* 1996
241. **HUGH PRINCE,** *Wetlands of the American Midwest: A Historical Geography of Changing Attitudes,* 1997
242. **KLAUS FRANTZ,** *Indian Reservations in the United States: Territory, Sovereignty, and Socioeconomic Change,* 1999

Italic page numbers refer to illustrations.

131, 245n. 46; Socialist Party in, 122, 128
Lucchesi, Ivo, 139
Lugard, Baron, 68

Macchiaioli, 43–48, 228n. 38
Machiavelli, Niccolò, 71
Mafia: conditions for development of, 234n. 56; in election of 1994, 202; and government contracts, 197; "new" Mafia, 198; in Northern League discourse, 171, 179, 198; and Sicily, 60, 71
Maier, Charles S., 233n. 53
Mair's paradox, 93
Mandrou, Robert, 68
Mannheimer, Renato, 154, 155
Mantova model, 116
Mantua, 156, 164, 208
Manzoni, Alessandro, 45, 70–71, 72
Maoism, 74–75
Marche, 167, *201,* 202
Maremma region, 44
La Margherita, 107, 124, 213
Maroni, Roberto, 178, 187, 207–8
Martinazzoli, Mino, 179
Martins, Herminio, 17
Marx, Karl, 7
Marxism, 90
Mason, Tim, 61, 64, 65
Mauss, Marcel, 74
Mazzini, Giuseppe, 44, 65
media of communication: political influence of, 24; television, 24, 56, 197, 204, 210, 211
memory, sites of, 37, 39–40
Menchise, Vincenzo, 139
meridionalismo, 63
Merton, Robert K., 181
Messina, 86
Messina, Patrizia, 118, 119
methodological nationalism, 17
Michigan model, 27
microgeography of everyday life, 22–23
I miei ricordi (D'Azeglio), 45–46
Miglio, Gianfranco, 181
Milan: Christian Democrats in, 160; economic recovery, 84; electoral mobility in, *79;* and industrial triangle, 161; in Italian urban system, 86, *86;* metropolitan region of, 162; new right in, 165; Northern League in, 154–65, 170; population rank, 55; regional party in, 63; vs. Rome, 154; scandal, 91, 144, 145, 155, 167, 207; small-scale production near, 161; Socialists in, 160; southern and foreign-born populations in, 163–64; spatial economy of, 161–63; and unification, 48, 50

Milano a Roma (Diamanti and Mannheimer), 154, 155
Misericordia, 130
modernization: Americanization, 75; European view of, 67–70; as neutral, 69; and political development, 59–76; as rational and secular, 66–67. *See also* industrialization
Molise, *201*
Monarchists (PNM), 88, *89,* 96
Monsummano Terme: Communist Party in, 122, 130, 135; cooperative membership in, 129; election results, *123–24;* Fascist violence in, 126; location, *122;* party organization in, 130; political change in, 135; population, 122
Montalberti, Cesare, 187
Montanelli, Indro, 208
Montecatini, 126, 129
Movimento Sociale Italiano (MSI): and Christian Democrats, 149; in election of 1983, 101; in election of 1987, 101; in elections, 1948–87, 88, *89, 90;* and *lottizzazione,* 81; reborn as Alleanza Nazionale, 106, 208–9; in South and Sicily, 96, 142, 199, 209
MSI. *See* Movimento Sociale Italiano
multiculturalist school, 2–3; and "active socialization," 217; on difference, 28–30; and spatial siting, 14, 27
multimember districts, 91, 106
Mussolini, Benito: Berlusconi compared with, 213; National Alliance members and, 209; office in Piazza Venezia, 52, *54*
myth: backward Italy as, 66–67; in founding of nations, 176; of place and political identity, 171–75

NAFTA, 190, 193
The Name of the Rose (Eco), 232n. 36
Naples: economic losses, 83; electoral mobility in, *79;* in Italian urban system, *86;* Monarchists supported in, 88; population rank, 55; as regional capital, 86
National Alliance (Alleanza Nazionale; AN), 208–10; drawing votes from Northern League, 161, 165; in election of 1994, 199–204, *200, 201;* and geographical restructuring of Italy, 188; and Movimento Sociale Italiano, 106, 208–9; normalization of, 210, 257n. 68; and Northern League and Forza Italia, 107, 146, 167, 207, 212, 213, 252n. 37; as post-Fascist, 106, 142, 209, 210; southern support for, 164, 209–10; and strong national government, 214
National Front (France), 209